Bite Me!

An Unofficial Guide to
the World of Buffy the Vampire Slayer

Bite Me!

An Unofficial Guide to
the World of Buffy the Vampire Slayer

Nikki Stafford

ECW PRESS

Published by ECW PRESS
2120 Queen Street East, Suite 200, Toronto, Ontario, Canada M4E 1E2

NATIONAL LIBRARY OF CANADA CATALOGUING IN PUBLICATION DATA

Stafford, Nikki, 1973
Bite me!: An unofficial guide to the world of Buffy the vampire slayer /
Nikki Stafford. — Rev. ed.

ISBN 1-55022-540-5

1. Gellar, Sarah Michelle 1977– 2. Buffy the vampire slayer (Television program). 3. Television actors and actresses — United States — Biography. I. Title.

PN1992.77.B84S82 2002   791.45'028'092   C2002-903983-5

Cover and text design: Solo Design
Typesetting: Gail Nina
Production: Mary Bowness
Printing: Webcom
Front cover photo: Stephen Danelian/CORBIS OUTLINE/MAGMA
Colour section photo credits in order of appearance: Dale Berman/CORBIS OUTLINE/MAGMA;
Scott Weiner/SHOOTING STAR; Nathaniel Welch/CORBIS OUTLINE/MAGMA;
Challenge Roddie/CORBIS OUTLINE/MAGMA; Robert Trachtenberg/CORBIS OUTLINE/MAGMA;
Christina Radish; Gary Marshall/SHOOTING STAR; Ron Davis/SHOOTING STAR; Christina Radish;
Albert L. Ortega; Christina Radish; Marissa Love Stone/SHOOTING STAR;
Glenn Weiner/SHOOTING STAR; Christina Radish; Christina Radish;
Challenge Roddie/CORBIS OUTLINE/MAGMA

This book is set in Bulmer, Trade Gothic, and Twang

The publication of *Bite Me!* has been generously supported by the Government of Canada through the Book Publishing Industry Development Program. **Canadä**

DISTRIBUTION

CANADA: Stewart House, 195 Allstate Pkwy., Markham, ON L3R 4T8

UNITED STATES: Independent Publishers Group, 814 North Franklin Street,
Chicago, Illinois 60610

EUROPE: Turnaround Publisher Services, Unit 3, Olympia Trading Estate,
Coburg Road, Wood Green, London N2Z 6T2

AUSTRALIA AND NEW ZEALAND: Wakefield Press, 17 Rundle Street (Box 2066),
Kent Town, South Australia 5071

PRINTED AND BOUND IN CANADA

ECW PRESS
ecwpress.com

Table of Contents

Acknowledgments

First of all, thank you to Jack David and ECW PRESS for giving me the opportunity to do this book, as well as all of the people at the company who helped out along the way, especially Gail Nina, Mary Bowness, and Guylaine Régimbald. A big thanks to Stuart Ross, my editor, who manages to smooth out the rough edges of my writing, and makes me look like a much better writer.

When I finished the episode guide to *Buffy* and *Angel*, I recruited several dear friends and fellow *Buffy* watchers to read through and offer suggestions for improvement, and I'd like to thank Suzanne Kingshott, Kim Koller, and Kevin Courrier for catching all those little things that I missed. A warm thank-you to Tracey Millen, a recently converted *Buffy* fan, who proofread the final copy and also caught some important details.

When I was working on the first book, the following people offered their perspectives of the 1998 posting board party, and because it's included in this edition of the book, I wanted to thank them again: Erika Rottler (a.k.a. Sasheer), Erika Gilbert (Batra), Keith Miller (KAM), Tammie Purcell (greengirl), Viet My Nguyen (Samiel), Karri Phillips (Phoenix), and Will York (fenric). While working on this edition, which included the posting board parties from 1999–2002, I was helped out by Peter Hueser (Morbius), Joan P. Mendoza (friday), Liza Campbell (JustLiza), Terri (greeneyes), Karri Phillips (Phoenix), and Kim Antonio (Spookymagoo). A warm thank-you to the wonderful Karri Phillips, who is always helpful. Not only did she provide overviews of the posting board parties for each book, but she sent me great photos of all of the parties. Thank-you to the entire Posting Board Committee, who was very supportive of the book. Big thanks to Joan Mendoza for offering to assist near the beginning of the project and helping to round up the Bronzers to contribute to the chapter.

Thank you to Allie (Little Willow) for the help on her chapter, for contributing to the posting board section, and for running the best mailing list around. Thanks also to Kiba at jossisahottie.com, Connie Chang, and Jennifer Kaplan for their help with the Little Willow chapter.

Thanks to Amber Benson, who gave me permission to run her impassioned posting board speech in her bio; to Bailey Chase for taking the time to answer some questions for the episode guide; to Rana of Rising Stars Enterprises for being a lot of fun on the telephone and sending me fabulous signed photos of her clients; to Kristy, Virginia, Lilian, and everyone at CityofAngel.com for being a great group of people; and to Leslie Remencus at www.buffymusic.net for maintaining one of the best *Buffy* sites around and for allowing me to use the information on it for the episode guide.

Finally, a special thank-you to Robert Thompson, who helped me along the way and gave me a lot of love and advice; to Jonathan and everyone in my family who supported me; to Piquette and Sebastian, my muses who were always there to lend a paw when I was just about to give up; and, as always, to Jennifer Hale, without whom this book could not have happened. I don't know where I'd be without you.

This book is dedicated to *Buffy* fans everywhere, who manage to keep the Buffyverse thriving.

Introduction

SLAYERS AND WATCHERS:
A NEW VAMPIRE MYTHOLOGY

Buffy the Vampire Slayer first aired on March 10, 1997, and immediately exceeded everyone's expectations. Based on a largely unsuccessful film about a high school girl whose calling is to rid the world of demons, it carried the stigma that it would be a stupid television series for kids that was uncreative and imitative. Many people, including those who worked on the show, weren't sure it would last beyond the first season. But it did, and it continues to gain popularity among both fans and critics.

Vampires, in both fiction and folklore, have fascinated readers and moviegoers for centuries. With the publication of Bram Stoker's *Dracula* in 1897, the legend of the vampire moved into the mainstream, and in the 20th century Dracula became a movie icon. *Nosferatu* (1922) was the first of the major vampire movies, but it was Bela Lugosi, in Tod Browning's 1931 *Dracula*, who forever changed the monstrous demon into a more sexual metaphor. Dracula became suave and sophisticated, and his attacks on the necks of defenseless women were likened to a seduction. It was this image of the vampire as seducer that prevailed, reaching new peaks in the Anne Rice novels of the 1980s and '90s, which featured a romantic yet vicious vampire named Lestat. In 1992, the film *Bram Stoker's Dracula*, starring Gary Oldman and Winona Ryder, revived the idea of the vampire as a monster, remaining truer to Stoker's vision than most of the adaptations before it. In that same year, Fran Rubel Kuzui's *Buffy the Vampire Slayer* — starring Kristy Swanson and Luke Perry — was released, adding a new element to the vampire legend: the idea that someone exists to rid the world of vampires.

The fiction featuring vampires contains significantly different conventions than the folklore. For example, in vampire fiction, you become a vampire only if bitten by one. In the folklore, however, someone could become a vampire if an animal leapt over their coffin; if they'd been murdered or had committed suicide; if they'd been born with a harelip, or on Saturday, or between Christmas and Epiphany; if they'd been buried alive; if they hadn't been buried properly; and in other ways. In fiction, the vampire tends to be a rich nobleman; in folklore, he's a poor peasant wandering the countryside. In movies, the vampire is tall, thin, and debonair, with a cape, a white face, and sharp teeth. In folklore, the vampire has rosy-colored skin and is bloated because of all the blood he has drunk; his teeth are rarely mentioned; his left eye — or both — is wide open and staring, even while he's asleep during the day. In fiction, when the body of the vampire is staked, it disappears or mummifies; in folklore, the corpse must be disposed of. It was sometimes believed that the staking alone would not work, so the act was followed up with the cremation of the body. In both fiction and folklore, vampires are more often male than female, though in folklore the only female vampires are mothers who died in childbirth.

The folklore surrounding the vampire legend was based on real-life fears. Some aspects of the legend were invented during plagues — when people in a particular town died in large numbers, the locals would sometimes rationalize the deaths by blaming the first person who died. They would say that at night he roamed from house to house and sucked the life from others, who would be found dead the next day. These stories would prompt doctors to exhume the body of the first victim and stake it, and some medical reports of the time state that the hair and nails had been growing and blood came out like a river when the body was staked. There have since been many scholarly explanations for the doctors' "findings." When skin begins to decompose, it shrinks, exposing the fingernails and making them look longer. If the intestines become bloated with gas, blood will gush out with great force when the corpse is staked. Some later doctors suggested that so-called vampires suffered from porphyria, a disease that makes the eyes, skin, and teeth red, and causes cracked skin to bleed when it comes in contact with sunlight. It is also believed that to replenish the lost iron in their systems, victims of porphyria were instructed to drink blood, but there is no solid proof of that hypothesis.

In the 20th century, vampirism has moved into the realm of psychiatry, as in Stoker's *Dracula*. Stoker did a lot of research into both the folklore and medical vampirism, and the character of Renfield — a mental patient who swears his devotion to Dracula and eats insects for their blood — was modeled on real-life case studies. Vampirism is defined as the act of ingesting blood while gaining sexual pleasure from the act, and there have been many cases involving such patients; ironically, the majority of the patients are female. The most notorious case of vampirism — and many psychiatrists would hesitate to use that term in conjunction with the case — culminated in 1949, when Englishman John Haigh was executed for the "acid-bath murders." Between 1944 and 1949 he had killed nine people and drank a cupful of blood from each before putting the bodies in a vat of sulfuric acid to dissolve them. Of course, real-life instances of vampirism don't involve turning victims into vampires, flying about, and shape-shifting into bats. Those aspects remain solely in the fiction.

Buffy the Vampire Slayer is a welcome addition to the growing legend. The writers on the show follow some conventions of vampire lore while diverging from others. Joss Whedon's vampires don't fly around and change into bats — they drive cars and have relationships like mortals. But Whedon has created a whole new mythology with these demons, and he makes their "lives" and how they affect the lives of others the focal point of the show. Whedon's vampires aren't all faceless monsters, but people who were once victimized themselves.

Most importantly, he has altered the formerly defenseless figure of the young woman into a killing machine. But one who has problems of her own. However, her duty is her duty and she must learn to live with the very real fact that each new day could be her last. For, "In every generation there is a Chosen One. . . ."

'So a Werewolf, Two Lesbian Witches, and a Vengeance Demon Go into a Magic Shop...'

THE STORY OF *BUFFY THE VAMPIRE SLAYER*

Buffy the Vampire Slayer is a show that shouldn't exist. First of all, the title itself is risky, and the reason why many people won't watch it. "You watch a show called *Buffy the Vampire Slayer*?! Yeah, *that* sounds like a life-enhancing experience." How many fans have had to hide the fact that we watch this show, or have suffered derision from the masses of the un-informed? The title is meant to be funny, juxtaposing a name usually given to dumb blondes in beach movies with the incongruous phrase *vampire slayer*. But unless you actually watch the show, you don't under-stand the irony, and it just seems like a big joke.

In order to acquire the show, the networks allowed the executive producer almost full creative control, even though he takes huge risks. In the past five years he's done what no other show has: put a young flighty teenager in the role of "savior of the universe"; had an ensemble cast that includes a werewolf, two lesbian witches, and a vengeance demon; featured almost no adults, except Giles, who happened to raise a demon in his younger years; introduced shocking elements with no explanation for several episodes (Dawn); and written entire shows in the form of a dream that makes absolutely no sense ("Restless"). On regular network television, these kinds of risks just aren't allowed — the execu-tives find what sells and churn out that type of show. That's why we have countless shows about teenage angst (without vampires), sitcoms about families who just keep finding themselves in the strangest predica-ments (while, of course, taking time out to have that "extra-special episode" when Suzie is caught with the drugs), and so many shows about judges, lawyers, cops, and courtrooms that audiences are subjected to *three* different series with the words *Law and Order* in the title.

Buffy the Vampire Slayer is different, as any viewer will agree. How many of us have had someone make fun of the show, then become completely absorbed in it once we lent them a few videotaped episodes? *Buffy* is a show like none other on television, with its own unique mythology, an incredible ensemble cast, and a team of writers who keep the show on top creatively.

But in the beginning, it was all the brainchild of one man.

The Master of all Things Buffy

In the world of *Buffy* fandom, he is simply known as "god." The creator. The producer. The writer. The man who makes Buffy who she is, puts the words into the mouths of the characters, and shapes the storylines of one of the most original shows in the history of television. But he didn't always have so much control over the character. In fact, on his first time out, the character of Buffy was turned into his own nightmare.

Born on June 23, 1964, Joss Whedon came from a family of television writers and grew up in Manhattan. His grandfather had written scripts for 1950s and '60s television shows like *Mayberry RFD*, *The Donna Reed Show*, and *The Dick Van Dyke Show*, and Whedon's father had written for *Alice* and *Benson* in the '70s and '80s. But when Joss first tried his hand at writing, he wasn't as successful. "I wanted to write for TV, so I wrote a sickening number of TV specs, most of which were returned to me. The rejection notes usually said something like, 'Very charming. I do NOT wish to have it,'" he recalls. He continued to send out scripts for a year until the producers of *Roseanne* discovered him, and he says he literally was working at a video store on Friday and *Roseanne* on Monday. The experience was a mixed one. "It was baptism by radioactive waste," says Whedon. "[Roseanne] was like two people. One was perfectly intelligent and good to be around. One was very cranky. You never knew which would show up." After one year on the show (he wrote for the second season), he sold his first screenplay to Hollywood, and left *Roseanne*.

The story was one that had been in his head for some time. The basic premise was a cheerleader who realizes she is destined to be a vampire slayer when a mysterious man tells her of her vocation. The script mixed comedy with drama, and while the title was a humorous juxtapo-

CHRISTINA RADISH

Joss Whedon, the master of all things Buffy

sition of the words *Buffy* and *vampire slayer*, it was meant to be tongue-in-cheek, not an excuse for making the film an all-out comedy. Joss Whedon was about to get a harsh lesson about how little control a writer has in Hollywood.

Buffy the Vampire Slayer, released when Joss was a mere 27 years old, starred Kristy Swanson as the blond cheerleader. Donald Sutherland played her weary watcher, Luke Perry the love interest, Rutger Hauer (*Blade Runner*) the head vampire, and Paul Reubens (a.k.a. Pee-wee Herman) one of his lackeys. Working on the set, Joss had difficulty from the beginning. He later told *The Onion* that his biggest problem was Sutherland. "He would rewrite all his dialogue, and the director would let him. He can't write — he's not a writer — so the dialogue would not make sense. And he had a very bad attitude. He was incredibly rude to the director, he was rude to everyone around him, he was just a real pain. And to see him destroying my stuff. . . . Some people didn't notice. Some people liked him in the movie. Because he's Donald Sutherland. He's a great actor. He can read the phone book and I'm interested. But the thing is, he acts well enough that you didn't notice, with his little rewrites, and his little ideas about what his character should do, that he was actually destroying the movie. . . ." Reubens, on the other hand, was great, and seemed open to any of Joss's suggestions. It's probably why his is the funniest character in the film, and the only one who captures the strange sense of humor that later marked the television version.

The movie flopped at the box office, taking in only $16 million, and Whedon chalks it up to the fact that the final product no longer followed his original vision: "My original idea was a lot less silly. It *had* funny, but it was a much more serious action horror movie *with* the funny. Actually it was pretty gross, too. It wasn't just straight-on comedy, but that's how the film came off."

Whedon's talent as a writer, however, was not overlooked. He became Hollywood's Mr. Fixit and was brought in to jazz up scripts like *Speed*, *Waterworld*, and *Twister*, giving them more colorful dialogue. (In all of these movies, his writing went uncredited, and several of his suggestions were completely ignored, which is why *Waterworld* is, well, *Waterworld*.) Whedon gained more recognition when he co-penned the hilarious and clever *Toy Story* in 1995, for which he was nominated for an Oscar. In

1997, he wrote *Alien Resurrection*, but most of his dialogue was cut from the final product, infuriating him. "I'll tell you what the problem was," he says. "It was because Jean-Pierre Jeunet is the most unimaginative director I've ever seen. I could teach film with that movie, about how *not* to make movies. It was the most unimaginative directing I have ever seen. It was bad on every single level it could be bad on. Worst experience in my life. I was wanting to bomb France afterwards, it was so terrible. *Alien Resurrection*! I call it *Alien: We Bury the Franchise*." He would later rewrite the script for *X-Men*, and again most of his dialogue would be buried, prompting him to vow never to write again for something he couldn't direct.

While Whedon was coming to terms with the seedier side of screenwriting, *Buffy the Vampire Slayer* was released on home video, and the rental figures were far more encouraging than the box-office receipts had been. The movie was turning into a cult hit, and its producers were taking notice. Fran Rubel Kuzui, the film's director, and executive producer Gail Berman, who had thought the movie would make a great television show when she'd first read it, approached Whedon and asked if he'd be interested. He was very interested. As creator, head writer, executive producer, and occasional director, he would finally have the ability to do what he wanted with the series concept. Kuzui, Berman, and Whedon felt that if the show came out five years after the movie, it would avoid direct comparisons to its predecessor and viewers would recognize the difference between the two. The WB expressed an interest in the project, and auditions began. With Sarah Michelle Gellar (*All My Children*) in the lead role, and an ensemble cast that included young, raw talent and a theater-trained actor, Joss was confident that this time, his story of the cheerleading vampire slayer would be different.

Buffy the Vampire Slayer would not have a fall premiere, but would be added as a mid-season replacement in case another show didn't fare very well. Having a mid-season premiere gave Joss and the others more time to prepare. It also gave the actors more time to get to know one another. The members of the ensemble cast were mostly new to the business, with the exceptions of Sarah and Anthony Stewart Head, but they clicked right away.

Nobody knew if the show would be picked up for a second season, so the cast gave it their all in an attempt to win over the audience and the WB. Joss wrote the 12 episodes as one long story arc, and the final show of the season, "Prophecy Girl," completed the story, so viewers would know that the characters were going to be okay, even if they never returned. However, he intentionally left some story holes, so it would be very easy to start the show up again if it was renewed.

The ensemble immediately had an on-screen chemistry, as is evident in the first episodes. Xander and Willow seem like old friends, and if we do sense moments of discomfort on Willow's part, it can be attributed to the crush she's got on Xander. Cordelia is the perfect snob, Xander the wise-cracker, Willow the wallflower. Buffy has a sardonic wit about her, yet is vulnerable in certain situations, and Giles is the stuttery librarian who seems bewildered that his charge would rather date guys than slay vampires. Angel is brooding and mysterious, and the chemistry between him and Buffy is tense. The cast was perfect, and they were all delighted to be working with Joss, leading him to joke, "I don't think they fear me nearly enough."

Whedon knew he'd made the right choice with Sarah, and he refers to her as "like the best actress ever." He was delighted to see how she pulled off the role and how she was everything the movie Buffy wasn't. "Even though she's a vampire slayer," he says, "she still makes you feel everything she goes through, and that's not easy." He adds, "She is also great at pouting."

Alyson Hannigan, Charisma Carpenter, and Sarah Michelle Gellar doing promotion for season two of Buffy

As the filming for season one continued, Joss knew his original vision was being restored. He stressed that his show was not about "issues," like most teen shows, but that the subjects — no matter how many vampires or demons are lurking about — would be culled from the real fears of teenagers. Sarah agrees. "The scariest horror exists in reality," she says. "It's feeling invisible, date rape — these are situations teenagers understand and can relate to because it's happening to them."

When people ask Whedon why the townspeople of Sunnydale don't question the strange goings-on, he says his series operates under the same principle of suspended disbelief as shows like *Superman*. In *Superman*, people saw a man flying around in blue tights and a red cape, and they accepted he was there, just as the citizens of Sunnydale rationalize the vampire activity. Anthony Stewart Head remarked that he loves Whedon's unpredictable writing style, and joked that the cast has a constant fear of who will go next. "I thought it was wonderful last season when he bumped off the principal," he said during season two. "At that moment, you knew there weren't any lines he wouldn't cross, and anything goes."

There was some worry that the public wouldn't be able to handle a show this original and quirky, though. Sarah recalls the press conference they did to publicize the show, and the lukewarm reaction it received from the media: "In 1996 I was part of a cast of a mid-season replacement show based on a 1992 movie which didn't do that well at the box office. The whole cast was onstage for a press conference and nobody had any questions for us. We were all in tears." But once audiences saw the show, the critics were singing a different tune.

When the show finally premiered on March 10, 1997, it garnered a Nielsen rating of 3.4, meaning approximately 3,298,000 households were watching. It was one of the biggest ratings in WB history. Whedon attributes the show's initial success to the huge ad campaign the WB had launched to promote it. The series eventually became the biggest show on the network. And it wasn't just the fans who were loving it — *Buffy the Vampire Slayer* was a critical smash. Daniel Fienberg of the *Daily Pennsylvanian* raved, "Less cheesy than nearly every show on Fox, and edgier than every teen show that ABC, NBC, and CBS have put out in years, *Buffy* is (to create a TV *Guide* cover blurb) 'The Best Show on TV That You Would Make Fun of If You Didn't Know Better.'" Joe Queenan of TV *Guide* wrote that *Buffy the Vampire Slayer*, "far from being the stuff of fantasy or mere over-the-top satire, is the most realistic portrayal of contemporary teenage life on television today." Tom Carson of the *Village Voice* agreed, writing, "I can't think of a TV show that better captures how adolescence feels. . . ." He added that "the show's clear-eyed recognition that autonomy can be one hard row to hoe . . . puts it miles ahead of upbeat ads about girl Little Leaguers." Scott D. Pierce of *Deseret News* claimed, "*Buffy the Vampire Slayer* is the coolest show on TV." Thomas Hine of the *New York Times* called *Buffy* "television's most stylish female hand-to-hand fighter since Diana Rigg played Emma Peel on *The Avengers* three decades ago." He commented, "Being a teenager used to be the stuff of comedies. Now it's a horror show." Canadian Mark Kingwell, writing in *Saturday Night*, said that Buffy is "a true 1990s TV heroine" and "Gellar's edgy performances are a pleasure to watch." And last (possibly least), even Howard Stern told Sarah Michelle Gellar, "Your acting in this is perfect." He added, "It's one of the best hours on television."

Joss Whedon and Co. had a hit on their hands.

Slaying the Audiences

Following the popularity of the first season of *Buffy the Vampire Slayer*, the WB network allowed Whedon to write deeper situations into the series, develop the characters, alter their relationships, and tighten the ensemble cast into one of the strongest on television. The season two premiere featured an angry, depressed, and confused Buffy, setting the stage for a season that would delve into the characters' personal relationships and offer more continuity from episode to episode than in season one. The problems that teenagers have in high school would also be handled more seriously than in the first season. Because of the show's strong female following, Buffy's strength and intelligence would be made more prominent as well. "The problem with most high schools is they don't stress individuality," says Sarah. "Buffy shows girls it's okay to be different."

The new formula worked, and the ratings climbed steadily. The show was moved from the 9 p.m. Monday time slot to Tuesday at 8 p.m, midway through the season, and the new time slot stuck. Viewers tuned in week after week to watch the development of the relationship between Buffy and Angel, and the stars of the show were becoming recognizable faces. For the people who were watching the series, Buffy was a cultural icon of feminism and strength, which was exactly what Joss had intended. "I always wanted the character to be an icon," explains Whedon. "I wanted her to be a hero that existed in people's minds the way Wonder Woman or Spider-Man does, you know? I wanted her to be a doll or an action figure. I wanted Barbie with Kung Fu grip! I wanted her to enter the mass consciousness and the imaginations of growing kids because I think she's a cool character, and that was always the plan. I wanted Buffy to be a cultural phenomenon, period." In the second season, Joss included twists and turns that other shows wouldn't have had the guts to try. He killed off another major character, and had the love interest of the protagonist turn evil and become the villain of the season. Willow's character began to change and move in a Wiccan direction, while a new actor — Seth Green — was added to the mix.

Season one had introduced the characters and allowed the audience to become familiar with each one. Season two was about taking everything you knew about those characters and turning it on its head. Buffy went through her first heartache, Willow came out of her shell and began dating, Xander began to face his personal demons and his spiteful side came out, Cordelia became less a caricature and part of the Scooby gang, and Giles, well, didn't always wear tweed. Each of the characters fell in love (and we all know what happens to that on the hellmouth). The nail-biting finale of season two, "Becoming (Part Two)," had a Nielsen rating of 4.2 (about 4.4 million viewers), almost double what "Prophecy Girl" had garnered the year before. Joyce Millman of *Salon*, a longtime *Buffy* fan, urged her readers to watch what she considered one of the best shows on television: "Whedon energizes his metaphors . . . with a storytelling style that is both intensely emotional and devastatingly flip. *Buffy* approximates, perfectly, the mood swings of adolescence. . . . Indeed, one of the wonders of *Buffy* is how each member of Buffy's posse . . . has his or her own voice, unlike wb's higher-rated teen drama *Dawson's Creek*, on which everybody sounds exactly the same. You feel like you know the kids on *Buffy*. You've been there. Well, except for the vampires and stuff."

Season two also saw the first episodes written by Marti Noxon, who would later become co-executive producer of the show with Joss. She knew someone who had the same agent as Whedon, and was able to

Marti Noxon at the 2002
posting board party

finagle a meeting with him and co-executive producer David Greenwalt. "We just had a good meeting, although I was terribly nervous and thought it went badly," she says. "I was probably very lucky that I wasn't asked to pitch, because the show was still pretty young, so it wouldn't have been hard to get it wrong. We just talked about what I thought about the show and the influences that I saw working there and then a little bit about what I personally thought I could bring to it. I said, 'Pain, pain, pain,' and they said, 'Excellent, we can use some pain!'"

By season three, more viewers were catching on. *Entertainment Weekly* television critic Ken Tucker lauded the show in his column: "*Buffy*'s kickiness is both literal (its neck-snapping martial-arts scenes are simultaneously cartoonish and scary) and figurative; no show this side of *Seinfeld* loves the language of conversation (the wisecrack, the pun, the withering retort, and the muttered aside) as much." The season three arc included a new Slayer, Faith, that gave Buffy a new dimension: now she had to confront the Faith within, that leather-wearing, crass-talking girl who enjoys her job and gets off on the killing. For the next three seasons, other characters would tell Buffy she had a dark side and she should learn to embrace it. The season three Big Bad turned out to be the Mayor of Sunnydale (explaining why the police never questioned the large number of victims found with two holes in their necks), but the more important theme was graduation. The gang were trying to make it out of high school alive, Giles was relieved of his duties as Buffy's Watcher and had to figure out what to do with his life, and everyone had to prepare for the next stage in their lives: what to do after high school. To play the central guest character of Faith, Eliza Dushku was brought on board. The fans loved to hate Faith, and the brilliance of her character was that we only started to like her when she turned evil. Because of Dushku and co-villain Harry Groener, season three was one of the strongest seasons of *Buffy* ever.

However, season three also had its complications. Two of the episodes were pulled because of what the WB perceived to be inappropriate content, and for the first time, Joss Whedon wasn't singing such a positive tune about the network. The first incident occurred with "Earshot," an episode about violence in schools (see page 253 for a more detailed explanation of what happened). It was to air one week after the Columbine tragedy, and when the WB decided to postpone it, Whedon agreed because the timing would have been too close to what had happened, and people hadn't yet sorted out their thoughts. However, the WB didn't delay it by just a couple of weeks, they delayed it until the following September. WB CEO Jamie Kellner explained that a show like *Buffy the Vampire Slayer* just might be contributing to the violence.

Then the WB delayed the season finale, "Graduation Day (Part Two)" on the basis that it would be offensive so soon after Columbine. In an official statement, Kellner said, "It is out of sympathy and compassion for the families and communities that have been devastated by the recent senseless acts of violence perpetrated on high school campuses that we have decided to delay this broadcast. . . . Given the current climate, depicting acts of violence at a high school graduation ceremony, even fantasy acts against 60-foot serpents and vampires, we believe, is inappropriate to broadcast around the actual dates of these time-honored ceremonies." This time Whedon disagreed with the WB's stance. This episode wasn't about a student who had become homicidal and was going to take out the whole school, it was about a group of students fighting a giant reptile.

Whedon began to publicly challenge the WB's decision. When it was discovered that the episode had aired in parts of Canada (where it was aired on Monday, the day before the WB decided not to air it in the U.S.), Joss asked Canadians to "bootleg that puppy" for their American neighbors. The WB was not pleased. "I got in big trouble for saying I thought it was cool [that fans were bootlegging the episodes], but ultimately it was nice to know that people cared about the show," Whedon says. "[The WB] thought they would get terrible ratings, but they did fine when they finally aired. [The bootlegs] did not hurt us that much in terms of the network's needs." Fans bought a full-page *Variety* ad expressing their love for *Buffy the Vampire Slayer*, explaining that they knew the difference between right and wrong — even if the WB thought the audience were idiots — and that *Buffy* was a mature, important, and responsible show that should be aired. Whedon was flattered: "We were all just tremendously touched [by the *Variety* ad]; it was very cool. I have a framed copy of it in my office."

Sarah Michelle Gellar jumped into the fray to offer her own support for Joss Whedon by writing a mature Associated Press piece entitled "Stop Blaming Hollywood for Violent Behavior." In it she criticized the WB for its decision to pull the season finale, and right-wing organizations for blaming the media for Columbine. "I've always felt that, as an entertainer, my job is to tell a story and make people feel things, which may not always mean taking the moral high ground," Sarah wrote. "If a teenager can't discern right from wrong or fiction from reality, I'm pretty confident that it has little to do with whether he or she watches *Buffy* or plays aggressive video games and more to do with the fact that society has failed to teach him or her how to make those distinctions."

"Earshot" finally aired in September, one week before the season four premiere. If that wasn't confusing enough, season four took the neat little formula that we had grown accustomed to — Buffy as Slayer, Giles as Watcher, Willow as the smart computer girl, Xander as the bumbling friend who thought about sex, Oz as the cool guitar-playing werewolf, the Sunnydale High library as the meeting place — and changed everything, alienating the characters from each other, and viewers from a now-unfamiliar setting. Buffy felt disoriented at school, Giles was no longer her Watcher, Willow began undergoing major changes, Xander was separated from the group, and Oz disappeared. The show abandoned its format of the gang solving the mysteries behind the monsters through ancient texts and took on an *X-Files* quality, with Riley and the Initiative boys skulking around every corner. The show's writers realized partway through the season that the idea wasn't working and began de-emphasizing the Initiative and focusing on the alienation Buffy and her friends were feeling in their strange new environment.

That said, the season featured such classics as "Hush," which *finally* got Joss nominated for a writing Emmy, "Pangs," "Wild at Heart," and "A

ALBERT L. ORTEGA

The cast of Buffy the Vampire Slayer *hangs out in California. From left, Alyson Hannigan, Nicholas Brendon, David Boreanaz, Joss Whedon, Anthony Stewart Head, and Seth Green*

New Man," and introduced a new cast member, Marc Blucas. But Riley was a difficult role to step into. Buffy had just had her heart broken when Angel left for L.A., and Blucas had to fill the role of the squeaky-clean farmboy from Iowa. Fans didn't react well to his character — especially after the broody, volatile Angel — as Blucas discovered firsthand when he ventured onto the fan's message boards. But he remained cool: "I know that for the most part, people who have a problem with Riley, it's relational issues. I understand that they're protective of Buffy, and they know her with Angel. And it's understandable. I appreciate their wanting that." It was a tough situation to be in, since Angel was now gone, and many fans were uncomfortable with that.

An Angel Flies the Coop

Angel had left Sunnydale and moved to L.A. to try to make sense of his purpose in life . . . and to have his own television show. Joss Whedon got the idea to create a spinoff show for Angel when they were filming

"Becoming (Part Two)." The original idea was to have Angel move to L.A. where he would meet up with Whistler, his mentor, played by Max Perlich in the "Becoming" episodes, and have several flashbacks to how Angel came to be. However, as season three of *Buffy* unfolded, Whedon decided to bring in a new mentor, Doyle, whom Angel hadn't met before. The show was meant to be a darker, more adult show than *Buffy*, set in L.A., where Buffy had discovered the seedy side of the big city in "Anne." And the producers thought they should take at least one other character from *Buffy* to ensure viewers would watch both series. At the end of season three, we discover that Cordelia's father has been charged with tax fraud and the family is pretty much penniless, so it made sense to take that character and transplant her to L.A. as well, running away from her fashionable past in Sunnydale. Charisma Carpenter was a little worried about moving from such a successful show to an unknown one, but after reassurances from Joss that should *Angel* be canceled, her role on *Buffy* would be secure, she went ahead and made the leap. To round out the cast, Glenn Quinn was brought on to play Doyle.

The day-to-day duties on *Angel* were handed over to David Greenwalt, while Whedon would be an executive producer with him and oversee the scripts. Greenwalt had written "Angel," thereby creating the background to Angel, and "Nightmares," the first episode of *Buffy* to deal with darker psychological issues in the characters. He seemed like the perfect fit. Greenwalt explained where they were planning on taking the new series: "A lot of *Angel* deals with how Angel relates to this dark, dangerous, and sometimes glamorous world of Los Angeles. This is the city of law firms, and talent agencies, and gangsters, all very real, and at times extremely unsettling. . . . Just think for a moment about L.A. There's the quest for eternal youth and beauty in this town, people who will do anything to stay young forever. Then there's the incredible divide between haves and have-nots. The rich definitely live among the poor. You add demonology to that, and you've automatically got these great issues. And right in the middle of it all is Angel, a vampire with a soul, perhaps more of a soul than most of the people in the city."

Angel would not only look at L.A. and the darker elements of life, it would take us deeper into Angel's psyche. We had seen Angelus, the worst that Angel could be, but this series would explore the gray area of how Angel was struggling with his inner demons on a daily basis. Not that it wouldn't be without its laughs. "In addition to the morose, tormented Angel," said Greenwalt, "this time we also have an Angel with a sense of humor. In fact, all our characters, and all of our situations, have a dosage of dark, unexpected humor. *Angel* is almost like a film noir with a few giggles thrown in."

The show was an immediate success, although the ratings did dip mid-season, as some *Buffy* viewers decided it was too different from *Buffy*. Not only that, but in the ninth episode the writers took a surprising risk by killing off one of the only three regular cast members. Fans were shocked, and "Save Doyle" campaigns popped up everywhere. Joss supported his decision, saying it was in keeping with the spirit on the show. "He was an interesting character, but I just wanted to shake things up by getting rid of Angel's mentor," he said. "We were setting up someone who [the viewers] thought would be there the whole time and then killed him really surprisingly. We wanted to keep the audience on their toes, keep them frightened . . . and not let them feel safe in the world they are watching."

Soon Alexis Denisof was brought in as the newest cast member, and while some fans stopped watching, never to return, others thought Denisof gave the show more of a *Buffy* feeling, helping to steer it in the right direction. The first season relied on a lot of *Buffy* crossovers to bring in new viewers and was something of a monster-of-the-week show, but by season two *Angel* really found its legs.

Meanwhile, over on *Buffy*, things were changing rapidly and controversy was brewing. With Willow coming out as the first major gay character on the series, some fans were outraged that she would choose Tara over Oz, while others were delighted that homosexuality was finally being dealt with on television by a capable person like Joss Whedon — other shows had dealt with the issue but avoided the more serious implications. Not only did Joss feel it was time to take Willow's character in a new direction, but Seth Green had announced he was leaving, putting Joss in an awkward position. "I was like, 'Doesn't he have a contract?!'" Joss remembers. "But he left, and we sort of scrambled to fix that. And when he said, 'I'll do a couple more episodes,' and we said he should come back at the end of the year and we can do a thing, and he's like, 'Actually, I just wanna come back for *one*, I don't wanna do more than that.'

So I said, 'Okay, so that one's gonna be about how Willow loves Tara *and not* YOU! I realized I only had him for the one, so I had to resolve that plot. And I was pissed. But he showed up for his spot in the dream episode, 'Restless,' which was nice. You know, the thing is, if Seth had wanted to do the show we'd have used him. He's a wonderful actor and a fascinating character. But he bailed on our asses, he really did, and we had to scramble. And out of the heavens came Amber Benson."

But some fans of the Willow/Oz relationship thought differently, and came down hard on Amber, forcing her to let her feelings be known on the Bronze posting board (see the Amber Benson bio for her rebuttal). Joss stuck up for the relationship as well, and posted the now-infamous "apology" on the posting board:

> Okay. Let's be frank. Last Tuesday's episode was pretty controversial, and a real eye-opener for me. And despite my fervent hatred of criticism, I do understand when I've made a mistake. I thought the Willow arc made sense for her character, but the fact is, most people AREN'T like that, and it's hard for most normal people to understand a lifestyle that less than 10% of the population embrace. I don't want to be about issues — I just want to tell a story I think will engage and challenge, and this time I think I missed the mark. So I'm just hoping people understand we're feeling our way along here. We ARE listening. So we're going to shift away from this whole lifestyle choice Willow has made. Just wipe the slate. From now on, Willow will no longer be a Jew. And I think we can all breathe easier.

Whedon was shocked at the negative reaction (which, fortunately, represented a minority of viewers); he felt viewers of his show would be mature and open-minded enough to accept one of the characters coming out. When one interviewer suggested he was taking a big risk, Joss expressed his surprise: "It doesn't feel gutsy. In fact, I was shocked that everybody was making a fuss. I was like, 'Guys, do you live in the world?' I mean, honestly, some people are gay. I mean, a lot of them! Most of the gay people I know are gay." He explained on the posting board and to the media that he would handle the homosexual relationship differently from other shows — it would not become the focus of the show; it would just exist, as relationships do — and if they didn't like it, too bad. "My show is about

Alyson Hannigan and Joss Whedon

emotion," he wrote. "Love is the most powerful, messy, delightful and dangerous emotion. . . .Willow's in love. I think it's cool."

Season five would bring even more challenges, although many fans consider it the shining season of the series. By late fall, rumors began circulating that the WB was looking to cancel the show, which had viewers and critics scratching their heads. Why would a network cancel a show that was not only popular, but groundbreaking? The result was a season that could have been the end of the series (it had a sense of finality matched only by the first season finale), with Buffy finally admitting there are demons she can't fight, and they will be the ones that will leave the most lasting impression. There was a new arrival to the cast — and, oddly enough, Buffy's immediate family — with her new sister, Dawn, played by Michelle Trachtenberg. Meanwhile on *Angel*, the season finale the previous May had given Angel a purpose, and in the new season the show just got better and better.

But *Buffy* didn't make the papers in 2001 because of its great writing; the media jumped onto the big story that the WB wasn't going to renew the show in the fall. The network was offering 20th Century Fox, who owned the show, $1.6 million an episode for the following season, but Fox was asking $2 million. WB CEO Jamie Kellner became defensive in the media, stating that without the WB, *Buffy* would never have become so popular: "Nobody wanted the show; it didn't perform [at first] but we stuck with it." He added, "It's not a show like *ER* that stands above the pack." His flippant comments infuriated Whedon, who felt his show was not getting the kudos it deserved; after all, it was because of *Buffy* that the WB was suddenly attracting teenagers with other programs such as *Charmed* and *Dawson's Creek*. Only *7th Heaven* was performing better than *Buffy* in the ratings, and Joss said so in interviews. "For [the WB] to be scrambling to explain why it's not cost-efficient — it's their second-highest-rated show," he said. "They need to step up and acknowledge that financially."

Other networks realized that *Buffy* was a hot property, and ABC and UPN entered the discussions. Kellner made an extra effort to keep the show, even offering to give Fox every cent the show made. "We will take all the revenue we can generate with *Buffy* and we'll give it to you in a giant wheelbarrow," Kellner said. "And if that's not enough, then take it to somebody else. You've demonstrated you're not the kind of partner we should be doing business with."

Sarah Michelle Gellar publicly stated that if the WB didn't get the show in the fall, she would leave. Her comment generated a lot of gasps from the media, but she later stated that she made the statement to show her support for both the show and Joss, and to express how much it meant to her. Although it had raised eyebrows, Whedon understood the spirit in which it was said. "The fact is, she knew perfectly well that if we moved, she was going to move with us, and she's very professional," he said afterward. "I sort of shook my head when I saw that story, but I knew it was something that would just blow over."

In the end, it was UPN who picked up the show for a guaranteed two seasons at $2.3 million an episode, and agreed that if the WB cancelled *Angel*, they would also pick up that show for two seasons. Whedon and the cast were ecstatic — they finally felt appreciated after the WB had shown them so little respect in the media. "It's always been great at the WB," said Whedon. "But at the highest levels, they made a corporate decision that I found unfathomable. They decided not only to not step up financially, but to sort of diss the show in the press, and to me that was unforgivable. It really hurt. But the people I dealt with, the promotional people and the creative execs, they were great. I have no beef with them. But yeah, it's nice to see a network come up and say, 'We think you're an extraordinary asset and we're going to prove that by writing this large check.'"

As the season drew to a close, Joss had a few final arguments with the WB about how certain things were handled. In the critically acclaimed episode "The Body," where Whedon and the entire cast did an extraordinary job of depicting what it's like to lose a loved one, there was a throwaway same-sex kiss that just happened. The WB wanted it cut, but when Joss threatened to pull the episode, they relented. And viewers received a shock when the season finale ran as the "series finale" on the WB, prompting many to think the PR surrounding the move had all been a ruse and that season five really *was* the end of the show. At the end of the credits, the words "Five great years. We thank you." flashed across the screen, offering an eerie finality that made fans — and Joss — a little uncomfortable. Whedon called it "cheesy" in the press and reassured fans that the show was indeed continuing. The WB issued an apology, saying the message was meant as a sincere thank-you, not an insinuation that the show was over.

All Work and No Play Makes Joss a Pretty Cool Boy

Whedon wasn't being kept busy with just *Buffy* throughout the 2000–2001 year, though. He was also working on *Angel*, and developing his new comic-book series, *Fray*. Set in an apocalyptic, dark future where people can suffer mutation by radiation, the series is about Melaka Fray, a vampire and demon slayer of the future who is called to rid the world of evil. It was Whedon's first foray into the world of writing comic books, but he had been a comic-book fan all his life. "I've always wanted to write comics," he says, "and after establishing this relationship with Dark Horse on the *Buffy* books, I was thinking about it even more. I also saw how much fun the writers — including guys like Doug Petrie, who works with me on the show — were having with the comics, so I decided to abuse my vast power and force Dark Horse to let me do a series."

Joss was also developing *Firefly*, a new series that Fox would begin airing Friday nights in fall 2002. Set 800 years in the future, the show features

Joss Whedon holds up copies of his comic book, Fray

Nathan Fillion (*Two Guys and a Girl*), Gina Torres (*Cleopatra 2525, Alias*), Adam Baldwin (*X-Files, The Patriot*), Alan Tudyk (*28 Days, A Knight's Tale*), Jewel Staite (*Honey, I Shrunk the Kids: The TV Show*), Summer Glau (*Angel*), Sean Maher (*Party of Five*), and Ron Glass (*The Education of Max Bickford, Barney Miller*). *Firefly* is about Captain Malcolm "Mal" Reynolds (Fillion), a veteran who fought in a war to unite the planets, but was on the side that lost. Joss describes the show — which revolves around Mal's crew on his spaceship *Serenity* — as a "science-fiction Western," but with only human characters, unlike *Star Trek*. When Joss turned in the original pilot to Fox, they were very unhappy with it and made him go back to the drawing board. He tried again, and they were much happier with the second result, announcing late in May that they would pick up the first 13 episodes. They gave him a budget of $1.3 million per episode. For the first season at least, Joss decided to use the same team of writers that create *Buffy* and *Angel* each week.

As if that weren't enough, Whedon was also developing an idea with the BBC to begin a new show with Anthony Stewart Head called *The Watcher* or *Ripper*. Set in England, where Giles would return to hunt ghosts, it would consist of six episodes a season. *And* he was working on *Buffy Animated*, set back in season one when they were in high school, allowing writers who had come on board in later years to write scripts for the earlier characters. According to Jeph Loeb, former co-executive producer on *Buffy Animated* with Joss (he later left to pursue other projects), the later writers "never got to do stories where Willow likes Xander, Xander likes Buffy, Buffy has a crush on Angel, and Angel hadn't yet reciprocated. That's the fun part — to be able to go back and do that sort of thing." Almost everyone from the cast except Sarah Michelle Gellar and David Boreanaz signed on to provide the voices for the characters.

Knowing that running just two shows was extremely difficult, Joss enlisted help for season six, installing Marti Noxon as executive producer to run the day-to-day things on *Buffy* when he was on the set of *Angel* or *Firefly*. As season six began, fans were eager to find out how Buffy would be resurrected (after she sacrificed herself to save humanity in a gripping season-five finale), while seeing if the UPN move would prove to be a smart one. By August, posters everywhere around L.A. proclaimed "Buffy Lives," and UPN promoted the show in a way it hadn't been promoted in years.

Joss Whedon visits the set of Angel, *here with J. August Richards and Amy Acker*

The cast was very happy with the change. Nicholas Brendon saw it as a move toward viewing the show as one with an ensemble cast, rather than as a vehicle for one person. "We had relationships at the WB, so it's kind of weird to leave," he said at the time. "But we did get a lovely gift basket from UPN with a Cartier watch and champagne and beluga caviar. We didn't get much respect from the WB because they saw the show not as an ensemble, but as Sarah's show. When we had our 100th-episode celebration, they thanked Sarah, and then 10 minutes later they thanked the rest of the cast, too." Alyson Hannigan agreed: "UPN has picked up *Buffy* for two years. The WB treated the show as just being about Sarah — it's

KEVORK DJANSEZIAN/AP/CP PHOTO

Sarah Michelle Gellar shows her excitement about the upcoming season six in Pasadena, 2001, with Joss Whedon, Alyson Hannigan, and James Marsters

only the fans and Joss that view it as an ensemble, but hopefully the UPN will embrace that. There are lovely people at the WB, but I don't think they knew my name until *American Pie* came out! I never heard from the executives over there before, but then it was like, 'Oh sure, call me now!'"

Season six was about growing up and coming to terms with being an adult — and it showed more of the good than the bad. Every character ended up being his or her own worst enemy — Buffy can't live in the world because she's seen what Heaven is like, and she punishes herself by entering into an unhealthy relationship; Willow becomes addicted to the magic, and it compromises her happiness; Dawn turns into a kleptomaniac, turning everyone against her; Xander makes a huge but very human error and believes his life is ruined; Anya is torn between the human and demon worlds, and hates herself for allowing passion to rule her reason; Spike allows Buffy to abuse him, but struggles with the fact that he's neither a demon nor a man; and only Tara embraces adulthood, seeming to understand her place in the world. Of course, since Tara is the only one with a reasonable head on her shoulders, her character must be headed for certain doom. Giles, the only adult in the group who might have been able to help with the transition, returns to England, convinced Buffy no longer needs him because she has become independent.

The "big bad" of season six was unclear; some argued it was the Troika, while others said it was Willow. But instead the big bad appeared to be the process of growing up, and because Willow was the most unlike her younger character, she suffered the most. The season was a challenging one for viewers — the ambiguity in the plots divided fans and caused a lot of arguing and tension on the Internet mailing lists. But then again, that's what makes the show so great.

Back on the WB, *Angel* continued to shine; removing *Buffy* from the network was the best thing that could have happened to *Angel*. The networks refused to allow any crossover episodes between the two shows (although Joss says that could change), and *Angel* was forced to stand on its own two feet, which it did valiantly. The show came into its own: severed from the *Buffy* mythology, it rivaled *Buffy* for quality. Introducing Amy Acker as the new addition to the gang — and the potential love interest of two of its members — was a compelling development, as was the relationship between Cordelia and Angel (who would have seen *that* coming in season two of *Buffy*?!), the tensions between Wesley and the gang, and Angel's past and future catching up to him at once. At the end of what almost everyone considered the best season yet, David Greenwalt announced his departure to helm a spring 2003 show on ABC called *Miracles*. David Simkins (*Freakylinks*) will be joining the show as the day-to-day executive producer.

Buffy the Vampire Slayer has come a long way since its inception as a movie about a tough cheerleader in the early '90s. Asked what she likes best about being Buffy on the occasion of the 100th episode (the season five finale), Sarah Michelle Gellar answered, "Being part of really good television. Being part of a strong feminine role. We made 100 hours of not just *something* television — we made 100 hours of what I think is really groundbreaking television." And the critics agree. In May 2002, when TV *Guide* compiled its list of the "50 Greatest Shows of All Time," *Buffy the Vampire Slayer* was listed at No. 41, shocking everyone — including the fans, who are used to the show being overlooked. It placed ahead of such television classics as *Taxi, Bewitched,* and *Star Trek: The Next Generation*. It was about time somebody listened: while the acting prowess of Sarah Michelle Gellar, Alyson Hannigan, and the rest of the cast — as well as the writing and overall genius of Joss Whedon — were going unnoticed on awards night, there was, and is, an audience for the show.

The same month, Nicholas Brendon announced that the seventh season would be the show's last, explaining that Whedon's schedule was becoming stretched too thin running and developing five shows. "It's gonna be really sad for me, 144 episodes and it's my first job," he said. "I went through a lot of changes personally in that time, so it's gonna be a teary goodbye." The news wasn't a complete surprise to fans, considering that the actors had signed contracts for seven seasons. Marti Noxon, on the other hand, suggested in June 2002 that the show could continue after season seven, even without Sarah on board." It would be very hard to continue the show without her, but [UPN and 20th Century Fox] might try."

There will always be syndication, and as long as Joss Whedon can hold a pen or type on a keyboard, you can bet there will be more excellent television. Fans everywhere owe him a resounding thank-you for creating a world so complicated, so deep, and so wonderful that we don't mind the occasional derision from the non-converted who can't get past the show's goofy title. After all, they're the ones who are missing out.

The Cast of
Buffy the Vampire Slayer

SARAH MICHELLE GELLAR
Buffy Summers

Her big break is the stuff of Hollywood legend: she was "discovered" while eating in a New York restaurant with some friends. She was four years old at the time.

Sarah Michelle Gellar was born on April 14, 1977, in New York City. She was a bubbly and intelligent youngster, and her mother must have had a hunch that Sarah was destined for big things. Little did she know it would happen at such a young age. One day in a restaurant, apparently after watching the animated youngster for some time, a woman approached the table where Sarah and some friends of her mother were eating, and asked Sarah if she'd like to be on television. Gellar is slightly embarrassed when she remembers the encounter, recalling that she immediately turned to the agent and proudly rhymed off her full name, phone number, parents' names, and address. "I didn't know what I was doing," she laughs.

She impressed the woman nonetheless, and Sarah returned home and announced to her mother, Rosellen, that she was going to be on television. Her mother thought the whole thing was a prank, because her daughter didn't have any acting experience — that is, until she received a phone call from the agent setting up Sarah's audition. Rosellen's own curiosity (and probably some pleading on Sarah's part) pushed her to follow up. The next day she and Sarah were at Sarah's first audition.

The movie was called *An Invasion of Privacy*, and the cast boasted some notable names. The star was Valerie Harper, and Sarah would audition for the part of her daughter. Other cast members included Carol Kane (from *Taxi*), Jeff Daniels (*Dumb and Dumber*), Robby Benson (*Ice Castles*), and Jerry Orbach (*Law & Order*). The audition was held late in the afternoon, and Sarah was given a scene she was supposed to read with Valerie Harper, but Harper had already left for the day. The young-ster grabbed the script, said it was no problem, and started reading her part. When she came to one of Harper's lines, she lowered her voice and read it out, imitating Valerie. The casting agents found her irresistible and hired her right then and there.

Word spread quickly about this precocious young lady, and Sarah was soon made the star in a series of Burger King commercials that aired in 1981. Many years later, when she appeared on *The Tonight Show with Jay Leno* to promote *Buffy the Vampire Slayer*, Sarah laughed that they had to hire a speech coach to help her when she was doing the commercials: "I couldn't say 'burger.' I kept saying 'buga, buga.'" She eventually learned the proper pronunciation, though, and soon North America would be charmed by a little girl in a Burger King restaurant, sitting cross-legged on a chair with long dark pigtails. She was adorable, yet spoke in a very matter-of-fact way that made her seem beyond her years. Audiences everywhere loved her — with one exception.

One of her commercials led to a groundbreaking court case that would forever change the face of competitive advertising. In it, Sarah tells the audience that Burger King burgers are bigger than McDonald's ham-burgers and that the burgers are flame-broiled rather than fried like they are at McDonald's. This was the first time in television history that a company had used a competitor's name in a critical way. McDonald's sued Sarah, Burger King, and the ad agency that put out the commercials for slander.

"I was five," she remembers. "I couldn't even say the word 'lawyer' and a few months later I was telling my friends, 'I can't play. I've got to give a deposition.'" The lawsuit was settled out of court in 1982, but it set a precedent whereby companies could now name competitors' products in their advertising. Sarah did 30 spots in total for Burger King.

Sarah now had a recognizable face and was in demand. *An Invasion of Privacy*, which she had begun filming the week after her first audition, fi-nally aired in 1983. Sarah then appeared uncredited in a feature film called *Over the Brooklyn Bridge*, which featured a stellar cast, including Elliott Gould, Margaux Hemingway, Carol Kane, Sid Caesar, and Shelley Win-ters. After completing these movies, Sarah took a bit of a hiatus from acting in larger productions — she was, after all, only in Grade 2. During this time, she focused more on her schoolwork and her friends, although she continued to do commercials.

By 1986, though, she was back in business, appearing as Emily in an episode of *Spenser for Hire*. Sarah loved working with the show's star, Robert Urich. "I was eight or nine, and he was just wonderful to me," she remembers. The same year she appeared in her first theater production, Horton Foote's *The Widow Claire*. The play was at the Circle in the Square Theatre in New York City, and the cast must have been like a dream for a nine-year-old girl: her co-stars were Matthew Broderick and Eric Stoltz. She remembers that when she was first cast to work with them, they weren't big-name actors, but soon afterward, *Ferris Bueller's Day Off* and *Some Kind of Wonderful*, starring Broderick and Stoltz respectively, were released. "I was the most popular girl in school because I was working with both of them!" she recalls.

That popularity didn't last. When it was time for junior high school, Sarah enrolled in Columbia Preparatory School in New York and soon realized it would be difficult for her to fit in. Many of the students came from very wealthy families, and Sarah's mother was a teacher, with a more modest income. "Many students were used to having everything handed to them on a silver platter," Sarah says. "Everything I got I worked hard for and got on my own." As many children know, kids at junior-high age can be very cruel, and the students at Columbia Prep were no exception. Sarah became a loner because the other kids wouldn't hang out with her. Probably out of jealousy of Sarah's talent and success, they punished her for being famous by harassing her constantly. Sarah was miserable at school, so she continued putting most of her efforts into acting.

In 1988, she landed a small role in the Chevy Chase movie *Funny Farm*, in which she played a student. Her performance went uncredited there, as well. The following year she appeared in the feature film *High Stakes*, a thriller starring Kathy Bates and Sally Kirkland. Sarah starred as Kirkland's daughter, Karen, and this was the only time she was credited as Sarah Gellar. She found out that another actress used that same name, so from then on she went by her full name. That same year she hosted *Girl Talk*, a cheesy Saturday-morning TV talk show for young girls, where the hosts would sit and talk about clothes, guys, and other topics that could be considered "girl talk." Her co-hosts were Soleil Moon Frye, best known as Punky Brewster, and Rod Brogan, who went on to *Major Dad* and *One Life to Live*. However, the lighthearted talk show had a very small viewership and was soon canceled.

By this time, at 13, Sarah was so busy with everything happening in her life that her mother had her wear a pager so she'd know where her daughter was. Sarah shares a close relationship with her mother. Her parents were divorced when she was very young, and she was always reluctant to talk about her father, Arthur Gellar, except to say that they didn't get along and he was no longer part of her life. Arthur was found dead in his apartment on October 9, 2001, after a long battle with depression and cancer.

Despite Arthur not being around, Sarah did not grow up fatherless. Her mother remarried in the early 1990s, and Sarah says her stepfather has supported her in all of her achievements. "My stepfather always says that when he sees how many things I handle in a day, he'd be willing to hire a young person like me, because now he sees what an incredible thing it is to see kids so focused and how much they have to offer," she says proudly. She has said she considers him to be more of a father than her biological one.

Sarah always speaks of her mother tenderly, and it's clear that Rosellen attended auditions with her, watched out for her, and kept her grounded. However, she was not a typical stage mother who would make decisions for her daughter. Sarah explains, "My mother is not living vicariously through me. . . . It has always been my choice to act. If at any time I wanted to give it up, she would be behind me 100 percent." She adds, "My mom has always been behind me and we are very close." Rosellen recently moved to California to be closer to Sarah and they try to get together a few times every week.

It was Sarah's mother who realized how unhappy Sarah was at the prep school. Because it was a regular private school, the other students simply couldn't identify with her lifestyle. Sarah was beginning to rebel and started keeping to herself. "I went through this crazy phase where I had five holes in each earlobe and wore a navel ring," she says. "I'd dye my hair a different color each week. I really wanted to be a Gothic teenager, like one of the kids in *The Craft*. No wonder people tended to avoid me at school! I guess I was a bit of a nerd, really."

Sarah admits now that she had many of the same problems in junior high that Buffy has in high school, because she was misunderstood. Buffy has to slay vampires when she should be doing homework or dating, and Sarah faced a similar problem: "I had that same decision — do I go to a school dance or slumber party or do I go to an audition?" Her favorite movie of all time is *Heathers* — which probably says a lot about how she regarded her school years. (In *Heathers*, Winona Ryder plays a student who doesn't fit in with the rich girls she hangs out with. In a bizarre twist, Christian Slater's character conspires with her to kill their classmates.) Sarah was made to feel ashamed of her accomplishments and was never proud of what she did. "I never liked to talk about my acting," she recalls, "because if I did I was branded a snob, and if I didn't I was still a snob. I would cry because I didn't understand why people didn't like me."

Her mother transferred her to the Professional Children's School in Manhattan. Immediately there was a difference in how Sarah was treated, because the other students worked, just like she did. She made many friends and finally felt as though people understood her: "It's for anyone with irregular schedules — musicians from Juilliard, ballerinas from the School of American Ballet, and writers, and just the most talented group of young people where your talent is special, but it doesn't affect your schoolwork."

At this time, Sarah was acting, going to school, taking figure-skating lessons, and learning tae kwon do. She had studied the martial arts for four years, and was two belts away from her black belt, even placing fourth in competition once. "I would get up in the morning," she says, "go to the ice rink, then go to school, then go to auditions, then go to tae kwon do. I was cracking." Rosellen could see her daughter was over-worked, so she told Sarah it was time for her to make a choice — she could do two things at once, but no more. Sarah naturally chose school and acting. (Little did she know how important that tae kwon do would someday be for her.) Sarah graduated from the school with a 4.0 grade-point average after only two and a half years, but while there her career skyrocketed, setting the stage for stardom.

In 1991 Sarah was cast in the made-for-TV movie *A Woman Named Jackie*, which was about Jacqueline Bouvier Kennedy Onassis. Sarah played the young Jacqueline Bouvier, while seasoned stage actress Roma

Downey played her as an adult. Downey went on to play Hippolyta alongside Lucy Lawless and Kevin Sorbo in *Hercules and the Amazon Women* before landing the lead role in the hugely popular television series *Touched by an Angel*. Sarah loved Downey and recalls that she wanted to be like her. She began mimicking her movements on the set, and Downey was flattered. For the purposes of the movie, Sarah's imitation led to uncanny similarities in speech and action between the younger and older Jackies, making both performances believable and seamless. Interestingly, one of the cast members was Mark Metcalf, who would later square off against Buffy as the Master.

In 1992, shortly after starting at the new school, Sarah appeared in the premiere cast of the latest Neil Simon play, *Jake's Women*. Despite being 15, she played 12-year-old Molly, which began a pattern in her career where Sarah would play someone either older or younger than herself. A year earlier, she had won the role of Sydney Orion Rutledge in the Fox teen soap opera, *Swans Crossing*, although the episodes didn't air until a full year after the pilot had been filmed. Playing Sydney would help her win her next role in *All My Children*. Sydney is a manipulator, the daughter of the mayor in the tiny seaside town of Swans Crossing. Asked to describe her character, Sarah answered, "Well, Sydney is kind of like the town witch. She doesn't really care about anyone else's feelings and she feels that everything revolves around her, and it usually does. I guess there are always similarities and differences, but I try to keep the bad parts of Sydney out of my life." Ironically, a reviewer for *Entertainment Weekly* would describe Sydney as "a younger, blonder Erica Kane." The show, focusing on the lives of 12 young people, was mediocre at best — it made *Saved by the Bell* look like a high-quality program. The town boasted the Swans Cleaners, Swans Auto Shop, and Swans Café (which had a swan-shaped phone), and just made the viewer wonder if anyone in this town could live without those damn birds. Despite the near-ridiculousness of the show, it garnered a small but devoted following. Mira Sorvino even appeared in early episodes (before her Oscar, of course).

Swans Crossing prided itself on standing apart from other shows, especially *Beverly Hills 90210*, in that it didn't deal with "issues." For Fox, though, the only thing that mattered was the ratings, which were decent, but not stellar. How Fox imagined that a show geared to seven- to 15-year-olds would do well in a 2 p.m. time slot remains a mystery, but after three months of the daily soap, it was put on hiatus. To see if it could pick up any new fans, the network rebroadcast the first three months of the show — in exactly the same time slot. The series had a lot of potential among younger viewers, and the producers had even marketed *Swans Crossing* dolls. However, the ratings weren't high enough to cover the cost of producing a daily show, and the series was canceled. All was not lost, though, for after *Swans Crossing* was finished, Sarah moved on to an audition that would change her life forever.

Sarah had no idea what part she would be getting when she attended the audition for *All My Children*. She knew it would be for a young person, and she'd probably play someone's child. Then she was cast as the daughter of the manipulative Erica Kane, played by Susan Lucci. Sarah was very nervous the day she walked onto the set. After all, *All My Children* was one of the hottest soap operas on television, and Erica Kane was the diva of soap divas. Sarah's fears were quickly assuaged on that first day. Lucci was rehearsing a scene with Michael Nader, who plays Dmitri, but she stopped and came over to welcome Sarah. She then accompanied the younger actress around the set, introducing her to everyone. Sarah was very touched. "I couldn't have asked to work with anyone better," Sarah said at the time. "You can't not have a good working relationship with her." She would soon be singing a different tune.

Sarah's character, Kendall Hart, entered the show's story line just as Erica was about to get married. Sarah often jokes about the plot and what a whirlwind it was, and she's not kidding. From 1993 to 1995 her character went through just about everything. Kendall made her first appearance on *All My Children* on February 24, 1993. Erica had been raped and made pregnant when she was 14, but she'd given the baby up for adoption and tried to forget it had ever happened. Kendall shows up as someone who idolizes Erica, but won't reveal the truth about who she really is. Mona, Erica's mother, sees the birthmark on Kendall's neck that identifies her as Erica's daughter, but it isn't until Bianca, Erica's other daughter, is injured in a riding accident that Kendall tells Erica the truth. When Kendall then becomes obsessed with finding her birth father, Erica forbids it. When Kendall convinces Dmitri to help her, Erica finds out, kicks Kendall out of the house, and leaves Dmitri, demanding a divorce.

Kendall spends the night with Dmitri's assistant, Anton, and then tells Erica that Dmitri tried to rape her. In a blind rage, Erica returns and stabs Dmitri with a letter opener, remembering when she'd been raped as a teen. (Are you still with me?)

Kendall starts scheming with Del Henry, another guy in town, about writing a tell-all book on Erica Kane. In the attempted murder trial, Erica says she didn't mean to stab Dmitri, but had hallucinated that he was Robert Fields, the man who'd raped her. Kendall takes the stand and swears that Dmitri had raped her and that Erica's act was something he'd pushed her to do. However, during the trial she realizes her real father was a monster, recants her testimony, and is sent to jail for perjury, setting Erica free. Meanwhile, Mona kills Fields and later dies in her sleep (after the actress who played her, Frances Heflin, lost a long battle with cancer). Kendall finds out Anton is Dmitri's son and marries him, but later agrees to a divorce. She and Erica come to an understanding before Kendall leaves Pine Valley for Florida, from whence she came. Whew!!

Kendall's life was pretty complicated, but Sarah loved every minute of it (although she sometimes wished Kendall would calm down a bit). Kendall's crazed behavior allowed Sarah to try things she'd never done before. "It was amazing playing a psycho-loony," she said afterward. "I got to attempt suicide. I shot at people. It was great." Sarah probably enjoyed being on this show more than her previous work because of the challenge. The show was on daily, which meant the characters were given a new script every day, and she learned the importance of getting a scene right the first time. "You get a script a day in advance, you rehearse it once or twice, and you get one take, maybe two, and that is it," she explains. "Contrary to popular belief, we did not have cue cards."

The fans loved Sarah. As Kendall, she was deliciously evil, yet you really couldn't help but feel sorry for her because she had been abandoned as a child. In 1994, after having been on the show for less than a year, Sarah was nominated for a Daytime Emmy Award for Outstanding Younger Leading Actress in a Daytime Drama Series. She didn't win that year, but it was a thrill for her to have been nominated after such a short time. However, it was also at this time that the rumors began about her relationship with Lucci being less than perfect. Lucci had been nominated for Outstanding Lead Actress in a Daytime Drama Series 14 times,

Sarah Michelle Gellar wins the award for Outstanding Younger Leading Actress in a Drama Series in 1995, for her role as Kendall Hart on All My Children but had never won the award. Sarah would later admit, "It wasn't an easy time in my life. . . . We didn't have a perfect working relationship. We, um, weren't going out to lunch."

The tabloids and other papers began reporting that Lucci and Sarah hated one another. To this day Gellar insists that was not the case, that the papers blew things out of proportion. She says they worked well together on-screen, but they didn't have a very good personal relationship. Midway through the season, Sarah decided she would leave the show to move on to other projects (and, some say, to get away from Lucci). She must have wondered whether or not she'd made the right decision when in 1995 she was again nominated for the Younger Leading Actress award — and won (the Emmys were held the same evening as her prom night, and Sarah somehow managed to make it to both). Sarah insisted to Lucci that she had never been in competition with her. "I won for scenes I submitted with her," she explains. "You don't work alone — this was work we did together." The very next day, ABC announced officially that Sarah was leaving the show. This was six months after Sarah had told them, and she was very unhappy about the timing. "It made me look incredibly bad," she recalls. "I was told by ABC that I couldn't announce my leaving until they made an official announcement. . . . The timing was terrible."

Despite the ups and downs on the show, *All My Children* had taught Sarah a lot about show business. "It gave me an amazing understanding of the technical aspect of this industry — how to hit a mark, how to not shadow somebody, how to play to the camera," she says. "And that way, when I got to nighttime, all I had to worry about was the performance. I made some of the most amazing friends on that show — Eva LaRue Callahan and John Callahan and Sydney Penny — and I learned so much just about being a professional on the set, working those hours. Then it gave me the chance to grow up at home and not move to California until I was a fully formed adult and I could handle things better."

Sarah would later remember that, in 1993, after a strange comedy called *Buffy the Vampire Slayer* had hit the movie theaters, her make-up person on the set of *All My Children* joked about how much she looked like Kristy Swanson, the actress who played the title role in the movie. Perhaps Sarah was destined to become her younger, hipper television incarnation.

When Sarah was on *All My Children* she enjoyed playing a character who was seven years older than she was. She mentioned in an interview how on television it seemed like adults played kids, but never vice versa. "They just don't write for kids anymore," she said. "You always have older people playing younger people. . . . There are some very talented teenagers who can do it just as good, if not better, than any adults, but they're not given a fair chance." Later she would say she far preferred daytime television to prime time: "I don't mean to bash all these people who leave daytime for prime time, but I don't think those nighttime sitcoms are a hell of a lot better these days. In some cases, daytime has a lot more talented people than in prime time." One wonders if she regrets those earlier comments now. However, she can't really be blamed for making them. After all, she hadn't yet met Joss Whedon.

When Sarah's agent contacted her about a new show about high school kids battling real demons, she was excited about the concept and decided she had to play the part of Buffy. She could do comedy, drama — and tae kwon do. When she arrived at the auditions, however, the casting agents saw her long dark hair and pale skin and asked her to read for a different role. They said she would be perfect as the snobby and dominating Cordelia, especially after having done such a convincing job in the similar role of Kendall. Sarah went through the audition, but pleaded with the casting agents to let her try for Buffy. They finally relented.

Whedon remembers the experience. Sarah walked in and immediately seemed to possess all the qualities he wanted for Buffy — she had to be funny, tough, attractive, and weird. Now he had to see how her reading went. He was not disappointed. "She gave us a reading that was letter perfect," Whedon recalls, "and then said, 'By the way, it doesn't say this on my resumé but I did take tae kwon do for four years and I'm a brown belt. Is that good?' No, perfect," Joss thought to himself. He says she nailed the part right then and there, but Sarah has a different recollection of events. "It was the most awful experience of my life, but I was so driven," she says. After the initial audition, she went through five more auditions *and* five screen tests. But she prevailed, and the part was hers. She packed her things and moved to Los Angeles. The pilot episode was shot and the WB was convinced — this would be a very big show.

Sarah loved her new character, despite having problems with some of the dialogue. She told *Rolling Stone* magazine, "I still have to ask Joss, 'What does this mean?' because I don't speak the lingo. I think he makes it up half the time." (Joss admits that he does.) *Buffy the Vampire Slayer* was different from all the other high school shows because of its focus on a single, tough young woman. The mid-1990s saw a wave of empowered women on television: Peta Wilson's character on *La Femme Nikita* is a deadly assassin; *Xena: Warrior Princess* featured two women, Xena and Gabrielle, who have changed the face (and gender) of action shows; Captain Janeway became the first female captain of a *Star Trek* series on *Voyager*; and *The X-Files* introduced Dana Scully, a brave, intelligent woman who must fight powers much bigger than herself and stand up for her own beliefs. However, all of these female characters had made it past adolescence, whereas Buffy was still battling her way through high school besides having to take on vampires. "She doesn't know if she wants to be a cheerleader or fight vampires," Sarah says of Buffy, "and that is what makes her interesting and believable. Buffy is a person who is lost, who doesn't know where she belongs — and you feel for her." To make her character even more realistic, Sarah took up kickboxing, street fighting, boxing, and gymnastic training. The show debuted in March 1997, and Sarah Michelle Gellar was a full-fledged prime-time star.

After months of anticipating how television audiences would react to *Buffy the Vampire Slayer*, Sarah wasn't actually in Los Angeles to witness the huge summer promotional campaign the WB launched. When the show went on a five-month hiatus between the first and second seasons, Sarah found a side career as a horror-movie scream queen for wunderkind screenwriter Kevin Williamson.

Williamson can be credited with single-handedly reviving the horror genre for the '90s, despite having been told by a high school English teacher that he'd never succeed as a writer. He attended theater school on an acting scholarship, but was more interested in writing scripts than acting them out. His first script, *Killing Mrs. Tingle*, failed to make it to the big screen until 1999 as *Teaching Mrs. Tingle*. He returned to more well-known Hollywood jobs like temping and dog walking but recalls a very strange experience that happened when he was home alone one night. A noise in the kitchen prompted him to grab a butcher knife and a cellphone and call a friend, who began asking him trivia questions about

CHRISTINA RADISH

Sarah wins the Kids' Choice Award for Best Female Butt Kicker in 2002

1980s horror flicks. This surreal situation became the opening scene for a new script, which he penned in three days.

Scream was bought by Miramax and became the biggest-grossing horror movie of all time. Starring Neve Campbell, Skeet Ulrich, Courteney Cox, and Drew Barrymore, the film was an ironic look at the horror-movie genre, poking fun at its conventions while following them at every turn. Fans and critics loved it. Williamson's characters were different — smarter — than their counterparts in earlier horror films, and he is very conscious of how he writes dialogue for his teenage characters. He refers to the teenager of the '90s as "a very self-aware, pop-culture-referenced individual who grew up next to Blockbuster in the self-help, psychobabble '80s." His characters don't get scared as easily as victims in earlier horror films; for example, when the killer calls her house and says he's standing on the porch, Sidney (Campbell) throws the front door open to prove him wrong. With a cutting-edge writing style and at only 32 years old, Williamson was very similar to Whedon. It was probably inevitable that he would choose Sarah Michelle Gellar to be one of his stars.

I Know What You Did Last Summer, starred Freddie Prinze Jr., Jennifer Love Hewitt, Ryan Phillippe, and Sarah. When Sarah first read the script, she was a little wary about the role of Helen Shivers, the local beauty queen, because she disliked the idea of playing a dumb blonde. However, after thinking about the character for a while, Gellar realized there was more to Helen than she'd originally thought, and she accepted the part. Williamson immediately took to her the same way Whedon had. "You know that when you hire her to do a job she's not going to be in the trailer, complaining about everything," said Williamson. "She's going to be right out there at three in the morning, barefoot, in the freezing cold, giving you the tenth take." Sarah relocated to North Carolina for the duration of filming the movie, and realized how much easier feature films were than television series. On *Buffy*, she worked long hours, and a one-hour episode was filmed over eight days. However, the two-hour movie was shot over two months, so there was ample time to go back and change things. Helen Shivers was an exciting part for her because she was a big fan of horror films, having seen all the *Friday the 13th* and *Halloween* movies. "There's nothing like the adrenaline rush you get," Sarah says of horror films. "You know it's fake, that nothing bad is actually gonna happen, but it's still scary and fun. It's kind of like a roller-coaster ride."

In *I Know What You Did Last Summer*, an adaptation of the Lois Duncan novel, four teenagers spend a frolicksome evening on the beach. Driving home, they hit a person standing in the road. Desperate, and assuming the police will accuse them of drunk driving, they take the body and dump it in a lake. However, their problems don't disappear. The honors student can now barely get passing grades. The promising football player falls apart and quits the team. The beauty queen gets stuck working at a clothing store, haunted by the past. And the past catches up to them when they begin receiving mysterious notes that read, "I know what you did last summer."

The movie, while not as clever or deep as *Scream*, is filled with suspense and gore. The killer dresses as a fisherman and guts his victims with a huge meat hook. At one point, he chases Helen through the streets to her sister's clothing store, where she pounds on the glass, begging to get in. Her sister nonchalantly wanders away to get the keys, and the suspense created by Gellar banging her fists on the window is heart-stopping. Filming this scene was difficult for Sarah, because she had been conditioned over the previous months to fight back. Instead of running, Sarah kept turning to fight the killer. "I'd punch the guy, and it'd be like a right hook to the jaw — boom!" she laughs. "And [director Jim Gillespie is] like, 'No, you flail your arms.'" She would continue to fight later when she was working on *Scream 2*, and Wes Craven, the horror legend and director of that film, would joke to her, "Don't kill the bad man, because then he can't come back for a sequel."

So Gellar learned to run from the killers, but that posed another problem. She appeared to be too athletic for a beauty queen and kept outrunning the bad guys. So the director put her in six-inch heels, and Sarah put pebbles in her shoes, and she slowed right down. Once she got used to being helpless, Sarah enjoyed the challenge of playing someone so different from Buffy: "I don't think that Helen — I hope — [has] any Buffy traits. I hope I did a good enough departure that you don't sit there and think, 'Oh, there's Buffy.'"

Sarah enjoyed working on the film because she became very close to her co-stars. Considering that everything in Southport, North Carolina, closed at 9 p.m., there was really nothing else to do. She and Hewitt would wander around the town occasionally, but it became a frightening activity as filming went on, because every time they saw a fisherman in his rain gear they'd jump in fright. The other disadvantage to filming in Southport was that the townspeople were unhappy that a group of film people were shaking up their town, and began to resent their presence.

Meanwhile, back in the civilized world (i.e., cities with cable), *Buffy* was becoming a hit and Sarah didn't know it. Web sites devoted to the show and its stars were popping up on the Internet, and by the end of the first season, there were over 40 of them. *Buffy* posters were in subways, on billboards, and on the sides of buses, but isolated in Southport, Sarah had no idea of the phenomenon that was taking off. She got a clue, though, when she visited New York during a downpour and people still recognized her. "I have mascara running down my face," she recalls, "and people are going by in cars honking their car horns, going, 'Hey, Buffy.' I couldn't believe it."

On its opening weekend, *I Know What You Did Last Summer* grossed $16 million, almost recouping its budget of $17 million. Throughout its six-month run, the movie grossed over $70 million worldwide.

Partway through filming *I Know What You Did Last Summer*, Williamson offered Sarah a small part in his next big film, *Scream 2*. Many young actors in Hollywood had been hankering for a role in a Williamson film, so to be offered a part in two was very flattering for Sarah. To film *Scream 2*, Sarah again relocated, this time to Atlanta. She says she was a little intimidated at learning that the sequel would once again star Neve Campbell, because the cast of *Buffy the Vampire Slayer* watched *Party of Five* religiously. However, as she got into an elevator with the cast of *Scream 2*, Neve turned to Sarah and said that Jennifer Love Hewitt wanted her to say hello. Sarah knew everything would be fine. In fact, when she realized who the rest of the ensemble cast were, she described the shoot as a high school reunion, having attended high school with Jerry O'Connell and Rebecca Gayheart.

Sarah's role in *Scream 2* is actually very small, but it was convenient because she had to get back to California to begin filming the second season of *Buffy the Vampire Slayer*. In the movie she plays a sorority sister who gets a phone call from the killer when she's alone in the sorority house, being "sober sister" for the evening. Williamson had gotten used to Sarah's sense of humor and sarcasm when she was on the set of *I Know What You Did Last Summer*, so he'd written this part especially for her. Sarah's brief time on-screen is great and full of suspense. Williamson was on the set to watch her final scene, and Sarah laughs, "When he saw me on the set of *Scream 2*, he said he just loves the way I die." *Scream 2* was a fascinating experience for Sarah, because she worked for the first time with Wes Craven, who had directed the *Nightmare on Elm Street* films. She gained a profound admiration for how he directed. "Whereas most movies have some guy off camera going 'bang' to make you turn around," she explains, "Wes hides people in different places just to freak you out. And it works." *Scream 2* had a dark comic edge to it that *I Know What You Did Last Summer* lacked, so it was more up Sarah's alley. She was thrilled to do both movies because of the diversity of the characters, and because "they offered me the opportunity to do drama, to do horror, to do action, to do comedy. That's an actor's dream." No wonder she enjoys being on *Buffy the Vampire Slayer* so much.

Scream 2 garnered $33 million on its opening weekend, the biggest opening of any Miramax film and the biggest December opening of any movie in history. It grossed $96 million in its first month alone and was re-released into theatres the following April, raking in another $50 million worldwide. Sarah had just finished filming two of the most successful horror films in history, and when she returned to L.A. she realized she was also starring in a very successful television show. She was on a roll. By the time the second season began airing, Sarah had become one of the hottest young stars in the world. She was living proof that Hollywood was finally starting to write realistic parts for people her age, rather than making them caricatures. "What Kevin did with his scripts, and what Joss has done for me with Buffy," she said, "is written three-dimensional human beings: people who make mistakes, good choices, bad choices, have flaws." Talk shows began scrambling to get *Buffy* stars on, and suddenly they were all in demand.

Fame has its disadvantages, however. Sarah was used to doing many things at once, but she was busier now than she'd ever been. She had begun filming the second season of *Buffy* while finishing work on *Scream 2*, and then hit the talk show circuit and had newspaper and television interviews. One of her favorite stories, which she related in several interviews, was that one morning she was driving to the *Buffy* set with the top down on her convertible and she noticed a lot of people staring at her. Assuming that people were recognizing her, she thought nothing of it. However, the stares got weirder and weirder until she glanced down and realized she was wearing nothing but a slip — she had been so tired she'd forgotten to put her dress on! She knew then that she would have to start getting more sleep, but she takes it all in stride: "Yeah, I don't have much of a life beyond work, but how many other girls get to really release their inner demons for a living?"

On January 17, 1998, Sarah hosted *Saturday Night Live*. Although the show had been waning for a few seasons, with falling ratings, lame skits, and a lot of criticism, this episode was very funny. Even Rosie O'Donnell later said to Sarah of the show, "I think it was the funniest one this season." Sarah admitted to being extremely nervous beforehand, and she'd thought to herself, "I'm gonna be the first host to just get out there and go, 'Uh . . . uh. . . .'" However, Rosie was right. Sarah brought her sarcasm to many of the scenes, making otherwise flat skits absolutely hilarious.

Right after Sarah was on *Saturday Night Live*, the *Buffy* ratings passed the four million mark, and two weeks later it had surpassed five million. The show was taking off. To top it all off, it won three Petcabus awards, which are given to underappreciated shows that deserve awards. *Buffy the Vampire Slayer* won the Golden Petcabus, given to the best underappreciated show on television, as well as awards for Best Ensemble Cast and Best Recurring Character (Juliet Landau for Drusilla). On March 10, 1998, Sarah herself won a Blockbuster Award for Favorite Supporting Actress in a Horror Movie for *I Know What You Did Last Summer*.

During Sarah's second-season hiatus, she filmed two more movies. The first was *Cruel Intentions*, a modernized version of *Les Liaisons Dangereuses*, co-starring Ryan Phillippe. In it she plays Kathryn, the part played by Glenn Close in the 1988 version. Her stepbrother, Sebastian, is in love with her, so she makes a bet with him: if he can convince avowed virgin Annette Hargrove (Reese Witherspoon) to sleep with him, then Kathryn will let him have sex with her. But if he loses, she gets his car. Kathryn is evil and manipulative, and Sarah went back to her real hair color for the part, as if to show how much Kathryn had in common with Kendall. As far as Sarah was concerned, she was pretending to be the students with whom she'd gone to Columbia Prep School: "It's frightening what that much money and that much freedom when your parents aren't there can breed in a young child. It's real. It breeds terror. Not every school is like that, and not everyone is like that, but it does exist. There were kids in my class who had money clips that were monogrammed!"

The film was praised by critics, and audiences loved this new side of Sarah. The following year at the MTV awards, Sarah won Best Actress for her role, and she and Selma Blair won the award for Best Kiss, for a scene in the film where Kathryn tries to teach another girl

Selma Blair and Sarah demonstrate why they won the MTV Movie award for Best Kiss

MARGARET GREY/ZUMA PRESS

how to kiss properly. Sarah wasn't sure why there was so much hype over the two women kissing, although she remembers the actual filming to be a little uncomfortable. "Well, I had to kiss another girl," she says. "Big deal. It wouldn't have been so bad if it wasn't for the fact that we had to shoot that scene in Central Park on probably one of the nicest days in New York in seven years. We had quite an audience, but I guess I did a convincing job. My mother said to me afterwards, 'Did you have to use so much tongue?'"

As soon as Sarah was finished *Cruel Intentions*, she starred in *Simply Irresistible*, about a woman who suddenly gains magic powers after inheriting a restaurant. Unfortunately, the movie was filled with flaws (for example, it was a complete rip-off of the far superior *Like Water for Chocolate*) and non sequiturs that were never explained. Critics were decidedly cold to it, and the movie earned less than $5 million (it had cost $6 million to make). Sarah had starred in her first flop. "That was really hard for me," she recalls. "I read a script that I fell in love with and learned a very hard lesson — that it doesn't always work out. I've always wondered why good actors did bad movies. I'd think, 'Didn't they read the script? Didn't they know?' Now I understand what happens. Whether it's the direction or the production or some of the acting, it can change in the transition from the script you first read."

Finally, she also lent her voice to one of the characters in the computer-animated *Small Soldiers*, a very funny film where some toys develop superintelligence and wage a serious war. Sarah voiced one of the Gwendy dolls who get caught in the middle of the fighting.

Sarah was becoming a star outside her hit television show. As *Buffy* entered its third season, she was considered a role model to young women everywhere. Maybelline picked her up as a spokesmodel in 1999, because they saw her as a positive example for young women. She was identified as part of the new Brat Pack in Hollywood, but as far as Sarah was concerned, this new generation of young actors weren't your typical Hollywood brats: "We're not raucous, we're not wild, and we don't go out and party until two in the morning. You haven't heard one story about this new group of actors I run with beating up photographers or trashing a hotel room. We're not a partying group. We're a very sedate bunch: Ryan Phillippe, Reese Witherspoon, Selma Blair, myself . . . and I don't really know why. Maybe Hollywood's getting pickier and the studios are now giving opportunities to the few of us who can handle it."

As someone who represented a strong yet feminine woman who didn't get into trouble with the media, Sarah was perfect for Maybelline. When asked what her beauty routine is, she answers confidently, "I carry a bottle of water with me all the time. I don't really drink . . . anything except water and iced tea. I really believe vitamins can fix almost anything: skin and hair problems, energy problems, colds. I always take my vitamins, usually a multi and a vitamin C. When I'm not working, I rarely wear makeup. I just put on sunblock, moisturizer and lip balm. I'm very careful with my skin. I use Rembrandt whitening toothpaste." Emma Caulfield, who plays Anya, admitted that Sarah doesn't really need makeup because of her natural beauty: "She gets in at like 5 a.m. in the morning for makeup, and I swear, she doesn't look any different with the pancake makeup on. She's stunning. Oh, and she has a fetish for . . . she's gonna kill me but . . . toenail polish! Every hour she paints them a different color."

In interviews reporters would ask Sarah who she was dating, and she would say that she was taking time away from dating and that the only men she was around were actors, and she didn't like dating actors. She was seen around town with Jerry O'Connell and there were some untrue rumors spreading that she was involved with David Boreanaz (his marriage was breaking up at the time, so the tabloids went for the obvious lie). But by early 2000, her friendship with Freddie Prinze Jr. was blossoming into something more. They had remained friends after filming *I Know What You Did Last Summer*, and by the end of 2000, the media was starting to catch on that they were dating. In April 2001, Freddie proposed to

Sarah with her fiancé, Freddie Prinze, Jr.

CHRISTINA RADISH

Sarah, giving her an engagement ring designed by Cathy Waterman (who has designed rings for Gwyneth Paltrow, Meg Ryan, and Meryl Streep). Prinze has said, "Sarah's so smart. You just sit back and listen; and when she's done, you think: 'I'm a smarter person.'" And the feeling is mutual. "I love Freddie a lot," Sarah says. "Ever since we've been together I've felt more together and happy."

Sarah's movie career was still blossoming. She took a year off after *Simply Irresistible*. At the time she worried her movie career might be over, but friends convinced her that flops were just part of the business — she had to move on and make another movie. She chose *Harvard Man*, an indie film. Written and directed by James Toback (*Two Girls and a Guy, Black and White*), the film also stars Adrien Grenier (*Drive Me Crazy*), Joey Lauren Adams (*Chasing Amy*), Eric Stoltz, and Rebecca Gayheart. The story is about a basketball player, Alan, who becomes involved with a cheerleader (Gellar), who happens to be the daughter of a mob boss. Her father gets Alan involved in sports betting, not realizing an FBI agent is following their every move. The film was shot mostly in Toronto, Canada, in the summer of 2000. The producer of the film, Michael Mailer, told an interviewer that Sarah plays a "classic female manipulator, who is very smart, very street savvy, and very tough at the same time. And she is doing a remarkable job."

Sarah added that if reviewers thought they saw a trend in her character choices, they would be right: "To me, when I look for a character to play, I look for someone that would be interesting for me to watch, and watching a one-dimensional character — the bad girl, or the dumb girl — there is no interest in that for me." The film was screened at the Cannes Film Festival before going into limited release in summer 2002.

By the beginning of 2001, Sarah was finally getting recognition for her role as Buffy. She had won the Teen Choice awards in 1999 and 2000 for Best Actress on Television (and won the Extraordinary Achievement Award in 2001). She was nominated for the Best TV Actress Saturn Award every year since 1999, and won it the first year she was nominated. And she was (finally) nominated for a Golden Globe for Best Performance by an Actress in a TV Series — Drama. In the same category were Jessica Alba (*Dark Angel*), Sela Ward (*Once and Again*), Edie Falco (*The Sopranos*), Amy Brenneman (*Judging Amy*), and Lorraine Bracco (*The*

Sopranos). Although the award predictably went to Ward, it was interesting to see both Alba and Gellar nominated.

Later that year, Sarah was back to movies in the role of Daphne Blake in *Scooby-Doo*. The cast also included Sarah's beau Freddie Prinze Jr. as Fred, Matthew Lillard (SLC *Punk*) as Shaggy, and Linda Cardellini (*Freaks and Geeks*) as Velma. *Scooby-Doo* was filmed on an island off the Gold Coast of Australia, where she stayed in a solar-powered house with Prinze. If given the opportunity to live in a similar house full-time, Gellar

CHRISTINA RADISH

Sarah at the premiere for Scooby-Doo

would choose not to. She said, "There is nothing worse than having an 18-hour day in the sand and you're all gritty and want to come home and take a hot shower and there is no hot water because there was no sun." However, she loved the country. "I want to move to Australia," she told an interviewer. "There is something about Australia that is the best mix of everything. It has the culture and nightlife of New York and the cosmopolitan aspect, but it has the relaxed laid-back atmosphere of California and the people are so nice. I just think it's such an amazing place. Australia has an amazing way of life. They take everything with a grain of salt."

As for the filming, Gellar said she had a great time on the set. Internet rumors abounded that on *Buffy the Vampire Slayer* the gang would have to stop using the term "Scooby gang" because Sarah was appearing in the film, and the crossover paradox would just be too weird, but those rumors appear unfounded. Sarah was thrilled to be part of such an important part of pop culture, even if she did have to suffer the psychedelic get-up. "Daphne is a fashion plate: I get on a plane in one outfit, I get off the plane in a totally different outfit," she says. "Everything is purple — the scarves, the headband, the skirt. I was like, 'What if I look terrible in purple?' And then there were the knee-high purple boots. I hate knees — I think knees are ugly. I was an ice skater when I was younger. It's a big deal to get me to wear short skirts. The costume designer would ask, 'Don't we have something shorter?' And I was like, 'No!' But I'm doing all these running and chasing scenes with little short skirts and knee-high boots. And the crew always cracks up, because the second they yell 'Cut!' those boots are off and my sneakers are on." The movie became one of the biggest blockbusters of 2002, up against other summer fare such as *Spider-Man* and *Stars Wars Episode II: Attack of the Clones.*

Sarah Michelle Gellar is one of the hottest actresses in Hollywood today. As for rumors that she acts like a diva on the set of *Buffy the Vampire Slayer*, her co-stars say they're just creations of the media with no grounding in fact. Amber Benson, who joined an already tight and well-oiled ensemble cast, was immediately put at ease by Sarah's friendliness: "Sarah, here she is Buffy, and she's super-nice. She's never been anything except extremely sweet to me. I don't drive, and she calls me and offers me rides to work." And James Marsters has nothing but praise for his sexy co-star: "Sarah is an absolute dream. A lead of a TV series has the power to make the set a nightmare or heaven. Sarah has chosen to use her powers to make it heaven. She's always on time. She always knows her lines. She's always wonderful to work with. She's always fresh. She's always jovial. You know, nobody really wants to push her around, but other than that she's a dream. Truthfully. And kissing her was no chore!"

Sarah reacts to some kind words as she helps dedicate a home for Habitat for Humanity, a nonprofit organization that helps eliminate poverty housing

Sarah has proven that she's not a child star but a serious actress. She has starred in successful movies and in one of the hottest shows on television today. Is she in danger of being typecast? It's not likely, because in the past she has chosen very diverse roles. But, as Sarah puts it, so what if she is? "If this is typecasting, you know, God help me, I guess. . . . I should be so lucky."

What we can bank on is that Sarah will always be busy, taking on a million tasks at once with detailed precision. But that's okay with her. As she told *Rolling Stone* magazine, "If you want something done, ask a busy person to do it. That's going to be my epitaph."

ANTHONY STEWART HEAD
Rupert Giles

Though he may not be immediately recognizable to a North American audience, Anthony Stewart Head had an enormous acting portfolio, ranging from commercials to movies, before entering the picture in the first episode of *Buffy* as Giles, the intellectual Watcher and librarian.

Born on February 20, 1954, in Camden, England, Head is nothing like his stuffy television counterpart, Rupert Giles. He has worked in movies, television, and theater, although until he joined *Buffy the Vampire Slayer*, most people identified him as the Taster's Choice guy. From 1990 to 1997, a series of commercials ran in England for Nescafé Gold Blend and in the United States for Taster's Choice, in which a veritable soap opera unfolded. An attractive woman crosses the hall to ask her neighbor for some coffee and finds a handsome English gentleman — Tony. A love story evolves over their coffee mugs, and viewers see a son show up and an ex-husband unearthed. Ah, the woes of coffee drinkers. The commercials were huge, and within months of their airing in the U.S., sales of Taster's Choice coffee had increased by 10 percent. And they say looks don't sell coffee.

Tony's career has had far more illustrious moments. Onstage he appeared (as Anthony Head) in, among others, *Godspell*, *Henry V*, *Rosencrantz and Guildenstern Are Dead*, *Chess*, *Lady Windermere's Fan*, *Julius Caesar*, and *The Rocky Horror Picture Show*. This latter is a favorite role among fans, and several followers of the cult hit have said Tony was the best Frank N. Furter ever. Well, he was without a doubt the sexiest. In a long wig, tons of makeup, and fishnet stockings, Tony strutted across the stage, singing "Sweet Transvestite" and "I Can Make You a Man" to the delight of the audience. Singing skills run in Tony's family — his brother, Murray Head, had a hit in 1984 with "One Night in Bangkok." It was a skill Tony would put to good use in the *Buffy* musical episode after giving fans glimpses of his abilities when caught at a coffee bar by the gang in season four.

It was during the run of this show that Head perfected some of the more subtle aspects of his acting that he now uses on *Buffy the Vampire Slayer*. Anyone who has witnessed the live show knows that when Frank N. Furter — the gay mad scientist — struts out onstage, the audience shouts at him when he sings and heckles him when he talks, and sometimes the rowdier audience members throw things (although that behavior is usually saved for the movie). Frank, in return, insults the audience right back. Tony says he had to learn a whole crop of insults when he was rehearsing the part, and he refused to let any heckling go unanswered. "The show ran for hours because I answered everything!" he says. "After that, they said to me, 'Tony, you have to let some of them go.'

Anthony Stewart Head, looking unlike Giles

So I developed 'the look.' With it, I could put down a heckler at the back of a balcony. It was so empowering."

While working in the theater in England, Tony met the love of his life, Sarah Fisher. "We met backstage at the National Theatre 18 years ago," he recalls. "I was doing a play called *Danton's Death* and for the last entrance I had to come on as a soldier taking traitors to the guillotine. I'd wait in a corridor at the back with my musket, and one day this beautiful lady walked past carrying a pint of beer for some guy front of house. I got there earlier and earlier in the hope I'd see her again. Eventually, we'd sit and chat before I'd have to go on for a beheading." The two have been together ever since.

Tony starred in various BBC television movies, as well as the films *Lady Chatterley's Lover*, *Prayer for the Dying*, and the American-made *Royce*. In 1992 he moved to the United States for television work, and his first role was a guest appearance in *Highlander: The Series'* particularly violent episode "Nowhere to Run." Then he was offered the role of Oliver Sampson on the sci-fi television series, *VR5*. A woman discovers she has powers to access the subconscious of other people through virtual reality. She moves through the various levels of virtual reality on her way to level five, where she can alter events and people's behavior. Sampson is the head of the Committee, a mysterious organization that hires the woman to carry out dangerous assignments that use her ability for questionable purposes. *VR5* lasted only one season, but Tony then appeared in an episode of *NYPD Blue*, one of the first times he was credited as Anthony Stewart Head.

He noticed that there were differences between American and British styles of acting: "In the U.K., the way of coaching, for the most part, is a bit more stylized, more technical." In the United States, he says, it's more realistic, and he now prefers a more Method style of acting — like rolling on the floor to indicate he's been in a fight rather than having the makeup people simulate it. He laughs, "Alyson [Hannigan] still won't let me live down the time she tried to pick a bit of fluff off my jacket and I snapped at her, 'Don't touch that! I spent an hour getting that just right!'"

In 1997 Head was offered the role of Rupert Giles in the offbeat *Buffy the Vampire Slayer*. It didn't take long for him to realize this was a part he had to play. "When I read the script I just laughed out loud and I thought, 'This has to be something,'" he recalls. "I loved the concept. English people are often always cast as either the bad guy or the stupid stiff-upper-lip guy. This was just so different." When he auditioned for the part, he suggested playing Giles either as a version of Hugh Grant in *Four Weddings and a Funeral*, as Prince Charles, or as Alan Rickman "in his more decisive moments." Joss Whedon didn't want to choose, so Head settled on a combination of all three.

Head was particularly fond of the way Giles just "bumbles through life," and despite all his knowledge, Giles often looks like a deer caught in headlights when it comes to difficult situations. The *Buffy* cast love the way Tony is so non-Giles when he's off the set, and the online *Buffy* drinking game commands players to chug whenever they spot the earring hole (which is usually well-hidden by makeup) in Giles's left ear.

Nonetheless, Tony's understated turn as Giles didn't go unrecognized by the cast, who praised his abilities to subtly tackle the role. "He does the heavy lifting for the show with all that exposition," said James Marsters of Head's studious portrayal of Giles. "Every week he has to convince us that the world is going to come to an end again and again. He's got to talk about the Box of Tathor or the Talisman of Nigeria or whatever and sell it. He has to give it weight so it doesn't seem repetitious. He does that every time so well."

While filming *Buffy*, Tony split his time between Los Angeles and his home just outside of Bath, a midsize city in England's west country, where he lives with Sarah and their two daughters, Emily Rose and Daisy May. He continued to pick up guest-starring roles in English shows so he would be working on both continents. In 2000 he played the murder suspect in *Silent Witness*, a British series. He also appeared in *Best Actress*, an American made-for-TV film that aired on cable.

It was the travel that led to concerns that he might not stay on *Buffy*. His children urged him to remain on the program. "The kids absolutely love the show," he said in an interview in January 2001, as *Buffy* garnered greater popularity than anyone had expected. "The times when we've talked about maybe me leaving, they've said, 'Oh my God, no, you can't, you can't!' It's very hard, because they're growing up and Sarah has raised them as a single mother for six, seven years now." Tony's arrangement allowed him to spend more than eight months a year in Los

Angeles, coming back to Bath only when he had six days clear of work, which amounted to once every five to six weeks.

By *Buffy*'s 100th episode, it was becoming clear that Head could not continue with his hectic pace, and the actor began looking for a chance to remove Giles from the regular cast and return to work in the U.K. Eventually Whedon agreed to write him out of the regular role, though people questioned why Tony would want to leave such a popular program, which was getting a renewed promotional push with its move to the UPN network. It was a comment from his daughter, Daisy, that cemented his decision to leave *Buffy*. "It was all very emotional," he explains. "People said, 'How can you turn that money down? You've got a guaranteed salary for a year, 22 episodes a year, a good whack.' You go, 'God, am I really doing the right thing?' And then, in the car on the way back, Daisy said, 'Think about it: you've been away for more than half my life.' So I went, 'Jesus! Okay, I'm coming home.'"

Certainly Tony was planning to continue his acting career after *Buffy*, and rumors circulated about a second spin-off from the show in which he would star. So Giles fans can breathe a sigh of relief. Or can they? "Well, with Joss you never know," says Tony. Provisionally titled *Watcher* or *Ripper*, the Giles show is being touted as *Cracker*, the British crime drama, but "with ghosts." And although nothing is set in stone, Head is keeping his fingers crossed that plans to reprise his role as Giles this side of the Atlantic eventually come to fruition. "It would be an adult show, more about ghost stories and inner demons," he says. "The BBC is keen and have said they want it. They have a slot for it, but nothing is signed."

While the spin-off was discussed, Tony moved on with his acting, taking a guest-star role in the BBC series *Spooks*, which is about British secret service operatives. He also landed a role in *Manchild*, a six-part BBC series some critics called "a male version of *Sex and the City*." Head played James, a character who is dealing with impotence, and starred Nigel Havers, Ray Burdis, and Don Warrington. The show aired in spring 2002.

Acting wasn't the only thing on Head's mind upon being freed of the daily constraints *Buffy the Vampire Slayer* placed on his time. He also managed to record and release *Music for Elevators*, his tribute to musician/composer Brian Eno's *Music for Airports*. The album was released

CHRISTINA RADISH

*A family portrait: David Boreanaz, Anthony Stewart Head, and
Alyson Hannigan pose with their pups*

through the Internet in early 2002 (www.musicforelevators.com). "It's a little thing I did with this electronics composer, George Sarah," Head explained. "We brought in a bunch of friends: James [Marsters] and Amber [Benson] to do backing vocals, and Joss wrote a really sweet song for it. When I first played it to him I was very nervous, because his roots are the Grateful Dead. So when I recorded his track he didn't like it at all. But I played it again when we got the mixes and he said, 'Ooh, you made me funky!' I don't know if it'll ever hit England. I'm not intending to hype it."

ALYSON HANNIGAN
Willow Rosenberg

With the exception of Sarah Michelle Gellar, Alyson Hannigan is perhaps the most recognizable and successful of the cast of *Buffy the Vampire Slayer*. Though many know her from *Buffy* and her famed role as Michelle, the "band camp girl," on the two *American Pie* movies, Hannigan has long been in demand on both the big and small screen.

Alyson was born in Washington, D.C., on March 24, 1974, but she grew up in Atlanta, Georgia. Perhaps her introduction to show business came when her parents, who were photographers, needed a baby in a photo and used her. "When I got old enough where I knew what I was doing," Alyson remembers, "my mom asked me if I wanted to try doing commercials, and I said, 'Yeah!'" Alyson was only four years old at the time, but she enjoyed making commercials for companies like Six Flags and Nabisco so much that she focused on television full-time. Since then she has had several television roles, appearing on *Picket Fences*, *Touched by an Angel*, *Almost Home*, *The Torkelsons*, and *Roseanne*.

Alyson's break came in 1988, when she appeared with Seth Green in the Dan Aykroyd film *My Stepmother Is an Alien*. While acting, Alyson attempted to maintain a so-called "normal" life. But high school wasn't much fun for the budding actress. "My experience in high school was just crap," she recalls. "I went to North Hollywood High, and it was awful, and I was miserable, and I just wanted to get out. I was completely depressed and listening to a lot of Cure." It was an experience she'd later use in her roles in both *Buffy* and *American Pie*. Throughout the early 1990s, Alyson continued to play small roles in long-forgotten television movies like *Switched at Birth* and *The Stranger Beside Me*.

In 1997 Hannigan finally landed the part of Willow Rosenberg on *Buffy*, a role she had first heard about when a friend mentioned she would be perfect for it. "My agent had a breakdown that he read to me," she says, "and I think it said something like, 'She's a shy wallflower who's still wearing the dress that her mother picked out for her.'" However, at first she couldn't even get an audition, much less the part. The role of Willow was given to another actress, Riff Regan, who filmed the 30-minute pilot that was used to sell the show to the WB network. After the show was picked up, the producers decided to take Willow in another direction, cutting Regan loose. Hannigan finally had her shot at the role that would come to define her career.

In the same way Gellar recalls her auditions for the show, Alyson remembers that she had 10 of them, until finally it was down to her and an actress from New Zealand. In the final audition she had to read with Nick Brendon and Sarah Michelle Gellar, because the real test was to see how she interacted with them. She remembers the audition with horror — she messed up because she couldn't pronounce the computer terms in it, and she was convinced the other actress would get the role. Joss told her that although she'd flubbed the dialogue, she had a chemistry the other actress didn't. She was offered the role a few days later.

After filming had begun on the first season, Alyson felt a little out of place because the other actors had become friends over the summer, while she was new to the show. She quickly made friends with Sarah and Nick, though, and was delighted that the chemistry between the cast members was so perfect. She insists that she's very different from her character — she wouldn't know how to hack into a computer system if her life depended on it — but that she and Willow have the same sense of humor.

Whedon has mused aloud about how lucky he was to cast Hannigan in the role of Willow. The actress brings a depth to the character that even he didn't foresee. In the second season he said, "She treats Willow's lifelong love for Xander as a smoldering passion that she knows will never reach fruition. Another actress might make it a little more obvious, but Alyson's underplaying is just perfect." Willow fits in with the other characters in that she isn't part of the popular crowd, but her inherent shyness sets her apart from Xander and Buffy. And Alyson conveys this shyness perfectly. "I wanted Willow to have that kind of insanely colorful interior life that truly shy people often have," Joss explains. "And Alyson has that. She definitely has a loopiness that I found creeping into the way Willow talked, which was great. To an extent, all of the actors conform to the way I write the character, but it really stands out in Willow's case."

Alyson's success as Willow eventually translated into a break on the big screen. In 1998 she was cast in the role of the flute-playing Michelle in *American Pie*. The script sold Hannigan on the picture, and she was so impressed with the possibilities of the movie that she worked 20-hour

Alyson Hannigan shows off her tattoo, a Japanese kanji that brings luck and happiness

Thumbs up! Alyson participated in the 24th Annual Toyota Pro/Celebrity Race with Melissa Joan Hart, George Lucas, Josh Brolin, and several others (she came in 10th)

days so she could film it and *Buffy* at the same time. "I fell in love with it and I wanted to be any part of it," she says. "Especially because it was right around the time that all the other teen movies were out and it really stuck out of the pack. I just love the sense of humor . . . it's so funny." Alyson used the skills she had developed on *Buffy* to great effect in *American Pie*, ad-libbing one of the movie's most famed lines and stealing scenes throughout the picture.

Her role in *American Pie* garnered some controversy because of its adult themes, an issue Hannigan eventually had to address on *Buffy* as well. Following the breakup of Willow and Oz, Whedon decided to use Hannigan's character to explore the issue of same-sex relationships on *Buffy*. On the show, Willow falls in love with Tara, a novice Wiccan played brilliantly by Amber Benson. The storyline was drawn out to the point where Alyson says she just wanted some form of resolution: "Eventually, after weeks of tiptoeing around the issue, everyone concerned admitted that all roads led to the fact that the girls were in love, which

CHRISTINA RADISH

Alyson Hannigan

resulted in huge sighs of relief all round. Amber and I were sort of in the same position as Willow and Tara in that for the longest time we weren't sure what was going on and were like, 'What . . .? Are we . . .?' Then finally it was, 'Great! It's official. We're in luurrvvve.'"

Hannigan's personal life has also captured the attention of the public. For a spell, she dated Ginger Fish, the drummer in shock-rock band Marilyn Manson. Her relationship with Alexis Denisof, who played Wesley, the bookish Watcher on *Buffy* before moving the role to *Angel*, has also garnered some notice. Though the two were attracted to one another, Denisof wouldn't become romantically involved with Alyson while they were working on *Buffy*. But the relationship changed during the shoot for an ill-fated heist picture called *Beyond City Limits*. "During that summer," recalls Alyson, "we both worked on *Beyond City Limits* and we'd sit in each other's trailers, venting and trying to decide how we'd ended up in the worst movie ever! 'Why is the producer screaming his head off for no reason?' and so on. It was very traumatic and we were each other's salvation. We laughed all the time together and then the relationship I was in didn't work out. By that point, [Alexis] wasn't on *Buffy* anymore and I think it was just around the time he started on *Angel* and suddenly . . ."

Now happily dating Denisof, Hannigan looks forward to continuing her work on *Buffy* and being shrewd about her choice of movie roles. At a press conference in June 2002, she expressed her worry that the fans might hate her character after Willow's downward spiral in season six. "I just hope they forgive my evilness in the last few episodes." She can rest assured, though, that she will always be a favorite among fans, for she has brought to life one of the quirkiest, sweetest, and most original characters on televison.

NICHOLAS BRENDON
Xander Harris

From the day he was born, Nicholas Brendon Schultz boasted something that most people don't have: an identical twin brother, Kelly Donovan. Born April 12, 1971, the pair were inseparable, and to this day remain best friends. "You always had a person to play with," says Nick of Kelly. "You always had someone to confide in, someone to talk to. And someone just to beat up." His parents got divorced when he was young, and it brought him, Kelly, and their two younger brothers even closer together.

As a child, Nick developed a stutter, something that affects over three million Americans, and he feared that people were making fun of him, especially in high school. "I was seven or eight when it really became apparent. The more anxious and embarrassed I became, the worse it got," he told one interviewer. "Of course, the snowball effect of fear and failure soon took over and soon my life became a living hell." He withdrew from friends and didn't date until his early twenties.

After high school he worked as a receptionist at a talent agency and as a waiter, and was a pre-med student, but he knew he had to conquer his stuttering. So he decided to go into the one career for which a stutter would be unacceptable: acting. "One night I went out into the backyard," he recounts, "and I was talking to God — asking for direction — and acting was the answer I got. That was pretty terrifying, because I was not a confident kid. I had a stutter. I had ears that stuck out and acne. I was definitely not cut out for acting. But I decided to chance it." It took him over four years of saying tongue twisters and speaking more slowly, but when he finally stopped stuttering, it was the most rewarding accomplishment of his life. Today he is the spokesperson for the Stuttering Foundation of America, helping other people overcome the disability he has conquered.

Nick moved to Los Angeles to become an actor, dropping his last name and going by Nicholas Brendon, but he had a terrible time finding parts. He started getting bit roles in television shows and movies, but couldn't win anything bigger. But his resumé said something much different. "My whole resumé is pretty much a lie," he admits. "I did one day on *The Young and the Restless* and then, of course, I put on my resumé

Nicholas Brendon

'recurring' because it looks better. And now I've gone from that to being a regular. So it's out of control."

He hit rock bottom shortly before landing the role of Xander on *Buffy the Vampire Slayer* when, as a waiter, he could barely pay his rent, his girl-friend had left him, and he had all but given up hope of ever finding good acting work. He was then hired on as a production assistant on the TV series *Dave's World*, but he says it was more of a gofer job than anything else: "I had to go and buy Pop Tarts for the writers, and they wanted the cinnamon Pop Tarts, but not the ones with the frosting on top, so if I got the frosting on top I was in a world of hurt." When he didn't show a lot of enthusiasm in the workplace, he was ultimately brought into his boss's office and fired, with these last words: "You should be acting." Three months later, he won the role of Xander, essentially his first big break.

One of the reasons Brendon was attracted to the script for *Buffy the Vampire Slayer* was his own rotten time at high school. "High school isn't really great to many people," he says. "It's like a mandatory prison sentence. . . . In Israel they make you join the army; in America we go to high school." The character, described by one reporter as a version of a Greek chorus, since Xander is often treated as an outsider looking in, was originally based on Joss Whedon himself. "I think it was Joss when he was in school, but now he's God, so he has more say on what the outcome is," jokes Brendon. No wonder Xander gets all the good lines. And the gorgeous women.

Xander has undergone several changes during the course of the show, but the biggest one has been his maturity. Where in high school he was the goof who spun the one-liners, in season four he developed a real worry that his friends were moving on in their lives without him, since he was the only one who didn't go to university. His strange but sweet romance with cheerleader Cordelia had come to an abrupt end, as did communication between the two actors. As he told an interviewer in 2000, "When you're close with a character, you're often close with the people as well, and then when you guys break up on the show, you kind of break up a little in real life as well. I haven't talked to Charisma since we broke up, much at all really, because we were always in different scenes and then she was over on *Angel*. Kind of strange."

But in season five everything changed, and Xander became a man,

CHRISTINA RADISH

Nick kisses his wife, Tressa DiFiglia

declaring his love for Anya and moving toward wedding bells (or not) in season six. "It's nice to see him grow and mature," says Brendon, "because I've been the nerd guy for four years. . . . It's nice to go back and play a different character."

And it's not just Xander who's grown up, but Brendon as well. On September 1, 2001, he married his girlfriend, Tressa DiFiglia, at her parent's ranch in Carlsbad, California. The couple had gotten engaged earlier in the year. "I bought a ring, and I took her to Sausalito, in Northern California, and we got a hotel room that overlooked the water," recalls Brendon. "I sang a song we like — it's called 'And We Danced,' by Mark Paisley. And we kind of act out things sometimes, so we did. In the song, he takes a diamond ring out of his pocket, and I did, and she cried, and we were engaged." DiFiglia is also an actor, having played small parts in *The West Wing* and *ER.*

Today Nick lives in a Spanish-style home in the Hollywood Hills with DiFiglia. They fell in love with the house the moment they saw it, and bought it before they were married. "I just felt it was the right time," says Brendon. "We wanted to get out of our little apartment, and we found an awesome house. It was just the right time and the right fit. It's got everything we wanted in a house, so we wanted to jump on it."

And as for his twin brother, who is constantly mistaken for Nicholas and even tried dying his hair blond to avoid overzealous *Buffy* fans, Nick got the chance to act with him in "The Replacement." It was a fun experience for the two of them, and Kelly continues to act on other shows. When asked if he would work with Kelly again, Nick replied, "If something good comes up, but I don't want to be the adult equivalent of the Olsen twins. Or maybe we could do a TV movie with the Olsen twins and they could play our romantic interests! It would be very David Lynchy. I'll talk to my people and get right on it. Kelly has blond hair right now, so it's pretty easy to tell us apart. At least Tressa can. Except for that one time when she and Kelly had sex, but she apologized for that."

Nick hasn't done a lot of work aside from *Buffy*, although he did star in the 2001 summer film *Psycho Beach Party*. "Even though I played a gay guy, I was actually the straight man," he jokes. "I was not the funny guy, which is one of the reasons I wanted to do it. On *Buffy*, I am now considered the far-out funny guy. With *Psycho Beach Party*, I was so nice and philosophical, it was almost boring. But it was also a huge challenge because your natural instinct as an actor is to show off."

But things are never boring on the *Buffy* set. For Nick's 30th birthday in 2001, the cast threw him a big bash. *InStyle* magazine reported that Nick joked around a lot that night: "'I've still got all my hair!' crowed the birthday boy, which prompted his identical twin, Kelly, to plunge a metaphorical stake through his heart: 'Yeah, dude, but you have had all those facelifts.'"

SETH GREEN
Daniel "Oz" Osbourne

It's ironic that Joss Whedon was attracted to Seth Green because of his work in movies — film work would eventually force the actor to leave *Buffy the Vampire Slayer*.

Born on February 8, 1974, Seth grew up in Philadelphia with his math-teacher father, Herb, his artist mother, Barbara, and his sister, Kaela. He made his acting debut at the age of six in a production of *Hello, Dolly!* and decided he wanted to pursue a career in the field soon afterward. He has never wavered from that decision. Realizing her son was serious, Barbara made sure he got an education — he did correspondence courses and was tutored on the set — and he had plenty of opportunities as an actor. He tried acting classes, but attributes most of his acting knowledge to what he learned on the job. His first movie was *The Hotel New Hampshire*, with Rob Lowe and Jodie Foster, and that small part led to a large role in Woody Allen's *Radio Days*. Seth enjoyed working with Allen, and appreciated the fact that the director didn't expect him to be a little adult: "There was one point where we were running around with water guns and stuff, and he allowed that to happen."

His next film was *My Stepmother Is an Alien*, where he met and worked with Alyson Hannigan for the first time. They became very close friends, keeping in touch after the movie was finished. "We had a funny relationship," he says. "We would not see each other for a year, and then we'd get in touch and hang out really intensely for about three weeks, and then that would sort of peter off."

Following that film, Green appeared in several others, including *Big Business*, *Pump Up the Volume*, *White Man's Burden*, and *To Gillian on Her 37th Birthday*, while also taking guest-star roles in many of the hottest shows on television, including *Mad About You*, *The Wonder Years*, *Weird Science*, *The Drew Carey Show*, *Cybill*, and the pilot episode of *The X-Files*.

However, it was a part in a strange commercial that made him a recognizable face. In 1997 he appeared in a Rally's commercial as a drive-through cashier annoying the customers — he and another attendant would pretend they were ringing in the orders by yelling "Cha-ching!" after every customer order. The silly line became a popular catchphrase. Seth, who still gets recognized as that guy from the Rally's commercial, was stunned to find out how popular it had become: "It got out of hand. It was so silly. That's what happens with a catchphrase — people get caught up."

That same year he showed up for an audition with Joss Whedon, who recognized him from *My Stepmother Is an Alien*. "I had these big, crappy glasses on," he remembers. "I read with Joss and he asked me to take my glasses off." Unlike the others, Seth had to audition only once before he was given the role. He called Alyson that night to let her know they'd be working together again. No one was certain that his would be a recurring role, and when he was offered the opportunity to become a regular cast member, he hesitated at first, but decided to take the part. "I weighed my options as to what else I could be doing," he explains, "and decided that this was the best show I could be on right now, the best character I could be playing, the best potential." And despite all his other experience, he enjoys television more than movies because of the challenges it presents.

Seth was very fond of the Oz character, which he says is based on

Seth Green

someone Joss knew while he was at college. "The thing I love about Oz," he says, "is that he doesn't say anything unless it's important, so when he has something to say, it's really thought out. Smart." The biggest challenge on the show for the actor was when Oz turned into a werewolf. Although Seth was happy with the episode, he says the makeup people, headed by Emmy-award-winning makeup artist Todd McIntosh, had only two weeks to prepare the costume. Seth had to sit for hours for all the hair to be applied, and then the scene lasted a matter of seconds.

While starting *Buffy* in 1997, Seth was also offered a role in Mike Myers' first Austin Powers movie. He played Scott Evil, the son of Dr. Evil, played by Myers, and the role made Seth a full-blown Hollywood star. He enjoyed working on the movie, but said Myers was so funny it was difficult to keep from laughing all the time. "You can see me break in the movie at one point," he says. "He'd just done the 'Macarena,' then he walks over to me, you see me turn and almost smile, and then I got it together."

With his star turn in *Austin Powers*, Green had clearly managed to escape the "child star" trap that catches many other young actors. By taking smaller roles early in his career, he never became associated with a specific film, which allowed him to continue developing as an actor. "I'm fortunate that when I was younger I never had one particular project that made me a recognizable celebrity," Seth explains. "People have only recently started to know my name. The problem with a lot of child stars who have gotten into trouble is that they had too much too soon — stress, money issues, emotional issues. Suddenly you're not the same person everyone thought was so cute and funny."

Despite settling into a regular role on *Buffy*, by the fourth season it became clear that his film work and role on the program would present scheduling difficulties. In 1998, Seth appeared in *Can't Hardly Wait* with Jennifer Love Hewitt and the monster hit *Enemy of the State*, starring Will Smith, Jon Voigt, Ian Hart, Jamie Kennedy, Jason Lee, and Jason Robards, in which he played a secret service operative chasing Smith's character. More movies came in the following year, including *Stonebrook* and *Idle Hands*.

His biggest movie hit of all saw Seth reprise his role as Dr. Evil's son, Scott, as Mike Myers continued to push comedic boundaries in *Austin Powers: The Spy Who Shagged Me*, released in 1999. Seth continued to garner praise from those who worked with him. "Seth's improvisational skills are as good as anybody I've worked with — better than most. He comes to play," said Myers after working with Green for a second time.

Opportunities continued to come Seth's way, including several chances to record voices for animated television programs, as well as movies, and a regular spot as the voice of Chris Griffin on the *Family Guy*, which began in 1999. In 2000, he played himself on the short-lived television program *Tucker*.

That same year, Seth was clearly exiting *Buffy*, with Oz breaking up with Willow and leaving Sunnydale to find a way to control the wolf within. Strangely, the WB tried to downplay any move, initially claiming that Green would remain on the show in a semi-regular role. "He's not leaving," WB publicist Julie Kingsdale said. "He's just going to recurring status. He's gone to do [a] movie." Kingsdale added there would be a few episodes without Green. But Seth returned for only two more appearances as Oz in the fourth season (one as part of a dream sequence), apparently departing the show permanently. "It was all amiable," he says. "When you're a regular, the writers have to put you in every episode, even if it doesn't make sense."

Upon leaving *Buffy*, Seth proved time and again that he was firmly in control of his career, making it clear that he would not be your average movie star or teen idol. When his changing hair color became the fixation of too many teenage girls, he cut it all off during his return to television on *Greg the Bunny*. "I like it like this," he said at the time. "Kind of forces you to be present. No facade about it. Everybody got really preoccupied with my hair. So I cut it off."

The surreal comedy *Greg the Bunny* received mixed reviews from critics, but Seth clearly enjoyed making the program, which co-starred Eugene Levy, ripe from his hilarious performances in the *American Pie* movies. Seth seemed surprised that television critics didn't think a show about Greg, an innocent puppet bunny who falls into the world of a children's program that is populated by neurotic puppets and the humans who love and abuse them, would work. "Come on," he said. "It's a puppet show! Didn't you always say, 'Wow, if I could do the *Muppet Show*, that would be great!'"

Seth says a return to *Buffy* is unlikely, though never ruled out. "According to the Internet, I haven't had time or I've turned them down," he said in an interview early in 2002. "But the truth is I haven't ever gotten a phone call. It's not an 'I wouldn't do that' situation. It's just never come up. When I left, the show went in a lot of different directions. It's similar to [*Beverly Hills*] *90210*, [in that] the cast has completely changed over. There's like only three original characters on the show now. So I think it's just evolved. In a way, it's become something completely different that I might not be appropriate for."

Still, with or without *Buffy*, there's no slowing down for the diminutive actor, who made a clever cameo as a boy-band rock star in *Josie and the Pussycats* in 2001 before plunging into *Austin Powers in Goldmember*, released in summer 2002. "I've spent the last 20 years trying to get by," he said, demonstrating a level-headedness rarely seen in Hollywood. "Now all of a sudden I have all these opportunities, and I can't pass them up. But I've got savings now, so I can take some time to appreciate the stuff I have."

Seth also appears keen to continue making movies while maintaining television work, and continuing his long-term relationship with actress Chad Morgan, best known for a recurring role on the television program *The District*. Seth even joked about having a fictitious business card that played up his prolific profile. "On the front it says, 'He works hard for the money,'" he said. "And then on the back it says, 'So hard for it, honey.'"

JAMES MARSTERS
Spike

When *Buffy* fans first saw James Marsters in "School Hard," they instantly fell in love with his character, British bad-boy vampire Spike. His bleached-blond Billy Idol look and attitude made him so popular that, two years later, he became a regular character on the show. However, Marsters is a lot more than just Spike — he comes from a theater background, and he's not actually British. Or, for that matter, blond.

James Wesley Marsters was born in Greenville, California, and grew up in Modesto with his brother and sister. His birthday is August 20 (he won't say what year, but it's most likely between 1969 and 1971). He caught the acting bug early in life, when he played the part of Eeyore in a

James Marsters

Grade 4 production of *Winnie the Pooh*. "I was nine years old, attempting the role of Eeyore," says James. "I wanted the role of Pooh, but they denied me that. I think that I brought the existential angst of the character. I think that I did justice to the myth and legend."

After that precocious beginning, all James wanted to do was act. He attended David High School in Modesto and then enrolled in the Pacific Conservatory of the Performing Arts in Santa Monica. He eventually earned a coveted spot at the mecca of performing arts schools, Juilliard in New York (only about 8 percent of applicants get in). There he appeared in *The Tempest* and *Twelfth Night*. In New York, James not only learned more about his craft, but he learned how to fight. He tells a story of when he was attacked in Harlem: "This guy pulled a knife on me, and I wasn't carrying anything, so he chased me out of the stairwell. As I came out of the stairwell, I saw a two-by-four on the ground, and I hit him full on the head when he came out the door." James got the scar on his left eyebrow in New York, although he has a more impressive scar where he sliced his leg open in fifth grade on a sprinkler head and had to have skin grafts.

After Juilliard, Marsters went to Chicago, where he joined a theater troupe and again appeared in *The Tempest*. To this day he idolizes Shakespeare, and he's working on a screen adaptation of *Macbeth*, his favorite play. "It's a play I've done twice," he says, "and I think I have a pretty good handle on what makes it work and what doesn't make it work. I think it's a real audience pleaser if it's done correctly. All I need now is for some fool to give me $8 million so I can get it on film." In Chicago he cofounded the New Mercury Theatre Company, which eventually relocated to Seattle. He quickly realized he would never make a lot of money in theater, so he began setting his sights elsewhere.

In 1997 James moved back to California, quickly getting roles on *Northern Exposure*, *Medicine Ball*, and *Moloney*. He attended hundreds of auditions, and he got a call from Marcia Shulman, the casting director of *Buffy* at the time, to come and audition for the role of Spike. "When I originally got the audition, I went, 'Buffy the what?'" he laughs. "Then it was on that night and I absolutely loved it. I even got nervous for the audition the next day — 'God, I actually want this.'" When he arrived at the audition, he decided to have fun with it. The casting agents asked him to try it out using two different accents. "When I read for Spike, I also did it with a Southern accent, which would have been sexy but not as dangerous. I'd have been staked if they'd gone with Southern; I'd be dead by now." The casting director brought in Juliet Landau — who had just been cast as Drusilla — to the audition, and the chemistry was apparent from the start. James got the part.

Initially the idea was to have Spike around for three to five episodes, at which point he would be killed (presumably by Angel). As Joss has often done, he read the audience reaction to Spike and changed the course of the character, altering the scripts and storyline. But when he told James about the change in plans, he made sure the young actor realized his limitations. James recalls, "He said, 'James, this is not going to become the Spike show. I have many other fish to fry.' He was very clear with me about it, and it was nice to have that kind of honesty. But he did keep me busy. Spike was meant to be a transitory character and, thank God, Joss changed his mind."

After Spike tore off into the sunset with an unconscious Drusilla in "Becoming (Part Two)," he made one further appearance, in "Lover's Walk," before seemingly disappearing for good. Assuming his role with *Buffy* was over, James looked for other work. He got a small role in the film *The House on Haunted Hill* with Geoffrey Rush, and it was a thrill of a lifetime to work with such a talented actor. "He was fabulous," says Marsters. "An absolute gentleman. I expected him to be incredible but he was also just completely natural. I went out to lunch with him. He's just a great guy." James also appeared in an episode of *Millennium*, the Chris Carter show on Fox. Meanwhile, over on *Buffy*, fan pressure to bring Spike back was too overwhelming. By the beginning of season four, Angel had gone off to his own show, taking Cordelia with him. James got the call.

"Joss basically explained to me that he needed a new Cordelia — someone who stands around saying, 'We're all stupid — we're all going to die.'" James remembers. "Cordelia was going over to do *Angel*, so structurally they needed someone else in that role, and I said I would do it. Simply put, I'm basically a male version of Cordelia. It certainly explains my low body count. However, I get the better quotes — though she got the better clothes." Now a regular on the show, James is comfortable with the steady work and adjustments he's had to make to his life. To maintain Spike's platinum blond coif he bleaches his hair every nine days (and

CHRISTINA RADISH

Despite the Sweet 'N Low taking the edge off, Marsters doesn't bleach his hair during the summer hiatus

insists that four to seven packs of Sweet 'N Low lessens the burning sensation). He's not allowed to tan, which must be a difficult cross to bear in California. "I live three blocks from the beach," he says, "and I can't go there till twilight. I live like a real vampire." And he has to drink "blood" on the show every once in a while, a very sweet drink that's made either of Karo syrup and food coloring or Strawberry Quik.

But the job also has its perks — he still lists kissing Sarah Michelle Gellar as one of the highlights of his career. Also, Marsters wrote a comic book with Christopher Golden (author of several *Buffy* novels and comics) called *Buffy the Vampire Slayer: Spike and Dru*. The comic is set the day after the events of "Becoming (Part Two)," after Dru has awakened and she and Spike have left Sunnydale. "I was interested in having the characters torn apart in the beginning, have them not be together, and then have them discover through the book that they do need each other and that they are good for each other," James says. "It seemed to be kind of where the series was going as far as having their relationship being very complex with Angel." The comic has done well for him — it gave him a chance to contribute to something that interested him, as he'd been an avid comic book collector as a kid.

Although he enjoys playing Spike, he does worry that the character is being watered down a little, since he's not so scary after getting that chip in his head. After speculating for years that Spike must have been evil before becoming a vampire, he was shocked to read the script for "Fool for Love": "That episode was terrifying to me in the beginning," admits Marsters. "The character was revealed to be a nerd. And I did not want to be exposed in that way! I used to be a nerd in junior high school. I was short, I had fuzzy hair, and I was a theater geek." But once he got to the end of the script, he was relieved to see that Spike would get some of his cool back.

Today he continues his work on *Buffy*, while also showing off his musical side. He sings and plays guitar regularly at 14 Below, a bar in Santa Monica. He's put together a band called Ghost of the Robot with *Buffy* writers Doug Petrie and Stephen S. DeKnight, as well as members of local band Soccer Hooligans. He likes alternative acts like Radiohead, Belle and Sebastian, Beck, and The Cure, but also listens to a variety of other music. He was dating Liz Stauber (*Three Kings*, *Almost Famous*), but they have since broken up (he is divorced from Liane Davidson, who works in theater in Modesto).

He tries to find time for acting outside of *Buffy*, recently appearing in episodes of *Andromeda* and *Strange Frequency*. He also appeared in Amber Benson's writing and directorial debut, *Chance*. As to whether Spike will ever get his own show like Angel did, James jokes, "I have heard everyone talk about this except the one guy who can make it happen — Joss Whedon. I'm not holding my breath. I'm hoping he'll hire me for my next project. *Spike the Vampire Slayer Slayer*. Every week a new chosen one is born."

EMMA CAULFIELD
Anya

Born on April 8, 1973 in San Diego, California, Emma Caulfield is part German on her father's side, and part English and Irish on her mother's. No wonder Anya seems so worldly. Emma began acting when she was young, and in high school she won recognition for Excellence in Theater Arts from the Old Globe Theatre. "I really love what I do," she says. "I always have since I was a kid. I've always been the little drama queen. I studied it, did theater and loved theater. The best excuse I've had to be ridiculous was to be an actor. How else can you get away with doing things you can't do in a normal, structured society?" At college, however, she earned her degree in psychology, a subject that interested her because of her fascination with people. Her nontheatrical degree is a favorite topic among interviewers. Sounding a little like Professor Maggie

The lovely Emma Caulfield

Walsh, she describes her character on *Buffy* in psychological terms: "The id is our base impulse. We have the id, the ego, and the superego inside our psyche. The id is Freud's way of describing our animal instincts, the things that our ego and superego keep in check. I think Anya's struggle represents our id — and all the characters that surround her are the ego and the superego keeping her in check."

Psychology didn't lure Emma away from acting, and after college she attended the American School in Switzerland, where she studied theater. Back in Hollywood, she began auditioning while working in retail jobs on the side. Then she got one of those legendary Hollywood breaks. "I actually was stopped on the street," she recalls. "I had just moved to L.A. as a transfer student to UCLA, and I was leaving work — I was waitressing at the time — and my old agent came up to me and asked if I was an actress. One thing led to another, and next thing you know I was auditioning and dropping out of school. It just happened like that — I've been really lucky. I've been living out the Los Angeles urban myth."

She soon landed roles on several television shows, including *Burke's Law*, *Saved by the Bell: The New Class*, *Renegade*, *Silk Stalkings*, and *Weird Science*. Of all the parts, she remembers the *Saved by the Bell* experience the most fondly: "Actually, as silly as it sounds, [*Saved by the Bell*] is one of my favorite things I've ever done. It's the only thing I've ever done in front of a live audience. It's the closest thing to being in theater without actually being in theater. It reminds you of why you're in this business, because there's just such a kinetic energy that goes on with a live audience. It's always had a fond place in my heart."

Soon Emma got a major role on *Beverly Hills 90210* where she played Brandon's girlfriend Susan Keats throughout the sixth season. The following year she played Lorraine Miller on *General Hospital*. After garnering a lot of acting experience on two popular television series, Emma got a call from the casting agent on *Buffy the Vampire Slayer*. They were looking for someone to play a vengeance demon, and the character would be a one-off thing. Emma got the part, and "The Wish" became one of the most popular episodes of *Buffy*. She was called back to reprise the character in "Doppelgängland," and then again for "The Prom." Audiences loved her so much that Joss Whedon announced in March 2000 that she'd be a regular character.

Emma enjoys playing Anya, although she always reads through each script with some trepidation, worried that Joss will turn Anya into a demon again. And the worst part of that experience, she says, was the makeup. "The makeup for Anya was horrible," she says. "I wasn't lucky like James (Spike). He has a partial mask he can rip off when he's done. I had a full head, chest, and hair piece. It took over four hours to apply. Sometimes I felt like I was having an anxiety attack by the end of the day. It's incredibly claustrophobic!" Where Spike's purpose in season four was to embody the pessimistic side of Cordelia, Anya was brought in to be that frank side of Cordy that fans were missing. "She speaks her mind rather bluntly and feels a little bit on the outs with people, so it makes perfect sense," Whedon says. "And Emma's extremely funny. You don't usually get that much funny in a girl that pretty."

But Emma is very different from her outspoken character. She is extremely shy — she feels uncomfortable going to movie premieres and participating in photo shoots and interviews. Now that she's an actress in Hollywood and she's seen the bad that goes along with the good, she's a little less enamored of the field she chose. "I don't know that I want to act 15 years from now," she says. "I mean, I love the process of acting, but not the masochism. No matter how successful you get in Hollywood, you can't rest. Your next movie doesn't open well; they're looking for the next person to replace you; it's always something. You'll never have true peace."

That said, she admires the different facets of her character and has fun on the set. She says there's a lot of downtime on the set where actors sit around waiting for others to get their makeup on. During that time, she reveals, a lot of the actors have Scrabble tournaments. And they've gotten pretty ugly: "I've had some ferocious games with Marc Blucas where he'll beat me by one point. He's amazingly good at Scrabble. It's really annoying."

Emma appears in Amber Benson's film, *Chance*, and filmed *Don't Peek* in Australia during a season-six hiatus from *Buffy*. She often says she'd like to work with animals, and while filming *Don't Peek* she realized she might be able to do that some day. "I had this awakening there of what I'm supposed to do," she explains. "I made peace with the fact that this business is not what I'm supposed to do. It's really a stepping stone for other projects." But for now, she's happy where she is: "I'm on a great show, playing a great character, surrounded by great people. I'm so blessed."

MICHELLE TRACHTENBERG
Dawn Summers

Though only in her teens, Michelle Christine Trachtenberg has long been a recognizable face. She has hundreds of commercials under her belt, and roles on the big screen in pictures like *Harriet the Spy*, so the role of Dawn on *Buffy the Vampire Slayer* is just another in a series of acting successes for Trachtenberg.

Born on October 11, 1985, Michelle has been acting since she was old enough to walk. Her parents, Lana and Michael, both Russian émigrés, established themselves in Brooklyn, and Trachtenberg proved to be an exceptional talent at an early age. It wasn't long before her acting abilities forced the family to make a decision about remaining in the city. When Michelle was 12, her mother, a former actress herself, took her to Los Angeles while her father remained in New York, so Michelle could be at the center of the entertainment business. The gamble paid off.

Like Sarah, Michelle broke into regular television through a recurring role on *All My Children*. Gellar's tenure on the soap opera overlapped with Michelle's, as she was on from 1993 to 1995 while Trachtenberg performed from 1994 to 1996. Michelle played Lily Benton Montgomery, an autistic child. The role was difficult for such a young performer because Michelle had to act more through her body than through dialogue. She was very successful in the role, and her performances led Sarah to recommend Trachtenberg for the role of Dawn when Joss Whedon began his search for an actress to play Buffy's little sister.

At the time of her appearances on *All My Children*, Michelle also took a recurring role on the surreal and generally misunderstood children's program, *The Adventures of Pete & Pete*. The series detailed the lives of two brothers, both bizarrely named Pete, in the town of Wellville. The show gained a huge cult following during its time on Nickelodeon, and Michelle played the part of Nona Mecklenberg, whose father was played by rock legend Iggy Pop. Stars of both film and music lined up for roles on the series, which ran from 1994 to 1996, including R.E.M. singer Michael Stipe and *Reservoir Dogs* star Steve Buscemi. Just as Michelle had finally gained regular status on the show, she was forced to leave the series because of a conflict in the filming of her first major movie.

In 1995, Trachtenberg had been given the opportunity to play Harriet Welsch, the lead role in the film version of *Harriet the Spy*, co-starring Rosie O'Donnell. The film was a moderate success and vaulted Michelle into the limelight, including appearances on *The Rosie O'Donnell Show*. "She is simply a great actress," says Debby Beece, president of Nickelodeon Movies. "We looked at 350 girls, but there was no question in our minds that Michelle was the right girl for the job. Harriet is a well-defined, fully developed character, and we needed a fully developed young girl to play her. We needed someone to cover the range of emotions Harriet has to go through and who could appeal to both boys and girls. Michelle comes off as genuine because she really is a genuine kid. Everyone can identify with her."

Smaller roles in films like *Inspector Gadget*, as well as on television, followed Trachtenberg's appearance in *Harriet the Spy*. Then, in 2000, Joss Whedon found himself searching for an actress to play Buffy's little sister, Dawn. He quickly took a liking to Michelle. "I wanted to bring on somebody at a different stage of life, going through that younger adolescent pain," he says. "Sarah said that I should read [Michelle] for Dawn. We already had our eye on [another actress], but when Michelle read, it was clear she was the one."

It was a dream role for Trachtenberg, who had followed *Buffy the Vampire Slayer* because of her previous work with Sarah. In time, she became a diehard fan of the program. "I'm a huge fan," she admits. "I'm a walking encyclopedia of *Buffy*. I watched the show from day one because I worked with Sarah on *All My Children*. I was always thinking of little storylines for myself so I could guest star, like I could avenge Jenny Calendar's death by being her niece or I could be Giles's long-lost daughter. I would think of crazy things."

The reality was that Michelle would appear suddenly as Buffy's younger — and previously unmentioned — sister. Of course, as the fifth season developed, fans of the show became aware of the deception that

Michelle Trachtenberg

CHRISTINA RADISH

Looking a lot like big sis Buffy, Michelle poses for the camera at a premiere

was Dawn and how central it was to the plot. Michelle was joining a show with an established and long-standing cast. Despite the history of the series and the actors involved, Michelle found herself embraced by the cast. "Joining a show in its fifth year can be somewhat nerve-wracking," she says. "But like I said before, I was welcomed into the family with open arms. So it was a really comforting feeling, and getting to know all the stuff that happens behind the scenes isn't half-bad. It's actually really rather cool."

Michelle's familiarity with the show allowed her to appear comfortable among the older, more established performers, like Sarah Michelle Gellar and Nicholas Brendon. "On my first day on the set," she remembers, "I was saying to myself, 'Oh, right, this is the Initiative.' I knew every set, where everything is, where it goes. It was like, 'I know what's behind this door.' I knew the whole thing. And, like, if you ask me a *Buffy* trivia question, I'll not only give you an answer, I'll give you some of the history."

Now a star on a hit television series, Trachtenberg has tried to maintain a level of normalcy in her life. Much younger than the rest of the cast, she has to concentrate on passing math as well as memorizing her lines for upcoming episodes of *Buffy*. Still, she isn't worried about the impact of being a child star, and demonstrates a maturity well beyond her years. "I think the words *child actor* are often synonymous with bad things, there are so many bad stories," says Michelle. "I'm really lucky to be surrounded by people that love and support me. If you don't believe in yourself and work hard, you can't achieve anything. You have to believe in your actions."

AMBER BENSON
Tara Maclay

She's worked with the likes of Steven Soderbergh and Leonardo DiCaprio. She's hung out with teen heartthrobs before they were famous. She's become a gay icon on television, even though she dates men in real life. She's added actress, director, producer, and writer to her resumé, and she's poised to take the world by storm. And she's only in her mid-twenties.

Amber Nicole Benson was born in Birmingham, Alabama, on January 8, 1977. Her father is a psychiatrist, her mother a psychiatric nurse. Her sister Danielle is four years younger. Originally Amber wanted to become a dancer, and at age six she danced in the Alabama Ballet Company's production of *The Nutcracker Suite*. But soon her aspirations took a different turn. "I realized that it wasn't dancing I enjoyed doing," Benson says. "It was being on a stage and doing something that drove the audience crazy, made them feel something." She began to get involved with local theater groups and enrolled in vocal lessons.

When she was 12, her father's job moved the family to Orlando, Florida, where Amber attended high school with Joey Fatone, who would find later fame with boy band 'N Sync (she also did a TV pilot with A.J. McLean of the Backstreet Boys, but the show didn't get picked up). When Amber was 14, her family realized she had some serious talent, and they moved to California. She starred in one commercial, and the jobs began rolling in. Her first big film was Steven Soderbergh's third feature, *King of the Hill*, based on a memoir by A.E. Hotchner about growing up in Depression-era St. Louis. With his mother in a sanatorium and his father a traveling salesman, Hotchner was left alone in a hotel and got to know the other residents. Amber played an epileptic girl in the hotel. The film, which also featured Elizabeth McGovern, Adrien Brody, Lauryn Hill, Katharine Heigl, and Spalding Gray, garnered rave reviews.

From 1993 to 1995 Amber appeared in a series of made-for-TV movies about Sergeant Jack Reed, starring Brian Dennehy. In 1995 she starred in first-time director R.D. Robb's controversial *Don's Plum* with Tobey Maguire and Leonardo DiCaprio. Filmed over six days, the film is about a group of guys who get together at a place called Don's Plum every Saturday night, and have to bring a date. Amber was one of the dates, and the

The irrepressible Amber Benson

low-budget, indie flick was mostly improvised, with a lot of swearing and questionable behavior as the characters rant about life. In 1998, Robb tried to release the film and was halted by Maguire and DiCaprio. He tried to sue them for holding up his film, claiming they were using their fame to do so, and DiCaprio and Maguire launched a suit in return. According to DiCaprio's publicist, the two had agreed to be in the film as a favor, with the stipulation that Robb would never show it as a feature-length film. As Amber explains it, "I think the main issue is that it was all done improvisationally, so a lot of the actors were afraid that people would think that the characters they were portraying were really them, and some of the things they said and did were a little vulgar." Eventually the suit was settled out of court, with Maguire and DiCaprio winning the fight to keep the movie out of North America, although it has appeared at some festivals.

That same year, Amber had her first *Buffy* connection, starring with Eliza Dushku and Lindsay Crouse in *Bye Bye, Love*. In 1998, she appeared in the Seth Green film *Can't Hardly Wait* as a girl who is perpetually stoned in the kitchen, but her scenes ended up on the cutting-room floor. "They took [*Can't Hardly Wait*] to the ratings board, and they gave it an R, but they wanted a PG-13," Benson recalls. "So they had to cut out a lot of the drugs and drinking to get that rating. I played a girl who was on ecstacy. I appeared with Seth Green, and I had a couple of nice scenes with him where he tried to pick me up."

Then *Buffy the Vampire Slayer* came along. Amber almost missed the chance to play Tara when she didn't get her callback on time. "I auditioned for it, and then I was supposed to go visit my sister that weekend, so I left for the trip on Friday," she recalls. "They said it would be no problem, because my callback was going to be on Monday. I didn't even bother to check my messages until I was halfway there. Then I check my messages, and there's a message from my agent — the callback was going to be that evening, on Friday. I called my agent back and she said, 'It's in fate's hands now.'" Amber already knew Alyson Hannigan and when she returned the following week, she met Hannigan on the set. "When I came in for callbacks, I ran into Alyson and she got mad at me for not telling her I was up for a part. But you kind of want to do these things on your own, you know? She said, 'I'm going to tell them to give you the job!' So she marched in, and they told her I already had the part."

Amber first appeared in the now-classic episode "Hush," where she meets Willow at an on-campus Wiccan group meeting. Her shyness was similar to that of Willow in season one, and the two became friends. However, people really sat up and took notice of her when it was revealed that the two were more than friends. Amber wasn't aware of the direction they would take her character when she first auditioned for the part, but when Joss told her, she was happy to play a gay teen, as long as she was satisfied with the portrayal. "I was very happy with the way it was introduced — it wasn't about ratings or seeing two girls kissing," she explains. "It's about two people, regardless of gender, who fall in love and treat each other with kindness and respect."

But not everyone saw it that way. When "New Moon Rising" first aired, some viewers were shocked to see Willow choose Tara over Oz, and the posting board at the official *Buffy* Web site lit up with angry, cruel, and homophobic responses. Joss and Amber were completely unprepared for the closed-mindedness of some of the fans, and because Amber hangs out on the Internet regularly, she was exposed to the insults first-hand. Not only did some fans attack her for playing a gay teen, but they told her she was fat and ugly, perpetuating society's demand that women weigh under 100 pounds or else they're overweight. Amber was upset to see how cruel some of these fans were (though the more mature fans stuck up for her on the lists, shouting the other ones down). Her first instinct was to walk away and no longer post on the Bronze, the posting board of the official *Buffy* Web site. But after a few days, she changed her mind, and confronted the homophobia and cruelty head-on in one of the most impassioned posts ever to appear at the Bronze. Here, in full, is the post that appeared on May 4, 2000:

> I've been thinking a lot about what people said about Tara on the Internet after the last episode aired. At first, I was very hurt. I tried to disassociate myself from feeling bad by saying: This is Tara that they are talking about, not me.
>
> But I couldn't. I guess it hurts when someone calls you ugly or makes nasty comments about your weight whether or not it is really you they are referring to. I am just a human being and I feel like I deserve to

be treated as such. I also feel that Tara deserves to be treated with a little more kindness and compassion. Yes, I am not a STICK. I am a NORMAL, HEALTHY (I was gonna say Girl, but . . .) WOMAN. I have breasts and hips and I am very happy that they are part of me. I weigh 118 and I am 5'4". If you saw me in real life, you would think I was on the thin side. But on TV, next to my very petite costars, I do look heavier. I am PROUD to be NORMAL. A body is a beautiful thing to waste. Believe me, I have seen enough of my friends and peers waste away to NOTHING so that they could work in this industry. So that they could perpetuate the LIE that ANOREXIA is Beautiful. IT IS NOT. YOU ARE BEAUTIFUL. ALL OF YOU. Just for being. You all can judge me and Tara for being 'fat,' 'gay' and 'shy.' I suppose that my being on TV gives you that right. But I DO NOT have to read what you say. I have enjoyed being a lurker. But my feelings just can't take the criticism. Those of you (you know who you are) with sensitivity will understand. Thank you for sticking up for us. Tara and I both appreciate it. I think that being a beautiful, heavy, lesbian witch rocks! No matter what happens, I'm glad I get the chance to walk in Tara's shoes. All you girls and guys out there who think that starving, binging and purging and exercising yourself to DEATH is gonna change how you feel inside — It's NOT. Don't buy into all the media crap. Love yourself for who you are, not what others THINK you should look like. It's DEFI-NITELY more important in this life to love each other despite our imperfections.

Women everywhere sizes 8 and up cheered. Here, finally, was a woman on the show who looked like a real woman instead of someone who starved herself, and she was being called fat. Instead of dropping her weight to fit in, she fought back against the ridiculous notion that 118 pounds is heavy in *any* reality. While all the female characters on the show are strong, powerful, and good, and are amazing role models for young women, here was an actress who had the guts to speak out against the sizeism and homophobia in our society. Amber still talks about it during interviews, saying, "It was either that or just spew a bunch of obscenities at people. Seriously, I was really hurt and really upset. For somebody to sit in their home and write all this bile on their computer. . . . Okay, fine, actors are in the public eye, but to make a personal attack on somebody because you're not happy with what they're playing, or that this character came into a series and came between their favorite couple . . . it's just ridiculous. And the fact that the audience is perpetuating this idea that you have to look like a waif to be attractive is just sick."

After her brief encounter with the seedier side of fandom, Amber was soon overwhelmed with the positive response to her character. She's heard from dozens of young women telling her how Tara helped them come out. "I've gotten a ton of letters from young girls who have been questioning their sexuality," Amber says. "They're uncertain, they don't know what to do, they have no role models out in Middle America, and they watch *Buffy* and see Willow and Tara in a committed, caring relationship, and it can work and there's nothing wrong with them. They are perfectly fine and normal and good the way they are and they don't need to worry. It sets an example, and that's what I'm most proud of with this."

Aside from *Buffy*, Amber has been working on other projects. She filmed a movie with Vince Vaughn, Julia Ormond, and Ed Harris called *Prime Gig*, where she plays a telemarketer nicknamed Batgirl. "I play a psychotic telemarketer," she says. "She's young and very aggressive. They call her 'Batgirl' because she bludgeons you to death until you buy her products. She's a verbal bludgeoner." The film went into limited release in fall 2001. She also wrote a comic book for Dark Horse Comics called *WannaBlessedBe*, named after the derogatory term she and Willow use to describe the shallow Wiccans in "Hush." Co-written with Christopher Golden, the story is about a girl who becomes jealous of Willow and Tara's relationship and threatens to terrorize Sunnydale. "I'm really proud of it," Amber says. "Writing comics is a lot different than acting — for one thing, you have to come up with your own dialogue!" The comic was such a success that she wrote a two-part comic called *Wilderness* about Tara, Willow, and Dawn.

But Amber's biggest project is *Chance*. A film about a girl who's just trying to find Mr. Right, it was written, produced, and directed by Amber. Oh, and she's the main character, Chance. She gathered together several friends and costars to act in it. James Marsters was one of the first to agree to be in the film. "James Marsters is a friend, and he said he'd love to do it," Amber says. "He's so good — it's really neat because the character he is playing is kind of me. I'm a little backward, and the character he plays is very sweet and a little shy. He's funky and cool. James is such a talented guy, and it was so neat to see him play something other than Spike." The film also stars Tressa DiFiglia (Nick Brendon's wife), Andy Hallett (the Host from *Angel*), and Jeff Ricketts (who played Weatherby, one of the Council members in "Who Are You?") and there's a cameo by David Fury playing a pizza guy. Emma Caulfield also filmed some scenes, but an accident prevented her from continuing.

Amber put up her own money for *Chance*, and when she realized it was going to be far more costly than she'd anticipated, she started

Amber Benson with co-star Michelle Trachtenberg

a fund where fans who contributed money to the film would get their name in the credits. It was a huge undertaking, but a rewarding one for her. "It's always what I've wanted to do. Hanging out with Joss and [*Buffy* co-executive producer] Marti Noxon, I watch them do their thing. They're writing and directing and producing. They definitely inspired me to do my own thing. And now I'm doing it."

At the end of the fifth season of *Buffy*, Joss approached Amber and explained to her that her character would be killed in season six. The episode where it happened — "Seeing Red" — was a devastating blow to fans of both Amber and the lesbian relationship between Tara and Willow. After the episode aired, Joss Whedon had to endure criticisms from some fans that he and the writers were homophobic by killing off a lesbian character. As he had done so many times before, he came on to the posting board and explained that he was offended by comments that he had killed the character because she was gay. He said Tara's character had to die in order to bring about Willow's fury. He stated that he killed the character off *because* she was so important to him and the audience (and would therefore garner an impassioned response) and added, "I love Amber and she knows it." Benson accepted the fate of her character, although there are murmurings that Amber will return. Until then, she's happy taking some time off and enjoying life. "That's three years of my life, kind of over," she says. "But it's exciting to go on to new things."

The Cast of Angel

DAVID BOREANAZ
Angel

It's not surprising, given his "rebel with a clue" appeal and profile as a rising male lead, that David Boreanaz would be the first of the *Buffy the Vampire Slayer* cast to act his way into his own show. Stepping into the lead of *Angel*, which started in 1999, was natural — Boreanaz had risen rapidly to television stardom as the larger-than-life vampire with a soul.

He was born on May 16, 1971, in Buffalo, New York, to David and Patty Boreanaz, and his early life gave few indications of his later direction and career in acting. David's father is a well-known weathercaster in Philadelphia, and his mother works at a travel agency; Boreanaz grew up alongside two sisters and was consumed by football. Despite his abilities on the field, a knee injury forced him to drop his football dream and set his sights elsewhere.

What the other players didn't know was that David had harbored a secret love of theater ever since his parents had taken him to a production of *The King and I*, starring Yul Brynner, when he was only eight years old. "I was third-row, and I was just blown away by his performance," he said years later. "And I came out and I just knew I wanted to be the King, I wanted to be an actor."

After attending Ithaca College in New York, he decided to try his hand at acting. Upon graduation he moved to Hollywood, taking odd jobs like valet parking and house painting while getting cast in commercials. Though it might appear that he was an overnight success, Boreanaz caught only a glimpse of stardom at the start. Years later, on *The Keenan Ivory Wayans Show*, he admitted to working as a valet in a garage. David added he would pull away in the car very calmly, but in the garage he and the other valets would drag-race the cars, clocking each other to see how fast they could go.

The only break he got before landing the role of Angel was playing

Kelly Bundy's boyfriend in a 1993 episode of *Married . . . With Children*. Over three years went by after that appearance, during which David turned to theater. One day while he was walking his dog, Bertha Blue, he was approached by a Hollywood manager who asked if he was an actor. When David replied that he was, the manager said he knew the perfect role for him. The rest is a true Hollywood fantasy.

During his time on *Buffy*, Boreanaz developed several close relationships with those on the cast, especially Nicholas Brendon. He and Sarah Michelle Gellar shared a friendship offscreen as well as on, where practical jokes were the norm. "Before doing kissing scenes, we try to gross each other out by eating things like goldfish crackers or tuna fish," he said while in the cast of *Buffy*.

From the start, the character of the brooding, loner vampire Angel struck a chord with viewers, creating a large fan base for Boreanaz and making him a sex symbol. He was selected as one of *People* magazine's 50 Most Beautiful People on TV in 1999, and Boreanaz's star rose quickly, rivaled only by that of Sarah Michelle Gellar.

David's private life also became public when his marriage to screenwriter Ingrid Quinn disintegrated and ended in divorce in 1999. "Marriage is a tough institution," he said in an interview following the breakup. "Two people's love is much more powerful than [a piece of paper]; I did it the wrong way. That's why I got burned, and that's why it hurts. I'm healing from all that. It helps to put things in perspective."

Following the divorce, Boreanaz took himself out of the dating scene for a while, saying he needed time to "really heal and learn more about myself and what made me do the things that I did." But only months after making that comment, Boreanaz was involved with Jaime Bergman, a former *Playboy* Playmate who had moved into television, taking the role of P.J. on *Son of a Beach*, the HBO parody of *Baywatch*. The pair married on November 24, 2001, and Jaime became pregnant soon afterward. Just as Angel was dealing with his grown-up son Connor on the series, Jaime gave birth to their son, Jaden Rayne, on May 1, 2002.

David also took a stab at movies, including a role in the teen slasher flick *Valentine*, alongside Denise Richards. Most critics panned the movie, but those who worked with him on the picture praised Boreanaz. "On TV, David's this brooding guy," says *Valentine* director Jamie Blanks.

David Boreanaz

CHRISTINA RADISH

David with his wife, Jaime Bergman

"But offscreen, he is an absolute nut! And he's a terrific actor with a lot of chops. I really love this guy." It was Blanks who also staked the notion of Boreanaz as a dark, solitary figure, noting the actor liked to have fun on the set and make seemingly strange, offhanded remarks. "We named him Captain Non Sequitur for all the oddball comments he'd make," says Blanks. "Once, right before we were rolling, he looked at me with a straight face and said, 'You know, Jamie, sometimes I wake up early in the morning and I eat salmon.' I just went, 'What?'"

In time, it became clear that David would be given an opportunity to star on his own, slightly removed from *Buffy the Vampire Slayer*. Joss Whedon had the notion that he could push the *Buffy* storyline further while doing more with Angel if he spun off the character and created a show around the vampire. Typical of the fast-moving Whedon, Boreanaz said he was approached about the new show with little warning.

"We were just finishing up the second season of *Buffy* and Joss called me into his office and said, 'I have this great idea for this character — I want to spin him off and put him in Los Angeles and be the defender of evil in a city of lost souls,'" Boreanaz explains. "At the time my mind wasn't really into it because I was focused on the season finale we were shooting. I remember walking out of the meeting, saying, 'Oh, that's great,' and it didn't really hit me until we went to the Warner Brothers event for the show in New York. They did a presentation of [*Angel*], and I realized this was a show that could really happen and snowball. At the time, I found that the character really didn't have much place to go in Sunnydale so, succeed or fail, this was an opportunity that I definitely wanted to accept to grow as an individual. I kind of kept it at bay. I understood what it was and what the possibilities could be, but I looked at it one step at a time."

Angel initially relied heavily on its connection to *Buffy the Vampire Slayer*, making crossovers between the shows commonplace. Boreanaz and Gellar occasionally appeared on both *Buffy* and *Angel*, but in time it became clear that *Angel* would have to survive with its own storylines and on the star power of its lead actor. Gellar was also very supportive of the new show, and even brought a surprise to the set soon after *Angel* started filming. "I said to myself, 'I should go down and support David. It's

David goofs around for the camera

his big moment," Sarah remembers. She bought a cake and decorated it for St. Patrick's Day, complete with "little dead leprechauns" who had been staked ("I broke toothpicks and stuck them in the heart").

The synchronicity between the two programs was eventually phased out and all but severed when *Buffy* moved to UPN, leaving *Angel* as the top vampire show on the network. David saw the move away from *Buffy* as an opportunity for *Angel* to find a life and storyline of its own. "Crossovers are always tough to do," he said at the time. "Everybody is always asking, 'Are you going to do any more crossovers?' Well, obviously we can't. We're on two different networks. I think the ones we did this past season were difficult enough and weren't extremely powerful. There's no need to continue a *Buffy* [connection] after the first episode of this season."

While David was part of an ensemble cast built around the appeal of Sarah and the Buffy character, *Angel* is a show driven by his performances. It might not be *The David Boreanaz Show*, but clearly he feels more pressure to be the focus than he did on *Buffy*. "Before the onus was on Buffy and now it's all on Angel," he says. "I didn't really think about the pressure. At the time, I felt sadder about leaving the show. I thought of the relationships I built over three, four years on *Buffy* and then I had to leave to start whole new relationships on *Angel*. Having your own show, it's about forging a relationship with the crew, the cast. It really is an adjustment, almost like changing schools. But of course I love what I do, and succeed or fail, I was still acting."

CHARISMA CARPENTER
Cordelia Chase

Though she was once best known as a former cheerleader for the San Diego Chargers and the public face of Secret antiperspirant commercials, Charisma Carpenter has quietly evolved into a remarkable actress.

Born on July 23, 1970, in Rosarito, Mexico, Carpenter says she got her name from a "tacky bottle of Avon perfume from the 1970s." She grew up in Las Vegas, Nevada, in a strict household that her friends dubbed "Alcatraz," but she laughs that she found lots of ways to get in trouble with her parents: "I had my rebellious side. I was very difficult to live with. I didn't have good grades, I was often in detention, I invited boys over as soon as my parents were out the door. . . . One night I even borrowed — it was borrowing really — my dad's car for a little drive into town." This sort of behavior wasn't particularly unusual in Carpenter's family, she notes, adding that five of her uncles drove Harley Davidson bikes and regularly took her for rides. "Let's just say that I wasn't exactly your quiet type," she adds.

Her parents split in 1983, though they later reconciled, only to divorce in 1996. During that period, Charisma attended Bonita High School, before heading to the School of Performing Arts in Chula Vista, California. Clearly not at all like the snobby Cordelia on *Buffy*, Charisma appears sweet and charming in print interviews and on television. On *The Keenan Ivory Wayans Show*, she burst into a fit of laughter when she remembered that as a child she was part of the Young Entertainers, a group that went to lodges to perform inspirational songs (let's hope one of them wasn't "The

The always stunning Charisma Carpenter

Greatest Love of All"). She was also a child model, appearing in beauty pageants, but she insists her parents weren't like most beauty-pageant parents — they always gave her the option to quit if she didn't like doing it. In high school, Charisma became a cheerleader, enjoying it so much that she became a professional cheerleader for the San Diego Chargers in 1991.

During her teen years she worked in a video store, as a waitress, and as an aerobics instructor, but she decided to try acting by appearing in commercials, most notably for Secret antiperspirant. She moved to Los Angeles, but her first impression was not a good one — it was during the L.A. riots. "The day I came, there was all this outbreak and mayhem and there was a curfew and there was no food in the apartment," she told Keenan Ivory Wayans. "So I had to go to this store and when I go out of the apartment complex I turn the corner and there's like cars on fire, people running with sawed-off shotguns and looting. I was so scared, so I put the car in reverse, got back into the garage, and ate canned soup."

After appearing in dozens of commercials, she was noticed and offered guest-starring roles on *Baywatch* and *Pacific Blue*. But Carpenter is quick to note that it was tough to get her career off the ground. Even though her press bio says an agent discovered her while she was working as a waitress, she has tried to put the story into perspective. It wasn't as glamorous as it might first immediately sound, she says, noting that while working at Malibu on Sunset Boulevard, she was referred to an agent who was starting his own management agency. While other actresses submitted photos of themselves scantily clad, Carpenter was trying to get by on her talent: "I struggled. I was a waitress. I was a hostess. I rationed my [money]. And I slept side by side with a roommate for three years in an apartment the size of a matchbox. But I believed."

Her early guest appearances on television roles led Carpenter to the part of Ashley Green on Fox's short-lived Aaron Spelling production *Malibu Shores*, which she starred in with Keri Russell. She played a character similar to the one she later played on *Buffy* — a snobby rich girl whose daddy pays for her designer wardrobe. Following the cancellation of *Malibu Shores*, Charisma heard about a potential role on a new program being developed by Joss Whedon. But she wasn't initially interested in the part of the bitchy Cordelia; rather, she wanted to be the Slayer. For a short time it appeared that Carpenter would be lucky to get any role on the show. On her way to the audition, she became stuck in traffic, leaving her very late for her reading. Thinking quickly, she called her agent and told him to send pizza to Joss. While she didn't land the role of Buffy, she did manage to convince Whedon that she could play Cordelia. To this day, Alyson Hannigan jokes that it was the pizza that landed Charisma the role.

While Cordelia initially appeared one-dimensional, the character soon evolved, making the role of the snobby rich girl who joins the Scooby gang more difficult to play. Carpenter handled it with aplomb, nailing the part from the first episode and creating a character who is caring while still being self-centered. But Charisma assures everyone that while she loves Cordy's truthfulness and opinionated nature, the actress insists she's nothing like her character.

Strangely, Carpenter's success on *Buffy* hasn't translated into movie roles, although in 2001, she had a cameo in *The Groomsman,* which she called a cross between *American Pie* and *There's Something About Mary.* Despite her lack of extracurricular acting, Carpenter's jump to *Angel* kept her busy for most of the first three seasons. That's not to suggest that Carpenter wasn't at least a little bit concerned about leaving a hit like *Buffy* to join the fledgling cast of *Angel.* "Personally, I was flattered and willing to accept the challenge of a new show," she says. At the same time, she was "a little concerned and terrified at the risk of leaving such a critically acclaimed and well-accepted and well-received show such as *Buffy.* I mean, it's like flying the nest for the first time."

ALBERT L. ORTEGA

With Cordelia's flippant nature acting as a foil to Angel's brooding darkness, Charisma managed to take her character into a new realm. No longer weighed down

Charisma Carpenter in 1999, before she cut off her lovely locks

by the high school themes that permeated *Buffy*, she has played Cordelia on *Angel* as a mix of moxie and smarts. It has both improved Carpenter's acting and made the character of Cordelia more rounded and believable. "She's become more fleshed-out and three-dimensional," Charisma says. "She's really starting to be less selfish — although I hope she never completely stops thinking of herself, because that's what makes her so funny. But she's more dependable, more reliable. When I was on *Buffy*, I'd say, 'Oh, I want to do more dramatic roles.' But honestly, on *Angel*, I get all this range every single episode. I get to be vulnerable, funny, heroic, brave, resilient, scared. I have a chance to do it all. When the day comes and this show is over, I will feel so much more accomplished as an actor. It's the best learning ground I could have."

ALEXIS DENISOF
Wesley Wyndam-Pryce

While many think that actors are much like the characters they play, Wesley, the bookish "rogue demon hunter," doesn't have much in common with Alexis Denisof. For one thing, Denisof's English accent is fake; the actor grew up in Maryland and New Hampshire. And unlike the shy, almost reclusive Wesley, Denisof has lived a life in the limelight, even becoming a source of tabloid gossip. But like many great actors, Denisof has taken a role and made it his own, adding nuances to Wesley on *Buffy* and *Angel* that even creator Joss Whedon couldn't have foreseen.

Alexis Denisof was born on February 25, 1966, in Maryland, but grew up in Seattle with his mother, Christiana. His parents separated when he was 13, and soon afterward, Alexis went back to the east coast for boarding school, attending St. Paul's in New Hampshire.

But acting was in his blood from an early age, and Denisof trained for three years at the London Academy of Music and Dramatic Arts, before joining the prestigious Royal Shakespeare Company, and spending the next 10 years living in London. He also developed a spot-on English accent that he would later effectively employ as the nerdish Watcher on *Buffy*. "It's a plausible British accent," Alexis said during an Internet chat for AOL. "But, it's not the accent I speak with in my daily life. But I used

A jubilant Alexis Denisof, looking very L.A.

to. I lived in London for many years. As time went by, I started to sound more and more like a native. When I returned to America, it took me a while to recover the accent of my childhood. But Wesley's accent is my version of an educated, upper-middle-class Englishman from the south of England with boarding school and Watcher's Council and a few years' fighting demons in Los Angeles all thrown in."

It was during his time in England that Denisof continued to act in theater, including appearances in some of the most notable Shakespearean plays, like *Hamlet* and *Romeo and Juliet*, and a stage adaptation of Dickens's *A Tale of Two Cities*. Dozens of other roles followed, but it took his 1987 appearance in the George Harrison video "Got My Mind Set on You" for Denisof to take his theater skills to the small screen. He later said he took the role only to meet the Beatle, though that never actually happened. Roles in movies, both good and bad, followed, including the American film *First Knight* with Sean Connery and Julia Ormond, and the U.K.-made *True Blue* and *Rogue Trader*, in which he appeared alongside Ewan McGregor.

While known for his acting skills, Denisof also became the target of the British tabloids. In 1997, he began dating Caroline Aherne, the former wife of rock star Peter Hook of the band New Order. Aherne, who had been through several troubled relationships following her marriage to Hook and who starred in *The Mrs. Merton Show*, was a favorite of the London gossip rags. Aherne's breakup with Denisof also became fodder for the tabloids, and Alexis fled back to the U.S. to escape the constant media probing. (Aherne went on to star in *The Royle Family*.) Though he intended to remain in the U.S. for a short while, his trip lasted much longer. After staying in a divey hotel, he moved in with former *Cheers* star Ted Danson and wife Mary Steenburgen, who he'd met on the set of the critically panned television production *Noah's Ark* in 1999.

"I promised them it'd be for only two or three weeks, until I got an apartment squared away," Denisof says. "A year later I was still there, and they were wondering if it was time to fill out adoption papers. Ted and Mary are my saviors. I definitely wouldn't have made it without their psychological and emotional support." Alexis also did a pilot for Fox that never aired. His break on *Buffy the Vampire Slayer* came when Anthony Stewart Head suggested Denisof for the role of

Wesley. Head had previously worked with him in the play *Rope*.

"I just put his name up," Anthony says. "I remember the producer coming across the car park saying that they were looking for a James Bond type who thinks he's Pierce Brosnan but is actually George Lazenby, and I said, 'I think I know the man for you.' I went up to the casting office afterward and said, 'By the way, I just suggested [the role] to Alexis Denisof.' And they said, 'Oh, we already got a call from his agent and he's coming in tomorrow.' So he came in and there was absolutely no doubt. And like so many other characters on the show, he was only meant to come in for a short period and it grew because he's just fantastic."

The role of Wesley, the Watcher who is sent from England to take over from Giles, was expected to last for only two episodes before they "killed the character off in a glorious Joss Whedon spectacular death sentence," says Denisof. "But as we got working on it, we found this sort of uptight English guy was kind of funny. He had his own sense of humor, so they kept him alive, episode by episode."

While sparks didn't exactly fly on *Buffy* between the characters of Wesley and Cordelia, there was something brewing off camera. As it turns out, redhead Alyson Hannigan had her eye on the tall, dark-haired Denisof. "We were friends who flirted on *Buffy*," says Denisof. "But we didn't get together until after [I left]. She still teases me about my ethics at work. I think it's not a good idea [to date a co-worker], especially in the beginning. It would probably be fine now that we've been together a while, but it brings a weird kind of pressure to relationships."

The recurring role of Wesley finished at the end of the season. Alexis was uncertain of the direction he would take and was figuring

CHRISTINA RADISH

Alexis Denisof and Alyson Hannigan: don't they make an adorable couple?

out his next career move when Joss Whedon contacted him about reprising his role as Wesley in Los Angeles on *Angel* toward the middle of the series' first season. "I had just gotten back to L.A.," says Denisof, "and had been here for a day and was thinking, 'Gee, I should probably think about getting a job.' Then the phone rang, and it was Joss, with a job."

For Alexis, working on *Angel* wasn't exactly a continuation of his time on *Buffy*. Given the darker tone of the show, and the fact that the title character is a vampire who lives his life mainly after dark, *Angel* was often shot late at night. It took some getting used to, Denisof admits. "I actually have a little Polaroid taken by David Boreanaz on my mirror at work. It's a picture of me in my chair with my head resting on my hand, sound asleep. David wrote underneath it, '3:45 a.m., day one, Angel,'" he says with a laugh. "But I love working with him, and Charisma and David Greenwalt; they've really welcomed me and made me feel like part of a team. I have nothing but admiration and respect for everyone on that show. We're really, really having fun."

J. AUGUST RICHARDS
Charles Gunn

J. August Richards has created an acting career by battling the typical Hollywood convention, and in the process has deeloped a resumé that not only demonstrates his talent, but also his propensity to change the system from within.

Born Jaime Augusto Richards III (pronounced *high-may ah-goos-toe*) on August 28, 1973, he changed his name at the age of 16 to its current incarnation when no one could get the pronunciation correct. His parents had immigrated to Washington, D.C., from Panama, though Richards grew up in Bladensburg, Maryland, where his mother, Gloria, worked as a teacher, while his father, Jaime, worked as a mechanic. The couple split in 1985, when Richards was 12 years old. His interest in acting, even at a very young age, was encouraged by his mother, who took him to his audition for the University of Southern California. Not only was he accepted, but he was given a scholarship and finished his degree at the school.

J. August Richards

"I've always wanted to be an actor for as long as I can remember," he says. "I wanted to be an actor even before I knew what an actor was. I've always known I wanted to be an actor. The only other profession that I flirted with was becoming an inventor. When I was a kid I wanted to invent a light saber because my mom told me it wasn't real. I figured out how to make heat by using Tide and a couple of my mom's hair-care products. Don't try it at home."

By 1996, Richards had broken into the professional acting ranks with parts in a series of movies, including a small role in the forgettable *Good Burger* and a secondary role in *Why Do Fools Fall in Love* in 1998.

Following his big-screen breaks, he turned to television, showing up on a miniseries called *The Temptations*, as well as making guest appearances in *Clueless*, *Chicago Hope*, *The Practice*, *Moesha*, *The West Wing*, and *Nash Bridges*. All the while he continued to work on the craft of acting, taking classes and working to make his performances as believable as possible. It was this desire to improve his abilities that led him to take a workshop taught by Eriq La Salle, who was famous for his role as Dr. Peter Benton on *ER*. "We came down as hard as we could on him, in a very honest way," La Salle recalls. "He was ready to go to another level of truth. Overnight, after he had the courage to go there, his work went from a 2 to a 10. . . . If you realize 'I'm not really getting anywhere in this gear,' maybe you need to re-examine some things." In 2000 Richards was told of a role that had opened up on *Angel*. Though he was very keen for it, he had a hard time figuring out the motivations behind his character, a streetwise man named Charles Gunn who led a gang that fought vampires.

"My manager called me and told me I had an audition for a new character on *Angel*," relates Richards, "and when I read the scene that they wanted me to read at the audition, I wasn't sure what I was going to do. It was basically three whole pages of my character fussing at Angel, saying awful things to him. I was thinking, 'I don't know why I would curse this guy out for three pages. [Gunn] strikes me as the kind of guy who would just deck somebody right away.' I was on the phone with my manager saying, 'I'm not going to go in. I don't get it.' She said, 'Just go in! Just go in!'"

Using a technique he'd heard about while watching the television program *Inside the Actor's Studio*, in which stars discuss their craft,

Richards decided to play Gunn as a mixture of aggression and uncertainty: "I went into the audition and it was just incredible. It was one of the best auditions I've ever had — so much so that they called me immediately afterward and told me that they were interested in casting me for the role."

It was the break Richards needed, and he joined the cast as a regular. He also found love with Tangi Miller, who played Elena on another WB show, *Felicity*. All the while he never forgot his past struggles or the difficulties facing

J. August Richards with girlfriend Tangi Miller

CHRISTINA RADISH

other black actors in Hollywood. "I've been extremely lucky in auditioning for roles that aren't necessarily written for black actors," he says. "So I see a lot of opportunities open up for minority actors. And WB has been really kind toward me — they were even considering me as a star for the TV show *Popular*. I didn't get the role, but here I am with another great role on another great show. I would absolutely work within the system to change things. I like to play roles that are pertinent to plot, not the race of the character. I really just can't stand those roles that you know the black character is very tangential to the things that are going on — that offends me more."

AMY ACKER
Winifred "Fred" Burkle

Just like Fred, the mousy scientist who still manages to fight demons and vampires on *Angel*, there's more to Amy Acker than immediately meets the eye.

Born on December 5, 1976, in Dallas, Texas, Amy grew up as the eldest of four children. Acting wasn't her first ambition, as she'd aimed to become a dancer. When knee surgery finished her dancing dream, it opened a whole new area where Acker would eventually find success. "For all of my life growing up, I thought I wanted to be a ballerina," Amy says. "And then I got knee surgery in high school so I couldn't dance, and I started taking acting in high school, I guess my sophomore year. Right after that, I knew that was what I wanted."

In high school she began acting, taking roles in *The Crucible* and *Hello, Dolly!*, before following her newfound ambition to Southern Methodist University, where she spent three years studying the craft, eventually receiving a degree in Fine Arts Acting. As part of her education, she received training in weapons and combat, skills she'd eventually put to good use when she accepted the role of Fred on *Angel*.

Like Anthony Stewart Head and James Marsters on *Buffy the Vampire Slayer*, Acker followed her education with stints in theater. After graduation, she headed to work in a theater program in the mid-west U.S., where she performed in works written by some of the greatest playwrights, including Ibsen and Shakespeare. "I worked at the American Players Theatre, a classical repertoire theater," she says. "I left after graduating college and went to Wisconsin for eight months and did a bunch of theater in this beautiful place called Spring Green, which is in the middle of nowhere. It's a town of about 1,000 people, but the theater has 1,200 seats. Somehow it was pretty much sold out every night. People come from all over to see the shows. You hike up a mountain for about a half-mile and it's outside with the stars. It was pretty amazing."

By 2001, Hollywood had come knocking for Acker, and opportunities in both television and movies were presenting themselves. She did some voice work on *Wishbone,* a show about a talking dog, and moved to New York to take roles in two independent films, *The Accident* and *The Energy Specialist*. She also did the unseen pilot for *Hell House,* a television program that didn't find a taker, and won a role in the movie *Groom Lake,* directed by *Star Trek* icon William Shatner.

Eventually Amy received a call about a part on *Angel*. However, the role of Fred that she auditioned for turned out to be significantly different from how it would appear on the small screen. While Fred would eventually appear as a captive who was pulled into another dimension, the character Acker tried out for had a different name and her role in the

Amy Acker

show was not set. "The character has changed a lot from the audition," explains Amy. "First of all, her name was Logan in the audition, and she was working in the library, and it was a scene with her and Wesley. She was reading books and had kind of a little bit of the thing where she changes the subject real fast. But none of the history of being in the other dimension was developed at that point."

The role of Fred was intended only for the last three episodes of season two. But Joss Whedon and David Greenwalt liked Acker's performances as the shy, restrained, and frightened Fred so much that they decided to turn her into a regular character. Amy admits she was a little concerned about how she and her character would fit into a show that already had an established cast and storyline. "I kind of wondered about that," she says. "I was kind of worried about Fred becoming a regular. My old roomie is a big *Buffy* fan and she said, 'I was on the Web site and people are *not* excited about a new character joining the show.' It was before I'd even started, so I was like, 'Oh, no!' But it seems that everyone has been responding well to it."

Certainly Acker has come a long way from her work in classical theater. On *Angel*, every episode features strange new creatures and unique situations. But Amy says that's not unusual, given her film and television work so far: "I did a movie with an alien. I did a movie where someone was murdered. I did a TV pilot that didn't get picked up, but it was all about ghosts and a haunted house. So, for some reason, I seem to be drawn to these kinds of parts. So now [on *Angel*], it's like, 'Oh yeah, there's the demon. He should be there. The guy in the green face? That's perfectly normal.' It's definitely different, though. I was talking to one of my college professors, who called the other day. I was like, 'I think you need to add a class about acting with demons, because no one really taught us that in school.'"

A Night to Remember

THE BUFFY POSTING BOARD PARTIES

This report on the 1998 party was written with the help of the following posting board members who attended: Erika Rottler (a.k.a. Sasheer), Erika Gilbert (Batra), Keith Miller (KAM), Tammie Purcell (greengirl), Viet My Nguyen (Samiel), Karri Phillips (Phoenix), and Will York (fenric).

It was the kind of thing fans dream of, and the kind of thing celebrities tend not to do. Imagine this: You're in an Internet chat room one night talking with other people who share a love for a certain television show. You get to know everyone really well, and one day someone comes up with the idea that you should all get together at one big party. Then someone else says he knows the people on the show, and he might be able to get them to come. You fly in to California for a night of meeting your fellow posting-board members, only to be met with almost the entire cast of the show.

This is exactly what happened to almost 100 *Buffy the Vampire Slayer* fans on February 14, 1998.

Every day the fans would meet on the posting board, known as the Bronze, and discuss the show and the characters, or just chat about life in general. If you were lucky, you'd be in the Bronze when one of the "VIPs" would come in. The VIPs include David Boreanaz, Seth Green, Nicholas Brendon, Alyson Hannigan, and Joss Whedon, and the VIPs who post on the board regularly are Jeff Pruitt (stunt coordinator), Ty King (writer), and RD (the assistant to David Greenwalt, the show's co-executive producer). The fans were from all over North America, and since very few of them had met before, one of the posters, known as Blade, came up with the idea that they should get together and meet. Another poster, AKA Becker, immediately agreed, and said it should be held in L.A. because that's where the show is filmed. Todd McIntosh (the show's makeup artist) started spreading the word around the set, seeing if anyone was interested. Eventually RD stepped in to help out. The ball was now in motion.

Alyson was the first of the cast members who agreed to attend the party, and a committee of posters was formed to work out the details and coordinate who was coming. Although they knew about the VIPs who would be attending, they decided to keep the information under wraps, because they didn't want people to come solely to meet cast members. The purpose of the party was to meet fellow Bronzers — the VIPs were a bonus. RD came through and said that he got most of the cast to agree to come, and he also booked the spot for the event. Those posters who said they'd be there for sure and sent in their money (to cover costs of renting the venue) were given an invitation with the location of the event — Planet Hollywood in Los Angeles — which was kept secret from the other posters. However, the Posting Board Party Committee (PBP) were upset to learn that, the day before the event, Planet Hollywood publicly announced that cast members from *Buffy the Vampire Slayer* would be appearing there, and so fans from all over California would show up to see them.

On February 13, posters flew in from Texas, New York, Florida, Canada, Wisconsin, New Jersey, Illinois, Indiana, North Carolina, Washington, Georgia, and Washington, D.C. — one of the committee members estimates that 90 percent of the attendees were from out of town. (Is that true fandom or what?) AKA Becker lost all of his luggage upon arrival in Los Angeles, but he put his chin up and simply bought more clothes. Another member, Samiel, laughed when he remembered the problems that occurred when posters tried to meet up with people they'd never seen. Considering most of the posters go by amusing aliases, Samiel explains, "one does not go up to a stranger in an airport and ask questions such as 'Are you Dead Boy?' I guess that is one of the many disadvantages of knowing someone only by their Internet nickname." To make things easier, however, at the PBP everyone was given a name tag with his or her Internet handle.

The party was to start at 6, but the committee arrived early to set up. RD was there helping out the committee members, who worked out security and figured out where people would go. Initially Planet Hollywood said the party could be held on the second floor, but then switched it to

David Boreanaz, who was the first to arrive at the party,
receives a smooch from Seth Green . . .

. . . and gives one back to Alyson Hannigan

the first floor so it would be more readily accessible to the posting-board members. However, the committee had to rope off a special section to keep out people who hadn't been invited. Planet Hollywood provided them with finger foods, pasta, and free nonalcoholic beverages, and the committee had arranged for a huge chocolate cake designed to look like the posting board. The members of the posting board mingled, excited beyond words about the cast members who were about to arrive, and when the *Buffy the Vampire Slayer* theme began to play over the Planet Hollywood sound system, everyone broke into a cheer and turned the evening into a real party.

David Boreanaz was the first cast member to arrive (other VIPs had arrived earlier), and it was then that people realized what a madhouse the evening would be. Some of the posters mobbed him, wanting autographs, pictures, and just to shake his hand. As poster Batra put it, "It was as if David were a long-lost Beatle, the awed look on their faces, and one of the girls looked like she was about to cry." RD darted through the crowd to rescue David and lead him upstairs where he could have his dinner be-

What would you give to be the fan in the middle?

fore joining the party. Because he was the first actor to arrive, he probably garnered the most excitement. Erika Rottler remembers, "Seeing him for the first time was the only time I felt starstruck. There was Angel."

Soon after David's grand entrance, other members of the cast and crew arrived one by one — Anthony Stewart Head, Nicholas Brendon, Ty King, Jeff Pruitt, Sophia Crawford (Sarah Michelle Gellar's stunt double at the time), Joss Whedon, Todd McIntosh, Marti Noxon (writer/story editor), Alyson Hannigan, and Seth Green. Also in attendance was James Lamb, known as TV James, who had created the first official *Buffy the Vampire Slayer* Web site, which had brought all of the people together.

The posting-board members who contributed to this report had stories about every VIP who was there. Everyone said that Jeff and Sophia, who had met while working on *The Mighty Morphin Power Rangers*, made a very attractive couple. The two had gotten engaged a few weeks before the party, during the filming of "Phases." A regular on the posting board, Jeff often indulged the fans by talking about shooting the episodes and had even scanned in storyboards to show people. Erika, who has kept in touch with Jeff and Sophia since the party, had only nice things to say about Jeff: "Jeff is one of the coolest people around. If it wasn't for him I would have no idea about stunt people behind the scenes. He made me see a whole new side of Hollywood." The PBP wasn't the first time Erika had met Sophia Crawford, but she is always surprised by what Sophia looks like in person: "You would expect a big, tough, scary woman, but when you shake her hand and look into her eyes you see the true beauty in her. She is one of the sweetest people I have ever met."

David Boreanaz got rave reviews from everyone, and people kept commenting on how sweet he was. Karri Phillips recalls a group of girls, all about 13 years old, who had been eating at the restaurant and recognized David when he arrived. They dashed down the street to buy copies of a teen magazine whose cover David graced and returned in the hopes that he might sign them. Because they weren't part of the PBP, they had to stand aside and look on, until David finally spotted them behind the ropes. He walked over, signed all the magazines, and chatted with them, proving to everyone how gracious he was. Later, the father of a young boy approached one of the party members and asked if it would be possible to get David to sign an autograph for his son. David obliged, and found the little guy hiding behind a pillar out of shyness. Noticing the boy's Chicago Bulls jacket, David talked to him about the Bulls game the night before and put the boy at ease.

One posting board member couldn't make the party because she was studying for her bar exam, but the other Bronzers knew she was a big fan of David. One of the posters had been talking to her from his cellphone, keeping her updated on the evening's events, and he handed the phone to David so she could talk to him. Everyone was pleased to discover how genuine David was, and Keith Miller says that over the course of the evening David posed for numerous photos and talked to everyone. Tammie Purcell and Will York spoke with David, saying they preferred him as the evil Angelus. He was very open and animated with them, explaining how he prepared for the change in his behavior, but he wouldn't give away any of the upcoming episodes. Tammie joked that Angel needed to kill someone who was close to Buffy, but who wouldn't really shake up the storyline, like Buffy's father. David laughed out loud at the idea and said he thought it was very funny, but added, "Just wait." He was slyly referring to "Passion," which had not yet aired.

Karri, who also talked to David at length, recalls one trick he played on her: "At one point during the party, he walks up to me and says, 'Would you like a kiss?' and of course I look at him with a blank stare. Then he hands me a little Hershey's Kiss." She laughs that she ended up getting four real kisses out of him later in the evening, when her friend was trying to take a picture of David kissing her and the camera — luckily — wouldn't work.

Joss Whedon might not have an instantly recognizable face for most fans, but because he is the true mastermind behind the show he is treated with awe and respect among the fans and the cast and crew. Many fans got their pictures taken with him, but one Bronzer in particular, known as -mere-, was well-known as a big fan of Joss. Samiel recalls that when Joss first arrived, people started chanting for her to come over. "The chant was '-mere-' first softly, and finally so loud nothing else could be heard. . . . Joss and -mere- met in an embrace and the applause shook the room like thunder." Later, this particular Bronzer — now known to fans as Mere

Smith — would become one of the most popular writers on *Angel*. Talk about making your dream come true!

Batra was shocked when Joss recognized her name from the posting board. Will York said he got to talk to Joss at length, and remembers, "He talked of how he *wasn't* working on several projects that had been rumored (*Planet of the Apes*, *Avatar*, *Dr. Who*, etc.), because he was devoting his focus to *Buffy*. I also presented him with a membership card in Sarah-SOTA (the Sarah Society of True Adoration, a club I founded on the board), which he dug." Joss had brought along some behind-the-scenes and bloopers tapes, made especially for this event, which played on the screens throughout the evening.

Nicholas Brendon was very entertaining, and people mentioned him especially in conjunction with the Xander Dance Club (XDC). At the beginning of "Angel," Xander is at the Bronze doing a crazy dance, trying to get other girls to dance with him. Two of the posting-board members — KAM and Little Willow — thought that scene was so funny they formed the online XDC. The club began as a joke, but others joined in and it soon became the biggest club on the posting board (later to be surpassed by Little Willow's We Possess Willow Power club). To join the XDC you simply had to give a valid reason you wanted to be in, and you were assigned a number. Many members chose mottos as well, and they discuss the songs in the show and create scenarios where Xander must dance.

At the Posting Board Party, the XDC had bought a plaque for Nick. At the L.A. comic convention, an XDC member, Glitergrrl, had told Nick about the club, and he accepted an honorary membership as Member #0. So Keith had had the names of the club members engraved on the plaque with Nick's status as Member #0 placed at the top. They presented it to Nick in front of everyone at the party, but some of the women in the audience shouted out that he should earn his plaque by pulling off some Xander moves right there. Joss and Jeff started to coax him — Joss joked that he'd give him a raise — and Nick finally agreed. But he had one condition. Grabbing the microphone, he said he would dance only if David danced, too. Karri had been talking to David and his friend Patrick when this happened, and she said he kind of sighed to himself and relented. Patrick was floored, saying to Karri, "I can't believe David is dancing. He *doesn't* dance!"

As David walked toward the floor, Nick continued to joke around at the microphone. "Most of you guys know David as Brooding Guy," he said. "But I know David. He isn't really Brooding Guy, he's Happy Dance Guy. And why is that, David?" "Because of the '*fun*'!" David laughed. They performed a series of hilarious dance moves, with "Nick pulling an Elvis and David pulling a . . . I'm not quite sure what he was doing out there," laughs Erika. Keith remembers the scene clearly: "Amid screams and cheering, the two of them whipped around the dance floor in the fun and uniquely Xanderesque style. Nick, in a very Elvis-like routine, spun his arms, tap-danced, and even pulled off the splits, finally ending in an exhausted bow." After the two had finished, Nick graciously accepted his award, joking, "Number zero — is that a good thing?" For many, the dance was the highlight of the evening. David would later perform a similar version of the dance on the *Angel* episode "She."

Nick was a hit among fans on a personal level as well. Erika says, "Nick had that dark, charming quality with a dazzling smile to go along with it. He was very open to compliments and seemed to be truly enjoying the work he is doing on the show." "Bewitched, Bothered and Bewildered" had aired a few days earlier, and Erika congratulated Nick on what many fans consider one of the best episodes of the season. He was very touched and obviously loves working with Charisma. When Erika told him how happy she was that the two had become a couple on the show, he answered, "Isn't that great?" Tammie Purcell joked that momentarily she became Nick's drink holder when he was asked for an autograph. She laughs, "Was I tempted to take the straw? Yes I was . . . but I showed restraint."

Nick wasn't the only VIP to receive gifts. One of the committee members came up with a very clever idea that whoever came from out of town should bring a postcard from their hometown, and all the postcards were presented to Joss. Alyson Hannigan was given a glass dolphin, Beanie Babies, and a toy clapping monkey (because of the dream sequence in "Surprise"). Tony was given a scone mix and English toffees as a joke on how British Giles really is on the show, while David was given some Tasty Cakes, a videotape of *The King and I*, and other gifts, and Jeff and Sophia were presented with his-and-hers first-aid kits, a pair of handcuffs, and action figures.

COURTESY KARRI PHILLIPS

David dances to the delight of the audience, while Nick watches from the sidelines

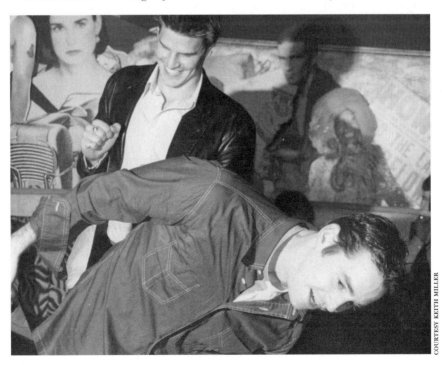

COURTESY KEITH MILLER

David and Nick show off the moves that get them the ladies

Alyson was a favorite with the fans. As Samiel says, "The guys crowded around Aly as thickly as the gals surrounded David." However, Aly was popular with both sexes. Erika was immediately drawn to her: "Alyson was as lovable offscreen as Willow is onscreen. She has a certain presence that draws you to her." She added that Alyson was "exceptionally beautiful. . . . She is truly genuine." In contrast, Keith thought she was very different from Willow, saying, "It may not be apparent without having met her, but Alyson's portrayal of Willow is brilliant, because in person she is confident and dynamic, in contrast to her quiet, reserved character." Tammie agreed that Alyson "is truly a delightful person."

Anthony Stewart Head seemed the most unlike his character. "Tony was stunning," Erika remembers. "He seemed to have the most fun, laughing and offering a smile to everyone. He probably made more hearts melt than Nick and David together." Tony's birthday was six days after the event, so Tammie got everyone at the party to sign a large card for him. As she said, it gave her a great excuse to talk to all of the VIPs, who also signed the card. When the card had been signed, everyone began singing "Happy Birthday to You," knowing that Tony was upstairs. He came down, having missed the song entirely, and everyone sang it to him again. Batra remembers that he looked embarrassed, but was very touched. Everyone thought he was a lot of fun to talk to, and one fan even commented that where before she couldn't imagine him as Frank N. Furter in *The Rocky Horror Picture Show*, she could now easily picture him in the role. Karri described him as a "hippie, a true child of the '60s. He was a trip."

One of the most popular guests was Seth Green. He was described as "down-to-earth," "sweet," "the definition of charisma," "a very great guy," and "a cutie." Samiel, who at one point became Seth's unofficial water carrier, says, "Of all the cast, Seth may be my favorite actor, not only for his acting abilities, but also for the kindness he displays." Seth had shown up unexpectedly and didn't have an official invitation. Karri recalls that AKA Becker, who had made up the invitations, jokingly threatened to kick him out, but promised to send him an official invitation in the mail. A few months later, he ran into Seth in New York, and Seth remembered him and wondered where his invitation was. When AKA Becker told him he still hadn't sent the invitation, Seth jokingly threatened to beat him up.

Alyson Hannigan and Seth Green, close friends in real life as well as on screen

COURTESY SAMIEL

David puts the squeeze on Alyson

COURTESY KARRI PHILLIPS

All night long, Seth met with fans, shook hands, and asked what people's real names were. He seemed genuinely excited to be there. One poster said, "If you ever meet him, it will change your thoughts on kids who grow up in the entertainment biz." It was at this party that fans first heard the news that Seth had been signed on as a regular character in the third season. After the excitement surrounding this announcement had died down a little, Erika asked him if he could call her cousin in Oklahoma, who had a Seth Green Web site. Without hesitation he picked up the phone and chatted with Erika's cousin for about 15 minutes about the site, then made it the official Seth Green Web site. A few people mentioned how well Aly and Seth got along together, saying you could tell they'd been friends for a long time by the ease with which they spoke to one another.

One of the posting-board members, Marcus, had the foresight to bring a laptop computer and cellular modem with him, which they hooked up to the Bronze. That night the posting board was filled with fans awaiting any news on the PBP, and David, Aly, and Seth all posted their hellos to those who couldn't make the party. Karri got the opportunity to show David the Web site that she has devoted to him, and he was so happy with it that he wanted to sign the guestbook. However, he explained that he was somewhat computer-illiterate, and Karri ended up doing the signing for him. The fans at the PBP also got the five cast members to pose for a photo, holding up a sign for the people who couldn't be there. The sign read, "Hi Everybody. I Miss you!!! Posting Board Rules!!!" They then posed for a mock photo of the four guys biting Aly's neck.

The party continued until 1 a.m. and many of the VIPs stayed very late. Not only did the fans get a rare chance to meet the cast and crew of their favorite television show, but they made a lot of friends among their fellow posting-board members. The cast and crew enjoyed themselves immensely, and as a thank-you RD invited the PBP committee members to the set of *Buffy the Vampire Slayer* a few days later. They got to watch a scene for "I Only Have Eyes for You" as it was being filmed, and they were shown the various sets, such as Buffy's bedroom, her house, the Bronze, and the Sunnydale High cafeteria, which was being built for the episode. In the past, all cafeteria scenes had been shot away from the set, and Joss finally decided to build a cafeteria so the cast and crew wouldn't

Tony, Nick, David, and Seth play vampires to Alyson's willing victim

have to leave the set. One of the people who got to see the sets couldn't believe how real they looked: "Buffy's room was homey, yet it was funny to look out her window and see her roof meeting up with the floor. The Bronze was smaller than it looks on TV but it was still cool. But my favorite was the library. It was just as it looks on TV. Big and booky. It was just so exciting to be in there, to look around and see the millions of scenes they have filmed run through your head."

A chance to meet their idols is something most fans only dream of, but for one evening the dream came true for 100 *Buffy the Vampire Slayer* fans. The crew and the fans worked together to pull off an event that has now become legend among online *Buffy* fans.

***

There has been a posting board party every year since the first one, and from 1999 onward the events were used to raise money for charity. The following brief accounts have been written with the help of Little Willow,

Peter Hueser (a.k.a. Morbius), Joan P. Mendoza (friday), Liza Campbell (JustLiza), Terri (greeneyes), Karri Phillips (Phoenix), Kim Antonio (Spookymagoo), and Kristy "Swoop" Bratton, who covered the 2001 and 2002 events for the excellent Web site "City of Angel" (www.cityofangel.com). I asked for their thoughts on each one, including their favorite moments, and I've listed who was there, how much money was raised for charity, and what the highlights were. As each person stressed, these parties aren't for meeting the stars of the show, but to meet other Bronzers. The Posting Board Parties are not meant for general *Buffy* fans, and the Bronzers look forward to these get togethers to meet the people they've been e-mailing all year, which is the real excitement.

"We'll Slay You"

February 6, 1999
   Sunset/Landmark, Hollywood

VIPS:	Joss Whedon and David Greenwalt; actors David Boreanaz, Anthony Stewart Head, Eliza Dushku, Seth Green, Elizabeth Anne Allen (Amy the rat), Danny Strong, and Larry Bagby III (Larry, the gay football player); Jeff Pruitt and Sophia Crawford; composer Christophe Beck; Karen Shepard (Eliza's stunt double)
Musical guests:	Velvet Chain and Four Star Mary (Dingoes Ate My Baby on *Buffy*)
Money raised:	$6,000

After the first Posting Board Party in 1998 had been such a success, Bronzers realized they could turn the event into a yearly occasion, but also decided to add a new element to the mix. By forming "The PBP Committee, Inc." they could solicit charitable donations from people attending the party, and from Bronzers online at the posting board. The

Seth Green hams it up for the camera during the presentation of the check to the Make-a-Wish Foundation. From left to right: Seth Green, Anthony Stewart Head, Eliza Dushku, Larry Bagby III, Joss Whedon

Eliza Dushku with Morbius

At one point in the evening, Seth Green was mistaken for a fan and reprimanded by security for hanging off the railing

committee formed an association with the Make-a-Wish Foundation in Los Angeles, and it was decided that all monies raised would go to this charitable organization. For the first time they incorporated the "pre-party" that happened the night before the main event.

Over 200 Bronzers attended this party from as far away as Europe, creating some fond memories. Peter Hueser, the president of the PBP Committee, remembers one in particular: "During the course of the party a young newlywed couple from Missouri approached me to thank me for helping to arrange the PBP. What made the conversation special was the fact that these two Bronzers (who admitted they'd never traveled outside the state of Missouri) had saved for almost a year to come to Hollywood to meet their Bronzer friends and help us raise money for MAW. Having experienced a real Hollywood-type event, they were eager to return and share their experiences with their friends and relatives back home."

Several others remembered how Seth Green entertained the audience by getting onstage with Velvet Chain and playing guitar, although according to Karri, he almost missed his cue: "Seth Green was supposed to play a song with the band and he was eating and they started the song without him being onstage. So they got to the part where he was supposed to join in and started singing, 'And we're waiting and waiting and waiting....' He finally got the hint and dropped his food and ran down so he could perform his song." Another highlight was when Joss Whedon and Eliza Dushku joined the Bronzers on the dance floor, and a week later, when "Bad Girls" aired, Bronzers were thrilled to see Eliza dancing just as she had with her fans.

"BY2K Party on the Hellmouth"

February 19, 2000
   El Rey Theatre, Hollywood

VIPS: Joss and Kai Whedon (Joss's wife); actors Alyson Hannigan, Nicholas Brendon, Emma Caulfield, Marc Blucas, Amber Benson, Alexis Denisof, Anthony

Stewart Head, Elisabeth Rohm, Danny Strong, Bailey Chase (Graham), Leonard Roberts (Forrest), and Larry Bagby III; writers David Fury, Doug Petrie, Tracey Forbes, Jane Espenson, Marti Noxon; makeup artist Todd McIntosh; Jeff Pruitt; authors Jeff Mariotte and Nancy Holder

Musical guests: Four Star Mary and Velvet Chain

Money raised: $11,000

The 2000 party attracted Bronzers from five continents, and once again the "pre-party party" was as much a hit as the main event. Darling Violetta, who perform the *Angel* theme song, played at the Friday-night party, and Four Star Mary and Velvet Chain entertained the crowd at the Saturday-night event.

It was the first PBP that Kim Antonio had attended, and she was more excited to finally meet her fellow Bronzers than anything else. "It was quite overwhelming, my first PBP. There were hundreds of us, and you couldn't tell who was a Bronzer in the hotel unless you wore your name tag. Fortunately for me, there were Bronzers from my area, and from there the networking began. It was kind of funny and cool meeting people face-to-face for the first time — when people find out who you are and vice versa, you scream and hug like you haven't seen each other for years. I guess it's because you get to know one another via the posting board and e-mail, and the last piece of the puzzle is the face. Plus, you can talk in real time and not have to wait minutes for an answer!"

Karri recalls the night being more of a blur because she was so busy getting name tags for everyone, but she remembers a few soldiers who delighted their fans. "Marc Blucas, Bailey Chase, and Leonard Roberts all came that year. It was fun to have the Initiative trio there. Those guys were total troopers. They never took a break once from the crowds. In fact, at the end of the night, we basically had to toss Marc out because the club we had it at was tossing us all out. But Marc was into hanging with his fans, which was very cool."

The feeling was mutual for Bailey Chase, who recalled, "The first one

Bronzer Karri Phillips with Alyson Hannigan at the PBP 2000

Karri with Anthony Stewart Head and Alexis Denisof

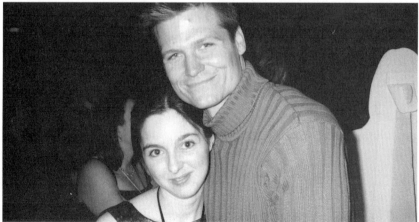

Karri with Bailey Chase

I went to was the most surprising. I had no idea what to expect and was blown away by the reception I received. I've gone in following years to give back to the fans who are so great and encouraging. There is nothing better than seeing someone's face light up when I meet and talk to them."

"2001: A Slay Odyssey"

February 17, 2001
American Legion Hall, Hollywood

VIPS: Joss Whedon and David Greenwalt; actors Anthony Stewart Head, James Marsters, Michelle Trachtenberg, Alexis Denisof, Clare Kramer, Andy Hallett, J. August Richards, Stephanie Romanov, Christian Kane, Danny Strong, Bailey Chase, and Leonard Roberts; writers Marti Noxon, Doug Petrie, Jane Espenson, Steven S. DeKnight, Tim Minear, and Mere Smith; makeup artists Dayne Johnson and Todd McIntosh; *Angel* composer Rob Kral

Musical guests: Four Star Mary (with James Marsters), Darling Violetta, Velvet Chain, Anthony Stewart Head and George Sarah, Andy Hallett

Money raised: $12,000

The 2001 PBP was bigger than the one before (which seems to happen every year), with over 300 fans arriving from 18 countries (the farthest away being New Zealand), more VIPS than ever, and television and print media showing up to cover the event. Almost everyone said the highlight of the evening was hearing Andy Hallett sing "Lady Marmalade," and he wasn't the only actor who got onstage. "My favorite memories of that year would have to be the musical acts," said Karri, who again was one of the organizers. "We had Darling Violetta play our pre-party. It is very cool to

Andy Hallett entertains the audience.
Joss Whedon's wife, Kai, is standing
behind him

hear the band that performs the *Angel* theme song perform an extended version of it live. Then, at the PBP, we had Anthony Stewart Head and George Sarah play for us. Tony can really sing. Then we had Andy Hallett sing some karaoke for us — he sang 'Lady Marmalade,' which totally rocked. That was my favorite section of the whole night. Our last band for the night was Four Star Mary, and they had James Marsters join them."

It was Liza Campbell's first PBP, and her favorite moment was meeting Spike himself: "He was so friendly, talking easily with the fans who surrounded him wherever he went. I was waiting in a group of fans to get my picture taken with him, and he was telling the girl in front of me how nervous he was about getting up onstage later that evening with Four Star Mary to play his guitar and sing a few songs with them. Then it was my turn; I went up to him and slid my arm around his waist and said, 'Don't worry, you'll be GREAT up onstage; we all love you!' (I'm still amazed I was able to be that coherent.) He looked at me with those melting ice-blue eyes and said, 'Thank you, that's so sweet!' and he hugged me right as the picture was taken, so now I have one of the GREATEST mementos ever!" James was the last VIP to leave that night, still hanging around signing autographs long after the others had gone.

Joss took to the stage at one point to express his appreciation for the posting board party and what it means to him: "Last year, I made a little speech. Everybody screamed a lot. It was really cool. [laughter] So I took that mike again, but I didn't have that much to say, but I'm sure I can think of something. . . . [Three] years ago we went to Planet Hollywood to meet with about 50 people who thought our show was cool, and that represented about a third of our viewers, [laughter] so it was a beautiful thing for all of us! And since then, every year you guys have been coming out,

*James Marsters hugs Liza Campbell
in a moment she'll never forget*

*James on stage, looking like
the rock star he is*

you guys have been raising money for a wonderful cause. You guys, you guys in particular —" he points to the PBP Committee — "have been organizing an extraordinary event that makes us feel comfortable and loved and appreciated and overwhelmed."

Mere Smith was the star of the party since, as a former Bronzer herself, she first met Joss at a PBP and is now a writer for the show. She told Kristy Bratton that she almost didn't make it there: "This is fantastic! I'm a little rushed because I was late and I drove like 90 miles an hour to get here and poor CCool and Gypsy Rat, I nearly killed them in my car like eight times but we got here. For now I'm just scoping everything out. I'm so inarticulate right now!"

Most of the people at the events were there to meet other Bronzers, and Joan Mendoza, who also attended the PBP for the first time in 2001, made an interesting observation, saying that someone who might seem unapproachable on the board often turns out to be the opposite in person, and as a result, she met a lot of Bronzers that she hadn't yet "met" on the board. She also got to meet Marti Noxon, her favorite *Buffy* writer: "I remember talking to her about the need for an Oriental character on

Buffy and that I already had an idea about the character's profile, history, and possible plotline association. She laughed, hugged me, and said, 'Wow, want a job?' To which I jokingly replied, 'I don't think Mutant Enemy can afford me.' This caused her to laugh even more." Terri also got to meet a favorite of hers, Marc Blucas: "Marc Blucas was kind enough to come to a luncheon that I organized for the Girls Who Love Riley. It was so thrilling to actually meet him in person. I enjoyed meeting the other VIPs, but I was so honored to actually meet Marc. He, in my book, is the greatest." She added that the charity aspect of the weekend was wonderful, and it made her proud to be a Bronzer.

"The Bronze Age"

February 16, 2002
American Legion Hall, Hollywood

VIPs: Joss Whedon; actors Alyson Hannigan, Alexis Denisof, Amber Benson, J. August Richards, Amy Acker, Danny Strong, Adam Busch, Tom Lenk, Michelle Trachtenberg, Andy Hallett, Robia LaMorte, Bailey Chase, Mark Lutz, Jeremy Renner (Penn in "Somnambulist"), Jarrod Crawford (Gunn's friend Rondell on *Angel*), and Amelinda Embry (Warren's ex, Katrina); writers Marti Noxon, Tim Minear, Jane Espenson, Steven S. DeKnight, David Fury, Rebecca Rand Kirshner, Drew Greenberg, and Mere Smith; Dayne Johnson and Diana Acrey (hair stylist); composers Rob Kral and Christophe Beck; authors Jeff Mariotte and Maryelizabeth Hart

Musical guests: Four Star Mary, Common Rotation (Adam Busch's band), and Andy Hallett

Money raised: $20,000

Joss gets on stage at the PBP 2002 to address the audience. Standing behind him are Jane Espenson, Marti Noxon, and Danny Strong

Michelle Trachtenberg and J. August Richards

This was the biggest and most successful PBP ever — over 400 people attended, raising a whopping $20,000 for the Make-a-Wish Foundation. Peter Hueser said the presentation of the check was the highlight of the weekend for him, and showed once again how strong the Bronzer community was. Bronzer Joan Mendoza was thrilled because she had played a part in raising some of the money: "This year, two of the Web sites I co-own donated auction items. The idea came to me while I was writing my donation check. I realized that contributing auction items would mean more money for Make-a-Wish than my personal donation. So, I contacted Peggy Li, of Peggy Li Creations, who creates jewelry for the show. I ordered two replica pieces of jewelry worn on the show and she generously donated two other pieces for a total of four items. It was a great feeling to know that our love for this show has some positive effects and benefits those less fortunate."

Little Willow was dubbed "Troika's Girl" at the end of the weekend, because she had attended a series of events that Adam Busch, Danny Strong, and Tom Lenk had appeared at throughout the weekend. On

Adam Busch's band, Common Rotation, entertains on stage

How many stars and writers can you spot? The VIP lounge at the posting board party

The men of Pylea: Mark Lutz and Andy Hallett

Alexis, get down with your bad self! Joss Whedon, Alyson Hannigan, and Alexis Denisof groove to the sounds of Andy Hallett's "Lady Marmalade"

The presentation of the cheque. From left, J. August Richards, Amy Acker, Alyson Hannigan, Alexis Denisof, Rebecca Rand Kirshner, Michelle Trachtenberg, Jeremy Renner, and Tom Lenk

The Duoka? Tom Lenk and Danny Strong

Sunday night, Common Rotation performed a two-hour set to a packed Hard Rock Café. "Then, out of the blue," says Little Willow, "they pulled me onstage. I ended up singing — at their request — 'I Love Rock 'n' Roll,' which at some point changed into 'We Want the Funk.' Cricket [another Bronzer] also came onstage and danced with me. Adam eventually asked for the microphone back — by getting on his hands and knees and begging."

As in previous years, the musical acts were the highlights. Danny Strong and Tom Lenk joined Common Rotation onstage to give Joss Whedon a bit of a surprise when they began singing a medley from "Once More With Feeling." Liza recalls, "I had the lucky chance of being right next to Joss Whedon when they started singing, and a look of sheer amusement just lit up his face. He took a moment from signing autographs to watch them and laugh uproariously." Andy Hallett once again entertained the audience with "Lady Marmalade," and added "I Left My Heart in San Francisco," while Joss, Alexis, and Alyson were onstage dancing. And Whedon, to the delight of the audience, performed Numfar's "Dance of Joy."

Shelley Ginsburg, the spokesperson for the Make-a-Wish Foundation, expressed to Kristy Bratton her appreciation for the great work Bronzers have done for the charity: "Someone wasn't sure how Make-a-Wish tied in and I thought, *Angel* and *Buffy*, in a way, have sort of a fantasy element to them, and we make children's fantasies come true. There is that storytelling aspect of one and the fantasy aspect of the other that kind of comes together that way. The shows have supported our Wish kids when they've asked to meet the cast or go on the shows, so it's really, really great and everyone is so dedicated."

The Posting Board Parties have been a resounding success for the Bronzers: a perfect way to meet the people you chat with year-round, while getting the added perks of meeting your favorite actors, writers, and crew. Since 1999 the Bronzers have shown their amazing generosity in collecting almost $50,000 for charity. As Terri says, "Bronzers really are a generous group. There isn't another group in the world quite like us."

Kim concurs that "the Bronze community is like a family — there are fights, there is drama, and there is love and respect for one another. So when we meet in L.A. once a year, it's a family reunion. The older Bronzers act like parent figures, watching out for the younger ones like their own children. When times are tough, your Bronzer buds are there for consoling, and even people you have never posted to before send their thoughts and prayers to you. Where else can you find a second family like that?"

Finally, Joan agrees that the Bronze is more than just a meeting place to talk about *Buffy* and *Angel*: "I'm so glad I stumbled upon the Bronze three years ago. It was instrumental in my meeting good people who have now become some of my closest friends, but also because it is one of the few online fan communities that afford their members the opportunity to make a real difference. And who said that the Internet is a bad influence?"

The Online Buffyverse

BUFFY AND ANGEL WEB SITES

I was a little hesitant to add a Web site section for the new edition of the book, simply because about half of the links I mentioned in the last book were outdated within months of the book's release. Such is the nature of the Internet. However, the Internet has provided *Buffy* fans with the perfect forum to show off their creativity, and it enriches the show so much I just had to include them. If any of the following URLs don't work when you type them in, try searching under the title of the site, and you'll usually find it.

Buffy Essentials

www.buffyupn.com

Buffy the Vampire Slayer Official Site
The official site doesn't offer the bells and whistles of most of the fan sites, but it's a good place to go to see trailers for upcoming episodes, see behind-the-scenes movies of "Once More, With Feeling" and other episodes, and get a brief rundown of the first five seasons. It also houses the Bronze, the official posting board, although the posting board had a lot of problems when it first went up, and several fans prefer the Bronze Beta, located at www.bronzebeta.com.

www.buffyguide.com

Buffyguide.com — The Complete Buffy Episode Guide
Without a doubt, the best place to find *Buffy* episode-guide info on the Net, including info about cast members and their characters; complete cast lists for the shows; goofs, music, pop-culture references; and a ton of other information about the episodes, as well as airdates for

syndicated episodes and lists of upcoming appearances. Unfortunately the episode-guide portion is a little behind, only recent for most of season five, but since other parts of the site are constantly updated, it won't be long until the rest of the site catches up.

www.buffymusic.net

The Buffy and Angel Music Pages

The best place to find lists of music used on *Buffy* and *Angel*. I used the information here to write up the music lists in my episode guide. The site is constantly updated, often a couple of episodes ahead of airing, and includes the title of the song, where it appeared in the episode, who performs it, and which CD it appears on. The Webmaster, Leslie Remencus, also includes information about the bands, including links to their official sites and their upcoming tour dates. You can even find the piano score to the gorgeous Buffy/Angel theme by Christophe Beck. This site is amazing.

Angel Essentials

www.cityofangel.com

City of Angel

The best of the *Angel* sites, "City of Angel" is much more than a fan site. Run by Virginia Obeius and Kristy Bratton, who oversee a large staff that includes writers, photographers, and a publicist, this site is a perfect example of what official sites should be (despite the fact it's actually an unofficial one). The writers have interviewed dozens of people affiliated with the show, including Joss Whedon, David Greenwalt, Tim Minear, Marti Noxon, Mere Smith, Jane Espenson, Robert Hall, Dayne Johnson, Robert Kral, Julie Benz, Elisabeth Rohm, J. August Richards, Andy Hallett, Mercedes McNab, Mark Lutz, Clare Kramer, Nancy Holder, Jeff Mariotte, and Maryelizabeth Hart. Phew! The exclusive interviews are accompanied by never-before-seen photos, reports of the Posting Board Parties, and a ton of behind-the-scenes *Angel* information. Hands down, one of the best television show sites around.

www.sanctuary.digitalspace.net

The Sanctuary Devoted to David Boreanaz and Angel

Another fantastic site, "The Sanctuary" boasts an excellent episode guide (The Screening Room) that is constantly updated and is as handy as the "Buffyguide.com" one. It includes pop-culture references, plot summaries, screen captures, cast listings, best lines, and lots of extra information. There is also a photo section (The Gallery), a fan fiction page (The Library), and some links. The pages are very stylish and dark, recreating the atmosphere of the show beautifully.

Buffy Search Engines

There are several good search engines, but a few that are specific to *Buffy* and *Angel*.

www.bitterwisdom.com/btvsurls

Sonia Marie's Links Page

With almost 3,000 links to *Buffy* pages, this site might be a little slow to load at times, but that's only because of the sheer number of links. Constantly updated, this is a great place to start your search.

www.buffysearch.com

BuffySearch.com

This site has over 4,000 links, including foreign or non-English sites, fan fiction sites, and relation "shipper" sites.

www.slayage.com

Buffy News

One of my absolute favorites. If you can get past the incessant pop-up ads, an unfortunate side effect of most larger fan sites these days, this is the best place to get all of the latest *Buffy* and *Angel* news, with new stories being posted every day from publications worldwide. A gem.

Cast Member Sites

Here are the best sites for each of the actors (in cases where I couldn't choose, I've listed two). Most include articles, photo galleries, and biographies and filmographies of each of the cast members.

Sarah Michelle Gellar Fan Page
www.smgfan.com

David Boreanaz
www.totallydavidboreanazuk.com
www.geocities.com/~angelsecrets/index2.html

Alyson Hannigan
www.network23.com/hub/ahas

Nicholas Brendon
www.nickbrendon.com (official)

Charisma Carpenter
www.charisma-carpenter.com

Michelle Trachtenberg
www.michelle-trachtenberg.com

Emma Caulfield
anya.org.uk

James Marsters
www.jamesmarsters.com
spike.jamesmarsters.net

Anthony Stewart Head
www.betsyda.com/ash/ash.html (also features an Alexis Denisof section)
www.ashead.com

Amber Benson
amberbenson.net (official)

Alexis Denisof
www.yeswes.com

Amy Acker
www.allstarz.org/~amyacker

J. August Richards
home.pacbell.net/jengod/buffy/jar/

Slaying Academia

www.slayage.tv

Slayage: The Online International Journal of Buffy Studies

A great site for people who always believed that *Buffy* was too intelligent for television, "Slayage" posts scholarly essays on the show, including ones on religious imagery, feminism, and the show's effects on popular culture. It also posts updates on *Buffy* academic conferences and where the professors who run the site do talks on *Buffy*. It'll take you right back to your college days (or let you know what's in store if you haven't gotten there yet).

www.atpobtvs.com

All Things Philosophical on *Buffy the Vampire Slayer* and *Angel: The Series*

Calling itself "Your complete compendium to all things mystical, good, and evil in the Buffyverse," this is an excellent site in the same vein as "Slayage," but with more discussion of the individual episodes and fewer academic theses. If you click on "Philosophies Represented," you'll get a season-by-season rundown of the occurrences of such philosophies as existentialism, feminism, dualism, relativism, and a bunch of other "isms." I love this site.

The Weird and the Wonderful: Miscellaneous Sites

www.risingstarsenterprises.com

Rising Stars

Rising Stars Enterprises is the talent agency that represents Andy Hallett, Mark Lutz, J. August Richards, and Daniel Dae Kim from *Angel* (and is currently acquiring some new *Angel*-and-*Buffy*-related clients). The great thing about this Web site is the fan directory, where you can send fan mail to your favorite actors and it will actually go to them. The people who work there are avid fans of the shows, constantly discussing them with fans who visit the message boards, and they are extremely helpful and generous with their time when fans have questions. A great site that other shows and talent agencies should emulate.

www.martzmountain.com/buffistafilk

BTVS and Angel Filk Collection

"Filking" is a common term among Internet types — it means parodying a song by using characters and information from a favorite TV show or movie. The limericks, haiku, poems, prayers, and songs range from quite poignant to downright hilarious. Here's an example of what you'll find:

> There once was a Watcher named Giles
> Who was charmed by a Gypsy's sweet smiles
> She died, which was cruel
> He blew up the school
> And now with Who covers, beguiles.

There are several other fan fiction sites — the search engines have listings for all of them.

www.vyra.cstone.net/

Buffy Dialogue Database

Buffy the Vampire Slayer is known more than anything else for its witty dialogue, and this is probably the best online collection of the best *Buffy* quotes from each episode. It includes a search engine where you can search for particular quotes based on keywords or who said it. The quotations almost as fun to read as they are to hear on the show.

www.studiesinwords.de

Psyche: Transcripts and Fan Fiction

An excellent link — people worried it would have to be kept secret to stave off the powers that be at Fox, which are often intent on shutting down sites that offer scripts. The complete scripts for *Buffy* and *Angel*, updated often, are available here as downloads or just to read on screen. You can also access the script of *Cruel Intentions*, listen to *Buffy* sounds, or read some great fan fiction. A very useful site.

Non-Buffy Sites

www.imdb.com

The Internet Movie Database

The most comprehensive database of actors and actresses and where they've appeared, the IMDB is a bible of sorts to many people. However, be aware that sometimes the information on the site is suspect, considering it was submitted by fans, not the shows themselves, and updates are often fueled by rumors.

www.tvtome.com

TV Tome — A Guide to the Television Shows You Love

By typing "Buffy" or "Angel" in the search engine, you'll be taken to a page with episode titles (including upcoming ones), cast listings, guides, and viewer comments. As with the IMDB, however, this is also compiled by fans who submit updates.

Little Willow

THE NET GODDESS OF THE BUFFYVERSE

The scene was one of the Posting Board Parties. Two fans were hanging out when they spotted a large group of people hovering around one spot. Eager to see which celebrity had been mobbed, they stepped a little closer. The taller fan leaned in to catch a glimpse of the *Buffy* actor, and then leaned back, and with a knowing smile said, "It's Little Willow." If you've spent any time on the online Buffyverse, you already know who he's talking about. Little Willow has developed a legion of fans on the Internet, and cast members of *Buffy* talk about how much they like her. She is a fan of *Buffy the Vampire Slayer* who has done more to promote the show and its actors on the Net than any other person.

Her real name is Allie, she lives in California, and she's 19 years old. Her age will shock many of the people who know her only over the Internet, because she acts far more maturely than the majority of people on the Net, and if you do the math you'll discover she was in her early teens when she started to get involved in the online *Buffy* community. "My age always throws people," she says. "If they just hear I'm 19, sometimes people won't give me the time of day, assuming that I'm some teenybopper. Or if they just see me, 90 percent of people guess I'm 12 based on appearance — on a daily basis. It's insane. Yet when people read things I've written, visit my sites, or correspond with me, they assume I'm much older. I always say I feel 28, look 12, and my age is somewhere in between."

Little Willow's resumé seems too diverse for someone so young — she's an actress, singer, dancer, writer of both fiction and nonfiction, journalist, and professional Web designer. Because she has become so well-known online, she maintains sites for bands, authors, and actors through her company www.rocktherock.com, with her associate, Paris_Angel. She runs the official Web sites for Amber Benson, Danny

Little Willow with Eliza Dushku

Strong, Christopher Golden (writer of dozens of *Buffy* novels and comics), Thomas A. Sniegoski (writer of the *Angel* comic book series), and Erika Amato (lead singer of Velvet Chain, the band that appeared onstage at the Bronze in "Never Kill a Boy on the First Date"). Her unofficial sites include Amberholics, Everlasting Eliza (an Eliza Dushku site), the Faith Dance Club and Xander Dance Club, We Possess Willow Power, Willow Keepers, and Be Back Before Dawn (a Michelle Trachtenberg site). Her premiere site (where you can find links to all the others) is the excellent Slayground (www.slayground.net), and she maintains nine mailing lists and five message boards. And these are only the *Buffy*-related sites — she runs dozens more for her other clients. Whew!

So why do so many fans of *Buffy the Vampire Slayer* love Little Willow? In a nutshell, she proves how much you can accomplish by being charming. Anyone who's spoken to her in person or via e-mail can vouch for her helpfulness, her sweet nature, and how accommodating she can be. As the listmistress for the JossBtVS mailing list (probably the best of the *Buffy* mailing lists), Little Willow (LW for short) keeps things under control and people playing by the rules without ever being condescending or rude, and deals off-list with anyone who misbehaves, to try to steer people away from flame wars. The reason JossBtVS is the most popular mailing list is because the conversation is always interesting, and when there's a lull, LW comes up with topics of discussion to keep things going.

That said, she has a ton of stories about people who haven't been so nice to her in return:

- "I have had people post on my boards or lists saying that I couldn't possibly know Amber, and though it's nice of me to be a fan, I shouldn't pretend like we're friends . . . to which the Amberholics just point those folks to Amber's acknowledgments of me in chats, interviews, and posts at the Bronze (which include: 'And Little Willow will vouch, too. She's very familiar with my dog and floor' and things like that!)."

- "I had someone curse me out violently on the JossBtVS list, and then post someone's name, address, and personal information on the list (saying it was mine), telling everyone I was some 39-year-old woman living with her mother in Florida or something ridiculous!"

- "I received some shockingly nasty (and absurd) emails after 'The Gift.' You see, weeks prior, I had written a speculatory post about who might die, and detailed how and why it might be Buffy, how she might sacrifice herself — so then after the episode, people acted like it was my fault, that I killed her. Yep, I pushed her off of that tower . . . riiiight!"

LW was watching *Buffy the Vampire Slayer* from the beginning, and in May 1997, soon after the first show aired, she visited the then-official site and discovered the Bronze, the official posting board. She posted that day and has done so every day since. At that time she began putting together her "Slayground" site, and it began her passion for creating online media for discussing all things *Buffy*.

Of course, part of the reason LW has so many official Web sites is because she's gotten to know several of the people on the show. The actor she's become closest to is Amber Benson, who suffered some unwarranted ire from fans when she first joined the cast. Little Willow was a fan of the character Tara ever since she first appeared, and has defended her countless times at the Bronze. She put up the first Amber Benson site in December 1999.

Amber attended the 2000 Posting Board Party, and while the rest of the audience was cheering for Emma, LW suddenly shouted Amber's name, and the audience began to cheer for her. Afterward, LW and Amber met for the first time. "After I introduced myself and praised her performance up and down," says Little Willow, "we clicked in surrogate sisterness. Someone told her over my shoulder about how I defend the character of Tara and Amber's acting, which was very sweet. We

Little Willow goes cheek to cheek with Amber Benson

discussed the site and I scribbled down the then-URL for it at her suggestion. We spoke of acting, *Bye Bye, Love*, the party, Eliza Dushku, upcoming projects, and a few other insightful things before I left so she could chat with others. She instantly became everyone's buddy. She's got an old soul and a sweet outlook on life."

But that wouldn't be the last time the two would chat. A few days later, Amber visited the Bronze posting board to thank everyone for such a warm reception at the party, and thanked LW in particular for making her night. "Shortly thereafter," LW continues, "she checked out the Web site and loved it. We then simply kept in touch. I feel blessed to call her my friend; she has had a profound influence on my acting as well as my outlook on life. She's going to make it quite far in this business, in this world, in this life."

Alyson Hannigan was another *Buffy* star that Little Willow had wanted to meet for a long time (she did, after all, borrow Alyson's character's name for her screen handle). She had been a fan of Hannigan's since long before she was on *Buffy*, when Alyson was guest-starring on television shows and appearing in movies. LW first met Alyson online at the Bronze. "In early 1997, the VIPs posted at the official BtVS board often," explains LW, "because then it was a very small community and, since the season one episodes were filmed way in advance, they had more spare time. I spoke to Alyson on the board many times and even once on the phone in August of that year. We chatted, we rambled, we laughed." But she still hadn't met her in person.

Alyson attended the first Posting Board Party in 1998, but LW was unable to attend. However, a friend made her feel like she'd been there: "My friend Hilary surprised me with autographs from Joss and Alyson — and pictures of them holding a sign saying, 'Hi Little Willow!'" LW attended the following Posting Board Party, but Alyson did not.

COURTESY LITTLE WILLOW

Little Willow meets Willow

Finally, they met face-to-face in 2000, the same year LW met Amber. "I was on the dance floor listening to the tunes of Four Star Mary," LW says, "when one of my Bronzer friends told me, 'Someone said Alyson's here, Little Will.' I grinned as I replied, 'Okay. Maybe.' Then people began running up to me, saying, 'Little Willow, Little Willow, your namesake is HERE! Go. Meet. Her. I told her you were here.' At this point, the lobby was filled with fans waiting for the newly arrived VIPs — Marc, Alyson, Tony, and Alexis — to scribble a note in their autograph books. I wanted to wait for her to come inside where she could breathe instead of being yet one more person to crowd her out there."

As two of Little Willow's friends began pushing and pulling her toward the lobby, LW watched as fans surrounded one of their favorite actors. She was about to meet Alyson Hannigan: "Finally, I was able to introduce myself by real name and board name. Alyson's initial reaction: 'OH MY GOD!' And thus began a conversation of 'It's so amazing to meet you,' 'Oh my god, it's so amazing to meet *you*!' and so forth. We compared our nearly identical bracelets and spoke of purple outfits — I had a dress; she had the top she 'stole from wardrobe.' Alyson exclaimed, 'I'm so glad

COURTESY LITTLE WILLOW

Little Willow with Danny Strong and actress Vicki Davis

I finally get to meet you! Ah! You're so cute!'" It was a night LW wouldn't forget (partly because her friends were videotaping the meeting!).

Danny Strong has become more than just an acquaintance, though. Little Willow first met him at the Posting Board Party in 1999 (and afterward he said he was shocked anyone knew who he was). They continued to keep in touch and are now very close friends: "Danny's like a brother to me — even my mother will tell me, 'Say hello to your brother for me,' and they get along famously. He is quite talented, but his most endearing trait is his modesty. . . . Well, that and his sense of humor. I will never forget the day we visited Chinatown with some friends. Danny had me laughing so hard that I was in pain. Every time I think of that day, I can't help but smile."

LW first met Christopher Golden at the Bronze (surprise!), and it's because of her that some of the *Buffy* comics have been written. LW was the first person to introduce Golden to Amber and suggest they do a comic book together, and the result was *WannaBlessedBe* (see the section on Amber Benson). When LW first chatted with Golden, she praised his

Buffy novels. "I then tracked down some of his earlier books," she says, "and continued to read his new books as they were released. In March 1999, he deemed me his 'West Coast Publicist.' I now maintain his official Web site and help promote his works. His writing is positively riveting and inventive. Like I've told him countless times, he's spoiled me — other authors or horror books tend to pale in comparison." She has also met Nancy Holder and is developing her official Web site as well.

Little Willow is an amazing person, and not only do the *Buffy* fans appreciate her, but the cast, the crew, and other Web site administrators are grateful for her work. Recently one Web site put up a special page called "Net Goddess: A Shrine for Little Willow" (www.jossisahottie. com/kibathediva/littlewillow), and people were invited to post reasons why they love Little Willow. The responses speak for themselves:

- "I am a HUGE Little Willow Fan. Her intelligence and work ethic are outweighed only by her talent. I just hope that when she is running the world she has some sort of cabinet position for me. She is truly an amazing person, and I feel honored knowing her." (Danny Strong)
- "Little Willow is one of the most enthusiastic, most charismatic people I have ever met. Her Web sites kick ass, but that's just the tip of her iceberg. She's a smart, savvy young woman with the brightest of futures." (Christopher Golden)
- "Little Willow . . . my brainwave twinnie, the Rory to my Lane, my American half. You are the Portuguese/Yugoslavian twin sister that I never had. You are amazingly smart, beautiful (inside and outside), funny, honest, and one of the kindest people I've ever had the pleasure of meeting and talking to . . . and I'm honored that I can call you a friend." (Connie)
- "I have been communicating with Little Willow online for quite a long time. Despite the fact that she is a very busy girl (I swear, she must know how to stop time!), she has always taken the time to read and reply to my e-mails. . . . She is intelligent, talented, compassionate, optimistic, witty, and giving; I am glad to consider her one of my friends and I hope that she feels the same way in return." (Heather)

- "I just have to say that when God packed that much energy into such a cute and adorable package . . . well, amazing things were bound to happen! She ROCKS!!!!" (Amber Benson)

So You Wanna Be a Slayer?

THE BUFFY AND ANGEL TRIVIA QUIZ

When the first edition of this book was published, it included a trivia quiz divided into sections — fill in the blanks, name that speaker, give the episode name, and so on. But as difficult as I thought the quiz was, I received several e-mails from people complaining that it was "too easy" and they had scored 95 percent on it. So this time around I'm asking 100 questions in four categories: easy, medium, hard, and very hard. I've watched the episodes several times now, and in most cases, the answers to the questions are obscure and were mentioned by one person in passing in the show. You'd better know your stuff — this quiz is meant for the serious Slayers among you.

At the end of each category, I've included a few *Angel* questions. If you don't watch *Angel*, skip those questions and score yourself out of 75 points instead of 100. (And dock your score by five points off the top for not watching both shows — for shame!) Write down your answers on a piece of paper and then check your score at the end, so you don't inadvertently see the answers to future questions. See page 407 for the answers and the rankings. And by the way, if you can score even 40 on this quiz, you have my undying respect. Good luck!

DIFFICULT, SCHMIFFICULT
Questions for Newbies

1. Who is the first member of the gang that Buffy speaks to in "Welcome to the Hellmouth"?
2. What is the team name at Sunnydale High?
3. What is the name of the newspaper in Sunnydale?
4. What is the name of Buffy's favorite stuffed animal?
5. What kind of demon does Drusilla leave Spike for in 1998?

6. Anyanka was the patron saint of whom?

7. What residence does Buffy live in at Sunnydale U in season four?

8. What is the name of the Fear Demon in "Fear, Itself"?

9. What song would Buffy want as the first dance at her wedding?

10. In "Into the Woods," Graham tells Riley about a mission away from Sunnydale. In what country is it located?

11. In "Life Serial," the Troika fights over who was the best James Bond. Which actor does each character like the most?

12. In "Older and Far Away," Xander gives Buffy a weapons chest he built. What added feature did he build inside the chest?

13. What does Rack say Willow tastes like in "Wrecked"?

Angel:

14. What is the Host's favorite drink?

15. What is Angel's real name?

16. In "Tomorrow," the Host gives Angel a copy of his CD. What is it called?

"TIME FOR A LITTLE RESEARCH"
The Next Level

1. Name Buffy's previous high school in L.A.

2. What is Buffy's astrological sign?

3. In what year did the earthquake occur that buried the Master in Sunnydale?

4. What special order of vampires does the Master belong to?

5. What is the Anointed One's real name?

6. What is the name of the cemetery in Sunnydale?

7. What is the drug Ted uses in his cookies in "Ted"?

8. What year does Buffy believe it is in "Halloween"?

9. What is the name of Kendra's Watcher?

10. What is Xander's code name in the group when Buffy is AWOL in "Dead Man's Party"?

11. What is the name of the psychiatrist in "Beauty and the Beasts"?

12. What was Buffy's score on her SATs?

13. Where was Buffy living in the alternate universe ("The Wish") when Giles contacted her for help?

14. How old is Anya?
15. When choosing courses for her first year at Sunnydale U, Willow switches from Modern Poetry to what?
16. What is Riley's Initiative code name?
17. What is the body temperature of a vampire, according to the Initiative?
18. What is the first dorm room that the Gentlemen attack in "Hush"?
19. When Buffy is first brought into the Initiative in "A New Man," how many hostiles does Riley say he's killed or captured at that point?
20. What item did Oz trade in Tibet to get Willow's skirt?
21. What is Spike's favorite food at the Bronze?
22. What is the street number of the Magic Box?
23. What is Tara's brother's name?
24. What food is Tara allergic to?
25. What is Buffy's address?
26. In "Life Serial," what score does the Troika give Warren for the challenge he presents to Buffy?
27. In the same episode, when Buffy is caught in the time loop in the Magic Box, how many times does the bell on the door jingle?
28. Where is the coven located that Giles mentions in "Grave"?

Angel:

29. What year was Angel born in his human form?
30. At what age did Doyle's demon side start showing?
31. What type of demon inhabits the boy in "I've Got You Under My Skin"?
32. In "Eternity," Angel meets actress Rebecca Lowell. What's the name of her television series?
33. What are the Groosalugg's favorite foods in L.A.?

IS IT GETTING WARM IN HERE?
The Slayer-Sized Questions

1. What school did Amy's mother go to after Amy's father left the family?

2. In "Never Kill a Boy on the First Date," Giles reveals the Anointed One will rise on the thousandth day after what?

3. Where did Cordelia and her parents go during the summer of 1997, against her will?

4. In "Some Assembly Required," Buffy goes to Daryl Epps' house and his mother is sitting on the couch watching one of his football games. How many yards does she say he rushed that night?

5. Where is the skating rink located in "What's My Line?"

6. What does Oz consider to be the Holy Grail of chords?

7. What grade is Xander hoping to score in his American Literature class in "Bewitched, Bothered, and Bewildered"?

8. How many churches are there in Sunnydale?

9. How much rent does Faith pay when she first moves to Sunnydale?

10. What flavor of chocolate bar does Giles buy in "Band Candy"?

11. Where was the retreat located that Giles went on in "Lover's Walk"?

12. At the beginning of "Gingerbread," Joyce recognizes the vampire that Buffy slays. Who was he?

13. What is Mr. Trick's favorite comic strip?

14. What is the mayor's wife's name and in what year did they get married?

15. What is the code word for the Watcher's Council?

16. What is the name of the demon that is raised in "Living Conditions"?

17. What is the frat house called where Buffy parties with Parker in "Harsh Light of Day"?

18. What is the name of the head of the science team in the Initiative?

19. On what date does Faith wake up in the hospital after being in a coma?

20. What is the name of the proprietor of the Magic Box before Giles?

21. In "Checkpoint," what does Anya say is her real full name?

22. The last guy Joyce dates is named Brian. Where does he work?

23. According to Spike, how many days was Buffy dead?

24. What is the debt Spike owes the loan shark in "Tabula Rasa"?

25. What gas is Jonathan allergic to?

26. In "Doublemeat Palace," the wig lady orders a coffee and an apple pie every day. What does it cost?

Angel:

27. How much money does David Nabbitt contribute to charities every year?

28. What is the number of the apartment Cordy shares with Dennis?

29. What is *Caritas* Latin for?

30. In "Blood Money," a group of soap opera actors dress up and pretend to hold up people at gunpoint for charity money. What soap are they supposed to be from?

31. In "Judgment," Angel explains the three things he won't do. What are they?

32. What is the password on Nathan Reed's computer at Wolfram & Hart?

33. At the beginning of "Heartthrob," Angel and Darla have just robbed someone in Marseilles in 1767. Who?

34. How many city code violations does Gavin say Angel has racked up in "That Vision Thing?"

35. What is the name of the retirement home in "Carpe Noctem"?

36. Where is the Host's heart located in his body?

37. What are the names of the members of Holtz's family?

38. As Holtz was trying to find Angel, how many vampires did he kill along the way?

39. In the files and records department at Wolfram & Hart, how many cabinets are devoted to Angel?

40. What is the address that Cordelia tries so hard to convey to everyone in "Birthday"?

TROIKIAN TRIVIA
Or, I Bow Before Anyone Who Can Answer These Questions

1. Name Oz's aunt, uncle, and cousin who are responsible for him becoming a werewolf.

2. When Buffy first wakes up in the hospital in "Killed by Death," what time is it?

3. In "Homecoming," Ian Abercrombie's character rounds up a set of twins from Germany. What crime are they wanted for there?

4. In "Amends," we flash back to when Angelus killed a servant girl. Whose servant was she?

5. What album does Oz pull out of Giles's record collection in "Harsh Light of Day"?

6. What is the expiry date of Joyce's credit card in "Who Are You"?

7. During kitten poker in "Life Serial," what cards does Spike lay on the table to win the hand?

8. What are the last four digits of Giles's phone number (as seen in "Living Conditions" when Willow calls him)?

Angel:

9. What is the address of Angel Investigations in season two?

10. What is the phone number for Angel Investigations?

11. What is Angel's licence plate number?

The Episode of Buffy You May Never See

THE UNAIRED PILOT

When Joss Whedon was trying to get networks to pick up his show, he filmed a half-hour proposal to give executives a taste of what was to come. This rough pilot, currently unavailable to the public, is an interesting piece of *Buffy* history. At times it seems very familiar, while other moments are so strange you can't help but laugh at how different the show turned out to be.

The episode follows the same storyline as "Welcome to the Hellmouth," where Buffy comes to the new school, meets Principal Flutie, encounters Willow, Xander, Cordelia (and her posse), and Rupert Giles. She's trying to escape her "destiny" because of how badly things turned out in L.A., but soon discovers a destiny is something you have to face.

The pilot opens just as "Welcome to the Hellmouth" does, with Darla sneaking into a school with a former student, although instead of the school hallway, they end up in the auditorium, where the stage has been fitted with an elaborate set, presumably for an upcoming play. She pretends to hear a noise, and when he reassures her, she turns to him – completely vamped out – and bites his neck. We cut to the outside of the high school the next day, which is the same front later used on the show, and Buffy, sporting light brown hair, looks bewildered as she checks her sheet for her classes. She meets with Principal Flutie and promises not to burn down this school. Willow has a crush on Xander, he wants her to help him with his homework, Cordelia and Harmony show up and Cordy utters her now-famous line about Willow's Sears clothing. Cordy and Harmony discuss going to the Bronze that night.

Xander and Buffy run into each other the same way, with her accidentally leaving her stake behind (the difference is, it happens outside in the courtyard rather than in the school hallway). Buffy goes to the library, and while it's different from the library we later see in Sunnydale

High, the dialogue is almost word-for-word what ended up in the real pilot. The two girls in the girls' change room discover the body of Darla's victim in the locker in the same way. When Buffy finds out what happened, she storms back to the library in the same way, and again the discussion between her and Giles is almost identical to what ends up in the final episode, showing that Joss knew where he was going to take Giles all along.

Buffy goes to the Bronze that night (Jonathan is standing in line in front of her) and runs into Xander, who tells her Willow left with some guy. Just as she figures out that the partygoer at the Bronze in "Welcome to the Hellmouth" is a vampire from his El Debarge clothing, in this episode she knows Willow's "boyfriend" is a vampire when Xander mentions his Lionel Richie getup. They follow them back to the same auditorium where Darla had taken her first victim, and Buffy faces the vamps and dusts one. Darla reappears, Willow is saved by using a cross, and Buffy accepts her duty. The next day at school Giles reprimands her by saying she let two people know her secret, almost didn't get to Willow in time, and was a sloppy fighter. Willow and Xander protest, and Buffy reassures him that "the world's in beauty hands."

While it sounds very similar to what we eventually saw, there were several key differences. One of the biggest is the fact that, with such a low budget, there is no action music or sound effects in the scenes. When Darla silently bites her victim at the beginning, there's no creepy music and he doesn't utter a sound. It ends up being almost funny. Even funnier, though, is the fight scene at the end. When Buffy stakes the vampire, the moment is *so* hilarious it's worth seeing the entire pilot for: the vampire falls back on the floor, steadies himself to stay really still, and then, with effects that resemble a series of slides, he changes to dust. First he's a big pile of dust (click), then a smaller one (click), then a flat spot of dust (click), then he's gone. There's no music — we just watch the hysterical slide show and thank our lucky stars the WB eventually gave Joss a moderate budget to work with.

Another jarring difference is the actors. Riff Regan plays Willow in this episode, and she has curly brown hair and a sweet round face. But no matter how good Regan is (and she's not bad), it just seems *wrong* that anyone but Alyson Hannigan should be allowed to step into Willow's shoes. Hannigan was able to nail a certain wacky behavior that sat just below the surface, and Regan didn't imbue her Willow with anything other than a shyness and jitteriness that wouldn't have been enough for this character. Principal Flutie is played by Stephen Tobolowsky (most recently seen as Sammy Jankis in *Memento*), and he is almost as good as Ken Lerner.

However, not only are some of the actors different, but certain key characters are missing altogether. There is no Angel in the pilot, nor is there a Master and an underground conspiracy to rise and take over Sunnydale. The vampires aren't organized, they just pop up. Of course, you couldn't fit all of that into 30 minutes and have a cohesive show, so perhaps Whedon explained the intricacies of the show to the executives instead. The high school is called Berryman High, and the school team is the Bulls, rather than the Razorbacks.

One scene is intentionally really funny, and it's a shame it had to be cut from the eventual pilot. Xander walks Buffy through the school courtyard and points out the various cliques — the rockers, the grunge kids, the surfers, the theater club, the "dirty girls." It's a hilarious scene with some great dialogue, and the two characters click as friends right away. Buffy uses her own unique slang throughout the episode, setting her L.A. character apart from the Sunnydale types, whereas in the eventual pilot they all speak in such a way that Giles can't understand a word.

There are moments in the unaired pilot that touch on things that come up later in the series, but not in "Welcome to the Hellmouth." Cordy and Harmony talk about how they're going to the Bronze to see Dingoes Ate My Baby, which is a great moment, considering this band never actually appeared in *Buffy* until season two. Joss must have figured that band name was too good not to use again. And in the second scene between Buffy and Giles, she tells him he doesn't understand what she's gone through, what it was like losing her Watcher, and what it's like being a 16-year-old with failing grades and no social life, and no real excuse to give to her parents. Instead of cramming all of that into the first episode, Joss stretched it out over the first two seasons.

The unaired pilot is a great look at what the show *might* have been, and luckily, the eventual series picked up on all of the best parts of this pilot and left the not-so-good ones behind. Perhaps someday the producers will stick this on a *Buffy* DVD set, and fans will be able to have a good laugh and see how so much of it was promising right from the start.

Buffy the Vampire Slayer
Episode Guide

The following guide contains spoilers for each episode (that is, the entries give away some important plot details), so, if you prefer to be surprised, avoid the entries for those episodes you have not yet seen. The episode guide offers background research into demonology to give the reader a richer understanding of each episode. The opinions expressed in the following pages are mine only, so feel free to disagree. These are intended as reviews of each episode, rather than plot summaries, so I often leave out parts of the plot. And when I list bloopers and nitpicks, I offer them only in fun, and not as criticisms of the show. I nitpick because I love.

At the end of each *Buffy* entry, you will find items of special interest. **HIGHLIGHT** includes one or two things that stood out in the show, but which didn't fit in the summary. **INTERESTING FACT** occasionally pops up, listing a tidbit of information about an actor or the show. **DID YOU NOTICE?** details something in the episode that either foreshadowed other episodes, was the first time we saw something that would become important later, or was an in-joke inserted for the viewer to find. **NITPICKS** are those things that bothered me after watching the episode, but that other people might be able to explain to their satisfaction. **OOPS** details the bloopers and continuity errors I spotted in the episodes. **WILLOW WICCA WATCH**, which tracks Willow's development as a witch, features more heavily in the later seasons. **RESTLESS MOMENT** lists something in the episode that appeared or was alluded to in season four's "Restless." Finally, **MUSIC/BANDS** lists all the music heard in the episode, and for that feature I am deeply indebted to Leslie Remencus, who gave me permission to use the information listed on her fabulous *Buffy* and *Angel* music Web site (see Web site chapter).

For each season I have listed the characters that will recur. If they continue to appear in following seasons, I don't list them again.

STARRING: Sarah Michelle Gellar as Buffy Summers
Anthony Stewart Head as Rupert Giles
Alyson Hannigan as Willow Rosenberg
Nicholas Brendon as Xander Harris
David Boreanaz as Angel
Charisma Carpenter as Cordelia Chase
Seth Green as Oz (Season Three)
Marc Blucas as Riley (Season Four)
James Marsters as Spike (Season Four)
Emma Caulfield as Anya (Season Five)
Michelle Trachtenberg as Dawn (Season Five)

Season One

MARCH 1997 • JUNE 1997

Recurring characters in season one: Kristine Sutherland (Joyce Summers), Ken Lerner (Principal Flutie), Mark Metcalf (The Master)

1.1 Welcome to the Hellmouth (Part One)

Original air date:	March 10, 1997
Written by:	Joss Whedon
Directed by:	Charles Martin Smith
Guest cast:	Brian Thompson (Luke), Eric Balfour (Jesse), Julie Benz (Darla), J. Patrick Lawlor (Thomas), Natalie Strauss (Teacher)

After being kicked out of her previous school for burning down the gym, Buffy Summers arrives in Sunnydale, only to discover that the high school is built on a hellmouth and she must resume her duties as a vampire Slayer.

This pilot episode was excellent! It first aired as a two-hour premiere, but because the two hours are generally rebroadcast separately now, they will be dealt with individually in this episode guide. "Welcome to the Hellmouth" contains all the elements of a good pilot: it offers an introduction to the main characters, background information that lets the viewer know what life was like before the story began, and a look at the major settings in which the story will take place, all while establishing the main themes of the show.

When the episode first aired on the WB, there was a teaser giving a brief history of former Slayers and explaining where the vampire activity was taking place in the past (the teaser does not appear in syndication nor on the DVD). It is interesting that all the Slayers were women, yet the phenomenon of the Slayer's gender is never explained on the show. The action then moves to a couple of high school kids breaking into the school and the viewer is led to believe that a demon will attack them. Until, of course, one of them turns into a vampire and attacks the other. *Buffy* is a show that will cleverly undercut many of our expectations.

The first trick played on us is that the television show is so different from the movie. While the television Buffy still has the "keen fashion sense" that her original incarnation boasted, she's younger, more sarcastic, more intelligent, and has more personal problems. The movie version of *Buffy the Vampire Slayer* was like *Clueless*, but near the end suddenly tried to be a serious film. The television show carries comedy, action, and drama simultaneously and features a far superior ensemble cast. (The movie is worth seeing, though, if just for Paul Reubens's death scene.)

Alyson Hannigan as Willow is perfect. She's shy and unsure of herself, but incredibly intelligent; considering that Willow remains consistent in later episodes, it would appear that Hannigan had the role figured out from the start. Giles is great as the *very* British librarian who, as a Watcher, knows his duties but seems completely unprepared for a rebellious Slayer (and there isn't a single cup of Taster's Choice in sight!). The way he confidently slams down the *Vampyr* book before an unsuspecting Buffy leads us to think he knows exactly what he is doing, a notion immediately undercut by his surprise when Buffy acts like she doesn't know what he's insinuating.

Sarah Michelle Gellar, like Hannigan, seems to know where she's going to take her character this season, so she imbues Buffy with confidence when trying to fit in, annoyance at the thought of slaying vampires, sarcasm with everyone she meets, and an uncertainty that she *should* be the Chosen One. It's amazing how the behavior and personality of this character in the first episode are consistent with Buffy in later seasons. Gellar had her character nailed from the beginning.

David Boreanaz, on the other hand, is good as Angel, but he doesn't seem as comfortable with the character as he is in later shows. He plays Angel with less brooding and more smarm (not to mention the black and green velvet blazers he wears, which make him look more like Oscar Wilde than the Angel we've come to know). By the episode "Angel," however, he will have polished the character into what we have today. Nicholas Brendon as Xander is immediately nerdy, and within moments of making his first appearance he falls (literally) madly in lust with Buffy. In the early episodes his character's self-deprecation becomes annoying, but, thankfully, that hang-up with his manhood (or what he sees as his lack of it) disappears in later episodes. Finally, Charisma Carpenter is wonderful as that popular girl we all love to hate, and Cordelia is so vicious — while completely oblivious to her own ridiculousness — that you can't help but be intrigued by her. The ensemble cast is top-notch.

Some of the situations are similar to the pilots of other high school television shows, but Joss Whedon always adds a subtle twist. For example, many shows feature the "enlightened" principal we all wish we had, the guy who's willing to erase the memories of the past and start fresh. However, Principal Flutie rips up Buffy's records before realizing she's burned down her school gym, and spends the rest of the scene frantically taping them together while he lectures her on responsibility. This hilarious scene establishes Principal Flutie as one of the funniest characters in the early episodes.

An interesting aspect of this episode is that at the very beginning, when Buffy is having one of her prophetic dreams, we see snippets of the rest of the first season — the *Vampyr* book, cemeteries, blood, candles, Angel's cross, Moloch, vampires — establishing the themes to come. Among those themes is Whedon's vision of high school: the students are not all "Ra! Ra! Go, Sunnydale!" but share a quiet angst and can't wait to get out of there. Cordelia is the popular girl, yet she's intelligent and quick-witted, often putting even our sarcastic Slayerettes to shame. Although Cordelia accepts Buffy into her fold because Buffy is from Los Angeles, Buffy quickly realizes that although she was popular in L.A., being a Slayer is going to change everything here in Sunnydale.

Whereas the *Buffy* movie only touched on the idea that slaying would seriously interfere with a teenager's life, this theme becomes the major focus of the show. Buffy returns to the library after seeing a dead victim of a vampire and tells Giles that she's retired and no longer wants to be a Slayer. Giles convinces her of her duty, though, and she reluctantly sets out to save mankind, making sarcastic quips along the way. Although Buffy might not have the book smarts or knowledge of history that Giles thinks is necessary in a Slayer, she and her friends will rely on their in-depth knowledge and awareness of the society around them to survive.

"Welcome to the Hellmouth" was a great introduction to the series, although newcomers should watch this and the next episode together for a fuller effect.

HIGHLIGHT: Buffy picking out the vampire based on his "Debarge"-like attire.

INTERESTING FACTS: Ken Lerner appeared in several episodes of *Happy Days*, including one in which he played Frankie, a bully who picks on Richie Cunningham. Also, Joss has admitted to basing certain characters on real-life people — Cordelia is named after a cruel girl with whom his wife attended high school, and Xander is modeled after Joss himself.

DID YOU NOTICE? Luke says the "blood of man will flow as wine" at the harvest, which is exactly what happens when the Master takes over Sunnydale in "The Wish."

NITPICKS: This nitpick is moving ahead to the end of season two, where we discover that by the time Buffy moves to Sunnydale, Angel has been following her for a while. In the pilot, when he first meets her, he says, "I thought you'd be taller." If he'd been following her for over a year, wouldn't he know how tall she is? Also, Cordelia explains that Sunnydale is so small (it's a one-Starbucks town, after all) that the good part is half a block from the bad part. So how the heck did it get a university that's so far away from Buffy's house she ends up living in residence in season four?

OOPS: When Buffy follows the vampire into the back of the Bronze, she breaks off the leg of a stool to use as a weapon. When she raises it up to Cordelia, it's been perfectly chiseled into a stake.

RESTLESS MOMENT: The outfit Willow wears in this episode will be the one she's wearing in "Restless," when she's at the front of the class and everyone is taunting her.

MUSIC/BANDS: The *Buffy* theme, written and performed by Nerf Herder, is available on the *Buffy the Vampire Slayer* soundtrack. When Buffy is trying to decide what to wear to the Bronze, the song in the background is "Saturated" by Sprung Monkey. When Buffy enters the Bronze for the first time, Sprung Monkey is playing "Believe" onstage, and later they play "Swirl." As Buffy leaves the Bronze looking for Willow, they're playing "Things Are Changing." All of these songs are on their CD *Swirl*. The scores for the first-season episodes were written by Walter Murphy.

1.2 The Harvest (Part Two)

Original air date:	March 10, 1997
Written by:	Joss Whedon
Directed by:	John T. Kretchmer

Guest cast (who did not appear in part one): Mercedes McNab (Harmony), Jeffrey Steven Smith (Guy in Computer Class), Teddy Lane, Jr. (Bouncer), Deborah Brown (Girl)

When Giles discovers that the Master is about to be set free through his vessel, Luke, Buffy must try to stop the harvest before it begins.

The second half of the pilot focuses less on the characters and more on the vampires. We learn that many of the vampires have been with the Master for centuries, but the Master has been trapped in a church that, during an earthquake in 1937, was swallowed underground, taking him with it. When Jesse, a friend of Xander and Willow, goes missing, we learn something of Whedon's vampire mythology: a vampire is actually a demon inhabiting the lifeless body of the person it attacked. The demon takes on the look and personality of the former owner of the body, but it's all part of the trick. In other words, becoming a vampire is more of a demonic possession than a transformation. Notice how easily Buffy and Giles explain to Xander and Willow that Jesse is no longer Jesse but a demon; yet later, when the question is whether or not Angel should be destroyed, they won't be so quick to make the same rationalization.

The Master ordains Luke as his "vessel" in a strange perversion of a Christian baptism ceremony. Instead of placing a cross of holy water on the baptised's forehead, the Master draws a symbol similar to a Mercedes-Benz logo in blood (which opens a myriad of possible interpretations, but let's leave that one alone). The fact that this hellish activity is happening in a church gives the writers the perfect opportunity to set up the scenes as reversals of Christian ceremonies. Later, the Master will preach to the "Anointed" as if he is a member of his hellish congregation.

Darla is a wonderful character — a female vampire who is deceptively cute. As we later discover, in each era she chooses an outfit that will draw men to her. In the 18th century, she wore the dress of a noblewoman, for example, and in the 1930s she wore a kimono. However, it is disturbing that the outfit she chooses for the late-20th century is a private schoolgirl's uniform — let's hope it's simply Darla taking advantage of the fact that her main targets are now high school boys. Despite the prominence of male vampires in vampire fiction, Darla is the first vampire to kill in this television series. My only nitpick would be the way she cowers before the Master and seems completely unsure of herself; by "Angel," she'll be the self-assured Darla of later episodes, but in the pilot it just doesn't seem like her.

Buffy's mother is a major figure on the show — as is typical with many television series aimed at a high-school-aged audience — and she's very different from her movie counterpart. In the *Buffy the Vampire Slayer* movie, Buffy's parents are flighty and stupid people who are never around, making it difficult to believe in them as real characters. In the show, however, Buffy's parents are divorced, she sees her father only on occasional weekends, and her mother is an intelligent woman who can't seem to connect with her 16-year-old daughter. The writers on the show allow the audience to see her from Buffy's perspective, and she often comes across as an annoying person who just doesn't care about her daughter, which is exactly how most teenage girls view their mothers. But in actual fact, Buffy is Joyce's biggest priority, as she reads a ton of books on raising children, tries to connect with Buffy on several occasions (and fails miserably), and finally chalks Buffy's reticence up to her being a teenager.

The action scenes at the end of the episode are amazing, and while Sarah Michelle Gellar does have a stunt double, you'd never know it in this episode — the editing is seamless. Not only is Buffy physically strong, but she uses her wits to overcome her opponent, weakening Luke by making him think he would be burned by sunlight. Even Angel is impressed when she averts Armageddon.

Now, you'd think a bunch of vampires with disfigured faces feeding on club kids and getting beat up by a sophomore girl would have some impact on the other high school students, but we find out that things aren't that simple in Sunnydale. As Giles explains, "People rationalize what they can and forget what they can't." In this case, Cordelia explains to her friends that the fiasco at the club was caused by rival gangs. And so life continues as usual at peaceful Sunnydale High, where a giant hellmouth waits below the surface to open and devour them all.

HIGHLIGHT: Willow tricking Cordelia into deleting her computer assignment.
INTERESTING FACTS: When this episode first aired as the second half of part one, the WB broadcast a Ford commercial starring Susan Lucci. Hmm . . . looks like Kendall's outdoing her mom.

NITPICKS: In this episode, Buffy leaps over the school gate and jumps down from the rafters at the Bronze, yet later in season two, she'll appear to lack these superhuman skills. Also, Luke says he was around in 1843 Madrid, but when we later see early scenes of Darla and Angel with the Master, Luke is nowhere to be seen. Finally, in these early episodes of Buffy, the teeth the vampires wear make it difficult to understand what they're saying. Later, Todd McIntosh, the makeup artist, will give the vampires teeth that aren't so intrusive.

OOPS: In many instances on this show, vampires get burned but are left with no scars. In this episode Darla has holy water thrown in her face, but the next time we see her there is no evidence of it. In "Angel," Buffy's cross will burn an impression into Angel's chest, but it will be gone the next time we see him, and in "What's My Line? Part Two," Drusilla will torture Angel with holy water, but again it will leave no scars. Yet at the end of this installment, Spike's face will be burned, and he'll be scarred for the next few episodes. Also, Cordelia tells Harmony she's going to the Bronze because it's Friday night and there's no cover, yet there is a cover (you can see people paying the bouncer at the door) and everyone's back at school the next day (it might be Monday, but Xander, Willow, and Buffy are talking about the events for the first time — wouldn't they have called each other over the weekend?).

MUSIC/BANDS: As Buffy talks with Principal Flutie at the gate, the song playing in the background is "Right My Wrong," by Sprung Monkey. At the Bronze, Cordelia exclaims, "Ooh! I love this song!" referring to "Wearing Me Down" by the Dashboard Prophets. As the vampires approach the Bronze for the harvest, "Ballad for Dead Friends," also by Dashboard Prophets, is playing and continues into the action scenes. Both songs are on their *Burning Out the Inside* CD.

1.3 The Witch

Original air date:	March 17, 1997
Written by:	Dana Reston
Directed by:	Stephen Cragg
Guest cast:	Elizabeth Anne Allen (Amy Madison), Robin Riker (Catherine), Jim Doughan (Mr. Pole), Nicole Prescott (Lishanne), Amanda Wilmshurst (Senior Cheerleader), William Monaghan (Dr. Gregory)

When members of the cheerleading team are felled by strange illnesses, the gang guesses that a witch is casting spells on them.

When we think of witches, we tend to think of the infamous witch trials in Europe and America, particularly those in Salem, Massachusetts. The witch hunt in Europe was initially sparked by the Church — both the Catholic Church, and especially (after the Reformation) the various Protestant churches. Although its beginnings in different forms stretched back to the 14th or 15th centuries, the hunt reached its peak a couple of centuries later. Scholars have had differing opinions on how widespread the slaughter was, and estimates of the number of deaths have ranged between 100,000 and nine million. If accused of witchcraft, a person would rarely escape execution or imprisonment. It's also surprising to discover that many children were put to death as accused witches. However, most of those charged with witchcraft were adults who were outcasts of society — generally peasants who did not attend church — and their deaths led to a countryside filled with starving beggar children.

Germany probably had more witch trials than any other country, but the most notorious were held in Salem, Massachusetts, in 1692. These were different from their European counterparts in that most of the accused were Puritan churchgoers who had been useful members of society. A group of girls began saying that they'd been possessed by the devil, and that they could identify the witches in their village. During the trials they would go into convulsions, claim possession, and point out people in the courts as witches. Why these girls acted in such a manner is not known, although some scholars speculate that their actions arose from being stifled by an overly strict society. At the end of one year, two dozen people had been executed and over 150 imprisoned.

Today, witches exist as pagan lovers of nature who belong to a religion called Wicca, begun in the 1950s by Gerald Gardner. Many witches perform good magic, or white magic, which promotes healing and gives its recipients strength. Witches and other pagans follow three important principles: embrace love and a kinship with nature; follow the pagan ethic, which is "An it harm none, do what you will" (see "Wrecked"); accept the presence of both god and goddess, without considering one gender superior to the other. Witches who perform black magic, or evil magic that aims to harm, are shunned by others in the religion. All magic follows the Law of Threefold Return — pagans believe that any act of magic will rebound on the magician threefold, meaning if a witch performs black magic, he or she will experience a negative impact with three times the force of the act performed (see "After Life").

In "The Witch," the writers do a great job of misleading the audience. The real focus of this episode, though, is the often precarious relationships between teenagers and their parents. Buffy tries to reach out to her mother, but Joyce is too caught up in her work to notice. When she, in turn, attempts to connect with her daughter, Buffy accuses her mother of trying to mold her into a miniature Joyce. The tension between Buffy and Joyce is caused by Buffy's envy of the relationship between Amy and her mother, which, unknown to Buffy, is actually violent and abusive.

Robin Riker, as Catherine the Great, is superb when playing the part of a teenager trapped in an adult body. She's jittery, the way Amy was at the beginning, making the two roles appear seamless. The scene where Amy (in her mother's body) tells Buffy what happened would have been more realistic if she'd said her mother had switched their bodies a couple of days before. Instead, she says the bodies had been switched a few months before, meaning the poor, dejected girl at the beginning of the episode was Amy's mother. However, it would explain how the first cheerleader caught on fire.

The fact that Buffy wants to be a cheerleader links her to the movie Buffy, and Giles is like Merrick (the movie Buffy's Watcher) in that he doesn't want Buffy to join. He calls cheerleading a cult and forbids her from trying out, but Buffy won't listen to him. As for Giles, we see how excited he is to be living on the hellmouth when he looks happy to hear about the cheerleader who catches on fire. "That's the thrill of living on the hellmouth," he says with an expression of glee, prompting surprised looks on the faces of the others.

Willow is a great character in this episode. Xander tells her how he feels about Buffy, and Willow is caught between her feelings for him and her friendship with both him and Buffy. When he gives Buffy a bracelet that reads, "Yours always," the hurt look on Willow's face speaks volumes, yet she doesn't hold it against Buffy or Xander. This is also the episode where Xander calls Willow his "guy friend" who knows how women feel, but Willow has a look of triumph on her face when Buffy calls Xander her girl friend. Willow and Xander also take a more active role in Buffy's slaying, calling themselves the slayerettes, and

Willow's strength comes through when she attempts to stall Amy's mother by standing in her way and asking, "Do you actually *ride* a broom?"

On seeing this episode for the first time, one might be confused — where are the vampires? However, as a metaphor for the pressure parents put on their teenage children, it is nonetheless a lot of fun.

HIGHLIGHT: Buffy's rendition of "Macho Man."

DID YOU NOTICE? This episode marks the first time we see Giles lie. He tells Buffy that the spell he cast was his "first casting," but we later discover that to be untrue.

NITPICKS: How did Amy get Buffy's bracelet?

OOPS: Amy's last name is Madison, and on the cheerleading trophy it lists her mother's name as Catherine Madison. But if her parents got married after they graduated from high school, the trophy should have listed Catherine under her maiden name.

MUSIC/BANDS: During Amber's dance routine and when the Razorbacks head out onto the basketball court, the song playing is "Twilight Zone" by 2 Unlimited, from their CD *Get Ready for This*. As Joyce and Buffy have their heart-to-heart talk, you can hear Humbucker's "Count the Time," from *My Snake*.

1.4 Teacher's Pet

Original air date:	March 25, 1997
Written by:	David Greenwalt
Directed by:	Bruce Seth Green
Guest cast:	Musetta Vander (Nathalie French), Jean Speegle Howard (the *real* Nathalie French), Jackson Price (Blaine), Jack Knight (Homeless Guy), Michael Ross Verona (Teacher), William Monaghan (Dr. Gregory)

Xander develops an infatuation for his biology teacher, not realizing she's not exactly what she seems.

"Teacher's Pet" takes the focus off Buffy and places it on Xander. For the first time we can truly understand his anxieties about his masculinity. After all, he's in love with a girl who always ends up protecting him and getting him out of sticky situations. This episode opens with a dream sequence where Xander fights off vampires to save a helpless Buffy, who adores him, only to jump up onstage and resume his position as lead guitarist in a rock band. While the daydream is very funny, it's also poignant, for as exciting as it is for women to see other women defending themselves, it must be difficult for a male raised in a society where he is supposed to be the hero and the female the damsel in distress. We also discover Buffy has a thing for Angel. Interestingly, he shows up to warn her about a man with big claws (an obvious allusion to Freddie Krueger) who will eventually be used to vanquish the bigger problem — the praying mantis who preys on virgins.

The idea of a high school guy being devoured by a praying mantis as a metaphor for losing his virginity is very clever. Women often complain about society's double standard toward sexuality — if a girl has sex, she's promiscuous, but a guy can have several "conquests" and he's considered cool. But what kind of pressure does that expectation put on a guy? In "Teacher's Pet," Blaine buys into the stereotype but covers up the truth by being a good actor. A member of the varsity championship football team, Blaine can easily convince others that he's slept with several girls. Xander, on the other hand, tries the same schtick and falls flat on his face. While Willow expresses her admiration for both of them remaining virgins, Buffy buys into the double standard, acting with shock upon realizing Xander is a virgin.

Enter Nathalie French. A beautiful woman who pretends to fall for Xander, she presents him with the opportunity not only to lose his virginity, but to do so with an older woman. Ms. French is symbolic of what society's expectations do to men — perhaps many lose their virginity against their better judgment simply to cater to that pressure. To make the metaphor even more explicit, Xander and Blaine are literally locked in cages, looking out at a creature who wants to use them only to fertilize her eggs and will kill them in the process. Xander, who will be her first prey, listens as Blaine recounts the mating procedure with grim horror. This may symbolize the reaction many teenage boys have to the realities of sex.

But why a praying mantis? The obvious reasons to choose such a creature are made clear in the episode — the female praying mantis often bites off the head of the male during mating, then eats the rest of him when she's finished. Also, the Greeks believed the mantis had supernatural powers because of the way it folds its front legs and looks up, as if praying. An important feature of the mantis that isn't broached in the episode is its ability to blend into its surroundings. The mantis is the same color as the leaves of the trees it inhabits, and is therefore camouflaged, hidden from its prey. Similarly, Ms. French is camouflaged as a substitute teacher, and the boys have no idea how dangerous she is. Also, a mantis can eat only live insects, hence Ms. French's cricket sandwich.

While this episode was clearly focused on Xander and his anxieties about his manliness, we also get a glance at Buffy's insecurity about herself. Dr. Gregory becomes important to her because he believes in her — no one else outside of the gang believes unconditionally that she can succeed. Even Buffy's mother constantly brings up her past to remind her of her shortcomings. When Dr. Gregory is killed, Buffy is left alone, having to prove herself by starting at square one.

On the surface, "Teacher's Pet" isn't as funny or interesting as other episodes, but it is far more clever than it first appears to be.

HIGHLIGHT: Principal Flutie lecturing Buffy on the importance of healing.

NITPICKS: Why were Dr. Gregory's glasses still on the front desk at the end of the episode? If they'd been cracked in the struggle, wouldn't the police have taken them as evidence? Also, when Buffy is hunting the "claw guy," why does she climb the fence? Can't she just jump over? And couldn't Angel have been a little more specific when warning Buffy about him?

MUSIC/BANDS: When Xander walks into the Bronze, the band onstage is Superfine, performing "Already Met You." When he smashes the mantis eggs, the song is "Stoner Love." Both are from Superfine's vinyl record *Stoner Love*.

1.5 Never Kill a Boy on the First Date

Original air date: March 31, 1997
Written by: Rob Des Hotel, Dean Batali
Directed by: David Semel

Guest cast: Andrew J. Ferchland (Boy), Geoff Meed (Andrew Borber), Christopher Wiehl (Owen), Paul-Felix Montez (Mysterious Guy), Robert Mont (Van Driver)

When Buffy catches the eye of a really cute high school guy, she quickly learns how being a Slayer interferes with having a normal life.

The vampires are back, and the Master is still plotting a way to escape his underground prison. We learn of a new twist on the ol' Master/Slayer prophecy — the coming of the Anointed One, who will lead Buffy into Hell. Giles conveniently discovers the prophecy at the same time, and the rest of the episode is spent trying to figure out which of the people who die in a bus/vampire accident has become the Anointed One.

This episode develops the relationship between Buffy and Giles — he seems more relaxed around her now, while coming to an understanding that she will undergo personal difficulties he hadn't anticipated. When Owen first arrives in the library, Buffy goes into cute flirt mode while Giles is curt with him. Buffy must remind Giles that a library is a place where people take out books, yet so far they've never been interrupted (apparently Sunnydale High doesn't boast a lot of readers). Buffy is trapped between her duty as the Chosen One and her overwhelming desire to have a real life, while Giles is caught between his duty to humanity — training and disciplining the Slayer — and the fact that he cares about her. When she begs Giles to let her go on a date with Owen, he stresses that her "fantasies" must be put on hold for the good of humanity. However, what she must explain to him is that at 16, a date with a good-looking guy seems more important than the fate of humanity.

Perhaps because of his new understanding of Buffy's situation, Giles does not put his foot down to tell her she must stop the Anointed One, and she goes to the Bronze with Owen. Giles is almost killed, Willow and Xander must lure Buffy back to save him, and Owen steps in to play the hero, almost getting killed himself. In one catastrophic evening, Buffy is forced to realize that she will never have a normal life, and that having a boyfriend

---

Giles's Head Trauma

In "Gingerbread," Cordelia asks Giles, "How many times have you been knocked out, anyway?" Here is a list of the episodes in which Giles has been knocked unconscious (how he's avoided brain damage is beyond me):

- "The Witch" (thrown against a wall by Catherine as he's trying to cast a spell)
- "Never Kill a Boy on the First Date" (knocked out by Andrew the crazy vampire at the morgue)
- "When She Was Bad" (kidnapped and hung upside down above the Master's bones)
- "Becoming" (knocked out by Drusilla)
- "Beauty and the Beasts" (accidentally shot with a tranquilizer dart)
- "Homecoming" (knocked out by Lyle Gorch)
- "Gingerbread" (passes out when Joyce and two cronies apply chloroform)
- "Spiral" (passes out in agony after being impaled)
- "Flooded" (thrown against the stairs of the Summers' house by a demon looking for Buffy)
- "Grave" (momentarily unconscious when powers are removed)

will only endanger his life. Giles comes to an understanding as well, and for the first time becomes a father figure in Buffy's life, explaining to her that when he was appointed the Watcher, he was told of the sacrifices he'd have to make. Unfortunately, no one seriously explained things to Buffy until this point.

The dialogue in this episode is top-notch, and in the span of one hour Buffy and Giles move from sarcasm to empathy. At the beginning, when Giles reminds Buffy of the serious consequences of telling people she is the Slayer, she reassures him that she won't wear her button that reads, "I'm a Slayer — Ask me how!" And when Buffy begs Giles to let her have the night off for a date, he sardonically replies that he'll go back in time and ask the demon prophets to please put off the Apocalypse for a day so Buffy can have a life. Yet, by the end, Giles realizes how serious that date was to Buffy, and Buffy realizes Giles was right that she must take her duty more seriously.

This episode was very well done, and its repercussions will echo in episodes to come.

HIGHLIGHT: Owen's reaction to seeing Giles at Buffy's house in the evening: "Wow, you really care about your work!"

DID YOU NOTICE? The slogan at the Sunnydale cemetery is "We'll take care of the rest." Obviously the motto doesn't take into account vampire activity.

NITPICKS: The writers should come up with a more detailed and specific history of past Slayers and Watchers. Previous Slayers are all women, yet Giles mentions his grandmother was a Watcher. Is it a hereditary thing? Why was his family chosen as Watchers?

MUSIC/BANDS: The band at the Bronze is Velvet Chain, performing "Strong" as Buffy and Owen walk out to the dance floor and "Treason" as they leave the floor to walk to the stairs. Both songs are from the band's *Groovy Side* CD. Cordelia and Owen dance to "Rotten Apple" by Three Day Wheely, from their *Rubber Halo* CD, and when Angel comes to warn Buffy about the impending disaster, the song is "Junky Girl" by Rubber, from their self-titled CD. Finally, during Buffy's last talk with Owen, the song in the background is "Let the Sun Fall Down" by Kim Richey, from her self-titled CD.

1.6 The Pack

Original air date:	April 7, 1997
Written by:	Matt Kiene, Joe Reinkemeyer
Directed by:	Bruce Seth Green
Guest cast:	Eion Bailey (Kyle), Jeff Maynard (Lance), Brian Gross (Tor), Jennifer Sky (Heidi), Michael McRaine (Rhonda), James Stephens (Zookeeper), David Brisbin (Mr. Anderson), Barbara K. Whinnery (Mrs. Anderson), Gregory White (Coach Herrold), Justin Jon Ross (Joey), Jeffrey Steven Smith (Adam), Patrese Borem (Young Woman)

Xander and four bullies become possessed by a hyena and begin attacking people.

"The Pack" focuses on school bullies and how cruel and thoughtless high school kids can be. On a school trip to the zoo (don't bullies always strike on school trips?), Buffy is mocked by a group of four bullies and later tells Xander and Willow how much she hates school trips.

After chasing a kid into the hyena exhibit, Xander and the bullies become possessed. We later find out that possession can happen during a predatory act — the bullies fall under the spell for chasing Lance, and Xander succumbs because he was chasing the bullies. Like the "cool kids" at school, the five maintain a pack mentality throughout the episode, always tracking down a member if he or she goes missing. The legend of a hyena learning a person's name to lure them away parallels the bullies and their prey — they learn the names of their victims, trick them into thinking they'll make them part of their group, and then pick on them ceaselessly, as happens with Lance. The dodgeball scene is brilliant; the mere mention of that barbaric "sport" is enough to send shivers down anyone's spine if they've been on the bad end of a game.

The fact that the cruel behavior of the possessed mirrors much of the bully activity in schools leads Giles to think everything is normal. He points out the three main traits of the "animal" behavior that Buffy has mentioned — picking on the weak; changing clothing and attitude; spending all spare time "lounging with imbeciles" — and understandably diagnoses Xander as a normal teenager. His sarcastic comment to Buffy, "Of course, you'll have to kill him," is wickedly funny in this situation. Buffy, however, knows something is wrong, not because of the others — their behavior is consistent with how they were before — but because of Xander. When he tells Willow he won't have to look at her "pasty face" any longer, he is acting out Willow's nightmare, and her face fills with horror. Hannigan is excellent in this scene.

Although this episode focuses on bullying in school, it also touches on another issue — date rape. Xander tries to rape Buffy, telling her she wants it because he's now dangerous and mean like Angel. Had she not been the Slayer, she probably wouldn't have escaped the situation, but she does. This scene is subtle and handled well.

It was reassuring that the first thing Xander did when the possession wore off was to save Willow, and also that Willow is mature enough to recognize that Xander acting like an animal is not really Xander. However, the ending could leave viewers a little uncertain about their relationship. If Xander, trying to rape Buffy, was acting out a tendency that stems from a genuine desire for her, then was his treatment of Willow based in reality? Was he speaking his mind? Also, Giles states that he can't find any mention in his reading on animal possession about amnesia afterward, and he's right. Yet, notice later in "Phases" how everyone accepts that Oz can't remember what he does while he's a werewolf.

Sadly, this episode was our goodbye to Principal Flutie, an absolutely hilarious character. It was such a shock to see the death of a fairly prominent character on the show, but exciting at the same time, for now we know how unpredictable this show will be. Goodbye, Principal Flutie . . . we hardly knew ye.

HIGHLIGHT: Herbert getting loose in the school hallways, and his very menacing get-up.
DID YOU NOTICE? Willow tells Xander he has to study or he'll wind up sweeping floors at the local pizza parlor, which is basically what he ends up doing after high school.
NITPICKS: Why is Buffy the only girl in gym class wearing a top with spaghetti straps? It seemed like an obvious ploy to make the lead actress stand out. Also, if the pack is supposed to remain tight, why does Xander keep separating from the rest of them and acting alone?
MUSIC/BANDS: When Xander is first acting strangely around Willow and Buffy at the Bronze, the song playing is "All You Want" by the Dashboard Prophets, and when Kyle and his friends enter the Bronze, it's "Reluctant Man" by Sprung Monkey. One of the best uses of music on the show is during the slow-motion sequence when Xander and the pack are

walking around the Sunnydale campus: the song is "Job's Eyes" by Far, from their CD *Tin Cans and Strings for You.*

1.7 Angel

Original air date:	April 14, 1997
Written by:	David Greenwalt
Directed by:	Scott Brazil
Guest cast:	Julie Benz (Darla), Charles Wesley (Meanest Vamp), Andrew J. Ferchland (Collin)

Buffy finally admits her feelings for Angel, only to discover he's a vampire.

"Angel" was a great episode and probably the most important to the second season. It opens with Buffy telling Willow how much she's fallen for Angel, yet she's never acted very interested in him before. Has she just been thinking about him more lately? It must be difficult for Willow — Buffy's feelings for Angel are much like her own feelings for Xander, yet Buffy has more of a chance with her crush than Willow does with hers.

We again see the Master, who now sends out the Three — three warriors stemming back to the mythology books who can take on anything and anybody. As exciting as the fight scene with Buffy is, the Three probably would have annihilated her and Angel pretty quickly, if their reputations reflect reality. However, Angel saves Buffy (as he does many times) and the Master is foiled once again. The Anointed One is being taught things by the Master, but you'd think the kid would begin to question the power of these vampires after realizing none of them can kill the Slayer.

Angel's first kiss with Buffy, where he accidentally transforms into a vampire, was an exciting one, but probably something many viewers foresaw. How else would Angel have known everything about the vampires? It certainly explains why he doesn't stay around for very long. We find out a lot of new information in this episode — Angel is 241 years old; he used to be the most vicious of vampires; a gypsy curse has left him with a soul and a conscience; he is a vampire who refuses to kill people. His face transforms when he gets angry, but the feelings he has for Buffy are probably ones he hasn't felt in a long time, so he transforms by accident (perhaps a metaphor for what happens to teenage boys when they get excited?). Buffy screams for the first time — she's used to seeing vampires, but not to having friends turn into them.

As if vampire slaying wasn't terrible enough for a 16-year-old girl, she now must accept that her boyfriend is a vampire. Xander — who will always be rather insensitive to Buffy when it comes to Angel — tells Buffy she has to kill him. Giles does it with more sensitivity, explaining as he did in the pilot when he was talking about Jesse that a vampire takes on a person's personality and appearance but that that person is dead. With Angel, however, this rationale isn't so clear: if Angel possesses his soul, there's a man inside that body with the demon. This situation doesn't seem to be explained in Giles's books, and if everyone else is having problems trying to figure out what's going on, imagine what Buffy must be dealing with! Her feelings for Angel are problematic, and always will be, and in a later episode she'll wish she'd killed him when she had the chance. But what if she had? Would she have been able to live with herself, not realizing what was really going to happen with him?

David Boreanaz

Meanwhile, Angel is going through a personal battle of his own, with no help from Darla. Darla was Angel's lover for centuries, and now that she senses his feelings for Buffy, she must remind him why he can't be with her. How do you date a person when you don't eat anything but blood, you can't stand sunlight, you have to be on guard constantly for fear you'll lose control and kill her, and you're over two centuries old? So, just as Giles, Xander, and Willow are reasoning with Buffy that she can't date a vampire, Darla is reasoning with Angel that he can't date a mortal. When Darla tricks Buffy into believing that Angel attacked her mother, what is most disturbing is the way Angel longingly gazes at the wound on Joyce's neck.

"Angel" cleverly demonstrates how most relationships work — outside forces like family and friends impose their values and opinions on the individuals in the relationships, not allowing them to work out their differences on their own. Here, those outside forces pressure Buffy and Angel to face off against one another, and they both realize that neither can kill the other.

This episode was well-written and beautifully acted. Boreanaz knows what he's doing with Angel, and rewatching "Angel" after seeing the second season shows us how these early episodes already contained hints about what happens in the future. The ending, where Buffy and Angel agree their relationship won't work, is very poignant, as is the burn that Buffy's cross leaves in Angel's skin.

HIGHLIGHT: The cockroach fumigation party.

DID YOU NOTICE? This episode was the first time Buffy was trained to use weapons other than stakes. She uses a staff, and immediately graduates to crossbow, which we will see her use again in "Prophecy Girl."

NITPICKS: When Giles realizes it was Darla who bit Joyce, not Angel, he immediately leaves the hospital to stop Buffy from killing Angel. Why? Angel is still a vampire, isn't he? Also, if Darla was the Master's "favorite" for 400 years, why didn't he act more favorably toward her?

OOPS: When Angel explains to Buffy how his soul was returned to him, he says he killed a gypsy girl in the Romani clan. It was the Kalderash clan; Romani is the gypsy language, not the name of a tribe. Also, Darla opens Angel's fridge to reveal hospital-issue packets of human blood, but later we find out Angel refuses to drink human blood.

MUSIC/BANDS: As Buffy and Angel say goodbye at the end of the episode, the song playing is the appropriately titled "I'll Remember You" by Sophie Zelmani, from her self-titled CD (notice how the title will be used for a later *Angel* episode).

1.8 I Robot, You Jane

Original air date:	April 28, 1997
Written by:	Ashley Gable, Thomas A. Swyden
Directed by:	Stephen Posey
Guest cast:	Robia LaMorte (Jenny Calendar), Jamison Ryan (Fritz), Mark Deakins (Voice of Malcolm/Moloch), Chad Lindberg (Dave), Pierrino Mascarino (Thelonius), Edith Fields (School Nurse)

Willow falls for a guy she meets on the Internet, not realizing he is actually a pagan demon who is taking over the world through its computer systems.

"I Robot, You Jane" is probably the most over-the-top episode in the first season, and the appearance of the robot at the end will have more than one viewer moaning, "Oh, puh-leeze!" However, the use of Moloch as the demon is an intelligent move, for he was one of the most feared of the pagan deities.

It is believed that the origin of the cult that worshipped Moloch is Canaanite, for when his name appears in the Bible it is in reference to the Canaanites. Moloch's worshippers would sacrifice their children — often the first-born — to him. In Leviticus 18:21, God explicitly forbids the Jews to follow this practice: "Do not hand over any of your children to be used in the worship of the god Moloch, because that would bring disgrace on the name of God, the LORD." Later, it is mentioned that King Ahaz and King Manasseh of Judah sacrifice their sons to him, and in 2 Kings 23:10, King Josiah destroys Moloch's temple to stop the human sacrifice.

Students of English literature will recognize Moloch as one of Satan's minions in *Paradise Lost*. When Satan battled against Heaven, Moloch was the strongest fighter, and when Satan's followers are listed in Book One, Moloch is the first to be named:

> First Moloch, horrid King besmear'd with blood
> Of human sacrifice, and parents' tears
> Though for the noise of Drums and Timbrels loud
> Their children's cries unheard, that pass'd through fire,
> To his grim Idol. (1.392–396)

Later, when Satan organizes his hellish council and asks his devils whether they should wage war on Heaven, it is Moloch, the general-in-chief of Satan's army, who first speaks, urging them to go to war, reasoning that the worst that could happen is death, which is better than being trapped in Hell.

It is fitting that *Buffy the Vampire Slayer*'s writers should allude to *Paradise Lost*, because the plight of the Master is similar to that of Satan. For revolting against Heaven, Satan and the angels who supported him are sent to Hell, a horrible underground pit of fire where they plot how to escape to fight God's army once again. Similarly, the Master and his followers are trapped underground, although the vampires have a way of going above temporarily. Many of the Master's speeches are strikingly similar to Satan's as well.

A disturbing element of this episode is the allusions — intended or not — to Nazi Germany. Moloch seems like Hitler reincarnated, and his various levels of control mirror Hitler's power over Germany in the 1930s and '40s. Moloch is a leader who tells his followers he loves them, but when they return that love and trust he kills them. The Internet seems to be a positive wave of the future — as Nazism was to many — but when its potential dangers become apparent, it's too late to undo. One of the computer hackers who does Moloch's dirty work is named Fritz, the word the Allied forces used for German soldiers. Moloch is the god of human sacrifice; Buffy is almost killed in a shower; Buffy and Xander become trapped in a gas chamber. And if these references are too subtle, the writers make a more obvious allusion when Moloch changes the thesis of a student's paper to read, "Nazi Germany was a model of a well-ordered society." And Moloch targets Willow, the Jewish girl. The parallels are interesting, but the writers' intentions are unclear. Was there a reason to make reference to Hitler?

There were a few inconsistencies with how the computers worked in the show. When Buffy is trying to find Willow's file to delete it, she types its name in the file finder program. Yet,

The first-season Willow we all fell in love with

if you look closely, the file was on the desktop to begin with. And Willow doesn't question the fact that her home computer tells her she has mail when she wasn't even online — the modem must be active for her computer to detect mail. When Malcolm is skimming the principal's records for information on Buffy, they wouldn't appear on the principal's screen. If Moloch is accessing the information from within the system, the file wouldn't necessarily open up on the screen like that. Finally, when Willow is scanning the pages, she's only got the scanner on part of them (and she wasn't scanning in a straight line), yet all the text gets scanned in.

This episode broached a very important topic — potential danger on the Internet. Many people use the Internet as their primary form of communication, so private or sensitive information is passed around on a daily basis. Of all the horrors and demons represented on the show, this is one of the most realistic.

"I Robot, You Jane" is our introduction to Ms. Calendar, who was not originally intended to be a recurring character. The banter between her and Giles showed a spark of chemistry and the writers decided to go with it. The arguments between the two, however, are very black and white — either you surf the Net or you read books — and don't allow for the possibility of the two worlds successfully overlapping.

"I Robot, You Jane" had a lot of potential, but the result is my least favorite episode of season one.

HIGHLIGHT: The gang realizing they'll never be able to date normal people as long as they remain on the hellmouth.

INTERESTING FACTS: Since appearing in this episode, Chad Lindberg, who plays Dave, has gone on to star in such films as *October Sky, The Fast and the Furious,* and *The Rookie.* A documentary called *Carving Out Our Name*, about him and his roommates (Wes Bentley, Brad Rowe, and Greg Fawcett) trying to make it in Hollywood, debuted at the Toronto International Film Festival in 2001.

DID YOU NOTICE? Chad Lindberg's character wasn't called Dave by accident; when the computer talks to him, the scene could have been plucked right out of *2001: A Space Odyssey*, where the computer, HAL, calmly threatens his operator, Dave, in the same monotonous voice Moloch uses in this episode.

NITPICKS: Alyson Hannigan mentioned in an interview that she felt strange talking to her computer while typing. Why didn't they just show us the screen while she typed? It worked on *Doogie Howser, MD.* Also, Buffy follows Dave to the CRD plant on foot, while he's driving a car, yet they arrive at the same time.

OOPS: Now, this is an error so obvious it must have been an inside joke. When Moloch finds Buffy's records on the principal's computer, it says she's a sophomore born 10/24/80. However, when he transfers the files to Fritz's computer, it reads she's a senior, born 05/06/79. (Both agree that her GPA is 2.8.) Perhaps this inconsistency is an allusion to the fact that Kristy Swanson's movie Buffy is a senior, while the television Buffy is a sophomore. Both are wrong, though, since we later find out her birthday is in January. Also, if you watch, frame by frame, the scene where Moloch is flipping through various records, you'll see the same five or six faces flash by in a loop.

1.9 The Puppet Show

Original air date: May 5, 1997
Written by: Dean Batali, Rob Des Hotel

Directed by: Ellen S. Pressman
Guest cast: Richard Werner (Morgan), Burke Roberts (Marc), Armin Shimerman (Principal Snyder), Lenora May (Mrs. Jackson), Chasen Hampton (Elliot), Natasha Pearce (Lisa), Tom Wyner (Sid's Voice)

When students are found dead with organs missing, the gang suspects a ventriloquist's dummy that appears to have come to life.

This may be the funniest episode in the first season. Sid, the wisecracking dummy, is absolutely hilarious. The setting is the annual school "talentless" show, where magicians can't perform their tricks, actors can't act, and Cordelia sings a wretched version of "The Greatest Love of All." It also features our introduction to Principal Snyder — or, as Giles calls him, "Our new Führer" — played by Armin Shimerman, who is best known as the Ferengi Quark on *Deep Space Nine*. He introduces himself with one of the funniest lines on the show yet, made funnier because of his seriousness: "My predecessor may have gone in for all that touchy-feely relating nonsense, but he was eaten." In "The Pack," the gang had discussed how the school would find a new principal and concluded the only way that one would come in is if he hadn't been told what happened. So the fact that Snyder accepted the job knowing what happened to Flutie immediately casts suspicion on him, reinforced by hints that he might be the demon the gang is searching for.

The ventriloquist's dummy is very eerie, and the speed with which he runs around Buffy's room is terrifying! (Sarah Michelle Gellar admitted to having nightmares about puppets after filming this episode.) The voice for Sid was perfect, as it captured the essence of a tough-talking, cigar-chomping gangster-type from the 1930s. Sid's deep voice is also unexpected, as we often think of dummies having high-pitched voices. One item that is left unexplained is why Morgan was chosen as the person who would own Sid. Why was Sid so cruel to him? Sid mentions that before he had been cursed into the dummy's body, he'd had a fling with a Korean Slayer; this tells us that Slayers are international, not just from the U.S. (as we will see up close in "Fool for Love").

Once again, as she did in "Teacher's Pet" when Dr. Gregory died, Cordelia goes into a melodramatic, self-absorbed mourning process for the dancer who is killed. We soon discover — unsurprisingly — that her biggest fear was that she could have been the victim. However, where Cordelia was hurtful to Willow in the pilot and downright vicious to Amy in "The Witch," she seems to have toned down to a self-obsessed comic device, and has become far more likable. In the second season she'll deliver some of the funniest lines.

This episode is the first and only time the show continues during the credits (on Angel, they will continue "She" into the credits as well). The gang's pathetic attempt at Greek tragedy is hysterical, as are the looks from the audience members. This great episode steered clear of vampires entirely, but contained some of the best lines yet.

HIGHLIGHT: Xander playing with the dummy and doing his own act with it in the library.
DID YOU NOTICE? When Buffy is looking for Morgan and she walks under the stage, look at the wall behind her — there's a picture of Moloch.
INTERESTING FACTS: Charisma Carpenter said in an interview that the writers purposely made Cordelia a singer in the talentless show because they knew Carpenter couldn't sing: "I was walking up to the production office and Joss stopped me. He said, 'Hey, by the

way, can you sing?' I said, 'No, but I can dance.' And he said, 'Good.' I didn't know if 'Good' meant, 'Good, you can dance,' or 'Good, you can't sing.' Well, I found out!"

NITPICKS: Joyce comes into Buffy's room and says she noticed something seems to be bothering her. A girl was just killed at school — what does she expect? Also, to test Willow's intelligence, Xander asks her what the square root of 841 is. How could Xander have chosen a number that has a perfect square root?

RESTLESS MOMENT: When Giles holds everyone in the "power circle" and shouts, "Fifteen minutes to showtime!" he's very similar to his stage-director character in "Restless."

1.10 Nightmares

Original air date:	May 12, 1997
Teleplay by:	David Greenwalt
Story by:	Joss Whedon
Directed by:	Bruce Seth Green
Guest cast:	Andrew J. Ferchland (The Anointed One), Dean Butler (Hank Summers), Jeremy Foley (Billy Palmer), Justin Urich (Wendel), J. Robin Miller (Laura), Terry Cain (Ms. Tishler), Scott Harlan (Aldo Gianfranco), Brian Pietro (Coach)

All of the worst nightmares of the people of Sunnydale begin coming true, and Buffy and the gang must find out what is causing this before the world is destroyed.

What's your worst nightmare? In most television shows or movies, it's getting caught in a burning building, falling off a cliff, boat, or roller-coaster, or some other disaster. But what about having your father tell you that you were a mistake?

"Nightmares" is eerie simply because Whedon has his finger on the pulse of teenage life. He knows what worries teens, what scares them, what makes them happy. So in this episode, their nightmares are extensions of their own personalities. Cordelia fears having a bad-hair day, wearing nerdy clothing, and being dragged into the chess club. Xander — the clown of the gang — ironically has a dire fear of clowns. Giles suddenly gets lost in his beloved stacks and can't read. Willow is faced with a crowd of people who expect her to do what she cannot. All of these phobias may not sound like appropriate devices for a horror film, but that's because they're far more realistic fears.

The worst of the nightmares is when Buffy's father shows up to tell her that he and her mother separated because of her. This would be devastating to any child of a divorce, and considering how many kids tend to believe all family catastrophes really are their fault, to actually hear one's parent tell them that in the cruel way Hank Summers does would be heartbreaking. During this scene, Buffy's face moves from a look of shock to one of being utterly crushed by the most important man in her life. Even after she realizes it's not real, the experience will probably leave a scar that won't heal right away.

Ironically, only Xander has the courage to fight against his demons. Only when he decides to stop running is he able to destroy the fear of a clown that has dogged him all his life. It's not clear why Billy's out-of-body experience is affecting everyone else, although things don't need explanations when you live on a hellmouth. His nightmare allows the writers to explore the far-reaching implications that child abuse can have on a person.

While it's understandable that the residents of Sunnydale rationalize the other weird occurrences on the hellmouth, it's hard to believe that all the biblical disasters that befall them could so easily be forgotten. Near the end the nightmares get worse, and Giles faces his worst nightmare, Buffy's death, while Buffy faces hers — becoming a vampire. The scene where Giles kneels before Buffy's grave is poignant, for we realize how much he cares about her.

"Nightmares" is a precursor to the amazing psychological depths this show will mine in later seasons. While season one, for the most part, happens on the surface, seasons two and onward will look at deeper issues, where our fears really lie. Sure, vampires are scary, but not half as frightening as being abandoned by a parent. The saddest part about this episode was that Buffy's nightmares outnumber everyone else's. It would seem that her problems with being a Slayer and a teenager aren't limited to haunting her waking hours. The hellmouth might produce a lot of scary demons, but nothing is as terrifying as our own imaginations.

HIGHLIGHT: The "Smoking Kills" poster on the wall in the basement and the dramatic irony it creates.

DID YOU NOTICE? One of Buffy's fears was of being buried alive and having to claw her way out of her grave, an experience that will, horrifyingly, come true. Her other fear, that her father will abandon her and no longer want to be part of her life, sadly also comes true (see "Helpless").

INTERESTING FACTS: Dean Butler, who plays Buffy's father, is best known as Almanzo Wilder on *Little House on the Prairie*.

NITPICKS: The audience boos Willow when she tries to sing, but the male opera singer is pretty lame, too. And how does Buffy retain her soul when *she* becomes a vampire (and somehow gets to the hospital during the day)?

OOPS: In "Becoming," we see a scene where Buffy's parents are fighting and she's in high school. Yet in this episode she tells Willow that they got divorced when she was in her freshman year of high school and had been separated long before that. And in "I Robot, You Jane," we find out Buffy was born either in 1979 or 1980, while in this episode her tombstone reads, "1981–1997." What gives?

1.11 Out of Mind, Out of Sight

Original air date:	May 19, 1997
Teleplay by:	Ashley Gable, Thomas A. Swyden
Story by:	Joss Whedon
Directed by:	Reza Badiyi
Guest cast:	Clea DuVall (Marcie Ross), Ryan Bittle (Mitch), Denise Y. Dowse (Ms. Miller), Julie Fulton (FBI Teacher), Mercedes McNab (Harmony), Skip Stellrecht (Agent Manetti), Marc Phelan (Agent Doyle)

When an invisible person starts attacking students, Buffy and the gang must try to figure out who it is so they can stop her.

Although "Out of Mind, Out of Sight" meandered in spots, it contained the best ending yet. Like "The Pack," this is an episode about popularity and what lack of acceptance can do to a person. As usual, the plight of an outsider mirrors someone in the gang, and in this case it's Buffy. Just as Marcie became invisible because the students and teachers treated her that way, Buffy often feels like an outsider. Xander and Willow share a joke that she doesn't understand and Cordelia treats her as if she's a complete loser. Buffy, who seems so quick-witted all the time, can't think of a single comeback when faced with an army of popular girls.

Cordelia is her normal "I am the center of the universe" self in this one, although for the first time she shows a hint of humanity, telling Buffy she feels just as alone as the unpopular kids. What is most shocking is the sincerity she exhibits, foreshadowing her character development in season two (although a lot of her earnestness has to do with the fact that she's speaking on her favorite topic — herself). Willow and Xander seem to shed the most light on what it's like to be unpopular. They immediately recognize the "Have a nice summer" inscriptions in Marcie's yearbook as the "kiss of death," which is a bit of a hyperbole, but contains truth. Their high school is more realistic than that of other television shows because there aren't just popular kids and unpopular kids but a hierarchy of popularity. Cordy and her friends are at the top, then Buffy and her friends, with various levels descending from there.

Angel appears again, as he did in "Teacher's Pet," for vampire-related reasons, rather than to enlighten Buffy on the immediate situation. He tells Giles he can obtain the Codex, a work that has been lost for centuries, although we never discover how he gets it (the Codex will play a more important role in "Prophecy Girl"). The disturbing thing Giles says about the Codex is that it contains the most complete prophecy of the Slayer in the last days. What does he mean by the "last days"? The Slayer's last days? The world's last days? Unfortunately, the phrase goes unexplained.

Fittingly, this is the episode where we see that Angel casts no reflection in the mirror, although this is inconsistent with vampire fiction. In the fiction, a vampire casts no reflection because he has no soul. So shouldn't we be able to see Angel?

The least convincing aspect of this episode is that no one in the gang knows how to interpret Marcie's messages. "Look" and "Listen" are almost always followed by "Learn" — it's a common saying in many schools. Even when they know how Marcie became invisible, they still can't figure out what she means by Look and Listen. Considering that Marcie was a student who once tried reaching out to others, why do they dismiss her as being insane and not try to reach out to her?

The scene with Cordelia is anticlimactic and unbelievable — first, Marcie would probably have started slashing at Cordy's face pretty quickly, rather than standing there holding the scalpel long enough for Buffy to escape. Second, when Buffy tries to "sense" Marcie's presence, she takes a long time doing so. With Buffy standing with her eyes closed and her back to Marcie, Marcie definitely has the upper hand and doesn't take advantage of it.

Like "The Pack" and the later "Earshot," this episode is an interesting examination of what happens when students are bullied. Perhaps instead of criticizing shows like *Buffy*, critics should look to Buffy for ideas about why certain students become violent. Not to mention an explanation of where FBI assassins come from. Overall, an entertaining episode.

HIGHLIGHT: Cordelia's never-ending May Queen acceptance speech: "Ask not what your country can do for you; ask, 'Hey, what am I going to wear to the Spring Fling?'"
INTERESTING FACTS: The alternate title of this episode is "Invisible Girl," and both have

been used as the official title. However, when the first season was released on DVD, the producers went with "Out of Mind, Out of Sight." Also, the concept of this episode was borrowed from the 1933 film *The Invisible Man*, and its many sequels. Finally, Clea DuVall has become a recognizable actress since her turn as Marcie. She's appeared in dozens of films, including *Can't Hardly Wait, But I'm a Cheerleader, Ghosts of Mars, 13 Conversations About One Thing*, and *Girl, Interrupted*.

NITPICKS: Considering that Cordy tends to repress her memories of bad events, how does she know to come to Buffy for help? Also, she says it's her first time in the library, yet she was the one who directed Buffy there in the first episode.

OOPS: While Cordelia is giving her May Queen speech, notice how Principal Snyder appears and disappears behind her. Also, if Marcie had put something in Cordelia's face to make it numb, she wouldn't have been able to raise her eyebrows, make facial expressions, and talk without hindrance.

1.12 Prophecy Girl

Original air date:	June 2, 1997
Written and directed by:	Joss Whedon
Guest cast:	Robia LaMorte (Jenny Calendar), Andrew J. Ferchland (The Anointed One), Scott Gurney (Kevin)

Giles reads the prophecy that Buffy will die by the Master's hand, and at 16 years old she is faced with the reality of her own death.

Whew! This was a fast-paced, well-acted, emotionally charged episode that brought the first season to a brilliant conclusion. If the ending of this felt like closure, it should: faced with the possibility of *Buffy the Vampire Slayer* not being renewed for a second season, Whedon had to reassure the fans that the gang would be all right. Ms. Calendar is back, foreshadowing her return as a major character in the second season. She and Giles exhibit more of the chemistry that was apparent in "I Robot, You Jane." She becomes the latest member of the "club," as Willow refers to it — if this keeps up, there will be fewer people in Sunnydale who *don't* know about the Slayer than those who do!

The best part of this episode is how the characters must try to come to terms with death. We all must die someday, but it's only when we are given a date that death assumes a horrific reality. Otherwise people tend not to spend every day thinking how they are getting closer to death with each passing minute. The same goes for Buffy: despite her job's extreme danger, she's never fully realized that there's a very real possibility she could die while carrying out her duty. Her reality is best summed up when she tells Giles, "I have to meet my terrible fate — biology." To a high school student, *classes* should be the most horrific thing in their lives, not their own mortality. However, when Buffy overhears Giles relating the prophecy to Angel, she reacts at first with laughter, then disbelief, and finally denial, refusing to fulfill her duty as the Slayer. She has her whole life ahead of her, and Sarah is wonderful in this scene, reminding us not to forget that a Slayer is still human. She also makes us wonder if the Codex was prophesying the events of season five, and Giles misread them.

Willow, too, is jolted into reality when her fellow students from the AV club are murdered. Until now she has reacted with disgust and disbelief to the strange occurrences around her, but so far none of the victims have been close to her. This loss is very real, however, and she'll be reminded of it each time she enters the AV room alone. Alyson puts in her best performance yet as the traumatized victim, crying to Buffy about how cruel and unfair life is. It is Willow's reaction to these grisly deaths that seems to spur Buffy on to face the Master.

The scene with Buffy and her mother is one of the few times they seem to connect. When Joyce shows her the dress, Buffy seems genuinely appreciative, whereas up to this point one or the other of them has always pulled away. Joyce tells the story of how she met Hank with no resentment, demonstrating that she seems to have gotten past the divorce.

Xander decides to take his crush on Buffy one step further, with devastating consequences. We've watched Xander pine for Buffy all season, and we understand the pain he's feeling. Turning him down must have been one of the most difficult things Buffy has had to do, and Willow's anxiety while waiting to hear the result must have been nerve-racking. A cheer should go out for Willow, though, for having the courage to also turn Xander down, knowing his proposal to her wasn't heartfelt. Poor Xander.

This episode was rated TV14, most likely for the gory exit of the Master. Buffy's death at the time was a shock, for, without knowing if the show was to be renewed for a second season, one might have thought there was a possibility (albeit a tiny one) that it would end that way. Buffy's state of paralysis when the Master stands behind her is an extension of her previous fear of death. As a single tear rolls down her terrified face, this is Sarah's best performance yet. Angel's inability to perform CPR is the first mention we get that a vampire has no breath, which will lead to inconsistencies in later seasons. The rooftop dialogue between Buffy and the Master is the funniest of the season, partly because Buffy is still shaken and the Master doesn't exactly understand what she's talking about.

The creature from the hellmouth was an amazing effect. In literature the hellmouth is the portal between Earth and Hell, the passageway through which one can move from one existence to another. Many Renaissance morality plays made mention of a hellmouth, and it is believed by some that when Jesus was crucified he traveled through the hellmouth to carry the souls of the just — such as Noah, Adam, and Eve — to Heaven, where they rightfully belonged.

"Prophecy Girl" was a superb episode, featuring standout performances by all involved. Despite Whedon wrapping the story up so well, it's possible there would have been a revolt against the network if the series hadn't been renewed — a television show this good demands continuation.

HIGHLIGHT: The rooftop banter between Buffy and the Master: "You have fruit-punch mouth!"

DID YOU NOTICE? Xander tells Buffy that she is turning him down because he's not dangerous like Angel, a mantra that will be repeated over and over in future seasons, especially by Riley and Spike.

NITPICKS: Buffy charging toward the library with her theme music playing has got to be the single cheesiest moment on *Buffy* ever. Also, Buffy says to Joyce that they can't afford the white dress. Who buys Buffy's clothes? They aren't exactly Wal-Mart brands, and considering Buffy doesn't have a paying job, Joyce must be paying for that designer wardrobe. Also, how did Xander know where Angel lived? Finally, there's never any explanation as to why the Master's bones stay intact — a vampire should be completely dusted when impaled the way he is.

OOPS: If there's a skylight over the library, why has the only sunlight we've ever seen there come from the side windows? There is never a beam coming from directly overhead (and, considering how many times after this we see Angel in the library, it wouldn't have been possible for him to stand in a room under a skylight). Also, when Cordelia is talking to Ms. Calendar in the car, her mouth isn't moving. And at the end, when Buffy is facedown in the water, her hair goes from being piled up on top of her head to being loose around her shoulders.

MUSIC/BANDS: When Xander goes home with the intention to listen to country music, "the music of pain," he listens to Patsy Cline's "I Fall to Pieces" (later the title of an *Angel* episode) from her 1961 album, *Patsy Cline Showcase* (the song is now found on *The Patsy Cline Story*). Later, as Buffy looks through her photo album, we hear "Inconsolable" by Jonatha Brooke and the Story, from *Plumb*.

Season Two

Recurring characters in season two: Robia LaMorte (Jenny Calendar), Armin Shimerman (Principal Snyder), James Marsters (Spike), Juliet Landau (Drusilla)

2.1 When She Was Bad

Original air date:	September 15, 1997
Written and directed by:	Joss Whedon
Guest cast:	Dean Butler (Hank Summers), Andrew J. Ferchland (The Anointed One), Brent Jennings (Absalom), Tamara Braun (Tara)

After being away in L.A. for the summer, Buffy returns to Sunnydale a very different person.

While "Prophecy Girl" ended on a relieved, upbeat note, "When She Was Bad" involves a lot of people getting hurt, mostly by Buffy. When Buffy makes her action-packed entrance, she seems normal, although perhaps a little distant. (When you haven't seen your friends for an entire summer, you might be a little withdrawn from them at first.) Once Willow and Xander mention the Master, though, gloom shrouds Buffy's face. Over the summer she has come to the sad realization that being a Slayer is her calling, and all she will ever be able to do with her life. She will never be a normal girl, and facing her own mortality in "Prophecy Girl" seems to have jolted her into reality. Regardless of her personal problems — which, admittedly, are immense — what she does to those around her is beyond insensitive, casting a suspicious light on how Buffy treats her friends. It makes her a more complex character, showing that even the good guys aren't always perfect. It's risky to make Buffy unlikable for an entire episode, but it's a risk that pays off by making her more human.

It's a little hypocritical, however, that Cordelia of all people should be the one to give her the pep talk. Where does she get off calling Buffy the bitch of the year? Sure, she's the only one who's been down that road, and we discovered in "Out of Mind, Out of Sight" that being popular has its downsides, too, but Buffy is nowhere near the bitch that Cordy has shown herself to be. The main difference between Buffy and Cordelia in this episode is that Buffy manipulates her friends and intends to hurt them as badly as she can, whereas Cordy picks on those who aren't her friends, and her insults drop people a notch or two without destroying them.

In this episode, Buffy hurts everyone around her, Angel worries that he may have hurt her, and Xander unknowingly hurts Willow by seeming to forget entirely that they nearly locked lips at the beginning of the episode. Why didn't the kiss have a greater effect on Willow and Xander? Does he really forget about it or just pretend to? It's difficult to tell whether they would actually have kissed, for they pull away from one another just before the vampire pops up. However, Xander's threat to Buffy — "If anything happens to Willow, I'll kill you" — proves that while his infatuations lie elsewhere, Willow is the one he truly cares about. And it also shows the huge burden that has been placed on Buffy's shoulders — she didn't ask for these vampires to come to town, but if she doesn't stop them, her friends will blame her for the vampires' carnage.

The fight scene at the end is great. In other action shows, like *Xena* or *Highlander*, the enemies tend to take on the hero one by one, rather than attacking en masse. In this episode, vampires attack Buffy in twos or threes, and she still holds her own. When she destroys the bones of the Master, she destroys the demons within her that have plagued her for months and she's ready to move on.

"When She Was Bad" was a good season premiere, but I find it hard to believe Buffy could have acted this way. It was a little disappointing to come back to the show like this.

HIGHLIGHT: When Xander mishears Willow's spelling of the swear word as "bitca."

DID YOU NOTICE? Charisma sounds like she was suffering from a cold throughout this episode. "When She Was Bad" was also the first time Snyder pegs Buffy as a troublemaker, and the first time Buffy feels Angel's presence before she sees him.

INTERESTING FACTS: The credits for the second season included David Boreanaz for the first time, and where the "In every generation . . ." speech had been read by the WB announcer for the first season, it is now recited by Anthony Stewart Head.

NITPICKS: Was it just me or did parts of this show seem like an extended ad for Cibo Matto? And why didn't Giles simply burn the Master's bones rather than bury them?

OOPS: When Joyce is driving Buffy to school, Buffy is wearing a pink tank top. But when she's in the school, it's a white top. The next day, she's wearing the pink top again, as if the car scene was supposed to have happened that morning instead. And when Willow, Cordy, Jenny, and Giles are rolled out hanging upside-down, Giles's hand brushes the Master's rib cage and you can see it move, as if it were made of rubber. Also, after Buffy stakes the first vampire, the camera is positioned over the skeleton for us to watch the fight, but the four are no longer hanging there. And Buffy breaks the Master's rib cage on the second blow with the sledgehammer, but when Angel walks around behind her, the rib cage is intact.

MUSIC/BANDS: As Angel leaves Buffy's room, the song playing is "It Doesn't Matter" by Alison Krauss and Union Station, from the CD *So Long So Wrong*. The song continues as Joyce drives Buffy to school. As Willow and Xander wait for Buffy to arrive at the Bronze, the band onstage is Cibo Matto (with Sean Lennon on bass guitar) and the song is "Spoon," from the CD *Super Relax*. Buffy does her sexy dance with Xander to "Sugar Water," from the same CD. The score for this episode was written by Christophe Beck.

2.2 Some Assembly Required

Original air date:	September 22, 1997
Written by:	Ty King
Directed by:	Bruce Seth Green
Guest cast:	Angelo Spizzirri (Eric), Ingo Neuhaus (Daryl Epps), Michael Bacall (Chris Epps), Melanie MacQueen (Mrs. Epps), Amanda Wilmshurst (Cheerleader)

A Dr. Frankenstein wannabe tries to reconstruct a woman after restoring his brother to life, but to obtain a head he must kill a living girl — Cordelia.

"Some Assembly Required" was creepy beyond words, and too obviously a takeoff of *Frankenstein* to be taken seriously. If the revivification of one's brother was supposed to be a metaphor for some high school problem, then its symbolism wasn't too clear. The basic plot is borrowed heavily from Mary Shelley's *Frankenstein*, where a scientist reconstructs a body from parts of corpses to try to create life. Science has often tampered with Nature, but when Dr. Frankenstein attempts to recreate the birth process, his efforts are met with terrifying results. He shuns the creature, who must go out alone and try to learn about the world. Eventually, after being spurned by a family he'd grown to love, the creature returns to Frankenstein and demands that he make a woman. Frankenstein reluctantly obliges, but before the process is over he realizes he cannot commit the same mistake he made before, and he destroys her, causing the creature to go on a murderous rampage.

In "Some Assembly Required," the story is similar, although it's used as a backdrop to an episode about relationships. Giles agonizes over whether or not he should ask out Ms. Calendar, Buffy and Angel's relationship sparks up again, and Willow and Xander complain that they always end up alone. When Xander rescues Cordelia, however, we see the first hint that she's attracted to him, although he misses it completely. There's also a certain sadness to the episode — where Buffy faced her own mortality in "Prophecy Girl," Chris has had to deal with his brother's death and his mother's subsequent depression. Chris — and everyone else, for that matter — becomes as invisible to his mother as Marcie was to everyone in "Out of Mind, Out of Sight." Chris Epps is arguably the smartest student in school, but in high school it is the sports figures who really matter, and Chris can never live up to his brother's reputation as an all-star running back. In other words, some assembly is required in all of these relationships.

Cordelia is rather dense in this episode, acting like the stereotypical horror-movie scream queen. Despite several warnings, she still takes no precautions. After hearing that female corpses have gone missing, she walks across a dark parking lot alone. Then she stays behind in the change room to apply her makeup, almost getting kidnapped. And after escaping *that*, she walks behind the bleachers alone to get a drink. Wake up, Cordy!

This episode was important to the development of everyone's relationships, and showed that in this series people keep trying to bring back their loved ones ("Forever," "Bargaining"), but other than that it was a gratuitous use of the *Frankenstein* story without adding anything to it.

HIGHLIGHT: Xander playing with the plastic head in science class.
DID YOU NOTICE? Buffy's cross isn't the one Angel gave to her, and after a couple more appearances, we won't see his cross any longer.

NITPICKS: Angel sees an open coffin in a grave and assumes a vampire has risen. Why? The vampires crawl up through the dirt, the families don't just leave the coffins there without replacing the dirt above them.

OOPS: The photos that Eric flips through don't match the poses the characters were in when he took them earlier. In Eric's shots, they all appear to be posing for him, yet earlier they were holding up hands, and caught off guard.

MUSIC/BANDS: Score by Christophe Beck, with Adam Fields. This episode marked the first time we heard the Buffy/Angel theme song.

2.3 School Hard

Original air date:	September 29, 1997
Teleplay by:	David Greenwalt
Story by:	David Greenwalt, Joss Whedon
Directed by:	John T. Kretchmer
Guest cast:	Andrew J. Ferchland (The Anointed One), Brian Reddy (Police Chief Bob), Alexandra Johnes (Sheila)

Sunnydale's newest vampire residents, Spike and Drusilla, arrive in town just in time for Parent–Teacher Night at Sunnydale High.

Spike and Drusilla are without a doubt the two coolest and creepiest characters on television. This co-dependent couple will wreak havoc on Sunnydale for the rest of the season, yet they'll have viewers begging for more. Spike is a Billy Idol lookalike, a British rebel vampire who has arrived from Prague with Drusilla, the mentally disturbed, childlike, weak vampire who depends on Spike for survival. Immediately there is something different about these two, a sense that perhaps Spike, too, has retained his soul but not a conscience. Why else would he care so deeply for Drusilla? When he makes his first appearance before the Anointed One, he talks tough and nasty, informing him he's killed two Slayers and he'll kill another. When Dru enters, his face changes back to normal — a special effect we haven't seen since Darla's face transformed in the pilot episode — and he talks in a cuddlier voice to her. Spike always keeps his game face off when he's with Dru.

As if the arrival of these two didn't cause enough problems for Buffy, Snyder is riding her again, telling her he's looking for any reason to expel her. Why is she sitting in the office with a girl who stabbed her teacher with pruning shears when the only offense he charges Buffy with is burning down the gym of her last school? First, she's already atoned for that, and second, why doesn't he instead attribute the destruction of the library to her? They never did explain who got blamed for that. However, this is an important episode in shaping your attitude toward Principal Snyder — it's hinted for the first time that he knows more about what's going on than we think. His standard response for strange occurrences is that they're PCP/gang-related, and that explanation keeps coming up a little too readily for comfort. At the end we're led to believe that the police are covering up the hellmouth activity as well.

The relationship between Buffy and Joyce is precarious once again, but Joyce's character is inconsistent in this episode. First she tells Buffy she doesn't want to be disappointed in her again, when Buffy hasn't done anything wrong. What kind of incentive is Joyce giving Buffy to be responsible when she clearly doesn't trust her to do anything right? At

The deliciously batty Drusilla . . .   *. . . and her co-dependent vampire*
boyfriend, Spike

Parent–Teacher Night, when the vampires jump through the window Joyce just stands there, exhibiting absolutely no surprise, leading some members of the *Buffy* mailing lists to speculate that Joyce was once a Slayer herself (she wasn't). After looking infuriated with Buffy immediately before the vampires enter, she allows Buffy to tell her what to do and doesn't drag Buffy into the locked classroom afterward, almost as if she knows that Buffy can handle the gang. For all of her pride and acceptance of Buffy at the end, she will soon forget and go back to badgering her daughter in subsequent episodes.

We discover that Spike — a.k.a. William the Bloody — was sired by Angel (a suggestion which will later prove to be false), which probably adds to Angel's enormous sense of guilt about his past. Not only is Angel responsible for the people he has killed, but for the people who die at the hands of those whom he has turned into vampires. The chain reaction Angel has caused is infinite. When Angel is first reunited with Spike, we get a glimpse of him as the evil Angelus, whom we will meet in all his horrific glory later in the season. He admits to almost sacrificing Xander to Spike, and yet people question why Xander hates Angel so much.

In the end, Spike blames his failure to kill Buffy on her family and friends. To this point in the series, Buffy has been told again and again that these outsiders are a hindrance to her, not a help, so it was comforting to know she's doing the right thing by getting her friends involved. Spike's treatment of the "Annoying One" is a relief, changing the ritualistic traditions of the vampire lair to an each-vampire-for-himself attitude and signaling the last we'll see of season one elements. Spike's rebellion is a refreshing change among the vampires, and fans everywhere applauded his and Dru's arrival. A terrific episode!

HIGHLIGHT: Willow's reaction to Buffy's lemonade.
INTERESTING FACTS: Joss Whedon refers to Spike and Dru as the Sid and Nancy of the vampire world. Sid Vicious was the bassist in the punk rock band the Sex Pistols. He died of

a heroin overdose while he was about to be tried for the murder of his girlfriend, Nancy Spungen, in 1979.

NITPICKS: Hasn't Giles learned by now that school is important to Buffy? As Buffy is on the verge of being expelled, Giles urges her to cut class and not attend the Parent–Teacher Night. Also, why has Cordelia started hanging out with the gang? A debt of gratitude?

OOPS: Technically, after Angel revealed in "Prophecy Girl" that vampires can't breathe, the fact that Spike smokes a cigarette should be a plot inconsistency. However, Joss has explained that vampires *can* breathe, they just don't *have* to breathe. Still doesn't explain Angel's comment in "Prophecy Girl". . . .

RESTLESS MOMENT: Joyce peers out of the hole in the doorway at Buffy, the same way she looks out of the hole in the wall in "Restless."

MUSIC/BANDS: When Willow is helping Buffy study French at the Bronze and Xander is dancing alone, the song playing is "1000 Nights," performed by Nickel. As the three of them hit the dance floor, "Stupid Thing" comes on. Both are from Nickel's album, *Stupid Thing*. Score by Shawn Clement and Sean Murray.

2.4 Inca Mummy Girl

Original air date:	October 6, 1997
Written by:	Matt Kiene, Joe Reinkemeyer
Directed by:	Ellen S. Pressman
Guest cast:	Ara Celi (Ampata), Jason Hall (Devon), Hendrik Rosvall (Sven), Joey Crawford (Rodney), Danny Strong (Jonathan), Kristen Winnicki (Gwen), Gil Birmingham (Peru Guy), Samuel Jacobs (Peruvian Boy)

Xander falls in love with a foreign exchange student who — surprise, surprise — turns out to be an ancient Incan mummy come to life.

This episode draws heavily from the history of the Incas and their practice of mummification. The Inca people were an immensely wealthy nation who prospered until the mid-16th century. The imperial capital was Cuzco (modern-day Peru), and the Incas ruled over Chile, upper Argentina, Ecuador, Peru, Bolivia, and south Colombia — an area larger than any current Andean nation. At its peak, the Inca nation consisted of 12,000,000 people, but only 40,000 of them were actually Inca, ruling like royalty over the others. It was partly the wealth of the nation that led to its downfall. Houses and other buildings were inlaid with silver and gold, and the nation's material wealth was one of the first things explorers recognized during the 1532 Spanish conquest. The Inca emperor was kidnapped and ransomed for a large sum of money — about $50 million by today's standards. However, it was mostly smallpox that destroyed the Inca people, killing about two thirds of the population upon contact with the explorers.

The Incas left no written records, and there is much debate about the nature of their religion. They worshipped nature gods, mostly sun and moon. In one of the only written accounts from the time, the Spaniard Father Bernake Cobo described the Incan practice of human sacrifice, which was rare and usually limited to children 10 and under. Occasionally, according to Father Cobo, they would sacrifice a maiden of 15 or 16 years, who had been raised in a convent to keep her unblemished. They would slit her throat or hang her, and sometimes remove her heart while it was still beating. However, considering the author of this account was a Spaniard who probably had to convince his people that the conquest was a *good* thing, we must take his words with a generous dose of wariness.

The Incas were one of many ancient cultures who practiced mummification. The mummy as a horror creature originated in film, unlike vampires and werewolves, which began as folklore. The original movie, *The Mummy* (1932), starred the incredible monster-movie actor Boris Karloff, and is about a mummified princess and an Egyptian who tries to restore her to life. One aspect of all mummy stories is reincarnation — either the mummy or someone who loved the mummified person is reincarnated in another life.

In "Inca Mummy Girl," the mummy is a princess who was sacrificed to a mountain god. This mummy was based on a real-life Inca female mummy discovered in 1995. The mummy was completely frozen, which had helped preserve the body. She was found on Mount Ampato in Peru, hence the name, Ampata, in this episode. Ampata is restored to life because of her overwhelming desire to have had a normal life centuries ago.

Once again, the plight of the "demon" mirrors Buffy's own life. When Ampata was a princess she sacrificed her life, love, and future for her culture. Buffy, too, has given up having a normal life, realizes she might not have a future, and will later sacrifice her love to save the world. The obvious connection is made when Ampata's guard refers to her as the Chosen One. After Ampata is destroyed, Buffy feels sorry for her, finally recognizing how similar they are: Ampata hides a corpse in her trunk, while Buffy hides holy water and stakes in her drawers.

This was another episode about relationships — poor Xander once again falls for a monster, and he is so comfortable around Ampata. Willow becomes depressed when she sees them together (and overhears Xander telling Buffy that Willow is just a friend, nothing more), not knowing that Oz has noticed her, and Cordy once again continues her superficial relationship with yet another good-looking guy for whom she couldn't care less. Her treatment of Sven, telling him to get a "fruit drinky" and ordering him around like a dog, is hilarious. When Willow dresses as an Eskimo — complete with harpoon — we realize it isn't her personality and looks that hinder her from a relationship, but the fact that she doesn't let the true Willow come out (see also "Halloween"). Ironically, it's when she's snug in her parka that Oz first notices her.

HIGHLIGHT: Buffy complaining about the Gilesmobile moving so slowly: "One of these days you're gonna have to get a grown-up car."

INTERESTING FACTS: Dingoes Ate My Baby is a reference to an Australian baby-murder case in which a woman named Lindy Chamberlain claimed a dingo had taken her baby from its crib. Her story kept changing until even her family started to disbelieve her, and she was charged with murder (and eventually acquitted). The 1988 movie *A Cry in the Dark*, starring Meryl Streep and Sam Neill, was based on her story.

DID YOU NOTICE? This is the first episode where we see Jonathan.

NITPICKS: Ampata locked lips with Xander for longer than the others — why didn't he turn into a mummy? And could Joyce maybe, just once, act like she's proud of her daughter? The way she gushes over how beautiful Ampata looks while snubbing her own daughter was downright annoying.

OOPS: At the end, when Ampata is choking Xander, from the front her face has turned into the mummy, but from the back she has her long shiny hair and from the side she hasn't become a mummy.

RESTLESS MOMENT: Xander expresses his concern that girls will laugh at him and pull out his still-beating heart to show to him.

MUSIC/BANDS: During the costume dance at the Bronze, the song is "Shadows" by Four Star Mary, and Xander and Ampata hit the dance floor to "Fate." Both are on Four Star Mary's self-titled CD. (Four Star Mary does the music for Dingoes Ate My Baby whenever they appear on the show.) Score by Christophe Beck.

2.5 Reptile Boy

Original air date:	October 13, 1997
Written and directed by:	David Greenwalt
Guest cast:	Todd Babcock (Tom Warner), Greg Vaughn (Richard), Jordana Spiro (Callie), Robin Atkin Downes (Machida), Danny Strong (Jonathan), Christopher Dalhberg (Tackle), Jason Posey (Linebacker)

When Cordelia and Buffy attend a frat party, they almost become lunch meat for a slimy creature the fraternity worships.

Although this episode was a little ridiculous, the concept of frat boys worshipping a creature in the basement as an analogy for fraternities is hilarious. On many university and college campuses, sororities and fraternities have gotten out of hand. Initiation rituals have caused deaths, the members often cling together with a pack mentality (see "The Pack"), and in some circles, if you don't make it into a sorority or fraternity, you're doomed to an unpopular existence. Meetings often involve rituals, chants, and candles, and to an outsider may appear very cult-like. Hence this episode.

Despite Buffy's rebellious behavior, she has always acted responsibly. When both she and Cordy drink underage and date older men, they fall into a vicious trap that threatens to destroy them both. The fraternity brothers pray to their god, Machida, who represents the fraternity itself. When they thank Machida for giving them all their wealth and possessions, the insinuation is that without their fraternity they would be nothing. Machida could also represent their masculinity and appeal to women — when Xander shows no interest in the "psycho cult," he is emasculated and forced to dance in drag. Machida itself is an obvious phallic symbol, slithering from hidden depths and standing up before the three helpless girls. We never actually see the end of the tail, as if it's connected to the frat house in some way.

Continuing the Willow arc in the subplot, she becomes a stronger character when she stands up and lectures Giles and Angel on how they treat Buffy. For the first time, Giles is forced to recognize that the pressure he's putting on a 16-year-old girl may be too much, and Angel realizes that it's difficult for Buffy to date a vampire — because she's so young, he must be more direct in telling her how he feels about her. When he invites her for a coffee, Buffy takes the upper hand, telling him she'll let him know when she's ready. But it was Willow who put the wheels in motion. This episode had its moments, but was a little too over-the-top.

HIGHLIGHT: Cordy's hilarious parking job and that terrific license plate: "Queen C."
DID YOU NOTICE? Just as Willow had done in "The Pack," Cordelia tells Xander he'll end up as a pizza delivery boy. No wonder the guy won't go to university in season four.

NITPICKS: Cordelia gives Buffy a set of rules to follow while at the party, the first of which is not to wear black. When Buffy shows up in a black dress, why doesn't Cordy say anything?
OOPS: Angel couldn't have entered the frat house if he wasn't invited.
MUSIC/BANDS: As Buffy becomes a wallflower at the frat party, the song is "She" by Louie Says. The track, which plays again at the end of the episode when Angel asks her if she'd like to get a coffee, is from the band's CD *Gravity, Suffering, Love and Fate*. Xander does his girlie dance to "Bring Me On" by Act of Faith, from the band's *Scream* CD. The score for this episode was written by Sean Murray and Shawn Clement, and featured the songs "Devil's Lair" (when Cordy and Buffy arrive at the frat party), "If I Can't Have You" (when they run into Richard at the frat house), "Wolves" (when Richard dances with Cordelia), and "Secrets" (when Cordelia lectures her boyfriend at the Bronze on how to get coffee).

2.6 Halloween

Original air date:	October 27, 1997
Written by:	Carl Ellsworth
Directed by:	Bruce Seth Green
Guest cast:	Robin Sachs (Ethan Rayne), Larry Bagby III (Larry), Abigail Gershman (Girl)

Chaos threatens to befall Sunnydale on Halloween, when people turn into whatever they've dressed as.

A Halloween episode was inevitable sooner or later on *Buffy*, and the result was excellent.

Halloween, or All Hallow's Eve, originated as one of the two great pagan festivals of the year. May Day was a great fertility festival that celebrated the arrival of spring and the promise of great harvest, whereas All Hallow's Eve was the beginning of winter, symbolizing death, cold, and darkness. It was believed that on this night chaos ensued — ghosts of relatives entered houses to be with families, fires were lit, fairies and nymphs created mischief. Yet Halloween was always a celebratory festival, and today exists as a fun event for children.

Ironically, Giles tells Buffy and the gang that Halloween is one of the quietest nights of the year for vampires, and that they tend to stay away. When she dresses as the person she'd like to become — an 18th-century French noblewoman — Buffy plays into the hands of Ethan Rayne, an acquaintance of Giles's whose significance will be explained in "The Dark Age." Willow and Buffy steal Giles's Watcher diaries only to discover a picture of the person Angel used to love. Cordelia then delivers a biting comment — "When it comes to dating, I'm the Slayer" — and Buffy assumes that to earn Angel's love she must become someone else.

Spike earns more of the viewers' respect because of his intelligence when it comes to slaying a Slayer. He watches her in alleys, videotapes her and watches each move carefully, and later he'll call on a group of bounty hunters to get rid of her. There's a reason he's killed two Slayers — he's vicious and very intelligent.

Ethan calls on Chaos — just as the pagans believed Halloween was a night of chaos — and worships the god Janus. Janus — later portrayed as a Roman god with two faces, one looking forward and the other backward — built a city on a hill, named Janicullum, and ruled it all his life. The period of his rule was a time of prosperity with no war and a surplus of food. It was believed that Janus invented money, and his face is emblazoned on the earliest bronze coins. After he died, his people turned him into a god and worshipped him.

It is said that when Janus was deified he became the guardian of doors, allowing certain people into the city and beating unwelcome people with a stick. His two faces allowed him to watch both directions. Perhaps it is because *Buffy the Vampire Slayer* is about a "doorway" — the hellmouth — that Janus is invoked here. Janus has also been used in modern literature to symbolize hypocrisy and the dual nature of things, or as Giles puts it, the division of self into female and male (anima/animus), good and evil. (Giles has always been more Jungian than Freudian.) In that case, the division of self becomes literal — on the outside Buffy is tough, but on the inside she wants to be someone with whom Angel will fall in love; Xander must let Buffy fight the battles, but deep down he wishes he could take charge; Willow is extremely shy and lets very few see her wonderful personality, and inside she's an attractive woman (with amazing abs) just waiting to be noticed. But as she says to Buffy, she's scared to show her true colors: "I don't get wild. Wild on me equals spaz."

The most surprising part of this episode is our first glimpse of Giles as the Ripper. We'll see more of this behavior with an explanation in "The Dark Age," but suffice it to say it was a shocker watching this "fuddy duddy" suddenly become tough *and* angry. Go, Giles!

"Halloween" was an intriguing episode, well-written, with great acting from all.

HIGHLIGHT: Giles's reaction when Willow, who has become a ghost, walks through the wall.

NITPICKS: As funny as it is, Willow opting to walk through walls is unrealistic. Since she doesn't feel any differently, wouldn't she instinctively use the door, as usual? And Giles explains that on Halloween demons lie low and refuse to come out, but wouldn't it be the perfect time for them to blend in? Also, we all know now that Ethan is a complete idiot, but even a moron should know better than to call his shop "Ethan's," knowing Giles is in town.

OOPS: Buffy's house door opens the wrong way in this episode and in "Inca Mummy Girl" — from inside the house, the doorknob should be on the right, not the left. And when Giles tells Willow to leave him and Ethan alone, she turns and brushes a curtain and closes the door. How can she do either of those things if she's a ghost? Also, Willow says Angel was 18 in 1775, which makes no sense. He was 26 when he was made a vampire in 1753, and even if Willow sees 1753 as the year Angel was reborn (which is unlikely), he would have been 22, not 18. Finally, a vampire sneaks into Buffy's house and is hiding in the stairwell, which is impossible because he was never invited in.

MUSIC/BANDS: As Angel waits for Buffy and gets caught up in a conversation with Cordelia, the song playing is "Shy" by Epperley, found on their self-titled album. As Willow crosses the street in front of Oz's van, his stereo is playing "How She Died" by Treble Charger, from their CD *Maybe It's Me*. Score by Christophe Beck.

2.7 Lie to Me

Original air date:	November 3, 1997
Written and directed by:	Joss Whedon
Guest cast:	Jason Behr (Billy "Ford" Fordham), Jarrad Paul (Diego), Will Rothhaar (James), Julia Lee (Chantarelle), Todd McIntosh ("Hi" Vampire)

An old school friend of Buffy's comes to town, but he belongs to a cult of vampire worshippers and wants to become a vampire.

One of the most important issues on *Buffy the Vampire Slayer* is that of trust. Buffy trusts that her friends won't betray her secret, that Giles will be there for her, and that Angel won't bite her. Her friends trust her to save them when they're faced with vampires, and Giles trusts that Buffy won't bail out on her duty. However, that trust has slowly been breaking down over past episodes. In "Reptile Boy," Buffy tells Giles that she and her mother are ill, when she really needs the night off to go to a frat party. In "Halloween," she and Willow steal one of Giles's Watcher diaries, while Buffy makes up stories about what Ms. Calendar said about him. Those lies pile up unstoppably in "Lie to Me."

In this episode, almost everyone lies to Buffy. Xander, Willow, and Angel look into Ford's past without telling her; Ford tells Buffy he killed a vampire; Angel tells her he stayed at home when he actually saw Drusilla. Spike also lies to Ford, and Ford subsequently lies to the vampire wannabes. After all that, Angel tells Buffy to trust him that Ford is no good. Can we blame her when she doesn't believe him?

The vampire club was an interesting aspect of this episode, and it's fitting that the writers would make fun of vampire wannabes, because in Whedon's mythology vampires are so vicious. However, occasionally Whedon *does* romanticize his vampires. Spike and Drusilla have a co-dependent relationship and both are attractive, while Angel — a vampire, lest we forget — is the male sex symbol of the series. The writers mock the Anne Rice/gothic mentality, where dressing in black, listening to Bauhaus, and holding up Lestat as the ultimate leading man is the norm.

There does exist, however, a vampire subculture that is hidden from the general population. While these self-described "vampires" crave and drink blood, they do not change into bats or live eternally or hunt victims. Vampire clubs have popped up worldwide, where these people can meet others with similar interests and engage in "vampire activity."

Buffy and Angel continue to play games with one another. After "Halloween" had such an intimate ending between the two, Buffy is once again making Angel jealous while he lies to her. First she danced with Xander to drive him crazy, then we saw her shrug off his date for a coffee, and now she hangs out with Ford in front of him. To her, Angel's lies and mystery cause suspicion, but it's also amusing to see a 242-year-old vampire going through the same mind games and manipulations that an 18-year-old guy would.

When we discover Ford's plight, it is difficult not to feel sorry for him, because in a roundabout way his fate is similar to Buffy's. Buffy complains that it's not fair for a 16-year-old girl to have to think about death, yet so far she's been able to beat it. Ford is dying and knows roughly how long he has left. However, unlike Buffy who, despite *all* her complaining, accepts that she might die and is willing to sacrifice her life to save humanity, Ford refuses to accept his fate and is willing to sacrifice his friends to extend his life.

The most important element of this episode is that we learn how Drusilla became a vampire. Like Ford, her life was sacrificed and she seeks revenge as a result. However, for the first time we realize how vicious Angelus was. He didn't attack only individuals, but also their families and everyone around them. Where other vampires kill because of their need for blood, Angelus had a sadistic desire to watch people suffer. This revelation foreshadows what will happen in "Innocence" and afterward. The writers make Angel's past so vivid that we just know we're eventually going to witness him in action.

"Lie to Me" was an important episode, and its message was clear at the end: sometimes telling a lie is much kinder than revealing the truth.

ALBERT L. ORTEGA

Alyson and David shoot some pool

HIGHLIGHT: Buffy's stunned reaction when Ford says he thought she was slaying a vampire. "What? Whatting a what?"

INTERESTING FACTS: The movie that Ford lip-synchs to at the vampire club is the 1973 version of *Dracula*, in which the Count is played by Jack Palance. Also, one of the vampires is played by Todd McIntosh, the show's makeup wizard. Jason Behr, who plays Ford, went on to star as Max in *Roswell*.

DID YOU NOTICE? After Willow dashes off because she can't lie to Buffy, there's a poster behind Buffy and Ford for Widespread Panic, a Grateful Dead-like jam band from Athens, Georgia. Someone on the staff must like them, because in dozens of episodes you'll see white and black WP stickers on lockers, walls, and everywhere else in the background. For the longest time online fans thought it meant "Willow Power," until it was revealed the stickers belonged to this band. Watch for more stickers and Widespread Panic posters in future episodes.

NITPICKS: Ford mentions Angel's hand is cold. Is Angel cold like a corpse? If so, the thought of him and Buffy together in "Surprise" is enough to give any viewer the wiggins.

And, Ford wasn't registered at Sunnydale, suggesting he came alone, without his family. Why, then, is he buried in Sunnydale?

MUSIC/BANDS: As Xander, Willow, and Ford shoot pool at the Bronze, the song playing is "Lois, on the Brink" by Willoughby, from the CD *Be Better Soon*. When Ford enters the vampire club the first time, it's "Never Land" by those Goth lords, Sisters of Mercy, from their album *Floodland*. While various Web sites suggest that this song was used only in the original airing of the episode, and repeats of the show feature a song written by Sean Murray and Shawn Clement, the current syndicated version still contains the Sisters of Mercy track. When Xander, Willow, and Angel enter the club, you can hear Creaming Jesus performing "Reptile," from *Guilt by Association*.

2.8 The Dark Age

Original air date:	November 19, 1997
Written by:	Dean Batali, Rob Des Hotel
Directed by:	Bruce Seth Green
Guest cast:	Robin Sachs (Ethan Rayne), Stuart McLean (Philip Henry), Wendy Way (Dierdre), Michael Earl Reid (Custodian), Daniel Henry Murray (Creepy Cult Guy), Carlease Burke (Detective Winslow)

Giles reveals his past as "Ripper," and a demon that he and his friends conjured up in university comes back to kill him.

Just when you thought Giles was the only adult you could trust, along comes a dark past and a strange nickname. This episode was great, if only to see Giles completely lose it for the first time. In a strange twist, throughout this show the roles of Buffy and Giles are switched, and while Giles becomes rebellious, refusing to talk to anyone and caring too much for Jenny to pay attention to anyone else, Buffy becomes practical and authoritative, forcing Giles to talk to her. This reversal is established at the beginning of the episode, where we see Giles's dream, not Buffy's, as we are used to. The difference is, Giles lacks Buffy's gift of prophecy because he is a Watcher, not a Slayer. Instead his dreams look back to a past he'd prefer to forget, although they do signal to him that his past is about to return.

The story of Eyghon, the tattoos, and the relapse is intriguing and acts as a metaphor for drug experimentation in high school and university. The experience with Eyghon got out of hand and one person "OD'd" on the demon and died. Giles thought if he could quit, then he would never have any problems, but he can't hide the marks on his arm. Eventually he has a relapse, separates himself from his friends, and pulls a "lost weekend," as Buffy puts it (a reference to the 1945 film where the main character goes on a weekend bender and isolates himself from everyone he knows). After his "relapse" threatens the lives of those around him — even passing the addiction on to one of them — he quits and the demon leaves him forever. It would have made a great Jefferson Airplane song.

Buffy comes through in a way we haven't seen before. Putting everything aside, she refuses to allow Giles to push her away, and it is she who instructs the others on what to do. Notice how Cordy steps up to receive her instructions from Buffy, something she never would have done a few episodes ago.

The special effects in "The Dark Age" were amazing. Robia LaMorte, who plays

CHRISTINA RADISH

Anthony Stewart Head

Jenny, said the Eyghon makeup almost brought on an anxiety attack: "They put this stuff all over your eyes and ears and all you have are two little nose holes to breathe out of. . . . Things start to go through your head, of seeing yourself jumping out of the chair and ripping the thing off." And the scene where Angel's demon fights Eyghon is superb.

Giles's lack of concern for anyone but Jenny is disturbing, though. He ignores Buffy, never thanks Angel, disregards Willow, Xander, and Cordelia and all the help they've given him, and instead comforts and helps out Jenny. Although, perhaps in this way he acts more like a teenager than ever before.

HIGHLIGHT: Willow yelling at Xander and Cordelia like a parent and telling them to get out of her library. Go, Willow!

INTERESTING FACTS: This episode was rated TV14, but it's not clear why. It contains no blood or especially gory violence. Also, Anthony Stewart Head revealed that to create the picture of the rebellious younger Ripper, they stuck a photo of Anthony's head when he was 17 years old onto a famous photo of Sid Vicious playing bass guitar.

DID YOU NOTICE? "The Dark Age" was not only the first time the gang uses the book cage to restrain a demon, but was the first direct mention we get of Xander's alcoholic Uncle Rory.

NITPICKS: After seeing Philip Henry walking when he's supposed to be dead, why would Giles not tell Buffy what was really going on? Shame or no shame, he knows Buffy is strong enough to handle herself and that she and the gang will come up with a plan. Also, why didn't Giles have his tattoo removed long ago? And Buffy says she's worried her mom will see the mark of Eyghon tattoo on her ... so she wears a tiny scarf and a tank top? Nice try, Buff. Finally, when Giles's phone is ripped out of his wall, it would not have registered at the phone company as being out of order, it would have just rung busy.

OOPS: The Saturday computer tutorial is at 9:15 a.m., but it's interrupted by Ethan and Philip. Allowing Giles time to get there, by the time Philip turns into goop and Ethan escapes, Giles and Jenny probably leave at around 10:30. Why, then, is it night when they arrive at Giles's place? Also, in the computer tutorial Cordelia says the police were questioning Giles about a homicide, yet she arrived after they'd said that. How did she know what they were questioning him about? Finally, when Giles came back into the costume shop at the end of "Halloween," it was empty, but now it's still full of the mannequins Ethan had been using.

MUSIC/BANDS: Score by Christophe Beck.

2.9 What's My Line?

Original air date:	November 17, 1997
Written by:	Howard Gordon, Marti Noxon
Directed by:	David Solomon
Guest cast:	Bianca Lawson (Kendra), Eric Saiet (Dalton), Kelly Connell (Norman "Worm-man" Pfister), Saviero Guerra (Willy), Michael Rothhaar (Suitman), P.B. Hutton (Mrs. Kalish)

Spike orders bounty hunters to come and stop Buffy while he plans to heal Drusilla, but one of the "demons" turns out to be someone quite unexpected.

This is one of those satisfying episodes where the diehard viewer is rewarded. To understand why Kendra shows up, you had to have seen "Prophecy Girl." The book Spike is trying to decipher was acquired in "Lie to Me," when it was first stolen by another vampire. Angel asks Buffy to go skating because of the chastisement he received from Willow in "Reptile Boy," where she told him to be more direct in his relationship with Buffy.

The highlight of this episode is that spooky, ghoulish relationship between Spike and Drusilla, but it begs a very important question. If a vampire is soulless, as Angel explains, and doesn't care at all about others, why does Spike care for Dru so much? In "Surprise," the Judge will tell Spike he senses a humanity about him, so it's hard to pin him down. Dru might be mistaken for a vampire with humanity as well, but she proves that theory wrong when she starts playing with Spike's emotions later. Perhaps it has something to do with who Spike was before he was turned into a demon (see "Fool for Love").

Aside from Spike and Dru, "What's My Line?" is about Buffy's future and the possibilities open to her. When everyone is taking aptitude tests to discover what career they are suited to, it hits them in a big way that slaying vampires will always be Buffy's career. How will she pay the bills? Will she be forced to get a second job? She'll be unable to have a family, Giles may die before she does, and her slayerettes will eventually move on to other jobs and she'll be alone. What kind of future is that? In part two of this episode we'll be given even harder questions to answer.

Willie the Snitch is an interesting character, but one who goes unexplained. How does he know so much about the vampire activity? Has he been Angel's source for all the information he has been passing on to Buffy? Willie's New York accent, along with the way Angel beats him up, is a humorous homage to gangster films.

This was a great lead-up to the second part of the episode, which deals with all of the issues raised in this one.

HIGHLIGHT: Willow's star treatment from the computer corporation. Canapé, anyone?

INTERESTING FACTS: When Buffy asks Giles what is meant by the phrase "the whole nine yards," he conveniently ignores her, probably because the meaning of the phrase is an ongoing debate among etymologists. Various theories have included the length of ammunition from a machine-gun belt, the length of cloth needed for a Scottish kilt, and the amount of cement held in a cement mixer.

DID YOU NOTICE? This episode featured the first time the slayerettes were referred to as the Scooby gang. (Xander refers to them that way when talking to Cordelia.)

NITPICKS: If Willow suffers from "frog fear," why was she able to remove the frog's eye in "The Witch" without hesitation, and why does she carry a green stuffed frog with her ("Inca Mummy Girl")? Also, the fact that Buffy gets into situations where she must be saved by others is becoming annoying. In this episode, "School Hard," and "Angel" (to name a few), she somehow ends up on her back, her eyes grow wide as the demon hauls off to hit her, and then someone saves the day. Why does she let herself become completely helpless?

OOPS: After Kendra slams Buffy into Angel's coffee table, the remnants of the table on the floor mysteriously disappear.

MUSIC/BANDS: As Willow is wined and dined by the computer corporation, the music playing at their "booth" is the Allegro movement from "Spring," from Antonio Vivaldi's *Four Seasons*. Score by Sean Murray and Shawn Clement.

2.10 What's My Line? (Part Two)

Original air date:	November 24, 1997
Written by:	Marti Noxon
Directed by:	David Semel
Guest cast:	Bianca Lawson (Kendra), Saviero Guerra (Willy), Kelly Connell (Norman "Worm-man" Pfister), Danny Strong (Hostage Kid, a.k.a. Jonathan)

Kendra turns out to be another vampire slayer, and Giles finds out that Spike and Drusilla need Angel to help revive Drusilla.

The most baffling aspect of this episode is that Buffy doesn't jump for joy when she discovers who Kendra is. We have watched 20 episodes up to this point where Buffy has complained and pitied herself almost to the point of being tiresome, and now she's faced with an easy way out and doesn't take it. Kendra is a textbook Slayer (if such a thing exists) and could probably handle the slayage on her own. Buffy has rebelled against Giles's wanting to do everything by the book, yet she is jealous when he shows genuine interest in how Kendra does all of her reading.

Willow is correct, though, when she reassures Buffy that the Sunnydale Slayer will always be Giles's favorite. We soon realize that Kendra is more like a robot than a human being, and her entire life has been shaped by her calling. Kendra is like many children who show potential or an extraordinary talent, whether it be in music, sports, or academics. Think of any classical pianist, for example, who is world-renowned. That person has probably been playing since age two, practicing three hours a day at age four, had little to no social life growing up, and is practicing 12 to 15 hours a day as a professional. These people are breathtaking to watch onstage, but probably wouldn't know the difference between Marilyn Monroe and Marilyn Manson.

Similarly, Kendra has no friends, no family, no social life, and no goals other than to rid the world of vampires. She is all a Slayer is supposed to be, but she sacrifices everything — including a personality — to do her duty. Her Watcher won't even let her talk to guys, probably to teach her that she can't have an honest relationship, anyway. Although Kendra's slaying technique is better than Buffy's, Buffy points out that, unlike Kendra, she has emotions, which help her fight harder. For proof, one need only think of "Never Kill a Boy on the First Date" and how angry Buffy became when she thought Owen had been killed. However, Buffy's emotions are a hindrance as well. Later, when Angel becomes Angelus, we'll see how Buffy's feelings for him indirectly cause a lot of grief to others.

Meanwhile, back at the bat cave, Dru tortures Angel with holy water and memories of what he'd done to her. Juliet Landau is so convincing in this scene that we realize just how insane Dru is. After she had lost her family, friends, and soul, her mind reverted back to that of a little girl. Angel becomes her new toy, and with delight she pours the holy water on him, burning his skin and causing the memories of what he did to come flooding back. The joy of torturing Angel seems to momentarily restore her strength.

The final scene is amazing. Kendra and Buffy make a great team, fighting as an unbeatable powerhouse. They stop the ritual before it kills Angel, and Kendra surprisingly helps Buffy save Angel. So why does she return to Africa? If she has no family to return to and the hellmouth is in Sunnydale, it seems strange that she would leave. Buffy is one tough Slayer, but she never would have won that fight without Kendra.

The Cordelia/Xander relationship is both strange and hilarious; this is the first episode where they start necking to the sound of violins, but they both deny there is anything between them. Thankfully, the writers develop the Oz and Willow pairing further, with Willow opening up when a guy she likes actually shows her some real attention for a change.

This episode marks a turning point in Buffy, and from now on she ceases to complain about her "job." "What's My Line? (Part Two)" had all the elements of a great show, and the gothic resurrection of Spike and Drusilla at the end promised us more excitement with our favorite vampires.

HIGHLIGHT: Oz talking about the stranger side of Animal Crackers.

INTERESTING FACTS: Buffy says to Kendra, "Back off, Pink Ranger!" a reference to one of the overly hyper fighters in *The Mighty Morphin Power Rangers*. This is especially funny because Sophia Crawford, Sarah Michelle Gellar's stunt double, was also the fight double for the Pink Ranger. Also, for some reason Jonathan appears in the credits for this episode as "Hostage Kid," which is strange since they've already used his name on a couple of occasions.

DID YOU NOTICE? Buffy tells Kendra to enjoy the in-flight movie on her trip home, unless it involves Chevy Chase and a dog. This is a reference to *Funny Farm*, a film Sarah appeared in, uncredited.

NITPICKS: Why do Kendra's parents know she's a Slayer and Buffy's don't? More important, Kendra's parents gave her to her Watcher when she was very young, while Buffy didn't receive her calling until she was in high school — doesn't that make Kendra the first Slayer? Speaking of Kendra, that has got to be the worst accent on this show ever. (Well, okay, until we hear Angel's in "Becoming." Yikes.) Also, Angel insinuates that he and Drusilla were a hot and heavy item in the past, which she seems to back up, but they weren't — Darla and Angel were the item, and Drusilla created Spike so she wouldn't be alone.
OOPS: Watch Kendra's braid in the goodbye scene with Buffy.
MUSIC/BANDS: Score by Sean Murray and Shawn Clement.

2.11 Ted

Original air date:	December 8, 1997
Written by:	David Greenwalt, Joss Whedon
Directed by:	Bruce Seth Green
Guest cast:	John Ritter (Ted), Ken Thorley (Neal), James G. Mac-Donald (Detective Stein), Jeff Langton (Vampire)

Buffy must look inside herself to try to understand why she hates her mother's new boyfriend so much.

Although "Ted" had one of the cheesiest wrap-ups of any *Buffy the Vampire Slayer* episode, the metaphor was brilliant. Ted is not only a salesman, but a guy dating Buffy's mom, and, as many children with separated parents can tell you, there is a fine line between the two. First the parent will try to sell the new person in her life to the child, telling the child how wonderful he is (Joyce skips that part because of circumstances beyond her control); then the boyfriend must sell himself, as Ted tries to do. He will ask about school, work, friends, clothes, and so on, in an attempt to befriend the child, and eventually will begin sounding like a robot.

However, one of the biggest fears a child has in this situation is that the parent will take more interest in the new person than in the child. Buffy feels this angst more than many children because she has no siblings and the only people she can talk to are her friends. What makes Buffy's situation more difficult is that her friends won't listen to her, either siding with Ted or Joyce or reasoning that she's overreacting. Things get out of control when Buffy "kills" Ted and for the first time thinks she has murdered someone who wasn't a demon. Has her slaying gotten the better of her? Has she lost control of her strength to the point where she'll attack anyone who angers her? And even if she was right — she *was* defending herself against someone inflicting mental and physical abuse on her — it will be difficult for her to convince others; she's not exactly helpless. The irony of the kids all talking about this incident at school is that although they've seen her slay vampires on a nightly basis, they rationalize that and block it from their memories, yet when she kills someone in the privacy of her own home, with no witnesses but Joyce, everyone treats her like a murderer.

When Ted dies, we see the effect it has on Joyce. Children tend to rebel against their parents dating other people, yet they rarely stop to consider why their parents are dating again. Joyce has been left to raise Buffy on her own, trying to steer her in the right direction while dealing with the challenges of being a single mother. Granted, she puts up blinders when Buffy tells her Ted threatened to hit her and takes her boyfriend's word over her daughter's, but Buffy is immediately rude to Joyce when she first walks in and catches them together. And we can only imagine what's running through Joyce's mind at the police station — first her daughter burned down a gym, and now she's killed Joyce's boyfriend.

One of the subtle things about this episode is the references to other episodes. "Ted" doesn't develop the characters, other than to reunite Giles and Jenny, but unlike many episodic television series, *Buffy the Vampire Slayer* has continuity and consistency. So Buffy, Willow, and Xander talk about how the bounty hunters were called off, Jenny says she has stayed out of mortal danger for three weeks ("The Dark Age" occurred three episodes before "Ted"), and Buffy is wrapping Angel's hand, which was stabbed in "What's My Line? (Part Two)." Not to mention the continuing snogathon between Xander and Cordelia.

The ending of this episode was weak. First of all, if you had killed four wives, would you be keeping them in the closet? Wouldn't the families of those women report them as missing and trace them back to Ted? Ted being a robot was strange enough; adding the serial-killer bit was just gratuitous. "Ted" had a lot of potential, and John Ritter was terrific, but the ending just fell flat.

HIGHLIGHT: The hilarious circumstance that Cordy's design sense — that the Persian rug didn't belong in Ted's room — would be the key to solving his identity.

DID YOU NOTICE? Ted tells Buffy that psychiatrists have a word for people like her — delusional — which hints at a future episode, "Normal Again."

OOPS: When the police officer asks Buffy where Ted first hit her, she points to the wrong cheek.

MUSIC/BANDS: The cheesy music playing in Ted's apartment was written especially for the scene by Los Angeles Post Music, a company that writes music for specific situations. Score by Christophe Beck.

2.12 Bad Eggs

Original air date:	January 12, 1998
Written by:	Marti Noxon
Directed by:	David Greenwalt
Guest cast:	Jeremy Ratchford (Lyle Gorch), James Parks (Tector Gorch), Rick Zieff (Mr. Whitmore), Danny Strong (Jonathan), Brie McCaddin (Cute Girl), Eric Whitmore (Night Watchman)

When Buffy and the gang are given eggs as part of a typical high school parenting project, their eggs become more of a burden than they could have imagined.

Even a fantastic show like *Buffy the Vampire Slayer* is going to have a bad episode once in a while. "Bad Eggs" is not one of my favorites, to say the least: it is a meandering and confused episode that attempts to offer up a metaphor for teen pregnancy. The metaphor is unclear, though, and begs a lot of questions. What exactly is that octopus creature supposed to represent? Why is it under the school? How did the health teacher get caught in its spell?

If you really stretch, you can work out some idea of what the show is trying to convey.

The sex ed teacher gives the students an egg to carry around, and the students must follow a checklist — feed it, burp it, and diaper it. Considering you can't literally do any of those things with an egg, most students do what Buffy does — check off each of the points before going to bed. This exercise in futility is precisely what makes it meaningless: it has no bearing on the reality of having children. Only when Willow and Buffy are under the spell of the egg do the burdens of teen pregnancy kick in. They become slaves to it, are tired and sluggish during the day, infect those around them (imagine how many teenagers ask their parents to baby-sit their children), and turn into zombies. To top it off, in many cases the male takes no responsibility (hence Xander boiling his "child").

The metaphor is an intelligent comparison, but the main plot fell flat. The little creatures in the eggs were ridiculous, and the subplot of the Texan vampires seemed tacked on so we wouldn't forget Buffy is actually a *vampire* slayer. However, the Texan vampires were far more interesting than the eggs, and this is the only time we've seen vampire siblings on the show.

The relationship between Buffy and her mother is used as a weak parallel for Buffy and her egg, but when Joyce hears Buffy on the phone she goes ballistic for no apparent reason. She's caught Buffy doing far more suspicious things, so her anger makes no sense, other than as a contrived way to show how tough parenting can be when you're dealing with an unruly teenager.

Although this episode had its problems, it was the script that convinced Joss Whedon and David Greenwalt to bring on Marti Noxon as a regular writer. "Joss and David Greenwalt called my machine and left a message," recalls Noxon. "I was sitting there and heard their voices, and the first thing they said was, 'We've read your script, and we really think it's been wonderful knowing you. We hope you don't take it too hard, but we don't think it's going to work out.' Of course they were laughing by that time, and followed that up by some very kind words, so I was quickly restored to a modicum of self-esteem, but they scared the hell out of me. It was actually one of the better phone calls I've gotten in my life."

One of the few reasons to watch this episode at all is for the great make-out sessions between Buffy and Angel. Their relationship is getting hotter, which offers the perfect lead-in to "Surprise" and "Innocence."

HIGHLIGHT: Cordelia's rant about her bear knapsack.

INTERESTING FACTS: Lyle and Tector Gorch are the names of two of the meanest members of the marauding gang in Sam Peckinpah's 1969 film *The Wild Bunch*. At the time of the movie's release, it was considered the goriest movie ever. Set in Mexico in 1913, it is a Western about a group of violent men who see the age of cowboys coming to an end. Despite an inherent code of honor that both they and the officials hunting them seem to follow, they are eventually pushed too far and invite an all-out massacre on a Mexican town (interestingly, Giles tells Buffy that Lyle and Tector massacred a Mexican village in 1886). *The Wild Bunch* is an amazing film and, not surprisingly, was apparently a big influence on Joss Whedon. The head of the bunch is Pike, the name of Luke Perry's character in the *Buffy the Vampire Slayer* movie, and another member of the bunch is named Angel, who, being Mexican himself, ends up caught between his gang and his people. It's clearly not a coincidence that Joss gave Angel that name, considering his own position.

DID YOU NOTICE? When the gang are in the science lab, you can see the words "Posting Board" on the chalkboard behind them, a tribute to the online community at the Bronze.

NITPICKS: After Buffy kills the mother creature, the squiggly critter detaches itself from Willow's back. Why don't we see the creatures falling from everyone else's back? Shouldn't they be all over the floor? And why is the ink gone from Buffy's clothing and body when she meets up with everyone after the incident?

OOPS: As Buffy fights with Lyle in the arcade, they collide with the pinball machine that a girl was playing moments before, yet the machine doesn't appear to be turned on.

MUSIC/BANDS: As Buffy and Joyce are shopping at the mall, you can hear selections from Mozart's *Eine Kleine Nachtmusik* and *Die Zauberflöte*. Score by Shawn Clement and Sean Murray.

2.13 Surprise (Part One)

Original air date:	January 19, 1998
Written by:	Marti Noxon
Directed by:	Michael Lange
Guest cast:	Brian Thompson (The Judge), Eric Saiet (Dalton), Mercedes MacNab (Harmony), Vincent Schiavelli (Enyos, Jenny's Uncle)

Drusilla and Spike reassemble the Judge, which will bring about Armageddon, and Angel and Buffy try to stop them. Meanwhile, we discover that Jenny has been harboring a dark secret.

"Surprise" was mind-blowing, it was so good. The WB was kind enough to schedule "Surprise" and "Innocence" on consecutive nights when it first aired, so audiences weren't forced to wait a week to discover what happened to everyone. The episode opens with Buffy's dream, one of the most realistic dream sequences ever filmed. Nothing makes sense, everything is disconnected, some elements are events that have actually happened to Buffy and others are prophetic, showing what will happen. The scene was absolutely brilliant.

The writers have set up a parallel between Drusilla and Buffy; in her dream, Buffy sees Dru killing Angel, but it will be Buffy who inadvertently "kills" Angel and resurrects Angelus. Both Buffy and Dru have parties — Buffy's birthday falls at the same time as Dru's coming-out party — and both are the leaders of their respective gangs. Spike, trapped in a wheelchair, is clearly furious with his lack of abilities, just as Xander has always resented that he must step aside while Buffy does all the fighting. Eventually Angelus will make Spike as jealous as he'd once made Xander.

We discover the gang has a traitor in its midst in the unlikely person of Jenny. She is actually Janna of the Kalderash gypsy clan, which adds a fascinating twist to the storyline. Gypsies originated in northern India, but through centuries of massacre and persecution they have scattered all over the world. The Kalderash gypsies, who are from the Balkans and are found mostly in central Europe, are the most numerous. Because gypsies were a migratory people, they were renowned for bringing new inventions, ideas, and folklore to other people. What makes a gypsy element in *Buffy the Vampire Slayer* so interesting is that much of the vampire and werewolf folklore originated with the gypsies. They have a rich oral tradition, and their language is Romani, a highly inflected tongue that likely descended from Sanskrit.

Many of the gypsies' oral stories reflect their anger after years of persecution and misunderstanding. Throughout history, gypsies have been blamed for strange occurrences and subsequently banished from the areas in which they stopped and set up camp.

Within the tribal groups, nothing is more revered than loyalty and cohesiveness, which explains Enyos's anger when he accuses Jenny of forgetting her people. Technological advances and urban culture are the biggest concerns of gypsies, who feel that these outside forces may threaten their lifestyle, and Jenny is a computer-science teacher who seems to have embraced urban culture. The other threat to the gypsy culture is intermarriage with non-gypsies. Thus, Jenny is torn between her loyalty to and love for a people that has raised her and provided her with a belief system, and the duty she feels toward her friends and the man she loves. Faced with probable banishment, she must act and keep Buffy away from Angel — but it's too late. We sympathize with Jenny, but at the same time she is responsible for not having told Buffy about the "one moment of true happiness" bit.

The scene with Buffy and Angel at the docks is beautifully executed by both actors, and even viewers who are no longer teenagers will recognize how difficult it is for these lovers to be separated for any amount of time, much less three months. The acting by Sarah and David in this scene will be surpassed only in the season finale. This was a wonderful, heartbreaking episode that must have had every Buffy fan on seat's edge waiting for its conclusion the following night.

HIGHLIGHT: Oz's reaction to seeing the vampire get staked.

INTERESTING FACTS: The Judge is played by the same actor who was Luke in "The Harvest." Also, in Buffy's first dream, Willow tells the monkey in French, "L'hippo a piqué tes pantalons," a very slang way of saying, "The hippo has stolen your pants." This is probably a reference to the Animal Cracker discussion she and Oz had in "What's My Line? (Part Two)." (Oz had said the hippo was jealous of the monkey's pants and that all monkeys were French.) Obviously Willow has told Buffy about the conversation for it to have made its way into Buffy's subconscious. Also, on August 30, 1998, *Buffy the Vampire Slayer* won the Technical Emmy for Best Makeup for a Series for the work done in "Surprise/Innocence."

DID YOU NOTICE? "Surprise" is the episode where we first see Spike drinking directly from the bottle.

NITPICKS: Why does the bookworm vampire wear glasses? Aren't a vampire's senses supposed to be heightened?

MUSIC/BANDS: This episode was scored by Christophe Beck. The song in the dream sequence is called "Anything," written by Sean Murray and Shawn Clement. When Angel tells Buffy he loves her, "Angel/Buffy Theme" is playing. During Drusilla's party the song she cues is "Transylvanian Concubine" by the wonderfully ghoulish group Rasputina, from their *Thanks for the Ether* album.

2.14 Innocence (Part Two)

Original air date: January 20, 1998
Written and directed by: Joss Whedon
Guest cast (who did not appear in part one): Ryan Francis (Soldier), James Lurie (Teacher), Carla Madden (Woman), Parry Shen (Student)

Buffy must deal with the fact that Angel has become the evil Angelus, and she must stop the Judge.

If "Surprise" brought a lump to your throat, then "Innocence" probably induced a wave of tears. This episode was an extraordinary blend of plot and metaphor, showing one of the possible aftermaths of teen sex. Buffy is devastated when Angel acts indifferent and crass after they had made love the night before, and as her face mirrors the emotions coursing through her, we watch her heart break before us. After 25 episodes of Angel being the good guy, the writers challenge our sensibilities, turning us against him in an instant (I mean, the guy won't even *call* her!). Boreanaz is brilliant as the evil Angelus, exceeding the work he'd done before as the good guy.

"Innocence" was a powerful episode about the complexity of relationships. In early scenes you can tell Cordelia is hurt that Xander still insults her in front of the gang. When Xander apologizes, it's the first time he and Cordy have come to an understanding about something, and their relationship takes a tiny step beyond simply being a gropefest. Willow catches them kissing for the first time and is devastated; she has just begun dating Oz, but Xander will always be her first crush. Meanwhile, imagine how Cordelia must feel as Xander chases after Willow, insisting that Cordelia means nothing to him. Buffy is trapped in a postcoital bewilderment, Giles finds out the truth about Jenny and the discovery causes a rift between them, and Oz senses that Willow cares for Xander and refuses to move the relationship forward until he's certain she cares for him more. Whew! Who ever said love was easy?

One of the great aspects of this episode was how Buffy acts the day after she loses her virginity. Joyce recognizes a strange look on Buffy's face, and Buffy seems to be covering something up. Like many girls, Buffy feels as though the loss of her virginity is stamped on her forehead and everyone will know. Only Willow senses what has happened, and she is sympathetic. Giles, too, will discover the secret and look appropriately flustered. Meanwhile, in other relationships, when Angelus enters the demonic fold of Drusilla and Spike they are both happy to see him, but Spike has no idea what he's in for. Angel will be far more problematic to Spike without a soul than he ever was before.

We instantly recognize what Angel is capable of doing. Where other vampires hunt because of their desire for blood, Angelus plays with the minds of his victims, torturing them for long periods of time. In other words, his return isn't an immediate threat to Buffy, but to all of her closest friends. As he puts it, he will kill her from the inside, rather than taking the pain away by killing her quickly. Buffy, on the other hand, is left with a material reminder of him — the Claddagh ring.

The creator of the Claddagh ring was Richard Joyce of Galway, who was on his way to a life of slavery on a West Indies plantation when he was captured by pirates and sold to a goldsmith. There Joyce learned the craft, and when he returned to Galway in 1689 he designed the Claddagh ring. If the wearer of the ring wears it on the right hand with the heart facing out, then he or she is free; worn with the crown out means that person is spoken for; and worn on the left hand with the crown out means the wearer is destined to be with his or her love forever. For that reason, Claddagh rings are often used as wedding bands. The heart symbolizes love, the crown loyalty, and the hands friendship. The right hand that holds the heart is supposed to belong to Dagda, the father of the gods of the Tuatha dé Danaan, a group of deities in Irish myth who were conquered and became fairies. The left hand belongs to Anu, the mother of the Celts in ancient Celtic lore. The Claddagh ring has become popular worldwide, although it is fitting that we later discover Angel, too, is from Galway.

Although Buffy's failure to kill Angelus at the end of "Innocence" will lead to immense guilt over the repercussions, we can't blame her. She let herself fall in love with a vampire, true, but many teenage girls fall for people they shouldn't, and no matter how badly she's treated, it's difficult for the girl to let him go.

The best part of this episode is the talk Buffy and Giles have in his car at the end. Giles tells her all the things teenagers long to hear from their parents but rarely do. He tells her he respects her and doesn't blame her for failing to kill Angel. However, his talk sounds a little *too* passionate — he agrees Buffy fell in with the wrong person, that Angel turned out not to be who everyone thought he was, but that she's not to blame for falling in love with him. Clearly, Giles also has Jenny in mind. Regardless, this was a wonderful scene, and I was disappointed only that it didn't end with a hug (although that would have been very un-Giles-like). The final scene — where Buffy shares a cupcake with her other parental figure — is sad: we realize Buffy is no longer a child. . . . in one day she's been forced to grow up and accept how difficult life can be. "Innocence" was an amazing experience and definitely in the top five episodes of the season.

HIGHLIGHT: Willow's explanation to Oz of why they're stealing a rocket launcher: "Well, we don't have cable, so we have to make our own fun."

INTERESTING FACTS: The first time this episode aired, it garnered 5.2, the highest Nielsen rating ever on *Buffy the Vampire Slayer*. In other words, over five million households were tuned in to the show.

DID YOU NOTICE? Jenny tells Enyos that they are fools for being so vengeful, and she's right. In "Passion" their vengeance will only compound what Angel originally did.

NITPICKS: Drusilla tortures Angel in "What's My Line? (Part Two)" for what he did to her family, yet now that the demon itself is standing before her, she couldn't be happier. Is this a character inconsistency, or a further indication that Dru has completely lost her mind? Also, if a five-foot-three girl stood on a jewelry counter in a crowded mall and shot off a rocket launcher, causing a huge blue creature to explode into tiny pieces, don't you think that would be a *little* difficult to cover up?

OOPS: Big continuity error. When Buffy goes home and cries herself to sleep, Willow, Xander, Oz, and Cordelia are getting together to break into the army barracks. Buffy wakes up, realizes Jenny knows the truth, and goes to school to force the truth out of her. *Then* we get the scene where the gang breaks into the army barracks *the night before*. Major oops. And when Drusilla slumps to the floor with the vision of Angelus's return, she's still in her party dress, but by the time she's lying on the table awaiting his arrival, she's back in the dress she was wearing the day before.

MUSIC/BANDS: Score by Christophe Beck.

2.15 Phases

Original air date:	January 27, 1998
Written by:	Rob Des Hotel, Dean Batali
Directed by:	Bruce Seth Green
Guest cast:	Camila Griggs (The Gym Teacher), Jack Conley (Cain), Larry Bagby III (Larry), Megahn Perry (Theresa Klusmeyer), Keith Campbell (Werewolf)

When a werewolf begins attacking people making out in Lover's Lane, Oz thinks he might be the creature.

So far we've had vampires, mummies, demonic possession, witches, monsters, even squiggly things popping out of eggs, so werewolves were inevitable. "Phases" takes on the werewolf legend with conventions from different werewolf movies.

The werewolf legend first became popular in Europe, and between 1520 and 1630 it developed into mass hysteria. In France alone there were over 30,000 wolf trials, and as was the case with the witch trials, many of the accused were poor peasants. When people began dying or crops failed, it was blamed on werewolves who were believed to be wandering at night, just as vampires have been blamed. By some reports, the werewolf could shapechange at will, but by others it was beyond the person's control.

The fact that Oz can't remember anything about the werewolf is a strange twist to the mythology. According to legend, even if the person doesn't realize he is a werewolf while transformed, usually something will happen during the day that triggers his memory, and the events come flooding back. In fact, those very memories are what make the existence of a werewolf so horrible — the person must live with graphic knowledge of his crimes, unable to stop them. No chains or prison can hold a werewolf, either, because he possesses superhuman strength. In other words, the gang's acceptance of Oz's condition ignores some very important elements of the lore.

As with vampirism, there have been psychiatric reports of people believing they are werewolves. This phenomenon is called lycanthropy, after the king Lycaon, who was turned into a wolf by Zeus. Most patients who show lycanthropic tendencies or beliefs are diagnosed with paranoid schizophrenia. Sometimes drug use is involved and the patients hallucinate, or there is an extreme mental disorder.

According to folklore, various signs suggest a person might be a werewolf (you can use the following list to check out your friends): having hairy palms or an extremely long index or middle finger; sleeping often because of the exhaustion brought on by his transformation; sleeping with his mouth open because he can't unclench his jaws once closed; often having a pentagram somewhere on his body that mysteriously appears after the first kill. There are several ways to become a werewolf: eating wolf or human flesh; eating the brain of a wolf; being bitten by a wolf or werewolf; being born on Christmas; and on and on. The only way to kill a werewolf is by using a silver bullet (and this method seems to be consistent in both fiction and folklore). In the folklore it is believed a werewolf becomes a vampire when it dies.

In werewolf films, many folklore beliefs have been altered. Oz's condition has more in common with Michael Landon's in *I Was a Teenage Werewolf* (1957) and Michael J. Fox's in *Teen Wolf* (1985), where becoming a werewolf is a metaphor for the changes a male body goes through during puberty. Even Willow spots this parallel when she compares Oz's condition to menstruation (making every female viewer laugh, and every male viewer squirm).

It was a daring move, but a clever one, that the writers chose to do an episode that focused on Oz right after airing "Innocence," which was the pivotal episode of the second season. The last four episodes have either focused on the relationship between Angel and Buffy or at least used it as a major subplot, and there are fans who don't care about them as much as they care about other characters. So it was the perfect time to switch gears and focus on another couple for a change.

Not only does the relationship between Oz and Willow develop, but after referring to Cordelia as a "skanky ho," Willow actually connects with her for the first time, as they sit and gripe about their boyfriends to one another. The very fact that Cordelia is complaining about Xander proves she is beginning to think of him as a boyfriend. Willow can't figure out if Oz cares for her since he hasn't even kissed her, which forces her to make the first move, a huge step in the continuing evolution of her self-esteem.

This episode featured some great references that fans who didn't see the first season might have missed. For example, Oz watches the cheerleading trophy and comments how the eyes seem to watch him back. You would have to have seen "The Witch" to understand the joke there (Amy's mom is actually trapped inside the trophy). His comment also foreshadows the next episode, where Amy returns as an integral character. More important, there is a reference to "The Pack," where Xander slips and Buffy realizes he remembers everything he did while possessed by a hyena. Unlike the bewilderment he expressed at the end of "The Pack," here he sees the possession as something that gave him power.

"Phases" was a strong episode that not only gave us a better look at Oz, but also explored the various relationships on the show and marked the beginning of Angelus's torture of Buffy.

HIGHLIGHT: Buffy attempting to play the weak girl in self-defense class.
INTERESTING FACTS: The werewolf costume in this episode looks more like a real wolf, yet walks like a man, but in later episodes the wolf will run on four feet rather than upright and will have the face of a demon.
NITPICKS: Buffy had just signed the funeral guest book when Theresa turns into a vampire and she must stake her. Considering there is no longer a body in the casket, wouldn't Theresa's family question Buffy if she was clearly the last person to see her? Also, Cordelia's car in this episode has a vinyl roof, but as it was screeching away in "What's My Line? (Part Two)" it had a regular roof.
OOPS: When Xander and Cordy are in the car arguing at the beginning, watch the left side of her bangs — they keep going up and down. However, the biggest continuity error of the show happens in the library right after Giles has loaded the tranquilizer gun. As the camera changes angles, watch how the glasses keep appearing and disappearing on his face.
MUSIC/BANDS: As Cordelia and Willow complain about their respective boyfriends at the Bronze, Lotion is performing "Blind for Now" onstage. The song is from their CD *Nobody's Cool*. Score by Shawn Clement and Sean Murray.

2.16 Bewitched, Bothered and Bewildered

Original air date:	February 10, 1998
Written by:	Marti Noxon
Directed by:	James A. Contner
Guest cast:	Elizabeth Anne Allen (Amy), Mercedes McNab (Harmony), Lorna Scott (Miss Beakman), Jason Hall (Devon), Jennie Chester (Kate)

A love spell that Xander intends for Cordelia backfires, with disastrous results.

"Bewitched, Bothered and Bewildered" (the title comes from a song in the 1940 musical *Pal Joey*) was a lot of fun, and it was exciting to see a first-season guest star return. The only disappointment is that after seeing what black magic did to her mother, why would Amy cast immoral spells? (See "The Witch.") You would think Amy would be suffering from some sort of trauma after losing her mother in such a violent fashion, but instead she seems to be following in Mommy Dearest's footsteps. Love spells are actually the most frequently requested form of magic, but as mentioned in the episode-guide entry for "The Witch," if the spell is impure, its implications can backfire on the witch threefold. Hence Amy's initial hesitation to carry out Xander's request.

Even when an episode of *Buffy the Vampire Slayer* features a self-contained story, rather than one that depends on an ongoing storyline (like "Innocence"), the writers still insert details to keep the action continuous with previous and future episodes. In this case, we discover Angel is especially vicious on Valentine's Day. Unfortunately, he seems to anticipate that Giles and Buffy will discover that fact and he waits until "Passion" to wreak havoc on the lives of everyone around Buffy.

Why doesn't Amy's love spell work? Perhaps she hasn't matured enough as a witch. Giles believes it's because she used Cordelia's necklace and it somehow protected her. However, it could also have had something to do with the goddess to whom Amy chants — Diana, whom she says is the goddess of love and the hunt. However, it is Venus who is the goddess of love. In addition to being the patron of wild beasts, Diana is also the goddess of childbirth. She had several temples that were presided over by priests, and what makes her temples stand out from those of other goddesses is the rite of succession from one priest to another. To become a priest of Diana's temples, one had to kill one's predecessor in hand-to-hand combat. Human sacrifices were also accepted on her altar. But there was no Roman goddess of love and compassion until Venus came along. So when Amy prays to Diana, she is praying to the goddess of the hunt, which would explain why Xander becomes hunted, not loved.

For the vengeance spells, Amy calls on the goddess Hecate, who was originally a kind goddess who promoted goodwill. However, gradually Hecate became associated with magic and sorcery, and would appear to magicians with a torch in her hand. She is credited with inventing sorcery, and statues of her were erected at crossroads, where offerings were left for her. Amy got it right, then, when she invoked Hecate.

One of the highlights of this episode is the huge step that Cordelia takes by telling off her friends so she can be with Xander. Suddenly we realize she sees him as more than just a toy, that she cares about his feelings. Although she and Xander will still argue as usual, this is a big step for her to take, putting them on a new course toward having an actual relationship. "Bewitched, Bothered and Bewildered" was a lot of fun, and perhaps the funniest episode of season two.

HIGHLIGHT: The Buffy rat.

DID YOU NOTICE? Angel suggests that ripping a person's lungs out lacks poetry, prompting Spike to say, "It doesn't have to. What rhymes with lungs?" It foreshadows a later episode where he'll ask, "What rhymes with effulgent?" and we find out what his past was really like.

NITPICKS: It's a given that Xander has done a stupid thing, but why is Giles so angry with him? It's not as if Giles never conjured up a demon like, oh, I don't know . . . Eyghon?!

OOPS: Xander and Cordelia run away from the school in the morning, yet when they arrive at Buffy's house it's evening and Joyce is at home. Exactly how far do these people live from the school?

RESTLESS MOMENT: Joyce comes on to Xander in this episode the same way she will later do in "Restless."

MUSIC/BANDS: As Xander waits for Cordelia to arrive at the Bronze, Dingoes Ate My Baby are playing Four Star Mary's "Pain," from their self-titled CD. Cordy breaks up with Xander to "Drift Away," by Naked, from their self-titled album. As Xander does his strut down the halls of Sunnydale, the hilariously appropriate "Got the Love" is playing, from the Average White Band's self-titled album. Score by Christophe Beck.

2.17 Passion

Original air date:	February 24, 1998
Written by:	Ty King
Directed by:	Michael E. Gershman
Guest cast:	Richard Assad (Shop Owner), Danny Strong (Jonathan), Richard Hoyt Miller (Policeman)

Jenny tries to decipher the restoration spell to bring back Angel's soul, but Angel gets to her before she can induce it.

"Passion" is one of those gems that makes watching television worthwhile. With its subtleties in acting, music, and direction, this episode definitely ranks highly on any fan's list of favorites. Usually voice-over narration is a distraction, jolting the viewer out of the story and reminding her that she's watching something that isn't real. Think, for instance, of the annoying narrator in the commercially released version of *Blade Runner*, who basically tells you what is going on, as opposed to the superior director's cut, which, without the voice-over, is far more powerful.

However, Angel's voice-over in "Passion" is perfect, representing the random thoughts brought on by events as they happen (this device will be used with the same effect in the "Becoming" episodes). Everything the characters do on the series is driven by passion — Giles's love of books, Xander and Cordy in the utility closet, Willow trying to make Xander jealous, Oz's love of music, Buffy's inability to kill Angel. As the narrator says, passion is what drives us and makes us who we are. At the beginning of the episode, Giles tells Buffy she doesn't have the luxury of letting her passion rule her, yet that's like telling her she doesn't have the luxury of breathing. Buffy's only human, and she doesn't *let* her passion rule her — it just does. Even Angel is ruled by passion — his passion for torturing Buffy. Passion can be good or bad, leading us to both follow our goals and do things we regret.

Although previous episodes have merely hinted at the evil acts Angel has committed in the past, now he begins Buffy's real torture, sneaking into the rooms of people she loves and watching them while they sleep. For the first time Buffy wants to tell Joyce she's a Slayer so her mother will be aware of the imminent danger lurking about. By using Giles's spell, she doesn't have to, but Joyce does find out that Buffy lost her virginity to Angel, which, for a teenage girl, is a far worse revelation. She is reminded that she created Angelus out of her own passion (a concept resolved in "I Only Have Eyes for You"), and poor Joyce must give Buffy the Talk, not realizing Buffy is mature far beyond her years. Like most mothers, Joyce fails to grasp that no matter how close a mother and daughter are, there are some things a daughter must keep to herself.

Unbeknownst to the gang, Jenny has quietly been suffering the guilt of lying to them, and decides to use her gypsy knowledge against her own people's wishes. The scene where she squares off against Angel is full of suspense, yet shocking when he actually does kill her. How many other television shows kill off a main character?

David Boreanaz is absolutely frightening, acting in a whimsical fashion before every kill. Even more amazing is Anthony Stewart Head's performance in the scene where he finds Jenny in his apartment. The only reason Giles will survive the physical torture he endures in "Becoming" is because nothing could be worse than what happens here. As he walks up the stairs, his face moves from surprise to anticipation to shock at what he finds. The music playing on the phonograph adds the final touch to a perfect scene.

Robia LaMorte, at the 2002 PBP
with her boyfriend

In the end, Buffy is overwhelmed by guilt, but Giles won't blame her because he succumbed to his own passion by hunting down Angel. However, this episode immediately recalls Buffy's failure in "Innocence," and for the first time Xander goes beyond mere jealousy of Angel and insists that he be killed. For its moral dilemmas alone, this episode stands above the rest. In my opinion, "Passion" ranks with the "Becoming" episodes as the best of the season.

HIGHLIGHT: Cordy's obsession that she let Angel in her car.

NITPICKS: Why does Jenny's tombstone read "Jennifer Calendar"? They all know that's not her real name. Just before Willow finds the fishkabob Angel left for her, she puts fish food in her aquarium. Wouldn't she have noticed it was empty? And how did Angel get into Giles's house if he's never been invited in? Are we to assume he's been in Giles's apartment offscreen? Finally, another nitpick about time. Giles and Jenny make plans to meet at his house, and he leaves her in the computer science room, dropping by Buffy's house momentarily before heading home. Meanwhile, Angel talks to Jenny, chases her through the school, kills her, takes her body to Giles's house, chills some champagne, arranges flowers, puts on the music, lights numerous candles, *and* draws a picture of Jenny's corpse before Giles gets home. Did Giles's car break down somewhere?

OOPS: Jenny asks Angel how he got into the school, yet she'd stopped him in the hallway in "Innocence," has seen him in the school numerous times, and knows that vampires can enter public places. And when the gang meets in the library first thing in the morning, the clock over Giles's shoulder reads 12 o'clock.

MUSIC/BANDS: As the gang dances at the Bronze while we hear the Angel voice-over at the beginning, the song is "Never an Easy Way," performed by Morcheeba, from their album *Who Can You Trust?* When Giles enters his apartment and expects to find Jenny upstairs, that soaring music is "O soave fanciulla!" from Puccini's *La Bohème.* Christophe Beck wrote the wonderful score to this episode, and at the end, when Giles lays the flowers on Jenny's grave, you can hear Anthony Stewart Head singing.

2.18 Killed by Death

Original air date: March 3, 1998
Written by: Rob Des Hotel, Dean Batali

Directed by: Deran Sarafian
Guest cast: Richard Herd (Dr. Stanley Backer), Willie Garson (Security Guard), Andrew Ducote (Ryan), Juanita Jennings (Dr. Wilkinson), Robert Munic (Intern), Mimi Paley (Young Buffy), Denise Johnson (Celia), James Jude Courtney (Kindestod)

Buffy discovers at the hospital that Death is materializing into a monster and killing the children.

It would have been tough to top "Passion," and unfortunately "Killed by Death" doesn't even come close. The only interesting aspects were the subplots — the main storyline was too episodic and looked like filler.

Given that, it was a great episode for fans of the Xander/Cordy relationship. Cordelia finally tells Xander straight out that she's sick and tired of him paying more attention to Buffy than to her. Cordelia's character has weathered a lot of changes this season, although the essential Cordy self-centeredness is still there. She has gone from being a vicious, snobby, selfish cheerleader to someone who cares more about her friends than about her own popularity. In this episode, there is a subtle moment that speaks volumes when she brings Xander a bag of doughnuts. She knows he's guarding Buffy's door, but she cares about him enough to get him something to eat.

This episode also featured the only face-off between Angelus and Xander, and Xander discovers that Buffy and Angel slept together. Angel rubs it in his face, making Xander feel like the lesser man. Nonetheless, Xander holds his ground and forces Angel to leave, reminding him that he'll never be mortal. Xander will do and say some pretty questionable things in upcoming episodes, but we have to keep in mind that he probably has Buffy's well-being first and foremost in his mind.

Buffy's flashbacks to her cousin's death were illuminating, and the fact that when Buffy was a child she played the superhero is very funny. Kindestod itself is a cross between Freddie Krueger and the Penguin, but if there was a metaphor here, it was buried pretty deep in the storyline. It's obvious the writers are offering a possible explanation of mysterious child deaths, but what does that have to do with the gang?

"Killed by Death" was uneventful, and the biggest shame is that when it originally aired, a seven-week hiatus of repeats followed it. The writers weren't exactly tiding us over with this one.

HIGHLIGHT: Willow using her frog fear to distract the security guards.
INTERESTING FACTS: The security guard was played by Willie Garson, now best known as the recurring character Stanford, Carrie's closest gay friend, on *Sex and the City*. Richard Herd, who played the doctor, is best known as Admiral Owen Paris, on *Star Trek: Voyager*.
DID YOU NOTICE? Giles tells the group that death and disease are two enemies Buffy can't fight, and she could be making up a demon that she can defeat, foreshadowing the storyline in season five.
NITPICKS: At the beginning, the gang throws a jacket over Angel's head to stop his attack on Buffy. Why didn't somebody stake him? Also, if Buffy is tougher than most people on account of being the Slayer, how can the flu cause her to pass out? Finally, if Sunnydale is such a little town, as Cordelia had said in the pilot, why does it have such a large hospital?

And notice how it looks like a different hospital every time they go there ("Nightmares"; "Graduation Day Part Two"; season five).

OOPS: Kindestod disappears through a door marked Basement Access, but that sign wasn't there when she looked in the room the first time. Also, the doughnuts Cordelia buys for Xander are from Krispy Kreme, but in 1998 there were no Krispy Kreme outlets in California (the first outlet in Southern California opened in 1999). Finally, watch Buffy's hair when she first sneaks down to the children's ward to peek in. As she peers around the corner, her hair is brushed straight back, but as we see her looking through the window, her hair has fallen forward.

MUSIC/BANDS: Score by Christophe Beck.

2.19 I Only Have Eyes for You

Original air date:	April 28, 1998
Written by:	Marti Noxon
Directed by:	James Whitmore, Jr.
Guest stars:	Meredith Salenger (Grace Newman), Christopher Gorham (James Stanley), John Hawkes (George), Miriam Flynn (Ms. Frank), Brian Reddy (Police Chief Bob), Brian Poth (Fighting Boy), Sarah Bibb (Fighting Girl), James Lurie (Mr. Miller), Ryan Taszreak (Ben)

A poltergeist is haunting Sunnydale High, forcing people to repeatedly reenact a murder that happened over 40 years earlier.

After seven weeks of Buffy Withdrawal Syndrome, "I Only Have Eyes for You" was a brilliant way to return to the show. We discover that Buffy feels guilty not because she couldn't kill Angel at the mall, but because she was the catalyst that took away his soul. When the gang discovers that the poltergeist haunting the school killed his teacher out of love, Buffy becomes furious and immediately turns on him. The fact that he will eventually use her to get out of his purgatory should come as no shock. (See "Where the Wild Things Are" for a more detailed description of poltergeists.)

The way the death scene is played out over and over never gets tiring — as we watch four couples do it (including the original one, in a flashback), it's interesting to see how each adapts to the scenario; only Buffy and Angel switch gender roles.

Giles's reaction to the poltergeist is sad — he so wants Jenny to return that he believes she is trying to contact him through paranormal activity. His inability to accept any other explanation forces the gang to find out for themselves what is really going on, and even as they are carrying out their plan, Willow can't bring herself to tell Giles his assumptions are misdirected. Only when the activity escalates to the point of putting their lives in danger does he admit to himself that he must be wrong.

"I Only Have Eyes for You" offers some essential developments. First, Spike clearly preferred Angel when he had a soul, although Spike didn't realize it at the time. Angel tortures Spike with as much glee as he tortures Buffy, and in this episode he and Drusilla flirt in front of Spike, who is still in a wheelchair. Angel's handicap jokes escalate, and Drusilla doesn't seem to care about Spike's feelings at all, although we can't forget that she has no soul and *couldn't* care about him. Spike's jealousy and anger, though, again reinforce the notion he's different from most vampires, who don't show emotion.

Also, we discover that Principal Snyder knows about the hellmouth, although he seems to be in the dark about Buffy being the Slayer. The mention of city council bringing him in as principal would explain his hatred for the students — he's probably not a principal at all. There's definitely something going on between him and city council — as we see in "Becoming (Part Two)" when he makes a mysterious phone call — and even though it's explored in season three, it's never really explained.

The love scene between Buffy and Angel is beautifully acted, especially by David Boreanaz, who is playing a woman. He displays feminine gestures without ever playing it over the top. For a brief moment, it appears as though we have the old Angel back. In acting out the scene, Buffy is able to put her conscience at ease, for just as Grace was able to forgive James, Angel tells Buffy, "I loved you with my last breath," and we know he means it.

This one was a tearjerker, and a great setup for the season finale.

HIGHLIGHT: Spike getting out of his wheelchair. Woo-hoo!

NITPICKS: Why have we never heard that bell tower before? Also, there's no way the students are blind enough to believe Snyder's "backed-up sewer" explanation for the sudden appearance of snakes on their trays.

OOPS: Willow mentions Jenny's lesson plans and bookmarks on her computer. Did the writers somehow forget the bonfire Angel made with Jenny's hard drive? Also, "I Only Have Eyes for You" was a big hit for The Flamingos in 1959, yet here Grace and James are dancing to it in 1955. One last point: in the opening credits, Meredith Salenger's last name is misspelled "Salinger."

WILLOW WICCA WATCH: This episode marks the first time Willow takes an interest in magic. As she's checking Jenny's computer for her lesson plans, she stumbles upon Jenny's bookmarks to various pagan and witchcraft sites.

MUSIC/BANDS: When Buffy turns down Ben's invitation to the Sadie Hawkins Dance at the Bronze, the music playing is "Charge," by the band Splendid, from *Have You Got a Name for It*. "I Only Have Eyes for You," performed by The Flamingos, plays when Buffy sees Grace and James dancing, and when she and Angel resolve the conflict, the song is playing again. The song can be found on numerous oldies compilation albums, and originally appeared on the 1959 album *The Flamingos Serenade*. Score by Christophe Beck.

2.20 Go Fish

Original air date:	May 5, 1998
Written by:	David Fury, Elin Hampton
Directed by:	David Semel
Guest cast:	Charles Cyphers (Coach Marin), Jeremy Garrett (Cameron Walker), Wentworth Miller (Gage Petronzi), Conchata Ferrell (Nurse Greenleigh), Danny Strong (Jonathan), Shane West (Sean), Jake Patellis (Dodd McAlvy)

Buffy and the gang must figure out what's going on when members of Sunnydale's champion swim team begin turning into sea creatures.

"Go Fish" was clearly a filler show before the season finale, so it lacked the clever ideas and symbolic parallels that most of the episodes feature. Nonetheless, it had its moments.

One of the biggest double standards in high school is the star treatment athletes get while the academics go largely ignored. Perhaps pep rallies are a way of giving football jocks something to cling to years down the road when they're pumping gas, but considering high school is when emotions are at their shakiest and lifelong impressions are made, the eggheads will never be treated as well as the athletes.

In "Go Fish," the writers explore the perks an athlete gets in high school, showing how those advantages have detrimental effects on others. Gage would rather play erotic solitaire than write computer programs, but Principal Snyder orders Willow to pass him. Knowing how difficult it is for Willow to lie about anything, and considering that she happens to be a brainy student who has always worked for her marks, he has given her a daunting task. Meanwhile, Buffy is almost sexually assaulted by Cameron, who is let off the hook because Snyder says her clothing was too provocative. The most disturbing thing about the incident is the lack of compassion the gang shows Buffy. As she stands and complains, they all give her that "won't you please shut up" look, as if being violated is an everyday occurrence. Sure, in that situation Buffy will always be far more dangerous than the perpetrator, but that doesn't negate the seriousness of the incident.

However, this episode also shows the downside to being an athlete. The members of the swim team are treated differently because of who they are, and are identified as Member of the Swim Team #1 and Member of the Swim Team #2. They all know if they weren't on the team, no one would pay attention to them. What happens to their bodies is a metaphor for what happens when you take steroids. It might make you the star athlete, but no one will be able to look past your exterior. The swimmers are completely defined by what they do, and are under immense pressure to be the best for the sake of the school.

The best part of this episode was the giant step Xander and Cordelia take in their relationship. In "Killed by Death" they moved beyond just kissing to actually caring for one another, but in this episode the speech Cordelia makes to "Xander" is astounding, to say the least. Faced with the possibility of Xander turning into a sea creature, Cordelia expresses her normal selfish concerns about how dating such a thing would affect her social status. Yet when she thinks the sea creature in the pool *is* Xander, she tells him she'll still date him and help him adapt to his new lifestyle. Does she say it out of fear? No, because if she truly feared the creature, she would have run, rather than follow him down the length of the pool pouring her heart out to him. Perhaps she has a newfound attraction to him after seeing him in Speedos (easily the most memorable scene in the episode), but her conviction seems to go beyond that.

Despite its lack of depth, "Go Fish" is an entertaining episode, offering viewers one last moment of levity before the series launches into its breathtaking season finale.

HIGHLIGHT: Willow's interrogation of Jonathan, showing her new sense of authority.

NITPICKS: Cordelia and Xander used the phrase "ran like a girl," when in fact the toughest person in their lives *is* a girl. "Ran like a wuss" would have been more appropriate. And at the end, when the sea creatures are swimming out to the ocean, why are they such exceptionally bad swimmers?

OOPS: There are four sea creatures, yet as you watch them swim out to the ocean there are only three. Also, Cordelia says it's about time the school excelled at something, yet way back in "Teacher's Pet" Blaine tells Ms. French he took the championships, and in "Some Assembly Required" Daryl Epps was on the championship football team.

MUSIC/BANDS: During the swim team's victory party on the beach, the song playing is

Naked's "Mann's Chinese," from their self-titled album. As Buffy spies on Gage at the Bronze, the song is "If You'd Listen" by Nero's Rome, from *Togetherly*. Score by Sean Murray and Shawn Clement.

2.21 Becoming (Part One)

Original air date:	May 12, 1998
Written and directed by:	Joss Whedon
Guest cast:	Julie Benz (Darla), Bianca Lawson (Kendra), Max Perlich (Whistler), Jack McGee (Doug Perren), Richard Riehle (L.A. Watcher), Shannon Welles (Gypsy Woman), Zitto Kazann (Gypsy Man)

As Angel and Drusilla try to open the hellmouth to engulf the earth, the pasts of the show's key players flash before our eyes.

The basis of "Becoming," like that of "Passion," is in the title. We see how Angel became a vampire, how he got a soul, how Buffy became a Slayer, and how Angel became her guardian. This absolutely brilliant episode gave viewers something they'd been begging for — a look into the past to see what made these characters who they are. The only downside is we don't see how Giles became a Watcher, but that's because it had no bearing on the plotline, which focused on the Buffy/Angel relationship. As wonderful as it is, though, any look into the past will emphasize a show's inconsistencies (see **OOPS** section).

Once again a voice-over narration is used to superb effect. This time it is Whistler, a great new character whose background and reason for being there seem to go largely unexplained, other than that he's some sort of good demon sent by somebody to help Angel (how's that for specifics?). Whistler is played by Max Perlich — a dead ringer for Thom Yorke of Radiohead — who is best known for his recurring role as Brodie on *Homicide: Life on the Street* and as a character actor in movies like *Maverick* and *Beautiful Girls*. Whistler is the third turning point in Angel's life, helping him become a useful member of society. Because he seems to know what is going on in the past and present, Whistler is the perfect candidate for narrator.

Going back in time is a fascinating experience (although we must thank our lucky stars that Angel lost that dreadful phony accent) as we see the torments Angel has caused other people, as well as the suffering that has been inflicted upon him. Joss Whedon brilliantly connects the past and present in these flashbacks — we move from a helpless Drusilla begging to be pure, to the Drusilla of the present, who is evil and completely out of her mind; Angel being given his soul cuts to Willow and Buffy finding Jenny's restoration spell; Angel watching Buffy in 1996 dissolves to Angel watching her now.

The biggest moral dilemma is raised when Xander voices his anger at the thought of Buffy and Willow restoring Angel's soul. Xander's reaction borders on viciousness, even causing Giles to lunge at him. Is Xander jealous, or does he have a point? Yes, Buffy is in love with Angel and it's the demon inside Angel that killed Jenny, but what if they do restore him? Will he lose his soul again if he achieves *another* moment of happiness? Or can Willow deliver the spell in a way that prevents that from happening? Buffy loves Angel, who was a good person to have on the gang's side. On the other hand, the evil Angelus is a very dangerous monster. This is one moment on *Buffy* where there is no clear right or wrong, and the characters are completely divided. Giles wants to cast the spell to fulfill Jenny's last wish, Buffy wants to be reunited with her love, and Xander doesn't want the spell to be cast, partly because of his jealousy of Angel — all of them are clearly ruled by their passions here. Only Willow refuses to take sides.

The end of this episode is very powerful, especially when the scene goes into slow motion to stretch out Buffy's arrival at the disaster scene. (Does Joss know how to savor the moment or what?) The music here is so effective, it almost becomes a character itself. Kendra is dead, Xander and Willow are unconscious, Cordelia is gone, and Giles has been kidnapped. Just as Whistler says, you can never be ready for moments like this one. Buffy has probably imagined such a moment many times, but she's never been prepared for it. This episode concludes with a real cliffhanger, one that Joss resolves beautifully in the finale.

HIGHLIGHT: Xander's fish-stick reenactment of Buffy staking the vampire.

INTERESTING FACTS: "Becoming" won the 1998 Technical Emmy for Music Competition for a Series (Dramatic Underscore).

NITPICKS: Giles uses something as important as an Orb of Thesulah for a paperweight? As funny as that is (since the shopkeeper in "Passion" mocked the "New Agers" who buy them for that purpose) it seems strange he wouldn't have offered it earlier for the restoration spell, or why Jenny doesn't see it in his office. Also, when they show Angel regaining his soul in 1898, he has relatively short hair, although in later episodes ("Darla") we'll see he had long hair at the time.

OOPS: Angel is 242 years old, which would place his birth date in 1756. Yet in this episode he is turned into a vampire in 1753 — someone's math is way off. The time line with other episodes is thrown off as well. In "Nightmares," Buffy tells Willow that her parents divorced the previous year (which would have been 1996) but were separated for a while before that. Yet in this episode her parents are fighting and still living together in 1996. And in "Angel," Angel tells Buffy he was a demon for 100 years, when it was closer to 150.

WILLOW WICCA WATCH: Willow tells Giles she wants to try the restoration spell, and he warns her that if she tries to channel the black arts, she could open a door she would be unable to close. Uh-oh.

MUSIC/BANDS: Score by Christophe Beck.

2.22 Becoming (Part Two)

Original air date:	May 19, 1998
Written and directed by:	Joss Whedon
Guest cast:	Max Perlich (Whistler), James G. MacDonald (Detective Stein), Susan Leslie (First Cop), Thomas G. Waites (Second Cop)

As Angel tortures Giles and Willow reattempts the restoration spell, Buffy prepares to kill Angel.

What can I say? The master of television has outdone himself again. Joss Whedon, you are a god. This season finale leaves the viewer breathless, depleted, and begging for answers.

Both Buffy and Giles show how strong-willed they are — the more that is taken from them, the more difficult it is to break them. As pointed out earlier, Giles survives the physical torture because Jenny has already been taken from him, which is the worst torture he's ever endured. Buffy becomes a fugitive, gets kicked out of the home, has friends in the hospital, and is expelled from school, but steels herself against it all to fulfill her duty. However, as Whistler tells her, she's got one more thing to lose, and even she couldn't have anticipated what that would be.

The biggest turning point in the show is that Joyce discovers Buffy is the Slayer. Next season will be very different now that Joyce is in on the big secret — the show's dynamic is forever changed. Buffy's secret represents all those things that teenagers keep from their parents, and now that the secret is revealed, it will be interesting to see where Buffy and Joyce go from here. Joyce reacts as if Buffy has just told her she is gay, first acting stunned, then asking if she has ever tried not being a Slayer, and finally blaming it on the lack of a father figure. It is difficult to imagine what it must have been like for Joyce to hear Buffy's news, and what's worse, Buffy doesn't take the time to explain herself. She's in the house and on the phone, leaving Joyce to sit in the living room with Spike and try to decide whether her daughter is delusional. Your first instinct may be to chastise Joyce for her treatment of Buffy or wonder why she didn't figure it out sooner, but ask yourself this: What would *you* do if your son or daughter told you that vampires were real and he or she had been chosen to defend the world from them?

Spike is wonderful here. From his attempt to reason with Buffy (while trying to fend off her blows), to his explanation that Buffy plays the triangle in his rock band, to his assault on Dru, he becomes a multifaceted character ripe for development. While Spike was largely ignored in "Becoming," he returns with a vengeance in this one.

And what of the end of the episode? Do we blame Xander for not telling Buffy the truth? Either he was jealous of Angel or he knew that Buffy wouldn't fight as hard if she thought Angel's soul would be restored. Notice how Buffy held back during their last fight, waiting for the spell to kick in. Do we blame Willow for trying the spell in the first place? If Willow hadn't restored Angel's soul, Buffy would have annihilated him and closed the hellmouth without having her heart ripped out. How about Giles? He is the one, after all, who told Angel the secret to awake Acathla, without which Buffy wouldn't have had to kill Angel. But can we blame someone who was so overwhelmed by love he momentarily lost his senses? The truth is, everyone was looking out for Buffy, but their actions ended up causing Buffy the worst pain imaginable.

Sarah Michelle Gellar delivered her best performance yet, as did Anthony Stewart Head. This season has been a roller-coaster for all the characters, and the writing, directing, and music were amazing. Cordy and Xander kiss for the first time in a meaningful and caring way, and Willow calls out to Oz rather than Xander. Everyone has moved ahead and "become" something new in this episode. Season three will show us they've all come a long way from season one.

All television shows should be this good.

HIGHLIGHT: The uncomfortable silence between Joyce and Spike in the living room, and Xander's speech to an unconscious Willow.

NITPICKS: How did Buffy know that Drusilla killed Kendra? And at the end, Spike appeared to be driving like he was in a bumper car, not on the road. Also, we've discovered that Angel had an Irish (or what passes for Irish) accent, but why did he lose it, yet Drusilla and Spike still have theirs?

OOPS: One of the many things that makes this show stand above all other action shows is

David Boreanaz and Sarah Michelle Gellar

how similar the body and stunt doubles are to the actors. Unfortunately, when Angel is swordfighting with Buffy, you can tell exactly when it's the double and when it's David Boreanaz: just look at the sideburns on the double. Also, notice how Buffy's hairstyle keeps changing during the fight scene.

WILLOW WICCA WATCH: As Willow is finishing the spell, she channels the energy and is taken over by it, allowing her to spew out the last part of the spell in Latin.

MUSIC/BANDS: As Buffy leaves Sunnydale, the beautiful song in the background is Sarah McLachlan's "Full of Grace," from her CD *Surfacing*. Score by Christophe Beck.

Season Three
SEPTEMBER 1998 • JULY 1999

Recurring characters in season three: Eliza Dushku (Faith), Harry Groener (Mayor Richard Wilkins III), Alexis Denisof (Wesley Wyndam-Pryce)

3.1 Anne

Original air date:	September 29, 1998
Written and directed by:	Joss Whedon
Guest cast:	Julia Lee (Lily), Carlos Jacott (Ken), Mary-Pat Green (Nurse), Chad Todhunter (Rickie), Larry Bagby III (Larry), James Lurie (Teacher), Michael Leopard (Roughneck), Harley Zumbrum (Demon Guard), Barbara Pilavin (Old Woman), Harrison Young (Old Man), Alex Toma (Aaron), Dell Yount (Truck Guy)

As Buffy tries to begin her life again in Los Angeles, her friends attempt to keep the demons at bay in Sunnydale while wondering what's happened to her.

I don't know about you, but "Anne" marked the end of one of the longest summers this viewer had to endure. Angel is gone forever (we presume), Buffy's in a deep depression, Giles has been tortured, and Buffy's friends don't realize what happened with Buffy and Angel. As we return to the gang in September, Buffy is hiding out in L.A. posing as "Anne" (her middle name), Giles is desperately following every lead he can to find her, Joyce is fearful of and angry with Giles, who she blames for Buffy's disappearance, Willow is wishing Buffy would just walk back in the door like nothing happened, and the Scoobies are fighting a losing battle against vampires.

Buffy's experiences in L.A. were a metaphor for what happens to runaways and other lonely people in big cities. These kids are begging on the street for money, fighting for food and their very lives, and basically endure a hellish existence that makes them old before their time as they repeat the same mantra, "I'm no one." Much of what is explored in this episode — despair, desperation, search for hope — will become the main themes for *Angel* next season, as he journeys to the city of lost souls to save some of them.

The response to Buffy's disappearance is interesting. Giles seems to be more bent on finding her than Joyce is — she stays around the house hoping Buffy will return. Her bitterness toward Giles is not only her anger that he, as an adult, should have been more responsible, but jealousy that Buffy had another adult role model the entire time, one in whom she confided while Joyce lived in denial for the past two years.

The scene of the gang trying to fight vampires opens the show on a comic note, which is needed since the show becomes so dark. As a season opener, it was satisfying in that Buffy had to admit who she was and reclaim her identity before she could escape the physical Hell she is in (which looked remarkably like Madonna's "Express Yourself" video). Her personal hell will be a little more difficult to escape.

HIGHLIGHT: Oz hurling the stake at the first vampire . . . and not even coming close.
INTERESTING FACTS: Carlos Jacott, the actor playing Ken, will appear in *Angel* in "The Bachelor Party" (as yet another human squareball who's a demon). And some of the footage from this episode — street scenes especially — later appear in the opening credits of *Angel*.
OOPS: When Buffy is fighting in Hell, she's wearing white running shoes. However, when she's climbing a chain to get out, she's wearing different sneakers.
MUSIC/BANDS: Bellylove performs "Back to Freedom" at the Bronze when Xander, Willow, and Oz are there; the song is from their self-titled CD. Score by Christophe Beck, as it is throughout the season.

3.2 Dead Man's Party

Original air date:	October 6, 1998
Written by:	Marti Noxon
Directed by:	James Whitmore, Jr.
Guest cast:	Nancy Lenehan (Pat), Danny Strong (Jonathan), Jason Hall (Devon), Paul Morgan Stetler (Young Doctor), Chris Garnant (Stoner #1)

Buffy's homecoming isn't as sweet as she'd expected, and her friends and family struggle to come to terms with their feelings about her disappearance. Meanwhile, a mask in Joyce's bedroom attracts a group of marauding zombies.

Where "Anne" didn't resolve any of the tensions from the end of season two, this episode had tense moments in spades. It's a difficult episode to watch — we love everyone in the gang, even Cordelia, and when some members gang up on another, we have conflicted loyalties and don't know where to turn. This chilling episode was disappointing because Buffy's friends don't just tell her what they think, they become so fierce they're not even acting like themselves anymore. It's a testament to Buffy's maturity that she ever speaks to her friends and mother again after what they put her through.

Willow, Xander, and Joyce are angriest with Buffy. Cordelia and Oz never lash out at her, but they were never as close to Buffy. And only Giles, dear Giles, realizes the life of a Slayer is so difficult that sometimes you have to walk away from it all. His look of happiness and almost overwhelmed gesture in the kitchen are the most touching moments in this episode.

Is the anger with Buffy justified? Buffy abandoned them without saying where she was going or what had happened, right after dropping a bombshell on her mother and having

ALBERT L. ORTEGA

Alyson and Sarah, friends off-screen as well as on

Giles tortured by her former boyfriend. But at the same time, when she felt the need to return, she gave her friends opportunities: she tries to get together with Willow and is stood up, and she tries to talk to Joyce in the house but Joyce doesn't know what to say. And even when Joyce invites everyone to dinner, they're so inconsiderate they invite most of Sunnydale High and a rock band. And people seem to forget she's a 17-year-old girl whose purpose in life is to protect the world from evil. Not exactly a small task.

The zombies, the personification of Joyce's and the gang's confusion, are straight out of *Night of the Living Dead* (or "Thriller," depending on your pop culture reference of choice). When the gang bury their feelings and try to forget about them, they only come back with more anger and pain. By the time Xander lashes out at Buffy in his oh-so-tactless way, you're ready to slap him into oblivion. And Willow tattling to Joyce that Buffy is leaving is very out of character. Willow is hurt, and we sympathize with her, but because of the setup we've had with "Anne," we can't help but yell "Tell them what happened!" through the entire episode.

And what about Joyce? She proves once again that she'll never win a Mother of the Year award when she chooses to confront her daughter in front of a crowd instead of quietly when they're gone. She insists she's not perfect (well, duh) and then tells Buffy she has licence to yell at her in public because she's had schnapps. Nice logic, Joyce.

HIGHLIGHT: Giles muttering away in his car about how stupid Joyce was for putting up her "pretty" mask.

INTERESTING FACTS: The zombies in this episode don't adhere to regular zombie characteristics. Zombies tend to be reanimated corpses who attack humans because they crave brains, but these corpses simply crave a mask.

DID YOU NOTICE? When Joyce buries the dead cat with the words "Goodbye stray cat who lost its way, we hope you find it," it sounds strangely like she's talking about Buffy.

NITPICKS: What kind of gallery allows its employees to remove ancient artifacts to decorate their home? Joyce doesn't even have an alarm system. And regardless of the fact that Joyce was knocking back the schnapps, shouldn't she have been aware of the underage drinking going on in her house?

WILLOW WICCA WATCH: Willow tells Buffy that she cast a small spell to cover a zit, and when she tried to communicate with the spirit world she felt like she was being pulled apart inside and blew out the power on her block, showing that she's messing with magic she's not ready for.

MUSIC/BANDS: Four Star Mary again perform the songs that Dingoes play at Buffy's party. The first is "Never Mind," from their *Thrown to the Wolves* CD, the second is "Sway," from their self-titled CD, and the third, played when Giles is on the phone, is "Pain," which appears on both CDs, as well as the *Buffy the Vampire Slayer* soundtrack. Score by Christophe Beck.

3.3 Faith, Hope and Trick

Original air date:	October 13, 1998
Written by:	David Greenwalt
Directed by:	James A. Contner
Guest cast:	Fab Filippo (Scott Hope), K. Todd Freeman (Mr. Trick), Jeremy Roberts (Kakistos), John Ennis (Manager)

As things begin to get back to "normal" in Sunnydale, Buffy and the gang are joined by a new Slayer — Faith — who is followed by the demon who killed her Watcher.

This episode features the arrival of Faith, the return of Angel, and a budding new love for Buffy. Many fans weren't sure what to make of Faith at first — our loyalties are with Buffy, after all — but looking at this episode you see how Willow, Xander, Giles, and even Joyce welcomed Faith into their world, while Buffy keeps her at arm's length. Faith is a sad and complex character whose mother is dead (although, other than when she mutters it at a vampire in this episode, it's never explicitly stated) and whose Watcher was killed before her eyes. She has no friends, no family, no money, and nowhere to go, and when she walks in on Buffy's seemingly charmed life it's *Buffy* who gets jealous. We, of course, side with Buffy because we don't yet know about Faith's past, and because we've been aligned with Buffy for two seasons now, we see Faith as a hindrance and just want her to go away. But that feeling will soon change, and the development of Faith's character is the best part of this season.

Meanwhile, Buffy tries to move on with a new guy, but will face difficulties as Scott does

The bad girl we fell in love with, played by Eliza Dushku

things that remind her too much of Angel. And Joyce, the ever-supportive mother, trash-talks Buffy in front of Faith before telling Buffy she can't deal with her "slayerness" any longer. Have some more schnapps, Joyce. No wonder it takes so long in the upcoming "Gingerbread" to realize Joyce is under a spell. Notice how Joyce tells Buffy it's a good thing she was an only child, foreshadowing a certain season five storyline.

One of the most interesting aspects of this episode is the relationship between Giles and Buffy. As he constantly flips through his books trying to figure out how the ritual with Acathla happened the way it did, he keeps hounding a rather reticent Buffy. When she finally admits what happened with Angel, he tells Willow he was only trying to get Buffy to open up, which would be the first step to her emotional healing. Joyce badgers and misunderstands Buffy — Giles is the more caring and understanding "parent."

Mr. Trick arrives in Sunnydale and makes the astute observation that the town is very Caucasian. That also goes for its demons. It's probably an unconscious thing on the part of the writers, but watch how the African-American characters on this show are like the infamous red shirts on *Star Trek* (you always knew when a crew member was going to be killed on an "away" mission, because he wore a red shirt).

"Faith, Hope and Trick" was a necessary episode to move the plot forward, but wasn't very interesting. After such a spectacular second season, the writers seem to be having some trouble getting season three off the ground.

HIGHLIGHT: Oz giving Scott points for saying "mosey."

INTERESTING FACTS: When Eliza Dushku was cast in the role of Faith, she had just graduated from high school in Boston, but had earned her acting stripes as Leonardo DiCaprio's sister and Robert De Niro's daughter in *This Boy's Life* when she was 12, and as Arnold Schwarzenegger's daughter in *True Lies* when she was 13. After such a precocious start, she realized she didn't want to give up her childhood to acting, so she took on smaller roles and concentrated on school until getting the part of Faith on *Buffy*. Even though she appears to be the oldest in the gang on the show, at the age of 18 she is actually the youngest actor there.

DID YOU NOTICE? The Bronze band is Darling Violetta, who later record the *Angel* theme song.

NITPICKS: Why do all of Buffy's crushes look exactly the same — Ford, Scott, and later Parker? Also, why is Angel's mansion still abandoned, complete with sculptures sitting in it?

OOPS: When Angel lands on the floor and we see his back, he doesn't have his tattoo.

WILLOW WICCA WATCH: Giles asks Willow what magic she's been trying and warns her that it's dangerous.

MUSIC/BANDS: As Willow and Oz wait for Xander and Cordelia by the curb, we can hear "Going to Hell" by the Brian Jonestown Massacre, from their *Strung Out in Heaven* CD. In Buffy's dream, she and Angel dance to "The Background" by Third Eye Blind, from their self-titled CD. At the Bronze, Darling Violetta plays "Cure" from the *Kill You* EP, and as Faith talks about slaying, they play "Blue Sun" from their *Bath Water Flowers* CD.

3.4 Beauty and the Beasts

Original air date: October 20, 1998
Written by: Marti Noxon
Directed by: James Whitmore, Jr.

Guest cast: Fab Filippo (Scott Hope), John Patrick White (Pete),
Danielle Weeks (Debbie), Phill Lewis (Mr. Platt)

When corpses are found in Sunnydale that have been mauled by wild beasts, both Buffy
and Willow worry it may be the work of their boyfriends.

This episode used Jack London's novel *Call of the Wild* as its reference point, and while
there are some similarities, Noxon's conclusion is the opposite of London's. *Call of the Wild*
follows the story of Buck, a dog who is kidnapped from his comfortable estate in California and forced to be a sled dog in the Klondike. He's passed from one vicious owner to the
next until he's rescued by John Thornton, to whom Buck becomes devoted. When
Thornton dies, Buck turns his back on civilization and becomes a savage beast, leading a
pack of wolves and showing no mercy to any being.

The book's kill-or-be-killed theme is celebrated by London, and Buck is lauded for
dominating everything around him. As he kills animals, dogs, and human beings, the
reader is supposed to look up to him. He learns no lessons, but rather uses primal instinct
to guide him. In "Beauty and the Beasts," however, the behavior of Pete, Angel, and Oz,
while under their various influences, is frowned upon. Deb, Buffy, and Willow make excuses
for their actions — "He's not usually like this" — while others believe they might have to
be chained up or destroyed. Deb and Pete have a relationship similar to that of an alcoholic
and his abused partner. And eventually, Oz and Angel fight against their primal instincts,
attempting to overcome them through meditation.

In the ongoing catastrophic emotional life that is foisted upon Buffy, she's finally able
to open up to someone who could help her — and then is unable to continue the therapy.
The therapist was essential to this plotline because he represents the psychiatric community, one that believes the mind is an untamed animal that must be controlled. Will Buffy
ever have that ability?

The most interesting aspect of this episode is how Buffy assumes the role of the lecturer
(and, in a way, hypocrite). She lectures Debbie on staying with a guy who's a threat to her
and her friends, and dismisses Debbie's pleas that something else is *making* Pete act this way.
This is the same argument Buffy's been making about Angel for about a year, and will continue to make throughout this season.

HIGHLIGHT: Giles's reaction to getting shot: "Right bloody priceless" . . . thunk.
INTERESTING FACTS: The "passages" from *Call of the Wild* — the one Willow reads at the
beginning and Buffy's voice-over at the end — aren't actually from the book, but are
loosely paraphrased versions of two sections of the book.
DID YOU NOTICE?: Willow's Scooby lunch box? And the anti-violence poster on the wall of
the locker room behind Buffy that says, "Most Women Aren't Attracted to Dead Guys."
NITPICKS: Giles completely loses it on Xander for falling asleep on Oz duty on "almost full
moon night," yet when he arrives in the library the following morning after "real full
moon night" and finds Buffy sound asleep, he doesn't say a word. Also, what kind of adult
sends three kids to a morgue to investigate a dead body? And when Oz changes into a werewolf with Pete, he does so in one shot, instead of the usual gradual transformation. How did
that happen? Finally, if Angel's a wild beast, how does he know to wear pants?
MUSIC/BANDS: Faith is listening to "Teenage Hate Machine" by Marc Ferrari on her Walk-
man. The song is from a grunge/punk CD put out by Master Source.

3.5 Homecoming

Original air date:	November 3, 1998
Written and directed by:	David Greenwalt
Guest cast:	Jeremy Ratchford (Lyle Gorch), Ian Abercrombie (The Boss), Danny Strong (Jonathan), Billy Maddox (Frawley), Jack Plotnick (Deputy Mayor Allan Finch), Joseph Daube (Hans), Jermyn Daube (Frederick), Lee Everett (Candy Gorch), Tori McPetrie (Michelle), Chad Stehelski (Kulak)

The Scooby gang's loyalties are tested when Cordelia and Buffy compete for the title of Homecoming Queen, but Mr. Trick and his cronies have a different evening in mind.

"Homecoming" is one of those episodes that moves the plot along, and if fans missed this one, they would have been pretty confused the following week. This episode introduces us to the wonderful Mayor: where else can you enjoy a character with *Leave It to Beaver* values who plans to destroy the world by transforming himself into an apocalyptic hellbeast? Writers today just don't infuse enough values into their shows and should pay more attention to shows like this one. Harry Groener is consistently wonderful in this role, one that would have been very difficult for many actors to maintain. No matter what the situation, Groener plays it to the hilt all season long. And he also answers a lot of questions we've had up to this point, such as why the police didn't seem to be catching on to the evil or arresting Buffy for killing demons that looked human, and so on. Ah . . . turns out Mr. Mayor knew about it all along.

The title of this episode refers not only to the annual high school ritual sacrifice that involves crowning a homecoming queen, but also to Buffy's own homecoming. When she realizes even her favorite teacher doesn't have a clue who she is, she begins to question her role in the school. She's their protector, but they don't even know she exists (or so she thinks), and this discovery takes her self-esteem down a notch.

This is also the episode where Xander and Willow realize their feelings for one another, a downward spiral that will have long-lasting consequences (see "Wild at Heart"). The episode is great on its own, though, and Cordelia shines — campaigning for Homecoming Queen is truly her calling. Buffy's more academic campaign is equally entertaining (the board with pro and con columns for her opponents is hilarious). Slayerfest '98, while very funny in a WWF kind of way, is a mere distraction to the rest of this very funny episode.

HIGHLIGHT: So many to choose from, but I'd have to say Cordy's version of the Vulcan Death Grip.

INTERESTING FACTS: This episode was full of great guest actors. Ian Abercrombie, who has been in dozens of movies (*Mouse Hunt*, *Army of Darkness*, *Wild Wild West*) and was Mr. Pitt on *Seinfeld*, plays the man who masterminds Slayerfest. Harry Groener, the Mayor, was best known as Ralph on *Dear John*, the timid little nerd who sat in the corner of every meeting and whined about everything. Jack Plotnick, who plays Alan, is an up-and-coming character actor whose recent roles include the gawky interviewer in the film *Gods and Monsters* and Jay Mohr's assistant Stuart on the short-lived but excellent television series, *Action*.

DID YOU NOTICE? The return of Lyle Gorch from "Bad Eggs"?

NITPICKS: There's a line in "Homecoming" that would have been funnier had it not been recycled from "Faith, Hope and Trick." In that episode, Faith asks Oz how he became a werewolf. Buffy replies, "It's a long story," and Oz interjects, "Got bit," to which Buffy answers, "Apparently not that long." At the end of "Homecoming," the exact same exchange takes place when the gang asks what happened to Buffy and Cordelia, the only difference being Cordy answering, "Got hunted."

OOPS: After Buffy discovers the gang has been helping Cordelia, she grabs a bottle of apple juice, takes one sip, and then crushes it, but the juice has magically disappeared.

MUSIC/BANDS: As the gang contemplates renting a limo, we can hear Lori Carson's "Fell Into the Loneliness" from her *Where It Goes* CD. "Jodi Foster," by the Pinehurst Kids, plays during the montage of people posing for the yearbook photos. The song is from their *Minnesota* CD. Lisa Loeb's "How," from her *Firecracker* CD, plays while Willow and Xander get dressed for the prom. Fastball's "Fire Escape" plays while Buffy and Cordelia campaign for homecoming queen. The song is from the band's *All the Pain Money Can Buy* CD. And finally, Four Star Mary performs the song that Dingoes play at the dance, "She Knows," from their *Thrown to the Wolves* CD.

3.6 Band Candy

Original air date:	November 10, 1998
Written by:	Jane Espenson
Directed by:	Michael Lange
Guest cast:	Robin Sachs (Ethan Rayne), Jason Hall (Devon), Peg Stewart (Mrs. Barton)

Buffy and the gang get a quick lesson in responsibility when all the adults in Sunnydale begin acting like teenagers.

"Band Candy" opens with Buffy acting more immaturely than usual — not paying attention to practice SAT questions, cruelly joking with Joyce that she could hop on a bus if she wanted to leave again — but leave it to Ethan Rayne to teach her a thing or two about where that behavior leads.

Jane Espenson — the great writer behind many of the comic episodes — comes up with the brilliant idea of giving us a flashback of the adults as teenagers, without actually going back in time. After eating chocolate bars laced with some ingredient that makes adults act like teenagers, Giles, Joyce, and Snyder respectively break out the Cream albums, the Juice Newton clothing, and perpetual geekiness. The result is absolutely hilarious, especially since the adults retain their present memories. Joyce knows Buffy is her daughter, and Giles knows she is his Slayer. Snyder is the only inconsistency in the episode, as he seems to forget that he hates Buffy with every fiber of his being.

The reaction of the children is equally hilarious. Buffy takes advantage of the situation by taking Joyce's Jeep for a spin, while Xander, Willow, and Cordelia are horrified by what their parents are doing (and by what happens at the Bronze). And I believe I speak for everyone on the subject of the Joyce/Giles coupling when I say, "*Ew.*" Buffy tells Joyce she never wants an explanation of the handcuffs (see "Earshot"), but in general Buffy and the gang wake up to their responsibilities and realize that, if they don't grow up, they could be just like their, um, parents.

HIGHLIGHT: Giles's victory hop behind Buffy when she punches Ethan.
INTERESTING FACTS: Anthony Stewart Head's real British accent is somewhere between the Cockney one he puts on here and the prim one Giles usually uses.
NITPICKS: Where is Faith? She would have had a blast in this situation. It's too bad she is missing from so many of these earlier episodes. And why do they always let Ethan get away? He's caused so much damage and it might seem funny, but people die whenever he comes in with his chaotic tricks, yet no one ever thinks to track him down afterward.
OOPS: When Buffy kicks the box, you can clearly see her stunt double's face.
MUSIC/BANDS: Mad Cow's "Blasé," from their *Eureka* CD, plays as the gang discusses their SAT scores. Giles and Joyce listen to "Tales of Brave Ulysses" from Cream's *Disraeli Gears*. Oz's band plays "Violent," from Four Star Mary's *Thrown to the Wolves* CD. As Willow, Oz, and Buffy watch the adults acting strangely at the Bronze, you can hear Every Bit of Nothing's "Slip Jimmy" from their CD, *Austamosta*. And finally, some of the parents make a dreadful attempt to sing "Louie Louie" at the Bronze.

3.7 Revelations

Original air date:	November 17, 1998
Written by:	Douglas Petrie
Directed by:	James A. Contner
Guest cast:	Serena Scott Thomas (Gwendolyn Post), Jason Hall (Devon), Kate Rodger (Paramedic)

Faith gets a new Watcher, and when Xander catches a glimpse of Buffy kissing Angel, the gang stages an intervention.

It's all out in the open — well, at least Buffy's secret is. And once again Xander acts like he's six years old and runs tattling to the others. But this intervention is different than the one in "Dead Man's Party." Buffy didn't just run away this time; she's been caught harboring someone who has tortured everyone in the room.

It's difficult for us to watch this because the writers have given us only Buffy's point of view, and unlike the gang, we know that Angel has been restored to his good, soulful self. We watch as she and Angel perform tai chi together, and their souls become interlaced once more. Tai chi chuan is an ancient Chinese form of self-defense that in the 20th century became popular as a relaxation technique. It is appropriate that Angel uses it for it stresses mental focus, the alignment of the body with the spirit (soul) and mind, and harmony between the self and the world around it. The technique is as much a philosophy as a physical exercise, and follows the tenets of Taoism, the most appropriate being "The hard and strong will fall [Angelus]/ The soft and weak will overcome [Angel, in the sense that he's more powerful with his mind than fists]."

Buffy learning the technique is her first step toward a more spiritual understanding of her calling. When the gang confronts her, it upsets her — and again, Xander throwing Jenny's death in Buffy's face is just cruel — but she shows a maturity at the end by refusing to hold a grudge. The only person who should be seriously hurt and appalled is Giles, but he has the decency to confront Buffy alone. Head shines in this very touching moment, and despite everything we've seen until this point, we're almost ready to condemn Buffy, too.

As for Xander's outburst, it's entirely in keeping with his character. Unlike Oz, who thinks about every word before speaking, Xander speaks first and thinks later. Probably the most emotional of the Scoobies, he wears his heart on his sleeve. During moments like this, you just want to throttle him, but you don't, because you realize he'll soon say something so thoughtful and caring you'll want to hug him. Xander is the opposite of Giles, who is all tact and very careful with his emotions. Xander rarely has any tact, but he says what he does because he cares about people. He truly is the heart of the group.

Finally, the spectacular fight between Buffy and Faith highlights the differences between them and sparks the rest of the season. When "Gwendolyn Post (Mrs.)" tells Faith she's an idiot, Faith's face completely falls, and we might agree with her Watcher from what we've seen. But think of it this way: Faith was trying to slay a vampire and protect her Watcher from danger; Buffy was trying to save Angel while her Watcher was knocked out cold somewhere. Which Slayer was actually fulfilling her duty?

HIGHLIGHT: Buffy's two-footed kick against Lagos, and all the damage it doesn't do.
NITPICKS: During the Slayer fight, why does Angel just lie on the table dazed and confused? He's gotten up from far worse. Also, Giles's explanation of what had happened to Gwendolyn makes you wonder how the Council could just let a Watcher go after what she'd done. Wouldn't she know too much and be such a danger to society that they should imprison her or something?
MUSIC/BANDS: When the gang's at the Bronze, Dingoes perform Four Star Mary's "Run" from *Thrown to the Wolves* (does this band get serious play on *Buffy* or what?). After they leave the stage, we hear Lotion's "West of Here" from *The Telephone Album*. At the end of the episode, we hear Man of the Year's "Silver Dollar," from *The Future Is Not Now*.

3.8 Lover's Walk

Original air date:	November 24, 1998
Written by:	Dan Webber
Directed by:	David Semel
Guest cast:	Jack Plotnick (Allan Finch), Marc Burnham (Lenny), Suzanne Krull (Clerk)

A drunken Spike returns to Sunnydale after Drusilla has left him in the lurch, and the Scoobies have to come to terms with their relationships after certain infidelities are revealed.

"Lover's Walk" is an excellent episode, one of the highlights of the season. We see the return of our favorite demon, a discussion of Buffy's future (after she didn't think she'd have one), and a turning point in everyone's relationships. Joyce once again does something stupid (if nothing else, you have to love her for her consistency), and at the climax of the episode, everyone's personalities shine through in the crisis situation.

Spike is absolutely hilarious as the drunken, dumped vampire, stumbling all over Sunnydale looking for his revenge. His warped nostalgia — remembering when he and Dru killed a homeless man, crying over Dru leaving him for a lesser demon — are a parody of how Xander and Willow will feel in upcoming episodes. He's also brutally honest with Buffy and Angel, forcing them to reevaluate their relationship and examine whether it's even realistic.

Alyson Hannigan once again shines in this episode as she makes a blunder that will change her life, and as she cowers before Spike when he threatens her. In the weeks to come,

Xander will try to justify his actions, while Willow will apologize over and over and realize her mistake, that it's Oz she really loves. As always with Xander, though, it's unclear whether he is really sorry, or if he just keeps his true emotions bottled up and refuses to apologize for things. Cordelia reacts rashly, as she often does, and Oz is the only person in that scene who doesn't say, "Oh god," but instead remains pragmatic and tells everyone they have to get out of there. He'll reserve his emotions for later, when no one is around.

The trick the director plays on the audience near the end — cutting from the factory to the cemetery — is cruel, but one we relish on future viewings. And everyone who always called Spike and Dru the Sid and Nancy of the vampire world is rewarded in the final scene, as Spike tears out of town screaming Sid Vicious's "My Way" at the top of his lungs. A terrific ending to a brilliant episode.

HIGHLIGHT: The Pez witch!

INTERESTING FACTS: James Marsters explains that it was really his hand on fire in this episode: "I lit my hand on fire," he says, laughing. "I did that in 'Lover's Walk,' which was my one season-three show. They were trying to figure out how to get the stuntperson's hand in the shot so they could do the fire gag, and I said, 'Let me! Let me!' I'm always trying to get into doing that stuff, and they let me. We did two takes. I burned the hell out of my hand, but I had a good time doing it."

DID YOU NOTICE? Spike's arrival, complete with breaking the sign, crashing the car, and falling out of the door, is a parody of his first appearance in Sunnydale in "School Hard," where he broke the sign (because he could, not because he didn't see it), screeched to a halt, and stepped out confidently.

NITPICKS: During the fight scene in the magic shop, why don't Spike and Angel have their game faces on?

WILLOW WICCA WATCH: Willow tries to put together a delusting spell for her and Xander, against Xander's will, showing that early on she was willing to use her magic on people who wanted to be left alone. Spike tries to force her to cast a spell for him.

MUSIC/BANDS: Spike sings Sid Vicious's "My Way" from the The Sex Pistols' *The Great Rock 'n' Roll Swindle*, although the music used for the episode is actually Gary Oldman's version from the film *Sid and Nancy*.

3.9 The Wish

Original air date:	December 8, 1998
Written by:	Marti Noxon
Directed by:	David Greenwalt
Guest cast:	Mark Metcalf (The Master), Emma Caulfield (Anya/Anyanka), Larry Bagby III (Larry), Mercedes McNab (Harmony), Danny Strong (Jonathan), Nicole Bilderback (Cordette #1), Nathan Anderson (John Lee), Mariah O'Brien (Nancy), Gary Imhoff (Teacher), Robert Covarrubias (Caretaker)

When Cordy wishes Buffy hadn't come to Sunnydale, we're given a glimpse of what life would be like if she'd never arrived.

CHRISTINA RADISH

Charisma Carpenter

Taking a cue from Hollywood director Frank Capra, the writers give us "It's a Wonderful Life When Buffy's Around." This fascinating episode opens up so much to us by using the old "What if?" notion, and it's an episode viewers will return to over and over again in their minds as things happen on this series. It's the debut of Anya (or Anyanka, as she's called in her demon form), the patron saint of scorned women. And man, Cordy is one scorned woman.

It's interesting that we feel sorry for Cordelia when she's called "Xander Harris's cast-off" — the term is far more offensive to him. Cordy's friends are cruel to her and treat her differently because she's been dating "beneath" herself, and when they put her in front of Jonathan and tell her he'd make a great date, her face falls and we're sympathetic toward her. But what about Jonathan? Could this have had any long-lasting effects on his self-esteem? (Actually . . . see "Earshot.") Willow feels terrible about what has happened and wants Oz to forgive her, but Xander refuses to admit he's done anything wrong.

The alternative universe is amazing: same characters, different personalities. Oz and Giles have teamed up with Larry and a girl to try to ward off the vampires, but it's never explained why Giles is such a failure and never became a true Watcher. Willow and Xander are excellent as the Spike and Dru of that universe (Willow is as strangely brutal, sadistic, and sexual as Angelus). Buffy looks like Lara Croft and is sporting one nasty scar; her signature line, "I don't play well with others," is ironic considering what we know. By being a high school student in Sunnydale, she has to have friends surrounding her, and she has figured out how to make them a unit. In Cleveland, she's turned into Faith. The Master is back in all his rat-faced glory, and his Brave New World with blood on tap is disgusting, but rather humorous — in a sick sort of way.

While much of this episode is very funny because we know what their world is really like, the ending of "The Wish" is devastating — people who care so deeply about others in our universe can so callously and unknowingly dispose of them in the alternative one. It makes you wonder if the demons and vampires they're dusting every night could have been their friends, had circumstances been different. David Greenwalt mimics Joss Whedon's style at the end of "Becoming" when he slows down the scene for effect; in "The Wish," it's heartbreaking.

HIGHLIGHT: Cordy calling Anya a "scary, veiny, good fairy."
INTERESTING FACTS: When asked if Vamp Willow was paying homage to a certain movie villain, Joss Whedon denied it on the posting board: "Did not mean to make Vampwill like Ursa in *Superman II*. There is NO CONNECTION! (However, I did see *Superman II* six times in a theater. Occasionally I am derivative and lame.)"
DID YOU NOTICE? When Anya first talks to Cordelia, she refers to Xander as "an utter loser."

OOPS: When Xander and Willow are talking at the Bronze at the beginning of the episode, her hair is tucked back one minute and falling forward the next.

MUSIC/BANDS: As Cordelia and Xander try to make each other jealous, the Spies' "Tired of Being Alone," from their CD *Toy Surprise Inside*, is playing. When Buffy follows Cordelia out of the Bronze, "Get Out of My Way" is playing (artist unknown). In the alternative universe, as Willow and Xander walk to the Bronze, we hear Plastic's apt song, "Dedicated to Pain," (not available on CD). As everyone dies in slow motion, the song is "Slayer's Elegy," written by *BtVS*'s Christophe Beck, with Bobbi Page. And finally, as Cordelia leaves Sunnydale High, making several new wishes, we hear "Never Noticed" by Gingersol, from their *Extended Play* CD.

3.10 Amends

Original air date:	December 15, 1998
Written and directed by:	Joss Whedon
Guest cast:	Robia LaMorte (Jenny Calendar), Saverio Guerra (Willy), Shane Barach (Daniel), Edward Edwards (Male Ghost), Cornelia Hayes O'Herlihy (Margaret), Mark Kriski (Weatherman), Tom Michael Bailey (Tree Salesman)

Angel, haunted by the ghosts of his past, makes a terrible discovery about why he's been brought back from Hell.

If "The Wish" borrowed from Frank Capra, then "Amends" goes the Dickensian route of Christmas specials. If you haven't noticed by now, Joss Whedon seems to alternate between Halloween episodes one year and Christmas shows the next. And this is a fantastic — and subtle — addition to that sometimes charming, sometimes dreadful oeuvre of Christmas specials.

Angel is haunted by demons that remind him of the sins of his past. Daniel, a man he'd killed in Dublin in 1838, is the Jacob Marley who begins the ghostly sightings. He and Margaret the servant girl are the ghosts of Angel's past; Jenny Calendar (it was so exciting to see Robia LaMorte's name in the credits) is the ghost of his present; and his nightmare about the threat he is to Buffy represents his future. Luckily, Joss only loosely bases this episode on *A Christmas Carol* so viewers aren't hit over the head with yet another Scrooge rip-off (in fact, you can enjoy it without seeing the parallel at all). Instead of showing Angel waking up and bouncing down the street, shouting that he loves his life, the ending is very quiet and beautiful, as if some higher power intervened to show Angel that he's needed. The climax where Buffy confronts Angel about what he's doing to himself is one of Sarah Michelle Gellar's finest acting moments in season three, and Angel's words, "It's not the demon in me that needs killing — it's the man," are sad and poignant; they set up his quest throughout *Angel*.

"Amends" also examines everyone else's feelings about Angel. Xander is still acting like an ass about Angel (Buffy tells him to stop not a moment too soon), and Giles once again is torn by his feelings. On the one hand he wants to help out Buffy, and knows that Angel means the world to her; on the other, he can't escape the fact that he knows, more than anyone, that Angel was a sadistic killer. After all, Giles has experienced that sadism firsthand on two occasions. The scene where Angel comes to Giles's house for help illustrates Giles's dilemma perfectly. Either Buffy just can't grasp the pain she's causing Giles by asking for his help, or she has decided that Angel's problem is more urgent than Giles's pain. It's one of the best conflicts set up this season, and because Giles is a mature adult, it never spins out of control or becomes a focal point.

The viewer gains new insight into every character in this episode. Willow and Oz trying to make another go of it is charming and sweet, and Oz again shows his maturity in his reaction to Willow's "arrangement." We always knew something was up with Xander's parents, but in this episode Cordelia announces why Xander tends to hate every holiday: his family consists of a bunch of alcoholics who become drunk and fight every Christmas, so he's forced to sleep outside in a sleeping bag. And finally, little things about Faith — like her lying to make Buffy think she's going off to a party or putting up little Christmas lights in her dingy apartment — deepen our sympathy for her character. No matter what she does after this episode, you can't get this image of Faith out of your mind: alone in her apartment over the holidays with nobody around her except the voices on her little television set.

HIGHLIGHT: The Barry White song starting up as Oz walks into Willow's house. Quite possibly the highlight of the season.

DID YOU NOTICE?: Giles keeps a little Christmas stocking with his name on it in the library!

NITPICKS: While I loved the ending of this episode, the timing seemed off. If Buffy left her house at around 8 or 9 p.m. to run to Giles's, and dawn was around 6 a.m., how could it have taken her almost 10 hours to find Angel? And why does everyone seem to be awake (or not to have slept) that early in the morning, but not look tired? And why is there about five inches of snow minutes after it's started snowing (especially if it was really as warm as they were saying it had been until then)? And finally, when Buffy and Angel walk down the main street at 6 a.m., the snow is covered in footprints. How is that possible?

MUSIC/BANDS: When Oz comes over to Willow's house, she's playing Barry White's "Can't Get Enough of Your Love, Babe," from his *Barry White All Time Greatest Hits* CD.

3.11 Gingerbread

Original air date:	January 12, 1999
Teleplay by:	Jane Espenson
Story by:	Thania St. John, Jane Espenson
Directed by:	James Whitmore, Jr.
Guest cast:	Elizabeth Anne Allen (Amy Madison), Jordan Baker (Sheila Rosenberg), Lindsay Taylor (Little Girl), Shawn Pyfrom (Little Boy), Blake Swendson (Michael), Grant Garrison (Roy), Roger Morrissey (Demon), Daniel Tamm ("Mooster")

When two children are found murdered in a local park, Joyce Summers rounds up a group of vigilante parents who want to take back the town and destroy everything supernatural — including their own children.

If you ever needed another reason to think Joyce Summers is a questionable mother, here's one on a silver platter. I loved this episode, and there are few that make me laugh as hard. All *Buffy* fans have had to endure the eye-rolling, "oh god you don't actually like that stupid show" responses from the uninformed and uninitiated, but probably very few of us went to school or work the next day and boasted, "So, last night Buffy managed to bring down Hansel and Gretel." We never would have lived that one down.

Up to this point, Joyce has tried to deal with this new idea of her daughter the Slayer, and her reaction has ranged from confusion to anger to lashing out at Buffy's skills as the Chosen One. So it's no surprise that she finally plays the outright terrible mother from fairy tales who has no faith in her daughter and wouldn't think twice about leaving her in the woods. Or burning her at the stake.

This episode shows the hypocrisy of parents who support censorship without doing any research first. Just as Joyce unquestioningly listens to two dead children, many fanatical groups today censor books and music without understanding what's in them. Of course, these same parents probably read the Grimm's fairy tales to their infants, but hey, those stories are just about witches boiling children alive to eat them. The *Harry Potter* books, on the other hand: now, *those* are dangerous! It's interesting how later this season, the WB committed the very things that were being parodied in this episode (see "Earshot").

The appearance of Willow's mother is wonderful, and it's the first time we see anyone's family but Buffy's. Her professorial criticisms of her daughter about witchcraft, acting out, and the patriarchal nature of children's shows are a perfect example of the parent who tries to understand her daughter through books and made-for-TV movies rather than actually getting to know her.

And finally, the vigilante parents: MOO. Are they completely wrong? Or is there something to Joyce stating that "silence is this town's disease"? By the end of this season, we discover that not only do the parents really know what's going on, but so do the police department and the students at Sunnydale High. So why don't people band together to fight rather than sit back and close the curtains, pretending there's nothing going on out there? Buffy's flip comment that "people die in Sunnydale all the time," so why make such a big deal about it, is more than a little disturbing.

HIGHLIGHT: The last 10 minutes of the show, from Giles and Cordy trying to "work together," to Oz and Xander being heroes, to the climactic kill, to Buffy and Willow attempting to turn the Amy rat back. Pure television gold.

NITPICKS: In "Bewitched, Bothered and Bewildered," Amy changes Buffy into a rat using *exactly* the same spell, and Giles helps her change Buffy back by the end of the episode. Yet here Buffy and Willow fail, and Amy will be stuck in that cage for three more seasons. Shouldn't they have gone to Giles?

OOPS: When Buffy wakes up at the stake, her arms are tied but her hands are free. A second or two later, you see her hands are bound as well.

3.12 Helpless

Original air date:	January 19, 1999
Written by:	David Fury
Directed by:	James A. Contner
Guest cast:	Jeff Kober (Zackary Kralik), Harris Yulin (Quentin Travers), Dominic Keating (Blair), David Haydn-Jones (Hobson), Nick Cornish (Guy), Don Dowe (Construction Worker)

Buffy is put through a test by the Watcher's Council, causing her to lose all of her powers and jeopardizing her relationship with Giles.

This episode's strength lies in the relationship between Buffy and Giles, and finally the direct comparison between Giles and Buffy's father is made. Hank Summers, who becomes less and less competent as the seasons go by, has again turned his back on his daughter (and kudos to Joyce for not falling into the single-mother trap of denigrating her ex-husband; instead she tries to explain to Buffy that it's not her fault). It's perfect that Buffy turns down Joyce's offer to accompany her to the Ice Capades, instead asking Giles if he can go. If he hadn't been so preoccupied with the Council's test, we know he would have (hey, if he could stomach the monster truck show with Jenny, he can do this).

Buffy is far more hurt and devastated by what Giles has done than what Hank did, because she counts on Giles and no longer counts on her father. Hank might have contributed to her birth, but we are led to believe he really hasn't had much to do with her since the divorce, and Giles has stepped in (unwittingly) as Buffy's surrogate father. While Hank probably didn't think twice about standing up his daughter, we know it's tearing Giles apart to have to lie to her. So much so, that he breaks and reveals what he's been doing to her in an attempt to save her life, proving that he cares for her first and foremost as Buffy, and secondly as the Slayer. His diversion from the strict rules of Watcherdom in this Slayer "right of passage" costs him his job as her Watcher, and it also signals to us that just as Buffy is very different from the Slayers before her, so too does Giles have to change to continue to work with her.

Another interesting aspect of this episode is the creepiness of Kralik, the psychotic vampire the Council has found to hunt Buffy. He had a problem with his mother, and it's turned him into a demonic, vengeful monster. He kidnaps Joyce, and even in Buffy's weakened state, she heads over to the house to try to rescue the one parent who really does care for her. At the end of the episode, Joyce shows some pride in Buffy for the first time, having seen how she can outwit a vampire rather than use brute force.

This episode is a turning point for both Giles and Buffy. She has now lived as a regular human being without any supernatural powers. She remembers what it's like to feel afraid, to bruise after hitting someone, and to run instead of staying to fight. While in seasons one and two, she just wanted to escape her life and would have given anything to have not been the Chosen One, in "Helpless" she gains a new appreciation for who she is. She actually *could* walk away from the life, since she is not the active Slayer, but she no longer wants to. Just as she chooses Giles to be her father figure, she chooses the life of a Slayer over the life of a normal girl.

HIGHLIGHT: Oz and Xander arguing about Superman's powers. If they weren't characters on *Buffy the Vampire Slayer*, they'd have a *BtVS* Web site.

INTERESTING FACTS: Harris Yulin, who plays Quentin Travers, has been in dozens of films, including, most recently, *The Hurricane*, *Rush Hour 2*, *Training Day*, and *Bean*.

NITPICKS: The premise of this episode is a little shaky — why exactly would the Watcher's Council put their Slayer through a test like this one? It doesn't help her training, it's extremely dangerous and she has a very good chance of dying, and the experiment isn't reality-based: they're trying to test what she'd be like with no powers, which is ridiculous because she *is* powerful. Then again, in "Checkpoint" we'll see that the Council is pretty much mentally challenged. Also, Buffy says that going to the Ice Capades with her father is a tradition they carry out every year on her birthday, but last year, in "Surprise," there was no mention of such a tradition.

O Father, Where Art Thou?

- Buffy's father divorced her mother before they moved to Sunnydale, and while he remained a small part of her life for the first couple of years, he eventually took off with his secretary, having nothing more to do with the family.
- Angel's father thought Angel (then called Liam) was a layabout and often derided him in front of others. Angel eventually kills him and the rest of his family.
- Willow's father appears to be nonexistent; she has mentioned Ira Rosenberg on a couple of occasions, but we never see him.
- Xander's father is a cruel alcoholic who seems bent on humiliating the family and beating down Xander's self-esteem.
- Cordelia's father was caught for tax evasion in 1999, and the family lost all its money. She moved to L.A. to escape the embarrassment.
- Wesley's father locked him in a closet under the stairs and apparently beat him. While Wesley still has contact with him over the phone, his father still makes him feel worthless.
- Tara's father made her believe she was a demon so he could keep her hidden in the house, waiting on the men in the family, as he'd done with her mother.
- Giles's father, who was also a Watcher, ignored Giles's plans as a child to become something other than a Watcher, giving him a speech about duty and sacrifice and having to follow in his footsteps.
- Spike momentarily believes Giles is his father in "Tabula Rasa," and immediately assumes he must have hated him.
- Virginia Bryce's father on *Angel* tried to scrifice her to a demon on his 50th birthday.
- Amy Madison's father left her family when she was 12, to run away with "Miss Trailer Trash."
- On *Angel*, Detective Kate Lockley became a police officer to impress her father, but no matter what she does, she'll always be in his shadow, and never get any praise from him.
- In "Untouched" on *Angel*, the suggestion is that Bethany's father sexually abused her.
- Faith's father appears to have left the family, and her substitute father, the Mayor, provides her with a lot of love, despite the fact he's an evil demon intent on taking over the world.
- Fred's father is very sweet, and loves his daughter very much.
- Giles becomes the father figure for everyone in the gang, most of all Buffy, and he single-handedly redeems the concept of fatherhood in the Buffyverse.

3.13 The Zeppo

Original air date: January 26, 1999
Written by: Dan Webber
Directed by: James Whitmore, Jr.
Guest cast: Saverio Guerra (Willy), Channon Roe (Jack), Michael Cudlitz (Bob), Darin Heames (Parker), Scott Torrence (Dickie), Whitney Dylan (Lysette), Vaughn Armstrong (Police Officer)

When the gang tells Xander to stay away from the fighting, he has his own adventures that threaten to end in disaster.

ALBERT L. ORTEGA

*Nick and David, close friends in real life
despite playing enemies on television*

Not since "The Pack" have we had such a great Xander episode. Although he's a main character, Xander is always in the background, generally gets only the goofy throwaway lines, and is the one we know the least about. But in "The Zeppo" he shines, and the episode is a very clever look at what goes on in his life when he's not with the others.

"The Zeppo" has all the elements of so many previous *Buffy* episodes: some evil has come to town and is threatening to bring on the ultimate apocalypse, Giles and Willow are doing the research but not telling others what is going on, Angel and Buffy have a "moment" where they pour their hearts out to each other, and Faith fights alone, absent from the gang for a portion of the night. But this time, we're with Xander, the guy on the outside who moves in and out of the scenes, watching the action going on.

The episode borrows its premise from the brilliant Tom Stoppard play *Rosencrantz and Guildenstern Are Dead*. In Shakespeare's *Hamlet*, Rosencrantz and Guildenstern are Hamlet's childhood friends, hired by King Claudius to spy on him. They move in and out of the play, appearing for brief moments to update the king on Hamlet's madness, but throughout the play they're interchangeable. Like Tweedledee and Tweedledum, there is nothing that sets Rosencrantz apart from Guildenstern. When Hamlet discovers a letter they are carrying from the king calling for his execution, he forges a letter calling for *their* execution, and Rosencrantz and Guildenstern are killed.

In the hilarious play *Rosencrantz and Guildenstern Are Dead* (later a film starring Tim Roth and Gary Oldman) written from the point of view of the two courtiers, Rosencrantz and Guildenstern — like Xander in "The Zeppo" — move in and out of the action of *Hamlet* (with dialogue from Shakespeare's play) and toward their inevitable fate. While they are minor players in *Hamlet*, in this play they become the focal point, and we discover what went on behind the scenes. Audiences of *Hamlet* didn't have a clue who the two childhood friends really were or what their motivation was, just as when Xander slips out of a scene, we don't consider what he could be doing. Now we discover he meets up with creepy demons, goes on adventures where he gets into trouble and has to get back out, and has interesting encounters in hotel rooms.

After a season where Xander has been increasingly hostile toward Angel and Buffy, it's refreshing to see him redeemed. We realize what we knew all along: that Xander is a true hero who keeps his achievements (both physical and sexual) to himself. However, was anyone else entirely creeped out by the serenity (almost happiness) that came over Xander's face when he thought he was going to die?

HIGHLIGHT: When Giles sees Xander in the cemetery and says he smells the "stench of death" in the air, Xander replies, "Yeah, I think it's Bob."

INTERESTING FACTS: Herbert "Zeppo" Marx was often considered "the other" Marx Brother, and complained that he was sick of being overlooked. He always played the straight man to his more famous brothers' wacky characters, but, according to Groucho, Zeppo was the funniest of the bunch.

DID YOU NOTICE? Cordy calls Xander the Zeppo and Jimmy Olsen, two references she could have gotten only from Xander. Notice how often she uses television and sci-fi references now. At least she got some good fodder for insults from their relationship.

NITPICKS: Willow says to Buffy, "It went good?" You'd think Willow of all people would grimace at such awful grammar. . . .

OOPS: That bomb seems to count down awfully slowly. At one point, it's at 11 seconds, then it's at 12 seconds (is it moving backward?) and about 15 seconds later, it's down to four seconds.

WILLOW WICCA WATCH: In one of the rare glimpses at the apocalypse that we do get, Giles argues with Willow that she can't cast a spell, because he's worried something will go wrong. Yet earlier, she did a clouding spell with no problem. It seems that if Willow's magic is helpful to the gang, they overlook it.

MUSIC/BANDS: As Xander comes up to the girls in his uncle's car, we hear "Dodgems" by Sound Stage Ltd., from the compilation CD *Alternative Volume I*. When Xander meets the blonde who is interested in his car, we hear an untitled song from Los Angeles Post Music (not available on CD). When he talks to her in the Bronze, "G-Song" by Supergrass is playing, from their *In It for the Money* CD. Tricky Woo's "Easy," from their *Enemy Is Real* disc, plays while Xander drives the zombies around town. At the end of the episode, Extreme Music's "For the Glory" plays (not available on CD).

3.14 Bad Girls

Original air date:	February 2, 1999
Written by:	Douglas Petrie
Directed by:	Michael Lange
Guest cast:	K. Todd Freeman (Mr. Trick), Jack Plotnick (Allan Finch), Christian Clemenson (Balthazar), Alex Skuby (Vincent), Wendy Clifford (Mrs. Taggert)

A line is crossed when Buffy joins Faith for a night of slaying and partying.

An excellent episode that shows the inherent differences between Buffy and Faith, "Bad Girls" marks a turning point in the season. They're both Slayers, but they are polar opposites on just about every level. Faith sees her calling as a blessing, the best thing that ever happened to her; Buffy wishes she could just lead a normal life. Faith dresses in black leather; Buffy wears colorful little outfits with matching flowers in her hair. Faith goes into battle with no plan; Buffy plans things out ahead of time to avoid errors.

To parallel our Slayers, we are introduced to a new Watcher, Wesley Wyndam-Pryce, a great addition to the show. While at first he seemed like a bit of a windbag, his character offers both a parallel and a contrast to Giles, also British, also a Watcher, also careful. Wesley is who Giles was at the beginning of season one, and from this point on watch Giles align himself with the gang and insult Wesley the same way they used to insult him.

The differences between the two Slayers and two Watchers become apparent when they're faced with danger. When Wesley and Giles are facing Balthazar (who looks like an

CHRISTINA RADISH

Alexis Denisof, looking very unlike the stuffy Wesley Wyndam-Pryce

obese version of the Master), Giles fights for himself while Wesley desperately waits for his Slayer to come and save him. Buffy is hurled back into her own world when Faith makes a fatal error, and she reverts back to her own values and morals to deal with the situation.

Because Buffy is an impressionable young woman trying to find herself, Faith appeals to her because she's something different. Just as Willow is coming out of her shell dating a guitarist and learning magic, Buffy wants to be dangerous for a while. But in doing so, she alienates her friends — once again Willow is left behind and has to deal with Buffy's rejection of her — and realizes she's made a mistake. For the first time, she's involved in the murder of an innocent human being, and she knows she wasn't meant to be a bad girl.

It's in this episode, where Faith seems at her most callous, that we suddenly start feeling sorry for her. That sympathy is what made the last third of the season the best storyline on television that year.

HIGHLIGHT: When Balthazar says to Giles and Wesley they know what he wants, Giles's response is priceless: "If it's for me to scrub those hard-to-reach areas, I'd like to request that you kill me now."

NITPICKS: Willow calls herself a great Wicca (it's the term everyone uses on the show) but Wicca is the name of the religion. The proper term for one who practices Wicca is a Wiccan. Also, why isn't Angel electrocuted when the live wire touches the person who's holding him? And Giles mentions a retreat that the Watchers go on every year, and he wishes he'd get invited. Wouldn't he have been the star Watcher, considering he had the one and only Slayer in the world for the longest time? And when Buffy gives Wesley the rundown of her fight with the Eliminati, she says the guy with the sword probably wasn't with the other two. Why would she say that, if they were all together and wearing the same outfits? And finally, why the heck doesn't Balthazar get a deeper tank of water?

WILLOW WICCA WATCH: Willow gives Buffy a protection spell as a gift, but adds lavender to hide the smell of the ingredients, showing she's able to alter spells slightly for pragmatic purposes.

MUSIC/BANDS: As Faith and Buffy dance at the Bronze, Curve's "Chinese Burn" from their *Come Clean* CD plays.

3.15 Consequences

Original air date:	February 16, 1999
Written by:	Marti Noxon
Directed by:	Michael Gershman
Guest cast:	K. Todd Freeman (Mr. Trick), Jack Plotnick (Allan Finch), James G. Macdonald (Detective Stein), Amy Powell (TV News Reporter), Patricia Place (Woman in Alley)

When Giles and the gang discover what Faith did, each tries to get through to her in his or her own way.

Another great episode for the development of Faith's character. Where Buffy is having nightmares about Allan's death, Faith is pretending it doesn't bother her, but it's clear she's just putting on a brave, tough face. Buffy, Xander, Giles, Angel, and Wesley all try to "help" out Faith because each believes he or she understands what Faith is going through. The problem is, none of these people tried to befriend Faith on unconditional terms before, and they really don't know where she's coming from. They don't know anything about her family life or what makes her tick; all they know is the little she told them at the beginning, and then her guard went up and they lost interest. Why would Faith listen to Buffy, who didn't like her until she realized Faith wasn't a threat to her? Only when Buffy realized her friends were *her* friends first and foremost did she start to hang out with Faith. Xander's "connection" with Faith is based on a mistaken assumption, and Angel tries to get through to her by drawing a comparison between Faith and himself as a demon. He believes that, like him, once she "gets the taste" of killing, it'll be in her blood. (Nice way to compare her to a dog, there, Angel.)

The moment where Xander explains that connection to everyone, and Willow realizes he and Faith have slept together, is painful — we're momentarily removed from the situation at hand and remember that these are teenagers trying to deal with their problems. As Willow sits in the bathroom crying, our hearts go out to her. It doesn't matter that she's now in a solid relationship with Oz, all that matters to her at that moment is that her first big crush has once again disappointed her. First he dated Cordelia, whom they both hated, and now he's slept with Faith, the enemy. Willow can't help but wonder why he wasn't attracted to her when he was single.

Eliza Dushku shines in this and subsequent episodes as the bad girl with a conscience who wears a mask so no one can figure her out. Faith is as complex a character as Buffy and Angel are a couple, and they all assume they know what she's thinking. It's no wonder she makes the decision she does at the end of this episode. When Buffy's in big trouble, she can cry on Willow's sympathetic shoulder or turn to understanding Giles, but Faith has no such companionship . . . until Mayor Wilkins comes along.

HIGHLIGHT: Cordy calling Wesley "Giles: The Next Generation" (again, a reference she's gleaned from Xander).
DID YOU NOTICE? The detective in this episode was the same one who questioned Buffy in "Ted" and questioned Joyce about Buffy in "Becoming (Part Two)." You'd think he'd have even more of a yen to catch Buffy in the act than Snyder does.
NITPICKS: Faith says her motto is "I see, I want, I take," but in "Bad Girls" it had been "Want, Take, Have." And couldn't Buffy have been a little gentler when breaking it to Xander that the guys Faith sleeps with are a "big joke" to her? Would she have said something like that to Willow? And finally, how does Wesley unlock Faith's chains? He has a key, but he didn't seem to get it from Angel.
OOPS: There's a major continuity problem in this episode. When the detective questions Faith and Buffy, he refers to the murder as happening the night before, when it appears to have happened two days earlier: the murder occurred, then Buffy went to Faith's apartment the next day (both happened in the previous episode), then she had the nightmare that night, then she went to school, and *then* the detectives questioned them. Also, Giles's calendar says April, when in fact it's February (we know this because in "Bad Girls" the Mayor says it was the commencement of the 100 days until the Ascension).
MUSIC/BANDS: As Willow cries in the bathroom, we hear Kathleen Wilhoite's "Wish We Never Met," from her *Pitch Like a Girl* CD.

3.16 Doppelgängland

Original air date:	February 23, 1999
Written and directed by:	Joss Whedon
Guest cast:	Emma Caulfield (Anya), Jason Hall (Devon), Ethan Erickson (Percy West), Andy Umberger (D'Hoffryn), Corey Michael Blake (Bartender), Megan Gray (Sandy), Michael Nagy (Alfonse), Norma Michael (Older woman)

In a botched attempt to regain her immortality, Anya brings Willow's vampiric alter ego into the gang's reality.

"Doppelgänger" is a German word literally meaning "double-goer," and in today's terms, an alter ego. The idea that a passionate version of ourselves was hidden within our more rational psyche was argued throughout the 19th century by several theorists, and the theory manifested itself in Romantic works such as Mary Shelley's *Frankenstein* and

Robert Louis Stevenson's *Dr. Jekyll and Mr. Hyde*. The idea lies at the center of this episode and the entirety of season three.

Just as evil, sexy, and "kinda gay" Willow is the doppelgänger of our Willow, who is quiet and shy, so too is Faith the alter ego of Buffy and Mayor Wilkins the alter ego of Giles. In this mad pairing of boss and daughter/warrior that goes on between Faith and Wilkins we see the same relationship as that between Giles and Buffy. Just as Giles reacts violently against the Mayor for threatening Buffy ("Graduation Day, Part One"), Mayor Wilkins tries to take revenge against Buffy for hurting Faith ("Graduation Day, Part Two"). If Buffy and Giles had given in to passion over reason, they could have been Wilkins and Faith; there's a very fine line separating the two.

Anya is back, and for once she's getting revenge for something that was done to her. She will eventually become a sweet and lovable character, but considering the mojo she tries to work on Willow in this episode, it's no wonder Willow will appear to hate her for a very, very long time.

When Angel starts to correct Buffy's statement that vampires don't have any of the personality of the original person, we know we could be in for quite a ride for Willow's ongoing character development. Alyson Hannigan is superb as Willow and evil Willow, and watching Willow pretending to be evil Willow is a delight. From her attempts to be sexy to her little wave at Oz, the scene in the Bronze is one of the highlights of the season. Hannigan has proven herself an actress who can rip your heart out when she's sobbing and have you doubled over when she's being funny. Sarah Michelle Gellar may be the star of the show, but Hannigan is truly the acting tour de force.

HIGHLIGHT: Giles's reaction when he realizes Willow isn't dead.

MUSIC/BANDS: When the other Willow first gets to the Bronze and is confused, K's Choice is onstage performing "Virgin State of Mind" from the *Buffy the Vampire Slayer* soundtrack. Later at the Bronze we hear Spectator Pump's "Priced 2 Move" from their *Styrofoam Archives* CD.

3.17 Enemies

Original air date:	March 16, 1999
Written by:	Douglas Petrie
Directed by:	David Grossman
Guest cast:	Michael Manasseri (Horned Demon), Gary Bullock (Shrouded Sorcerer)

Faith tricks Angel in order to make him lose his soul and become Angelus again, hoping that he'll fight on her side.

"Enemies" was the episode that turns that final corner and sends the season racing toward its thrilling conclusion. The gang now knows that Faith is evil, but the audience has already begun to sympathize with her. While torturing Buffy, Faith sneers in her face about why she dislikes her so much, but in doing so, opens up and lets us know why she feels so much anger. She thinks the others shunned her, and that no matter how hard she worked, Buffy was always seen as the hero and Faith the sidekick. We also find out about her parents; while we've always felt bad for Buffy because she had to go through a divorce at such a young age, Faith's past is far more harrowing, and Buffy's background suddenly seems pretty cushy.

In "Consequences," Xander thought he'd had a connection with Faith for all the wrong reasons, but in this episode we discover they actually do have a lot in common. Both have alcoholic parents, and both reached out to find friends. Xander was accepted into the fold; Faith was not, because Buffy was jealous and didn't want her to be too close. Both carry the anger within them, and Xander's anger comes out when he feels he can be superior. (His "I told you so" happy dance is so childish that we're shocked he would actually do it.) Faith, on the other hand, pretends to be friends with people but then latches onto the first person who will accept her for who she is (Wilkins). Xander's faults are pointed out to him and he refuses to admit he was wrong, often throwing it back in the other person's face. Faith is tortured inwardly about what she does, and eventually she apologizes. The difference is Xander values his loyalty to his friends above everything else because he has their acceptance, while Faith is so busy craving acceptance that she'll stab people in the back to get it.

The relationship between Angel and Buffy takes its first stumble toward its inevitable end in this episode. On the one hand, seeing Angel as Angelus is so painful for Buffy because his demon side haunted her only one year before. One of Buffy's biggest fears is that Faith could move in on her territory and claim her friends, so when Angel and Faith are canoodling in front of her, it's almost too much for her to handle. On the other hand, didn't he do everything he did because Buffy needed him to? How is he supposed to help out when every time he does he's punished for it? Buffy tells him she needs some time apart, and doesn't seem to understand how shattering that is to him; watch how *she* reacts when he does the same thing to her in "The Prom." Sometimes it's hard to forget that he's an adult who's been around for 250 years, and she's a passionate teenager who often doesn't think before speaking.

HIGHLIGHT: The looks on Buffy's and Angel's faces when they leave *Le Banquet d'Amelia*.
INTERESTING FACTS: I looked everywhere for mention of this film's existence, but it appears to have been made up for the show.
DID YOU NOTICE? Faith knew exactly where the light switch was when she went to the demon's apartment the second time. Too bad Buffy didn't notice that subtle little gesture.
NITPICKS: Why didn't Giles fill everyone in on what was going on with Angelus? Willow, Xander, and Cordy clearly have no idea, and they could have caused some major problems. It's also unclear at what point Buffy found out, since she seems to suspect Faith and Angel are having a fling. Also, Buffy says Faith is so late "she makes Godot look punctual." For someone who thinks *Of Human Bondage* is porn, where did she get that reference?
OOPS: Faith holds out her hands to Angel, showing him the demon's blood. Yet moments later, it's gone.

3.18 Earshot

Original air date:	September 21, 1999
Written by:	Jane Espenson
Directed by:	Regis Kimble
Guest cast:	Danny Strong (Jonathan), Lauren Roman (Nancy), Ethan Erickson (Percy West), Larry Bagby III (Larry), Justin Doran (Hogan), Wendy Worthington (Lunch Lady), Karem Malicki-Sánchez (Freddy Iverson), Robert Arce (Mr. Beach), Molly Bryant (Ms. Murray)

When Buffy touches the blood of a demon, she gains the ability to hear people's thoughts.

This episode is infamous not only for its content, but for the events surrounding its airing. On April 20, 1999, two students of Columbine High School in Littleton, Colorado, walked into their school and killed 13 students, then themselves. It was a devastating tragedy that became the focus of every discussion for months afterward, and the biggest lingering question (as in all major tragedies) was why. Why did they do it? What made them do it? Everything from how they were raised, to the Internet, to Marilyn Manson was blamed, and the entertainment industry fought back to prove it was *not* to blame, that the children themselves were responsible.

Enter the *Buffy* dilemma. "Earshot" is an episode where Buffy, who can hear thoughts, overhears someone threaten to kill everyone in the school. Bigger problem: it was scheduled to air on April 27, 1999, one week after the Columbine tragedy. Was it too soon? Yes, probably. The WB's decision? To pull it indefinitely and maybe never air it, because it's too hot a topic right now.

But what did this say to viewers? Basically that television *was* to blame, that on seeing an episode like that, viewers might say, "Wow, what a great idea! I'm going to go take out everyone in my school, too!" Joss Whedon agreed with the decision, although he probably didn't agree with just how long they decided to postpone the show for.

It made sense to delay it a couple of weeks, but the episode should have aired sooner — what it had to say was absolutely crucial to the ongoing debate. If you were not part of some right-wing parents' organization looking to ban everything in sight, you were probably arguing that the problem was not in goth clothing and *The Matrix*, but in the children themselves and their own mental problems resulting from societal pressures. What terrible thing made them do it? In "Earshot," Buffy's ability to hear thoughts probably makes her the most qualified person to enter the debate. She hears girls worrying about their hair, weight, clothes, and whether they'll ever get their first kiss; jocks worrying about dating and their image, and whether they can keep their place on the football team; bookworms thinking they'll never be noticed by anyone else; teachers wishing they had other jobs. All Buffy hears is worrying and upset, and if a thousand people are so bogged down in their worries that they can hardly think of anyone else, how are they going to notice when one person decides they can't take it anymore? The show was an excellent commentary on the tragedy in schools, arguing that bullying can be more damaging to a person than being in a car accident, that low self-esteem can be very, very dangerous, and that we have to learn to listen to one another and accept others if we're ever going to stop the violence.

Jonathan, the school nerd who has been bullied, is pushed to the brink. We've seen him accosted and then rejected by a beautiful woman ("Inca Mummy Girl"); treated like Cordelia's lapdog ("Reptile Boy"); held hostage by a police officer and then thrown aside, with no one asking him if he's all right ("What's My Line? Part Two"); treated like dirt by Xander when he wanted a library book ("Passion"); bullied by school athletes and interrogated by Willow ("Go Fish"); referred to as "you by the dip" by Buffy, who already knows his name but chooses not to use it ("Dead Man's Party"); sucked up to by Buffy and Cordelia when they want his homecoming queen votes ("Homecoming"); and taunted by Harmony and company when they're teasing Cordelia about scraping the bottom of the barrel when dating ("The Wish"). And this is just the stuff we've seen onscreen. We can only imagine what else has happened to him. After three years of being bullied by even the not-so-cool kids, Jonathan snaps, and the action he takes in this episode speaks volumes about the bullying problem in schools — far more than any right-wing parenting organization did at the time.

But parents didn't take notice, the episode was pulled, and the media spent the summer arguing that we should discriminate against people in black trenchcoats. The episode finally aired on September 21, 1999, two weeks before the season four premiere.

HIGHLIGHT: Buffy's surprise comment to Giles at the end of the episode and the way he slams into the tree when she says it.

INTERESTING FACTS: Joss Whedon supported the WB's decision, and said so on the posting board: "On the inevitable subject, as far as pre-empting the ep, I agreed with the decision and when you see it you'll agree, I think, that it was just badly timed. But it WILL air. I'm proud of it. It comments on that type of sitch, and obviously we come down AGAINST massacring people, but ANY comment after so desperate a tragedy would be offensively trite. Needless to type, this BLAME THE MEDIA thing makes me crazy. Remember when Dan Quayle blamed the L.A. riots on Murphy Brown? Everybody laffed, but NOBODY TALKED ABOUT THE RIOTS ANYMORE. It's just a way of avoiding the subject — and of making sense of something too ugly to deal with by latching onto a scapegoat. Sigh. (But it is Marilyn Manson's fault.)"

DID YOU NOTICE? That although the most silent member of the group, Oz has the most thoughts? Also, when Willow interrogates Jonathan, she tells him we all have fantasies that we're respected, powerful, and people pay attention to us, and that sometimes you have to *make* people pay attention. Could this have been the suggestion that sparked his later behavior in "Superstar"?

NITPICKS: Angel tells Buffy that in 243 years he's loved only one person. If he went to hell and suffered literally thousands of years of torment, why does he still see his age as 243 years? And Xander discovers the Jell-O problem after many people have already finished eating lunch. Did no one actually eat it? And finally, the WB assured viewers that this was a stand-alone episode, but with Buffy being so upset with Angel at the end of "Enemies" and suddenly affectionate with him in "Choices," a lot of viewers were left scratching their heads. Same goes for Jonathan giving the speech to Buffy in "The Prom."

OOPS: Watch how the clock tower drastically changes times whenever Buffy looks at it (it even moves backward). Also, when Buffy gets into the fight in the cafeteria, the lunch lady's stunt double appears to be a man in lots of padding.

3.19 Choices

Original air date:	May 4, 1999
Written by:	David Fury
Directed by:	James A. Contner
Guest cast:	Keith Brunsmann (Vamp Lackey), Jimmie F. Skaggs (Courier), Jason Reed (Vamp Guard), Bonita Friedericy (Mrs. Finkle), Michael Schoenfeld (Security Guard #1), Seth Coltan (Security Guard #2), Brett Moses (Student)

Faith retrieves a box for the Mayor that is essential to his Ascension, but when the gang tries to take it from him, Willow's life is put in jeopardy.

Another one of those episodes where things happen to each of the characters that will spark future plotlines. We find the unfortunate Cordelia working in a dress shop (and the reasons for this will eventually force her to L.A. rather than on to college); Xander discovers Jack Kerouac's novel *On the Road*, which inspires him to take his road trip; and the Mayor has some words for Buffy and Angel that will send their relationship spiraling to its conclusion.

But the hero of the story is Willow, who not only escapes the clutches of the Mayor with some big news for the gang, but confronts Faith, who is bigger and stronger. And not one but *two* of her spells go just the way she wants them to. That's got to be some sort of record. Willow really comes through for everyone, never shows any fear, and her strength and cunning in this episode make Giles's words in "Flooded" seem so much more harsh.

As is obvious from its title, this episode is about choices. Faith becomes the Mayor's full-fledged lackey by following through on some dicey business for him, and when she meets up with the Scooby gang and has the choice of moving back over to the good side, she walks out on them. Buffy decides to turn down Northwestern and stay in Sunnydale, and Willow chooses to go to Sunnydale U so she and Buffy can be together. The Mayor explains to Angel that things won't always be so sweet with him and Buffy, forcing Angel to make a difficult choice in the next episode.

But the most uncomfortable choice is when Wesley argues the greater good is holding on to the Mayor's box and not sacrificing other lives to save Willow. Although Willow is the most important person in the group besides Buffy, maybe he has a point. We later see a few characters die because of the Mayor's Ascension, not to mention what happens to the school. None of that would have been possible if they hadn't handed over the box in this episode. It was a choice they all felt was necessary, but was it the right one?

HIGHLIGHT: Willow telling everyone she got into Oxford: "That's where they make Gileses."
DID YOU NOTICE? The City Hall rooftop was the same set used for the library roof in "Prophecy Girl."
NITPICKS: Buffy says at the end that the Mayor should be disregarded when he comments about Angel and Buffy's relationship (which is two and a half years old) because he's never been in a lasting relationship. Did she somehow miss the part when he said he was married to the same person for decades until she died? And as for Cordy working in the store, why is she the only person in the gang who actually has a part-time job? How do Willow and Buffy expect to pay for college? And who will pay for Xander's road trip? Are their parents — whom they all claim are so evil — footing the bill for everything?
OOPS: When the Mayor walks into the room where the gang is ready to make the switch, he acts like he's never seen Buffy before, but he's actually seen her on a few occasions ("Band Candy," "Gingerbread," "Consequences").
WILLOW WICCA WATCH: Willow performs a spell to remove the protective barrier from the Mayor's box, and later she levitates a pencil to kill a vampire.

3.20 The Prom

Original air date:	May 11, 1999
Written by:	Marti Noxon
Directed by:	David Solomon
Guest cast:	Emma Caulfield (Anya), Danny Strong (Jonathan), Brad Kane (Tucker), Andrea E. Taylor (Salesgirl), Mike

Kimmel (Butcher Guy), Bonita Friedericy (Mrs. Finkle), Joe Howard (Priest), Tove Kingsbury (Tux Boy), Michael Zlabinger (Student at Mike), Damien Eckhardt (Jack Mayhew), Monica Serene Garnich ("No" Girl), Stephanie Denise Griffin (Girl in Store)

Buffy's excitement about the prom is shattered when Angel gives her some bad news.

If you thought Sarah Michelle Gellar's acting couldn't possibly get any better than it was in "Amends," watch this episode. Sarah makes Buffy run the gamut of emotions from excitement to confusion to heartbreak to resolve to resigned sadness. The Mayor's words in "Choices" strike a chord with Angel because they're exactly what Angel has been thinking for months now, especially after his bout as Angelus. And then Joyce steps in, a mother worried about her daughter dating a potential monster, and she makes his anxieties more personal. We can't help but wonder if this has been haunting Buffy, too. It must break her up that her friends don't trust Angel — he's hurt so many of them that no matter how much they love her they can't forget what he's done. Or that she is in the prime of her life and can never have sex with him or get married or have children. But the simple fact remains: Buffy is 18 years old and in love, and for her, that's all that matters right now. Her notebook, with "Buffy and Angel 4Ever" scrawled all over it, reminds us that she hasn't really absorbed what "4Ever" means.

"The Prom" has elements of that great horror-movie tradition of a high schooler's greatest night being overshadowed by tragedy. Marti Noxon borrows from *Prom Night* (and *Carrie* and *Pretty in Pink* and the other movies that Tucker uses to rile up his dogs) in an absolutely hilarious way to offset the sadness of the doomed Buffy and Angel relationship. The weredogs (who look remarkably like Snyder) respond to all the old prom standbys, and the guy's reason for trying to turn the prom into a disaster is classic.

The awards ceremony comes as a bit of a shock, as most viewers have assumed the other high schoolers didn't notice all the weird goings-on at Sunnydale High. Now we know they do, but why haven't any come forward to help out? In a clever turn, the director films Buffy accepting the award the same way Sissy Spacek accepted her flowers in *Carrie*. Was anyone else waiting for a bucket of blood to drop on her head?

HIGHLIGHT: The dance between Buffy and Angel at the end is one of the most heartbreaking moments of the series.

NITPICKS: Willow eventually agrees with Buffy that it would never work out between the two of them because Angel's a loose cannon and Buffy could get hurt. Has she somehow forgotten that her boyfriend is a *werewolf*?! And at the beginning of the episode, Buffy walks into Angel's house and throws the curtains wide open, almost incinerating him. Doesn't she know better by now? She did it as recently as "Earshot," and you'd think she'd peek in first.

OOPS: When the hellhound attacks the guy trying on the tuxedo, we see only a few things fall off the rack. But when the gang watches the attack on the security camera tape, most of the outfits fall off. Also, when Wesley is at the prom, he's holding a red napkin; the camera cuts away, and when it cuts back, the napkin is yellow.

MUSIC/BANDS: "Praise You," by Fat Boy Slim, the first song we hear at the prom, is from the CD, *You've Come a Long Way, Baby*. When the hellhounds are outside, they hear Kool and the Gang's "Celebration" and start running back toward the school. The song can be found on the band's *All-Time Greatest Hits* CD. When Buffy comes into the gym, Cracker's "The Good Life" is playing, from their disc, *Gentleman's Blues*. When Wesley tells Giles he'd like to dance with Cordelia, we hear the Lassie Foundation's "El Rey," from their *Pacifico* CD. Finally, Buffy and Angel dance their last dance to the Sundays' version of the Rolling Stones song, "Wild Horses," from the Sundays' *Blind* CD.

3.21 Graduation Day (Part One)

Original air date:	May 18, 1999
Written and directed by:	Joss Whedon
Guest cast:	Emma Caulfield (Anya), Mercedes McNab (Harmony), Ethan Erickson (Percy West), James Lurie (Mr. Miller), Hal Robinson (Professor Lester Worth), Adrian Neil (Vamp Lackey #1), John Rosenfeld (Vamp Lackey #2)

Faith wounds Angel in the hope that Buffy will become too preoccupied to prepare for the Ascension.

Once again, the magic combination of a *BtVS* season finale and the words "Written and directed by Joss Whedon" creates television magic. Anya joins the Scoobies as the only person who might have the information they've been looking for. The only question is, why didn't they think of using her before? At the prom she showed that she knew more about demons than even Angel, yet no one thought she might know the key to the Ascension? Emma Caulfield is a great addition to the gang; she brings background knowledge that gives her a place in the group, but she also has that indifferent flakiness that only Cordelia has been able to embody so well to this point, and will be able to fill some of the void left when Charisma Carpenter defects to *Angel* in the coming season.

Graduation day will not just be about graduating from high school. Buffy becomes a free agent, stating she no longer needs a Watcher. Willow and Oz take the next step in their relationship and make love. If the Ascension goes smoothly, the Mayor will "graduate" to an impervious demon, and Faith will go from being his lackey of sorts to his right-hand warrior. Anya makes her first step toward being a human being, as she feels pain and love for the first time. And David Boreanaz will get his own show.

The cliffhanger in this episode was excruciating (made worse when the WB postponed the showing of part two). Eliza Dushku, who has shown us all season that she's an actress of the highest caliber, puts in a showstopping performance. Buffy reaches her breaking point and moves in for the kill. It's interesting from a psychological perspective that Buffy wears Faith's clothes and trash-talks her when she's about to kill her. Has she realized that she's become like Faith, willing to take a human life?

HIGHLIGHT: Xander's comment about how lucky they are that none of the students ever take out any of the "library" books that the gang needs week after week.
NITPICKS: Angel gets increasingly worse, and we see the wound spreading further and further, but his blood doesn't flow. How exactly is the poison moving throughout his system if his blood is unable to take it anywhere? Also, Buffy is again the queen of insensitivity when she announces to Wesley that she's not going to sit and watch her lover die. Standing nearby

is Giles, whose lover was tortured and murdered by Buffy's "lover." The fact that he stands by her side makes him the noblest character on the show.

MUSIC/BANDS: When Buffy enters Faith's apartment, Faith is listening to Spectator Pump's "Sunday Mail" from their *Styrofoam Archives* CD.

3.22 Graduation Day, Part Two

Original air date:	July 13, 1999
Written and directed by:	Joss Whedon
Guest cast:	Larry Bagby III (Larry), Danny Strong (Jonathan), Mercedes McNab (Harmony), Ethan Erickson (Percy West), Paulo Andres (Dr. Powell), Susan Chuang (Nurse), Tom Bellin (Dr. Gold), Samuel Bliss Cooper (Vamp Lackey)

Buffy and the gang recruit other members of the student body to try to stop the Mayor's Ascension.

As if postponing "Earshot" indefinitely wasn't annoying enough, the WB declared at the 11th hour that "Graduation Day (Part Two)" was inappropriate to show and they delayed that, too. Of course, they showed part one just so fans would go completely nuts for weeks waiting for the subsequent episode (except in Canada, where it accidentally aired the Monday night before it was canceled; Canadian fans were kept busy the next few weeks bootlegging tapes for their American neighbors). And where the delay of "Earshot" was justified because of the subject matter, the WB *really* had to stretch to come up with a reason this time: Apparently seeing the students armed with weapons was too inflammatory, and they feared students would see this episode and take up arms in schools. Yeah, right. Against the huge reptiles that threatened kids across the U.S. that year at their high school graduations? It's too bad the WB assumed most of its viewers had the mental capacities of gnats.

When it finally aired, this episode was a thrilling conclusion to the first part, featuring stellar performances from the whole cast. Harry Groener is fantastic as the creature intent on world domination who will put it all on hold to grieve for the daughter figure he has come to love. Oz and Willow are charming, and now that Buffy and Angel are splitsville, this couple becomes the one to watch. Buffy rides an emotional roller coaster, and forgives Faith for what she's done, realizing that it was the Mayor who pushed Faith to such extreme behavior. At the same time Buffy bravely puts her life in danger to save the one she loves (who's a bit of a hog, under the circumstances — for once, Xander's comment is pretty accurate).

This episode featured the most talked-about sequence of the series' history to that point: the dream sequence between Faith and Buffy. People couldn't figure out what was going on, but in hindsight the scene is dazzling. Fans asked, "What does Faith mean by 'Little Miss Muffet counting down to 7-3-0'?" and theories abounded on the Internet and at the water coolers. But we would later find out, and the payoff would be immense (see "The Gift"). Thank you, Joss, for having faith in the intelligence of your viewers, even when the network didn't.

The filming of this episode was beautiful. From the erotic scene between Angel and Buffy filmed in slow motion, to the fabulous fight scene involving all the students and creatures, to the climactic explosion, "Graduation Day (Part Two)" was a nailbiter to the bitter end. This was truly their graduation day: the gang learned more in cemeteries, on patrol, and in the library with their research sessions than they ever did in math, chemistry, or English classes. The Ascension was their final exam, and they passed it. What a perfect way to end the high school years on the show. There wasn't another season finale in 1999 that even came close to this one.

HIGHLIGHT: Snyder's brief speech at the graduation ceremony (may he rest in . . . Oh, who am I kidding? Good riddance, Snyder!).

DID YOU NOTICE? The yearbook has the slogan of Nazi Germany — "The Future Is Ours" (see "I Robot, You Jane"). Even without the Nazi reference, the motto is an ironic one. This graduating class might have had the lowest mortality rate in the school's history, but they also didn't think they'd have a future beyond graduation day. Also, in the dream sequence, Faith quotes the same line from Robert Frost that Buffy does in "The Prom."

NITPICKS: If we say the graduation ceremony starts at three in the afternoon, and the eclipse happens about 10 minutes into the ceremony, how is it still as dark as night over an hour later? By the time the fight is over, the emergency vehicles have come and gone, and the gang walks off, the sun should have been out again. Also, at graduation ceremonies the students are grouped together by last name. So why is Oz (Daniel Osbourne) sitting behind Willow Rosenberg and Buffy Summers? His last name starts with O — he should be sitting in front of them.

OOPS: Anya told everyone in the previous episode that when the Mayor ascended, he'd be pure demon, yet Buffy says in this episode that she could play on his human weakness. He wouldn't have a human weakness if he were pure demon. Also, in the previous episode Oz was wearing black nail polish when he began kissing Willow, and in this one, which is supposed to take place immediately afterward, he isn't wearing any.

RESTLESS MOMENT: In "Restless," Buffy looks at the digital clock beside her bed and it says 7:30, a reference to Faith's enigmatic "7-3-0."

Season Four

OCTOBER 1999 • MAY 2000

Recurring characters in season four: Lindsay Crouse (Professor Maggie Walsh), Leonard Roberts (Forrest Gates), Bailey Chase (Graham Miller), Mercedes McNab (Harmony), George Hertzberg (Adam)

4.1 The Freshman

Original air date:	October 5, 1999
Written and directed by:	Joss Whedon
Guest cast:	Dagney Kerr (Kathy), Pedro Balmaceda (Eddie), Katharine Towne (Sunday), Mike Rad (Rookie), Shannon Hillary (Dav), Mace Lombard (Tom), Robert Catrini (Professor Riegert), Scott Rinker (R.A.), Phina Oruche (Olivia)

Buffy has to make the difficult transition from high school to university, and she feels left out and lost.

To continue the parallel between Buffy's slaying and her education, Joss opens this episode in a perfect way. Buffy is confused, has left things to the last minute, and feels a little left out, while Willow is excited about college. At the same time, a vampire sneaks up behind her and only by sheer luck decides not to have Willow and Buffy for dinner. Buffy is unsure about her future academic life, and it's showing in her slaying: in all areas, Buffy's not at the top of her game. She can't talk to guys, she's not living at home, Giles seems distant, she and Willow are no longer excited about the same things, she doesn't have a boyfriend, and she's humiliated in front of the whole classroom. Toto, we're not in Kansas anymore.

"The Freshman" marks the beginning of a season that contains some major character shuffling, the introduction of new characters and settings, and a shake-up of what we've come to know and love. No longer is Giles always around as the Watcher and father figure to the group. As a "man of leisure," he doesn't seem to have a job or a purpose, or to play a key role in their lives anymore. And as the season continues, Giles undergoes a quiet midlife crisis as he struggles to make Buffy more independent. Angel and Cordy are gone; Wes is no longer in the picture (although he was never around long enough to be an established character); Willow will suffer a serious trauma; Xander will be effectively separated from the gang; Anya will become a main character; and Spike will, uh, join the group. Joyce will become a non-character, and we'll be given Riley as a poor substitute for Angel. It's like . . . we're in our first year of university or something!

And maybe that's where the cleverness of this season lies. It makes us uncomfortable, we feel dislocated, and we long for a time when things were simpler. We were so used to things the way they were, and now they're all different. Unfortunately, for that reason (and many others) the season is my least favorite. That said, as we all know, *Buffy*'s weakest season is still better than 99 percent of everything else on television, and this season still contains some of the best episodes of the series.

Buffy's troubles in "The Freshman" are very realistic, showing that at least one of the writers on the staff has been through this before. From the opening scenes of the clubs passing out so many flyers Buffy's head is spinning, to the roommate from hell, to the proliferation of Klimt and Monet posters, to the professor making a scene with Buffy in front of everyone (we all saw that happen and thanked God it wasn't happening to us), this first episode brings back a lot of painful and all-too-real memories for older viewers, and perhaps scared younger ones away from college altogether. (I'm glad I wasn't the only one who thought some professors were unduly cruel to first-year students in an effort to thin out the ranks for upper years.)

Xander makes a much-needed and hilarious appearance as Buffy's support system and imperfect Yoda figure. While Giles and Joyce have cut the cord and are forcing Buffy to be independent, and Willow is so caught up in the excitement of academic bliss to notice Buffy's unhappiness, Xander gets right to the research and helps her fight the big bad. It's only when her friends regroup that Buffy gets back into her game.

The displacement of the characters and Buffy's confusion make this an excellent season opener and a great way to establish what will happen. Unfortunately, the season as a whole is disjointed and takes too long to find its legs. However, this episode contains one horrible moment of inadvertent foreshadowing: when Buffy's buying her books, she says to Will, "I can't wait 'til Mom gets the bill for these books. I hope it's a funny aneurysm." Eek.

HIGHLIGHT: The banter between Sunday and Buffy during the final fight.

INTERESTING FACTS: This episode is one of only a handful this season that will feature Kristine Sutherland as Joyce Summers. Sutherland informed Joss at the beginning of the season that she was taking the year off to live in Europe, so he kept her character's appearance to a minimum. Also, before playing Riley, Marc Blucas was a relative newcomer to acting. Born in 1972, he had spent most of his life playing basketball, and attended university on a basketball scholarship. When he wasn't chosen for the NBA draft, he moved to the U.K. and played basketball professionally for the Manchester Giants. In 1996 he returned to the U.S. to start up a company designed to help athletes through their contract negotiations, and began studying for a law degree to help him run the company. The night before his LSATs, he saw the film *A Few Good Men* and realized it wasn't law he wanted to pursue, it was acting. After a few small roles (mostly playing basketball players) in *Pleasantville, Clueless* (the television series), and *Eddie*, he landed the role of Riley.

DID YOU NOTICE? The rooftop with the skylight above Sunday's lair is the same set used in "Prophecy Girl" for the rooftop above the library.

NITPICKS: Why exactly is Buffy staying in a dorm? She must live about 10 minutes away. Also, why would the vampires' lair have a skylight? Wouldn't vampires prefer something that's a little darker during the day?

MUSIC/BANDS: As Buffy wanders around the campus, confused by all the activity, we hear Stretch Princess's "Universe" from their self-titled CD. As she walks through the hallways of her dorm, we hear Paul Riordan's "Freaky Soul," from the compilation *Alternative Volume 1*. The Muffs' "I Wish That Could Be You," from *Alert Today, Alive Tomorrow*, plays while Sunday's vampires discuss Buffy. When Buffy goes to Giles's house, he's playing David Bowie's "Memory of a Free Festival" from *Space Oddity*, and as Buffy enters the Bronze Splendid is onstage performing "You and Me," from *Have You Got a Name for It*. Score by Christophe Beck (throughout the season).

4.2 Living Conditions

Original air date:	October 12, 1999
Written by:	Marti Noxon
Directed by:	David Grossman
Guest cast:	Dagney Kerr (Kathy), Adam Kaufman (Parker), Paige Moss (Veruca), Roger Morrissey (Taparrich), Clayton Barber (Demon #1), Walt Borchert (Demon #2), David Tuckman (Freshman)

Buffy believes her annoying new dorm roommate is evil, while everyone around her assumes she's just starting to lose it.

Marti Noxon has written an absolutely hilarious account of the ultimate cohabitation from hell. Kathy is the Cher-loving, egg-labeling, toenail-clipping Goody Two Shoes, while Buffy is the gum-chewing, milk-chugging, paranoid basket case forced to live with her. Kathy has turned Buffy, who is generally a tolerant person, into someone with the impatience of a postal worker.

Dagney Kerr is wonderful as the incredibly annoying Kathy, and her singsong voice and nervous giggle are enough to drive anyone batty. Oz and Willow desperately try to come to terms with their friend, whose erratic behavior has them all worried she's going to pull a Faith on her roommate. The parallel of Willow's roommate, who is so much worse than Kathy, makes it even funnier. Giles seems to be changing even more, taking up jogging and getting subscriptions to strange magazines. And Xander is so desperate to be a part of the group that he gets a happy when Buffy simply mentions a demon.

The ending revelation is the perfect end to the story. Anyone who has been in Buffy's situation knows that it's like the roommate is sucking the living soul from them (we should have assumed from the get-go that Kathy had no soul, considering how much she loved "Believe").

And hey, what's with those shifty army guys . . . ?

HIGHLIGHT: The hilarious father–daughter fight between Kathy and Taparrich: "I'm 3,000 years old! When are you going to stop treating me like I'm 900?"

NITPICKS: Why weren't Willow and Buffy roommates from the beginning? It seems strange they both ended up in the same dorm, but not together.

OOPS: When Buffy is talking to Giles after his run, he flips a towel onto his shoulder. He sits down and it's gone, but when they cut back to him, it's back on his shoulder. Also, when Oz and Xander slowly approach Buffy, Oz is standing to the right of Xander, but when they land on the floor, they've switched sides.

WILLOW WICCA WATCH: Giles does a spell and asks Willow to help him with it.

MUSIC/BANDS: To our unending horror, Cher's "Believe," from the CD of the same name, plays over and over and over again throughout the episode. As Willow hangs up her Dingoes Ate My Baby poster at the end of the episode, we hear Four Star Mary's "Pain," from *Thrown to the Wolves* (it is also on the *Buffy the Vampire Slayer* soundtrack). Throughout the episode we also hear "Shakie Fakie" and "Freestyle Hombre" from a Skate Punk CD compilation.

4.3 Harsh Light of Day

Original air date:	October 19, 1999
Written by:	Jane Espenson
Directed by:	James A. Contner
Guest cast:	Adam Kaufman (Parker), Jason Hall (Devon), Melix (Bryan)

Harmony returns to Sunnydale as a vampire, Buffy's relationship with Parker gets serious, and Spike searches for a gem that will make him impervious to all harm.

It was a fleeting moment in "Graduation Day (Part Two)" when Harmony got bitten by a vampire, and perhaps some viewers assumed it was a quick bite and she got away. But Harmony returns in all her ditzy and vampiric glory to fawn over Spike in her pathetic way (so much for personalities changing in vamp form). Spike has returned to find the Ring of Amarra but, as usual, he screws things up pretty quickly.

The search for the ring in this episode is secondary to Buffy's relationship with Parker. In an eerie case of déjà vu, Buffy takes the relationship to a level she'd had with Angel . . . only to endure a similar result. It's so sad seeing her go through the pain again, considering it's taken her almost two years to get back in the game. But in the end, she's still loyal to Angel, and always will be. Parker might have been a fling, but we wonder if she could have ever gotten serious with anyone. If he hadn't been a "poophead," is there a chance the relationship could have worked? Or is any relationship with Buffy doomed from the start? After all, she's met her soul mate but is unable to stay with him. Will she always be single?

And finally, in a case of déjà also, Xander is reunited with Anya, who has returned to beg his forgiveness in her oh-so-blunt way. What doesn't make sense is how the writers draw parallels between her and Harmony and Buffy, as three women who are pretty much ditched after sex. Can we really believe Xander is as bad as Spike and Parker? (See "In the Dark" for the conclusion of this episode on *Angel*.)

HIGHLIGHT: Xander squirting the cranberry juice when Anya disrobes.
NITPICKS: Harmony says Drusilla left Spike for a Fungus Demon, but it was a Chaos Demon (he's said it before and he says it again). And why would someone as famous as Bif Naked play a frat party?
OOPS: Parker notices the ugly scar on Buffy's neck, which was from Angel's big guzzle in "Graduation Day (Part Two)." In later episodes, the scar will disappear. Also, Spike rips the necklace off when he realizes it isn't the gem of Amarra, but in the next shot it's back on.
MUSIC/BANDS: At the beginning of the episode, Dingoes Ate My Baby are performing Four Star Mary's "Dilate" from *Thrown to the Wolves*. Later, we hear Psychic Rain's "Take Me Down" from their *Spun Out* CD. At the frat party, Bif Naked performs "Moment of Weakness," "Anything," and "Lucky" from *I Bificus*. As Harmony tries to seduce Spike, we hear "Faith in Love" by Devil Doll, from *Queen of Pain*. And finally, Dollshead's "It's Over, It's Under" from *Frozen Charlotte* plays while Buffy looks for Harmony.

4.4 Fear, Itself

Original air date:	October 26, 1999
Written by:	David Fury
Directed by:	Tucker Gates
Guest cast:	Adam Kaufman (Parker), Marc Rose (Josh), Sulo Williams (Chaz), Walter Emanuel Jones (Edward), Adam Bitterman (Gachnar), Aldis Hodge (Masked Teen), Darris Love (Hallmate), Michele Nordin (Rachel), Adam Grimes (Lobster Boy), Larissa Reynolds (Present Girl)

When the gang enters a haunted house, their worst fears end up coming true.

My favorite of the holiday episodes. This episode has everything — fear, sadness, and big laughs. "Fear, Itself" is very similar to "Nightmares," and even gives it a subtle nod when Joyce reassures Buffy that the divorce didn't happen because of her (Buffy's biggest fear in "Nightmares"). This episode shows us how much everyone has matured. Willow's biggest fear used to be stage fright, now it's that a spell she casts will go terribly wrong and turn on her and her friends. Xander, whose childhood was marred by a severe fear of clowns, now worries that he's not part of the gang, that they'll forget about him and he'll become invisible to them. Oz worries that he'll transform into a werewolf at the wrong moment and put Willow's life in danger. And Buffy fears that, like Joyce hinted in "Gingerbread," no matter how much she fights, the demons will keep coming and she won't be able to save people.

In each case, the character's earlier fears stemmed from the basic human fears of childhood, and were very personal. As adults, their fears involve others — will they put their friends in danger? Will their friends abandon them? The Scoobies are going through big changes in their lives, and while this episode showed that Franklin Delano Roosevelt was probably onto something with his famous quotation, "The only thing we have to fear is fear itself," fear will fester within each of them throughout the season. Each has identified himself or herself as a member of this fighting team, and now they worry that their lives will change so much that the team will fall apart.

But, like "Nightmares," this episode had its share of humor to keep things from getting too serious. Anya faces her fear of rabbits by dressing up as a big, fluffy, pink bunny. Giles figures out a way into the haunted house in a rather rough and non-Giles way. And of course, the ending, where everyone has to face the biggest fear of all: Gachnar. The final moments of the episode hearken back to "Nightmares" one last time, when we realize that if Giles had actually read the text, things wouldn't have gotten out of hand. The first great episode of season four.

HIGHLIGHT: The sidesplitting last five minutes.

NITPICKS: At the beginning of the episode, Buffy hits what she suspects is a demon, but it turns out to be a guy in a mask, and he freaks out and asks what her problem is. Gee, I don't know, maybe that you jumped out of the bushes at her?! Also, Anya never knocks on anyone's door, so why, at an urgent moment, would she stop and knock? Wouldn't she have just walked into Giles's house like any other time?

OOPS: When Giles pulls the Frankenstein doll, it begins swinging wildly, but when the camera cuts back, it's almost still.

WILLOW WICCA WATCH: In this episode we discover that for all her confidence, Willow is worried about her ability to make her spells work, and at the beginning Oz expresses his concern about her dabbling in the dark magicks.

MUSIC/BANDS: As the frat boys set up for the party, we hear "Kool" by 28 Days, from *Kid Indestructible*. As people begin arriving at the party, we hear Third Grade Teacher's "Ow Ow Ow" from their *Greatest Hits Volume 1* CD. And Verbena's "Pretty Please," from *Into the Pink*, plays as the gang arrives at the party.

4.5 Beer Bad

Original air date:	November 2, 1999
Written by:	Tracey Forbes
Directed by:	David Solomon
Guest cast:	Adam Kaufman (Parker), Paige Moss (Veruca), Stephen M. Porter (Jack, bar manager), Eric Matheny (Colm), Kal Penn (Hunt), Jake Phillips (Kip), Bryan Cuprill (Roy), Lisa Johnson (Paula), Joshua Wheeler (Driver)

When the beer at the campus bar is poisoned, it turns the students into a bunch of cavemen.

Oh my God, call the papers! It turns out that consuming too much beer — wait for it — turns you into a Neanderthal! Who would have thought? The only surprise of this ridiculous episode is that Joss Whedon would have let it ever be made. I couldn't believe this show would ever sink so low. "Beer Bad" is the worst *Buffy* episode of season four, and probably of the entire series.

The strength of *BtVS* has always been its subtlety. Joss uses metaphors for real-life events, couching them in demon stories and teenage angst so viewers aren't banged over the head with any concept. In past episodes such as "Beauty and the Beasts" and "Reptile Boy," he introduced the concept that alcohol can make you crazy by letting a potion stand in for alcohol. But "Beer Bad" smacks the viewer in the face with the first chug of beer and doesn't stop whacking. And, of course, no one ever questions why Buffy, who's 18, is even being served beer in the first place. This episode was such an insult to both the characters and the viewers that I really don't want to waste any more paper talking about it.

HIGHLIGHT: I'd like to say none, but Willow letting Parker have it was a small victory for womankind.

INTERESTING FACTS: Hold on to your hats for this one: of all the episodes, this one was nominated for an Emmy for Hairstyling. O...kay.

NITPICKS: Too many to mention.

OOPS: At one point when the Neanderthals are all drinking, you can see the beer level in the pitcher rise and fall, even though no one is pouring any.

MUSIC/BANDS: There are several songs throughout this episode: Paul Trudeau's "People Will Talk," "I Can't Wait," and "It Feels Like I'm Dying" (*Kid Gloves Music Sampler*); Lauren Christy's "Perfect Again"; Ash's "I'm Gonna Fall" (*Nu-Clear Sounds*); Smile's "The Best Years," (*Girl Crushes Boy*); and Collapsis's "Wonderland" (*Dirty Wake*). When Veruca's band Shy is onstage, the actual band is T.H.C., singing "Overfire" from *Adagio*. At the bar, Kim Ferron's "Nothing But You," from the *Buffy the Vampire Slayer* soundtrack, plays on the jukebox, and Buffy watches Luscious Jackson's "Ladyfingers" (*Electric Honey*) video on television.

4.6 Wild at Heart

Original air date:	November 9, 1999
Written by:	Marti Noxon
Directed by:	David Grossman
Guest cast:	Paige Moss (Veruca), Lindsay Crouse (Maggie Walsh)

Oz discovers that Veruca is a fellow werewolf, and Willow makes a painful discovery of her own.

This episode ranks right up there with "Passion" for the pain it causes the characters and the viewers. I know I rave about Alyson Hannigan a lot, but in "Wild at Heart" she runs the gamut of emotions, and is absolutely amazing. From the opening scene where she's joking around with Buffy about her grades, to the uncomfortable lunch with Veruca and Oz where she fidgets and keeps saying the wrong thing, to her attempted seduction of Oz (she's come a long way from playing Barry White in her mother's living room), to her breakdown when she discovers Oz with Veruca, Hannigan was put through the wringer on this one (and the puffiness of her eyes at the end makes you wonder how many times she had to keep doing the scenes). *No one* on television cries like Hannigan. Her sobs come from the soul,

CHRISTINA RADISH

The sexy Alyson Hannigan

like she's really experiencing the pain, and there are few things more upsetting on *BtVS* than a weeping Willow. Emmy, are you paying *any* attention here??

Seth Green was great, too, and it's because of the chemistry between him and Hannigan that these scenes work so well. The emotional turmoil he goes through is as painful as what she's put through, and we know that leaving Sunnydale will be the most difficult thing he'll ever do. And, of course, while we cringe when he brings up her transgression with Xander, we understand why he does it. Seth Green left *Buffy* because his movie career had begun to flourish to the extent that he couldn't work in both television and film anymore. Unfortunately, since leaving the series, he's done fewer movies than he had while on the show, and none of them were of the caliber of *Buffy*. Oz, come back!

Paige Moss, on the other hand, was pretty flat in most of her scenes, her lip-synching is *terrible* (word of advice: you don't need to open your mouth like you're going to scream when mouthing words to a quiet, seductive song), and her slinking around the lab threatening Willow would have been a little scarier if she hadn't overacted every word.

The one comforting thing in this episode was how the characters turned to those closest to them, as they would have in high school. So far this season everyone's been isolated, so it was heartwarming to see Willow confiding in Xander and Buffy talking to Giles at the end.

HIGHLIGHT: Willow faking her bad dream about raspberry hats.

NITPICKS: Why would Professor Walsh — who we later discover knows everything about demons — tell Buffy about the "big dogs" she saw, as if she's never seen one before? And it's interesting that Oz agrees with Veruca that he doesn't like women who pick at salads, when by the looks of it, Willow and Buffy have been turning down a lot of salad dressing themselves.

MUSIC/BANDS: We hear Eight Stop Seven's "Good Enough" (*In Moderation*), and Veruca's band plays T.H.C.'s "Dip" and "Need to Destroy," both from *Adagio*.

4.7 The Initiative

Original air date:	November 16, 1999
Written by:	Douglas Petrie
Directed by:	James A. Contner
Guest cast:	Adam Kaufman (Parker), Mace Lombard (Tom), Scott Becker (Lost Freshman)

Unbeknownst to the gang, a military organization — involving Riley and Professor Walsh — is operating in Sunnydale against the demons.

Well, we finally discover what those camouflage-wearing stormtroopers are up to, but it's creepy, confused, and doesn't exactly work on this show. The idea is interesting — a military organization sets up shop on the hellmouth to capture demons, experiment on them, and try out techniques to render them harmless. But the Initiative clearly doesn't know too much about what it's doing, or it would have had a history of Sunnydale, would have known about the several near-apocalypses Buffy had averted, and about Buffy herself. Wouldn't the government have been scoping out this area for years? Wouldn't they have massive files on Buffy? At the end of "Out of Mind, Out of Sight," the FBI agents hinted to Buffy that they were watching her closely, but here it seems like they don't have a clue who she is.

As I mentioned earlier, season four suffers from some weaknesses, and the military element is the biggest one. The entire plot device is confused and disjointed, unlike the nemeses of other seasons. The best episodes of season four — "Fear, Itself"; "Pangs"; "Hush"; "A New Man"; "This Year's Girl" — are Initiative-free. The military aspect is too *X-Files* and goes against everything the series stands for: Chris Carter, the creator of *The X-Files*, should have been taking notes on *Buffy* at this point, not the other way around.

At first it would seem that now Riley and Buffy are the perfect match. Both secretly hunt demons and are determined to keep Sunnydale safe. But it's the *way* they hunt these demons that makes them polar opposites. The Initiative, in its government way, captures and dissects the creature, keeping files on it. The Scooby gang researches ancient texts written by superstitious village folk, opens up Grimm's Fairy Tales, and figures out how to kill these creatures by reading to the end of the nursery rhyme (see "Hush"). Among them are a witch and a Slayer, both "fairy tale creatures" to the Initiative. It's the way the Scoobies do their research that makes this show unique; adding the Initiative just makes *Buffy* like any other show. There's no need to contrast the way the gang and this organization hunt for demons, because we've been contrasting the gang's methods with every other sci-fi show on television for years. And it's clear the writers recognized the weaknesses of this plot:

Marc Blucas, looking sexier than his farmboy-from-Iowa character ever did

watch how the Initiative plays a relatively small part later in the season, and the writers focus on other plots, characters, and themes (such as the gang breaking up). No other nemesis of Buffy's has gotten such short shrift.

HIGHLIGHT: The hilarious slo-mo hair-pulling, slapping, and sissy-kicking scene between Xander and Harmony. Absolutely brilliant.

INTERESTING FACTS: Joss Whedon has acknowledged the nitpick many people have with the show: that for a guy with a chip in his head, Spike comes out a-swingin' when he's trying to get away from the Initiative. On the posting board, Joss had this to say about the inconsistency:

> Spike fighting his way out of the Initiative? Funny you should ask. This was one of the great foul-ups in *Buffy* history. When I saw the show cut together I went ballistic. Spike was hitting everybody — in the initiative, in the dorm hall, it was insane. Now, I surround myself with smart people (and then take credit for their efforts, a plan brilliant in its simplicity), but the ball got dropped there. We couldn't reshoot most of it so we edited it so that all he did was throw people,

not punch them, and when he did punch someone he went 'Arrgh my head' and whatnot. Mostly, we got away with it. It's like every time I see Angel walking in what looks like sunlight, I just cry and realize I can't possibly run two shows. But I press on after someone drags me drooling and muttering from the men's room and try to do my best. So for the love of god, DON'T MENTION THE SPIKE THING!!!

NITPICKS: I was going to mention the Spike thing, but see above. Also, Forrest says a vamp's body temperature is 62.3°F, which is room temperature. Is it just me, or is that one cold room?

OOPS: Spike says he's only 126 years old in this episode, but in season two Giles said he was 200. Later, in "Fool for Love" we discover he's actually 120 (if you count from the day he was turned into a vampire), which would have made him 119 in this episode.

MUSIC/BANDS: When Riley comes to talk to Willow, she's listening to Jake Lee Rau's "Welcome," from the disc *Joy*. When Spike finds Harmony, she's listening to Nikki Gregaroff's "Like We Never Said Goodbye." We can hear Moby's "Bodyrock," from *Play*, when Buffy and Willow arrive at the frat party. Buffy dances to That Dog's "Never Say Never," from *Retreat From the Sun*, and the Dingoes song that Willow hears is Four Star Mary's "Fate," from their *Thrown to the Wolves* CD. As Riley begins to talk to Buffy, we hear Deadstar's "Lights Go Down," from *Somewhere Over the Radio*.

4.8 Pangs

Original air date:	November 23, 1999
Written by:	Jane Espenson
Directed by:	Michael Lange
Guest cast:	David Boreanaz (Angel), Tod Thawley (Hus, The Chumash Spirit), Margaret Easley (Curator), William Vogt (Jamie), Mark Ankeny (Dean Guerrero)

When Xander accidentally awakens an ancient tribe of Native Americans, the gang is forced to recreate Thanksgiving the way it originally happened.

"Pangs" is a brilliant holiday episode, laying out both sides of the Thanksgiving debate without ever taking sides. Willow is upset that no one is taking Thanksgiving — that yam sham — seriously by realizing it was all about the massacre of an indigenous people. Spike and Giles roll their eyes at what they perceive to be her naïveté — as Brits, they believe that if you conquer a people, you should celebrate. Xander doesn't have an opinion on the issue, Anya bluntly states the holiday is about the ritual sacrifice of a bird to be eaten with pie, and Buffy wants them all to just shut up and enjoy the damn meal.

In "The Initiative," we discovered that Spike has now been fitted with an electronic chip in his head that gives him a painful shock if he tries to hurt anyone. It's the only good thing to come out of the Initiative plotline — an ingenious way to finally make good ol' Spikey part of the group. The ensuing friction between Spike and Giles is amusing — although they hate each other, they have similar reactions to things because of their British backgrounds — and having a vampire back in the mix (even if he's hated) helps fill that void that Angel left.

Speaking of Angel, this episode wasn't merely a crossover, it tied up the loose ends left dangling when he just disappeared with no goodbyes. Giles still hates him, Willow just wants to ask him about Cordelia, and although Buffy can't see him, she can feel his presence, again reminding viewers that he is her soul mate, and she'll never be entirely happy with anyone else. This episode and "I Will Remember You," the *Angel* episode that followed, will be the farewell between Angel and Buffy that we didn't get at the end of season three; they try to put their relationship to rest and move on. (See "I Will Remember You" for the conclusion to this episode on *Angel*.)

HIGHLIGHT: Spike's reaction to the Native American turning into a bear: "You made a bear! Undo it! Undo it!"

INTERESTING FACTS: Bailey Chase, who plays Graham, says that the first time he met with Joss Whedon, he nearly made a big mistake: "My audition was pretty comical. I went in and met with Joss at the callback and made fun of him, not knowing who he was — he doesn't strike you as someone who's created a $100 million icon — and I got the part." Marc Blucas had to catch up Chase and Leonard Roberts on the fact that their characters had been seen in previous episodes running around in ski masks, since neither actor watched the show.

DID YOU NOTICE? The arrows went into Spike in almost the same places where Angel was impaled during his torture session in "In the Dark."

NITPICKS: Doyle's vision signaled that Buffy was in trouble, but when is she not? And why are Xander and one other guy manually digging the foundation for the mission? Anyone ever heard of a backhoe?

OOPS: At the end of the episode, despite being hit by three different arrows, Spike's shirt has no holes. And Anya says, "So this is Angel?" like she hadn't met him before, but he was at the Bronze in "Doppelgängland."

4.9 Something Blue

Original air date:	November 30, 1999
Written by:	Tracey Forbes
Directed by:	Nick Marck
Guest cast:	Elizabeth Anne Allen (Amy), Andy Umberger (D'Hoffryn)

When Willow tries to cast a spell allowing her will to be done, things begin to go awry.

Although "Something Blue" was written by the person who subjected us to "Beer Bad," it's actually very good. Unfortunately, in the scene at the Bronze near the beginning, we see Willow stumbling all over with a — gasp! — beer, and Buffy reminds us of her earlier experience with the toxic substance (just when we were trying to forget). There are few things worse on television than writers reminding their audiences of their earlier "masterworks."

Fortunately for us, the episode gets better from there. Spike is very funny as Buffy's paramour, foreshadowing his later feelings for her (although Buffy is less believable; her behavior changes completely, while everyone else stays pretty much in character). In fact, "Something Blue" foreshadows a lot of season six. Aside from the Spike/Buffy thing, Xander's a demon magnet (engaged to Anya), Giles is blind (he's in England and can't see what they're doing), and Willow is performing magic beyond her control and making life seriously difficult for her friends.

This episode is the beginning of Willow's descent into magic addiction (it's a good thing she put the beer down or things could have gotten dangerous). We will watch throughout the season as she begins to do magic for her own selfish reasons, rather than to help the gang. That said, her magic is used 90 percent of the time for good, and very rarely for reasons like this one, which is why the way the writers treat it in season six is almost ridiculous. The ending of the episode was hilarious, showing that maybe the reason Willow doesn't like Anya (aside from the fact she's with Xander) is that she realizes they're a lot alike.

HIGHLIGHT: The brief return of Amy.
INTERESTING FACTS: D'Hoffryn is played by the same actor who played the doctor in "I Fall to Pieces" on *Angel*.
OOPS: In the span of one day, Buffy's hair keeps switching back and forth between crimped and straight. And when Spike passes in front of Giles's glass bookcase, you can see his reflection in the glass.
WILLOW WICCA WATCH: Willow casts a spell that hurts her friends, and Giles warns her that she can't do spells when she's upset, because she's unfocused and they'll go awry.
MUSIC/BANDS: In this episode we hear Blink 182's "All the Small Things" from *Enema of the State* and Sue Willett's "Night Time Company" from *Stories From My Head*.

4.10 Hush

Original air date:	December 14, 1999
Written and directed by:	Joss Whedon
Guest cast:	Phina Oruche (Olivia), Amber Benson (Tara), Brooke Bloom (Wiccan #1), Jessica Townsend (Wiccan #2), Camden Toy (Gentleman), Charlie Brumbly (Gentleman), Doug Jones (Gentleman), Don W. Lewis (Gentleman), Carlos Amezcua (Newscaster), Elizabeth Truax (Little Girl), Wayne Sable (Freshman)

Sunnydale is visited by the Gentlemen, who take the voices of everyone in town so they can torture them but no one can scream.

This mind-blowing episode is one of the best hours of television ever. The writing, direction, costumes, makeup, and acting are second to none. Joss came up with a brilliant and horrific concept, creeping out the audience as they had never been creeped out before. And just when you thought these floating, grinning creatures were about as scary as they could get, he throws in psychotic beasts in straitjackets that lumber foolishly beside them. The scene where Tara drops her books in the street is so suspenseful you can barely watch. (This episode marks Amber Benson's first appearance.)

When the WB advertised this episode with trailers suggesting it was going to be 29 minutes of silence, viewers scratched their heads in confusion, but when it all came together it was perfect. We take for granted that if you're being hurt or chased, you cry out, but in taking away that defence mechanism, Joss has created a nightmare. And a new classic. The Gentlemen are not part of a nursery rhyme, but a figment of Joss's imagination, and the reason they seem so familiar is because he's borrowed from aspects of other fairy tales and horror films. The atmosphere of this episode is reminiscent of a Tim Burton film, with the creepy Danny Elfman piano music, the darkness, and the black and white costumes. And

Joss used that all-powerful Number 7 from so many stories and fables before (seven dwarfs, seven seas, seven deadly sins, Seven Sisters). Watch for the person holding the sign that says "Revelations 15:1," a verse that states, "Then I saw in the sky another mysterious sight, great and amazing. There were seven angels with seven plagues, which are the last ones, because they are the final expression of God's anger." This person has obviously assumed the Gentlemen are the seven angels, and the hearts they are collecting will become the seven plagues.

It's not just the writing that made this episode so brilliant, but the acting. Even when they can't utter a sound, the Scoobies are completely in character. The scene in the psychology classroom is the highlight of the season. Giles goes on and on and on (complete with illustrations and music); Xander's mind is in the gutter; Willow offers helpful suggestions; Buffy simply assumes they can go off and kill the creatures with a stake — and, of course, complains she's too hippy in the pictures; and Anya couldn't care less. What's even more intriguing is the way Whedon contrasts the gang's education with the debriefing the Initiative is getting with Maggie. Giles uses primitive drawings and an overhead while Maggie uses a computer voice. The Initiative don't know anything about the creatures other than what has been shown by the previous murders and other scientific proof; the Scoobies, on the other hand, know how to combat the Gentlemen by following instructions they heard in a nursery rhyme. And the audience already knows which method will work.

"Hush" was a fantastic *Buffy* episode, and the only one that truly scares me every time I watch it.

HIGHLIGHT: Buffy's staking motion during Giles's "seminar."

INTERESTING FACTS: The weekend before the episode aired, Joss went into the posting board to talk about how he came up with the Gentlemen: "Inspiration for the bad guys: *Nosferatu* (Shreck), *Dark City*, *Hellraiser*, *Nosferatu* (Kinski), Grimm's Fairy Tales, the *Seventh Seal*, and Mr. Burns. And much Victorian influence. And yeah, about 29 min without dialogue, scary as hell to pull off, but if I have failed, IT'S SOMEONE ELSE'S FAULT. I'm fairly certain." Also, Amber Benson and the other stars have talked about how scary those monsters were to have on the set. "They were the nicest guys, but they looked so scary," Amber says. "We were shooting those scenes on location at a really scary spot, and the crew guy who led me to the set was telling me all these creepy stories about working on the movie *Se7en*. Then I saw them, and I just about died! Usually, you can see things on TV and you figure they can't be that scary in person, but they were. Alyson kept looking over at them during lunch and saying, 'I can't look at them. They look like dead people.' A lot of the cast and crew were scared by those guys."

NITPICKS: It's a little hard to believe that everyone on this show is an expert police sketch artist. Every time someone spots a demon, they're able to produce an exact portrait to show someone else (as Olivia does here). But notice how Giles has also done it in the past, yet his drawings on the overheads are so bad? And was it just me, or was Buffy's scream at the end kind of pathetic? It's the only time I really wished for an overdub on the show.

OOPS: We see Anya eating popcorn in the classroom, but she doesn't have any when the group walks in. Also, the clock on the tower the Gentlemen are in reads one time from the outside, but another from the inside. Finally, when Spike grabs the mug of blood from the fridge, it's filled almost to the brim, yet when he takes a swig he tips it so far up he should have been covered in it.

MUSIC/BANDS: During Giles's talk, he puts on Camille Saint-Saëns's "Danse Macabre."

4.11 Doomed

Original air date: January 18, 2000
Written by: Marti Noxon, David Fury, and Jane Espenson
Directed by: James A. Contner
Guest cast: Ethan Erickson (Percy), Anastasia Horne (Laurie)

The gang (minus Giles) discovers that Riley is one of the commandos, but must stop an impending apocalypse. Again.

After "The Zeppo," it's hard to take one of those "Some demon is going to open the Hellmouth thus ending the world" episodes seriously. When Giles says, "It's the end of the world, everyone dies," we can't help but ask, hasn't he caught on by now? The only difference between this aversion of the apocalypse and previous ones is that Spike is there. Wearing a Hawaiian shirt.

The theme of this episode is that high school is something that follows us long after we walk across that podium and grab that piece of paper. Willow overhears Percy calling her a geek and is immediately back in Grade 10, sitting alone wearing her Sears clothes. Spike tells Xander he's useless to Buffy, and Xander is reminded of all the times in high school when Buffy told him to go away or he'd get hurt. And inevitably, they go right back to high school to confront those demons head-on (and, for the first time, Spike realizes he can confront demons, too). Buffy tells Riley their relationship will never work and all she wants is a normal boyfriend. Is she haunted by her high school romance, too?

Forrest comes up with the interesting opinion that the Slayer is a fairytale creature. She's about as real as Superman to the Initiative, and this presents Riley with his first crisis of faith. Does he believe Buffy, who claims to be something that his "family" suggests is not real? Or does he forget Buffy and continue on the way he was in the Initiative, taking down Polgara demons while assuming a strong female demon hunter is a myth?

HIGHLIGHT: Spike's Southern drawl when Riley thinks he recognizes him: "I'm a friend of Xanderrrr's."
NITPICKS: One thing that often comes up on this show is Buffy's self-centeredness. She's quick to blame Riley for not being honest with her, but she was pulling the same ruse on him. And after Willow has suffered such a serious trauma earlier in the season, why would Buffy leave her alone at a party, Willow's first excursion back into the land of the living?
OOPS: In the scene where Giles is showing Buffy a map of where the commandos have been spotted, his voice appears to have been dubbed. Also, when Willow finds the dead guy, his eyes are open, but later they're closed, and then open again. Finally, when the gang is doing research on the demons, Xander's shirt is open, then buttoned, then open again.
MUSIC/BANDS: In this episode, we hear the Hellacopters' "Hey!" from *Payin' the Dues*, and Echobelly's "Mouth Almighty" from *Lustra*.

4.12 A New Man

Original air date: January 25, 2000
Written by: Jane Espenson
Directed by: Michael Gershman

Guest cast: Robin Sachs (Ethan Rayne), Elizabeth Payne (Waitress), Michelle Ferrara (Mother)

Just as Giles is feeling like Buffy no longer notices him, Ethan Rayne strikes again and turns Giles into a Fyarl demon, making him unrecognizable to the gang.

Jane Espenson has always had the magic touch when it comes to the comic episodes, and "A New Man" is no exception. It's Buffy's birthday again, so things will inevitably go terribly wrong. Giles has been on the periphery this season, coming to grips with no longer being a librarian or even a Watcher, and wondering if he even has a place in Buffy's life any longer. Ethan's mojo simply personifies how Giles has been feeling: like an old creature who is not recognized as part of the gang (and Wesley's not there anymore to make him feel cool). Anthony Stewart Head is brilliant as always in this episode, and somehow makes the Fyarl demon come across as a stiff librarian type, which is hilarious.

Giles meets his nemesis in the form of Maggie Walsh, that "fishwife" who will become Buffy's new mentor; she shrugs him off as an absent father figure who should just leave Buffy alone. Poor Giles discovers that everyone but him knew about the Initiative, which makes him feel even more alone (and Buffy was complaining in the last episode about Riley not being up front with her?). It's interesting that Buffy jumps headfirst into the Initiative without discussing it with Giles or anyone, despite the fact that they do their "research" in a completely different fashion than she's used to. And even when Giles gets the 314 tip from Ethan, she doesn't question that maybe this army outfit isn't all it seems on the surface.

The final scene is touching, as are many scenes with Giles and Buffy. Giles realizes he might not fit in with the group as one of their buddies, but is more like a stern father to her. Just as Joyce no longer takes an active part of Buffy's life but is still important to her,

---

Buffy's Birthdays

In "Older and Far Away," Spike says to Buffy, "Have you ever thought of *not* celebrating your birthday?" It's a good question, considering her birthdays are usually exciting for all the wrong reasons:

- 17th birthday: Angel becomes Angelus and begins hunting Buffy and her friends. ("Surprise")
- 18th birthday: As a Watcher's Council rite of passage, Giles drains Buffy of her powers without telling her, putting both Buffy and her mother in serious danger. Her father cancels on her for the first time, which leads to the disintegration of their relationship. ("Helpless")
- 19th birthday: Giles is turned into a Fyarl demon, and not recognizing that it's Giles, Buffy hunts it with the intent of killing it. ("A New Man")
- 20th birthday: Dawn discovers she's not real, and cuts her arm open in front of everyone to try to prove she's human. Glory kidnaps Dawn, and the gang must save her. ("Blood Ties")
- 21st birthday: Upset that everyone's ignoring her, Dawn inadvertently wishes that no one would leave her, trapping Buffy and her friends in the Summers' house in a never-ending birthday party. ("Older and Far Away")

Giles will always be the one she'll turn to, the one who means the most to her. This episode is the first of several that explore the individual characters' inherent doubts about their importance in Buffy's life.

HIGHLIGHT: Demon Giles chasing Maggie down the street.

INTERESTING FACTS: Anthony Stewart Head was happy to finally be rid of the suit once the shoot was over: "There are certain key smells like the smell of the latex glue. It's not particularly noxious, but by the third time it went on I really, really got to not like that after a while. It's just like Copydex, but there's something about it being all over your face."

NITPICKS: Why does Giles just happen to open that one dusty old book that just happens to tell him that a demon will be awakening after hundreds of years that very night? It's a little too unbelievable, even for this show. And when Giles goes to Xander's apartment, watch the pair of briefs hanging on Xander's clothesline: it keeps switching from one clothespin to two.

OOPS: Spike chastizes Anya for suggesting he could use a lamp in his crypt; he explains that there's no way to get any electricity in there, yet later he'll have a television and working lights.

MUSIC/BANDS: At Buffy's birthday party, we hear "In Good Time" (artist unknown), from a Dreamworks Demo Master CD, and 12 Volt Sex's "Over Divine" from *Pop Formula*. When Ethan's at the bar with Giles, we hear Other Star People's "Then There's None" (*Diamonds in the Belly of the Dog*) and "Lucky Man" (artist unknown). This episode also features Scott Ellison's "Down Down Baby," from *Live at Joey's*.

4.13 The I in Team

Original air date:	February 8, 2000
Written by:	David Fury
Directed by:	James A. Contner
Guest cast:	Jack Stehlin (Dr. Angleman), Neil Daly (Mason)

As Buffy becomes more ensconced in the Initiative, the gang fears she might be in over her head. Meanwhile, Professor Walsh worries that Buffy might be a bad influence on Riley and decides to put an end to their relationship.

This episode features a battle between those always seeking answers and those who never ask questions. Buffy once again (remember Faith?) abandons and endangers her friends — Willow in particular — when something juicier comes along, and this time it's going head-to-head with Riley and the Initiative. Professor Walsh involves Buffy in the war games to help train her "boys," but soon discovers Buffy is a complex person she can't understand. Unlike the demons, she can't cut Buffy open to experiment on her, and she sees Buffy as a threat to the team.

"The I in Team" contains one of the coolest alternating sequences of the season: a parallel is drawn between Buffy fighting alongside Riley and their lovemaking. While in Riley's world, the two are very separate things, Buffy's love life is usually as dangerous and violent as her patrolling. Riley is a Milquetoast compared to her other men, and soon she'll realize that a "normal" guy like Riley isn't in the cards for a not-so-normal gal like herself. The juxtaposition of the fighting and sex scenes, accompanied by that dreamy ethereal music, is beautifully shot.

In this episode, the relationship between Riley and Walsh becomes decidedly creepy, as Walsh takes on the persona of the mother-in-law. Buffy has taken away her "son" and Walsh believes no woman will be as good for her boy as she is, so she attempts to get Buffy out of the picture. Riley seems to realize that Walsh is his mother figure, but doesn't question how strange that is. At one point, when he gets paged, he says to the other guys, "Mother wants us."

But sometimes even your own family can turn on you, and Riley finds out what Walsh is capable of the hard way. And when her evil plan falls through, we finally find out what "314" stands for. And it ain't pretty.

HIGHLIGHT: When we see Buffy's face on the monitor behind Walsh's back, and her subsequent threat: "If you think that's enough to kill me, you really don't know what a Slayer is. Trust me when I say you're gonna find out." Brilliant.

NITPICKS: When the gang is trying to get the tracking device out of Spike he says he doesn't care if it's playing "Rockin' the Casbah." Considering he was a punk, Spike should have known the Clash's 1982 song was called "Rock the Casbah." Later, we watch Buffy's pulse on the monitor while she's engaged in the fight. Even when she's fighting at her hardest, the pulse doesn't change. I don't care how supernatural she is, her pulse would at least go up a point or two.

WILLOW WICCA WATCH: Willow's spell to ionize the atmosphere works well, even if it has some strange side effects.

MUSIC/BANDS: This episode featured "Trashed" by Lavish, from their Polaroid CD, Black Lab's "Keep Myself Awake," from the *Buffy the Vampire Slayer* soundtrack (at the Bronze), and the amazing music playing during the fighting/lovemaking sequence is Delerium's "Window to Your Soul," from their *Karma* CD.

4.14 Goodbye Iowa

Original air date:	February 15, 2000
Written by:	Marti Noxon
Directed by:	David Solomon
Guest cast:	Jack Stehlin (Dr. Angleman), JB Gaynor (Little Boy), Saverio Guerra (Willy), Amy Powell (Reporter), Andy Marshall (Scientist #1)

Riley is forced to face up to who he is, what the Initiative has turned him into, and whether or not the Initiative is the best thing for him.

After spending so many years under Walsh's thumb just accepting what came to him and not questioning anything, Riley has to face some awful truths in this episode, things that have him asking so many questions he could be spending the rest of his life searching for the answers. The Initiative not only kept "314" from him, they pumped him with vitamins, mind-altering drugs, and probably steroids that kept him strong and prevented him from asking too many questions. They truly are the Testosterone League, and Maggie keeps them that way (notice the not-so-subtle poster on the back of Riley's door that says BALLS in big letters . . . ahem). Marc Blucas is great as the confused soldier going through major physical and emotional withdrawal, and while the character is pretty unlikeable just because he's, well, boring, the viewer feels genuine sympathy for him in this episode.

The relationship between Willow and Tara has become more interesting in the past few episodes. Since "Hush," Willow seems to have found a kindred spirit in Tara, and little hints are dropped here and there that their relationship is a lesbian one. Their first spell together has them plucking flowers. Willow keeps Tara a secret from the gang, as if there was something about Tara she needs to hide. And in this episode, Willow mentions how much she enjoyed their "spell" the day before, and how she'd been thinking about it all day. And they're thinking of conjuring the goddess "Thespia" . . . ahem. It's about time there was a serious homosexual relationship on this show, and while other shows tend to make fun of it — on *Xena*, for instance, it became more of an in-joke than a serious lesbian relationship — or touch on it in a "very special episode" and then move on to more "important" things, the writers deserve major kudos for the wonderful way they handle it. It's kept subtle at the beginning, and when the gang eventually finds out they're a little surprised, but accepting, and instead of making a big deal about Willow and Tara's first onscreen kiss ("The Body") or their getting into bed together, the writers simply let it happen. Finally . . . someone who knows how to handle a homosexual relationship on television as if it just is, rather than it being something to gawk at. Although, when Tara deliberately ruins the spell for searching out demons, it makes you wonder . . . .

Xander is introduced to the Initiative, and along with Buffy and Riley, he sees Adam for the first time. Adam. The first man. Frankenstein's monster. Again. Yes, folks, just two seasons after "Some Assembly Required," the writers have given us yet another Frankenstein episode. The part of Adam that is most like Dr. Frankenstein's creature is his willingness to learn about the world around him. Just as the biblical Adam named things and came to understand the world through that evil aspect of humanity — knowledge — so too does Adam dissect creatures, ask many questions, and try to figure out why other people are on earth. He already knows why he's here, but he needs to know what everyone else's purpose is, and why Maggie gave him emotions. It's interesting that Maggie Walsh — Ms. Mother Says Shut Up and Don't Ask Questions — would create a monster that's so darned inquisitive.

Within 24 hours, Riley has lost his "mother," realized that everything he believed in is a lie, and has met the brother from hell. And just when he thinks he has no one to hold on to but Buffy, he's ripped away from her again by Forrest and Buffy's other evil brothers-in-law. Riley's character came under fire by a lot of fans because he was so far removed from Angel, but sometimes it was hard not to feel for the guy.

HIGHLIGHT: Spike giving Riley the thumbs-up to kill Buffy.

INTERESTING FACTS: Joss Whedon is very specific about how you pronounce Tara's name. Amber explains, "Joss [says] you can't call me 'Tahr-ah.' He's very adamant that it's 'Tear-ah.' Someone said, 'Is it Tahr-ah or Tear-ah?' and he's like, 'There is no Tahr-ah on this set!'"

NITPICKS: Maggie Walsh is dead and many people in the Initiative believe Buffy is responsible. Could she really have just tiptoed in there wearing a pair of glasses and thought she was properly disguised? And for some reason that demon that throws Spike out of Willy's bar has exactly the same voice that Adam had. Finally, Riley says they'd captured the Polgara demon a week ago, but if this episode immediately follows last week's, shouldn't he have said they'd caught it the day before?

OOPS: During the fight at the Initiative, Buffy is thrown against a door and you can see her stunt double's face straight on. Also, Buffy tells everyone that the gate slammed shut and then she used the gun in the sewers, when it happened the other way around. And Buffy uses the bandanna in her hair to wrap Riley's hand, but a few moments later it's back on her head. Finally, when Adam changes computer disks, he doesn't take the previous one out before loading the new one.

MUSIC/BANDS: This episode featured Lou Reed's "Romeo Had Juliette" from *New York*, Paul Singerman's "My Last Romance," and Mark Cherrie's "Big Ed."

4.15 This Year's Girl

Original air date: February 22, 2000
Written by: Douglas Petrie
Directed by: Michael Gershman
Guest cast: Chet Grissom (Detective), Alastair Duncan (Collins), Jeff Ricketts (Weatherby), Kevin Owers (Smith), Mark Gantt (Demon), Kimberly McRae (Hospital Visitor), Sara Van Horn (Older Nurse), Brian Hawley (Orderly), Jack Esformes (Doctor)

Faith wakes up from her coma and attempts to exact revenge for what Buffy put her through.

She's back! Just when you thought that coma was a handy plot device to get Faith out of the picture permanently, she returns after a series of weird dreams. In each of them Buffy stabs her over and over again, and it's only when she fights Buffy and wins that she's able to wrest herself out of the coma. The dream sequences are great (Joss is a master of them: see "Surprise" and "Restless"), and it's a thrill to see Harry Groener again as the Mayor. And Faith shows us just how strong a Slayer is when she gets up from her bed and walks into the hallway to speak to someone, without her legs buckling or her voice cracking.

"This Year's Girl" had some amazing moments. Buffy tells Willow that every police officer in Sunnydale is on the lookout for Faith and that she's probably hiding somewhere, when Faith suddenly turns around to confront her in broad daylight. Only Faith would have the guts to do something like that. And when she first gets out of the hospital, she goes straight to Giles's house and watches through the window as Buffy gets the phone call. Just as Angel watched through Joyce's window to see Buffy and Willow get the news about Jenny in "Passion," Faith revels in their discomfort and the fact that she knows where they are, but they can't find her. Her sadism hasn't changed, but neither has her sense of guilt that what she's doing might be wrong, and if things had gone a different way, she could have been Buffy instead.

Faith is also still Buffy's conscience, telling it like it is and pointing out Buffy's flaws. In this episode, we see Joyce for the first time in ages, with Faith telling the audience what we've already figured out: Joyce is no longer a presence in Buffy's life. In "Goodbye Iowa," when Buffy feared that her friends' lives might be in danger, she hid everyone she cared about at Xander's place. Notice Joyce wasn't there. So what better way to conclude the Faith/Buffy storyline than to let them walk in each other's shoes for a while. It's brilliant. Faith has always wondered if, by the grace of God, she could have been Buffy, and Buffy often tries to come to grips with why Faith is the way she is — what makes her tick and what's going on in her brain. So, voilà! You're now in each other's bodies. It's an inspired concept that makes the anticipation for next week's episode that much more exciting.

HIGHLIGHT: The Slayer fight on campus.

INTERESTING FACTS: The title of this episode isn't just a reference to Elvis Costello's "This Year's Girl," which appears on his 1978 album *This Year's Model*, but also to Japanese kitsch-pop band Pizzicato Five's song of the same name, from their 1994 American debut EP, *Five by Five*.

DID YOU NOTICE? The dream sequences had some great hints and winks in them. In the first one, Faith tells Buffy she has to get ready for "little sis" to come (season five). At the picnic with the Mayor, a snake slithers across the blanket, and the Mayor tells him he doesn't belong there. And finally, when Faith wakes up, her monitor says 30-97. Some fans speculated this could be the 7-3-0 (all the numbers are there) she had referred to in the "Graduation Day, (Part Two)" dream sequence. Nope, try again.

NITPICKS: Why is it that eight months after the Sunnydale High destruction, the build-

CHRISTINA RADISH

The return of Faith was something fans longed for all season

ing is still standing there with nothing but some yellow police tape around it? Every time the gang enters, the place creaks and groans; wouldn't it have been demolished by now? And Harry Groener has lost some weight and sports a different hairstyle, so it's not as believable that he would have made that videotape seven months earlier. Also, since Faith is wanted for questioning in a series of murders, shouldn't there have been at least one security camera on her room? And when she removes the wires that are monitoring her, the medical equipment should have started beeping or showing a flatline — it did neither.

OOPS: When Faith is running away from Buffy on the school campus, she leaps over a "brick" wall, which sways back and forth when she hits it. D'oh. And when Faith and Buffy take their fight into the Summers' dining room, they clear off the table, yet a moment later the tablecloth and a few other items are back on the table.

RESTLESS MOMENT: In "Restless," Buffy will look at the messy bed and comment, "Faith and I just made that bed."

4.16 Who Are You?

Original air date:	February 29, 2000
Written and directed by:	Joss Whedon
Guest cast:	Alastair Duncan (Collins), Chet Grissom (Detective), Rick Stear (Booke), Jeff Ricketts (Weatherby), Kevin Owers (Smith), Amy Powell (Reporter), Rick Scarry (Sergeant), Jennifer S. Albright (Date)

With Faith and Buffy in each other's bodies, Buffy has to prove to the Watcher's Council that she's not actually Faith before they ship her off to England.

Eliza Dushku and Sarah Michelle Gellar are outstanding playing each other in this funny, tense, and sad episode. It's clear they've watched each other act out the scenes first, and then mimicked each other's actions to make Eliza seem like Buffy and Sarah like Faith. Sarah has Eliza's laugh down pat when she's at Giles's house, while Eliza nails Sarah's stutter in the back of the Council van. And Eliza keeps the constant worry lines that Buffy would have, always looking like she's in fear of her friends being hurt, while Sarah adopts the Faith strut, swagger, and "Because it's *wrong*" sarcasm.

But not only do they have to mimic each other's actions and words, they have to evoke each other's subtleties. When Buffy (in Faith's body) confronts Giles and tries to convince him she really is Buffy, she's earnest one minute, and then does the off-topic, "What's a stevedore?" questioning that makes Buffy so charming. Meanwhile, Sarah has to show the guilt that Faith feels. She's awful to Tara, but she's putting on a show, and only later when she's alone will she feel the remorse for what she's done. Unfortunately, Eliza is superior at Faith in this sense because even when she's being mean, we can see the pain she's masking beneath, whereas Sarah as Faith just comes across as mean.

An interesting aspect of the body-switching is the effect of Buffy's absence on her friends. Giles, Willow, Riley — even her own mother — don't recognize her. Buffy is acting so strangely, and no one seems to catch on. Joyce probably assumed she's picked up the new behavior at college, Willow and Giles likely suspect she's gotten it from the Initiative, and Riley, well, he's just happy she's got it. It takes Tara — someone who's never even met Buffy — to figure out what's happened.

The shining moment of the episode is in the church, where Adam's vampire legion has taken the small congregation hostage. (And Riley, the little church-going goody-goody, has arrived at church late. Does he realize he's going to Hell for that?) Faith is on her way to a life of Caribbean freedom when she hears the news, and despite her "evil" nature she chooses to help the hostages over saving herself. When she and Buffy square off in the church, Faith reaches her low point, beating on her own body and declaring her hatred for the person she's become. Sarah is excellent, as is Dushku, who shows Buffy's shock at what Faith's doing to "herself." It's a poignant moment, and — conveniently, in a church — the one that will lead to her salvation. (See "Five by Five" and "Sanctuary" for the conclusion to the Faith storyline on *Angel*.)

HIGHLIGHT: Giles trying to distract the officer by flailing his arms about as if he were the Fyarl demon again: "Damn it, man! We have to get inside! Our families are in there! Our, uh, mothers and tiny, tiny babies!"

NITPICKS: Does Buffy always have to get so self-righteous on her boyfriends? She gets so jealous and insecure around Faith, and when Angel works with her to uncover Faith's secrets in "Enemies," she doesn't forgive him for doing what she told him to. Here she says to Riley, "You slept with her?" like he should have assumed some body-switching had been going on behind his back. And when Faith says to Spike, "You're a vampire," why exactly does he go ahead and explain that yes, he's a vampire, who happens to have a chip in his head, which happens to render him powerless, etc. when he should just assume Faith (who he thinks is Buffy) knows everything already? A little too convenient.

MUSIC/BANDS: "Vivian" by Nerf Herder (the guys who do the *Buffy* theme song), from *How to Meet Girls*, plays as Faith in Buffy's body dances at the Bronze; the Cure's "Watching Me Fall" from *Bloodflowers*, plays as Faith talks to Spike; and Headland's "Sweet Charlotte Rose," from *Headland 2* plays at the Bronze when Tara, Willow, and Faith are talking.

4.17 Superstar

Original air date:	April 4, 2000
Written by:	Jane Espenson
Directed by:	David Grossman
Guest cast:	Danny Strong (Jonathan), Robert Patrick Benedict (Jape), John Saint Ryan (Colonel George Haviland), Erica Luttrell (Karen), Adam Clark (Cop), Chanie Costello (Inga), Julie Costello (Ilsa)

When Buffy and the gang find themselves unable to handle a lair of vampires, they turn to the greatest mastermind/basketball player/writer/singer/all-around smart guy, Jonathan Levinson. Huh?

You can always count on Jane Espenson to write a clever episode that is consistent with the characters while giving us something to laugh about. Except this time. "Superstar" was a ridiculous episode that broke up the two-month hiatus before the final five episodes. I love Jonathan's character as much as the next guy, but this episode was just silly. I kept waiting for the general in the *Monty Python* sketches to break in and say, "Stop that! Stop that at once! This is just childish and I won't have it!" Unfortunately for us, he didn't.

This episode had its funny moments though: watch the opening credits to see Jonathan magically appear looking very James Bond-like and cool after each star is shown. And the show becomes a sort of "Where's Waldo?" game where you try to spot all the background Jonathan references. And, in light of Jonathan's recurrence in season six, it's funnier in retrospect because he just goes about things *so* badly. (A basketball star? To quote Buffy, he's like three feet tall!) But in the end, this episode was nothing beyond its surface, and just caused utter confusion. Does Jonathan dislike Buffy for some reason? What did she do to him (other than save his life) that made him want to render her almost helpless? Does he hold a grudge, or does he actually want to be Buffy? When we find out that in his ideal universe, he has the Class Protector Award, it diminishes the sincerity with which he presented it to her at the prom. When he was onstage at the prom, did he mean what he said to her or did he secretly wish he were getting that award?

CHRISTINA RADISH

What makes this episode important is that it introduces the concept that someone could brainwash people into believing different memories, a clue to a certain character who will suddenly appear in season five.

HIGHLIGHT: When Jonathan appears in the Initiative, and he's half the size of everyone else.

Superstar Jonathan Levinson, a.k.a. Danny Strong

NITPICKS: Some of the memories he has endowed people with are things he couldn't possibly know about, such as that he, not Buffy, was the one who smashed the Master's bones. How could he have known she'd done that? Unless his curse was that people would take everything they know to be true about Buffy and think that he did it instead (in which case, the events in "Surprise" take on a whole new meaning . . . .)

OOPS: The mark on Jonathan's shoulder in the calendar is slightly different than the one we see on him.

MUSIC/BANDS: Onstage at the Bronze is Royal Crown Revue, who perform "Trapped (In The Web of Love)" and "Hey Sonny (Where'd You Go?)" from their CD, *Walk on Fire*. Jonathan joins them onstage and sings "Serenade in Blue" (the vocals were done by Brad Kane).

4.18 Where the Wild Things Are

Original air date:	April 25, 2000
Written by:	Tracey Forbes
Directed by:	David Solomon
Guest cast:	Kathryn Joosten (Mrs. Holt), Casey McCarthy (Julie), Neil Daly (Mason), Jeff Wilson (Evan), Bryan Cuprill (Roy), Jeffrey Sharmat (Drowning Boy), Danielle Pessis (Christie)

When people notice apparitions and strange sexual behavior at a college frat party, the gang realizes the frat house is haunted and sets out to find the root of the problem.

This was a very spooky episode, although the premise — Riley and Buffy having constant sex — was a little strange. At first the gang thinks that the orgasmic wall, the vines covering the doors, and the "girls going all Felicity with their hair" are being caused by a ghost, but it turns out to be a poltergeist. Poltergeists are caused by negative energy from emotional turmoil in people. Experts believe the majority of poltergeist activity is created by hormonal upheaval in teenagers (think *Carrie*) and that females under the age of 20 are the leading causes, often unbeknownst to them. Teenagers who have encountered poltergeist activity often think they have become telekinetic, but in fact the poltergeists are triggered by a severe trauma in a living person (setting them apart from ghosts) and the activity can last a few hours or a few years. The activity builds up to a climax, then starts over again (much like a sexual act). Poltergeists can be extremely dangerous at their climax.

In this episode, the trauma was triggered by the sexual frustrations of the teenagers under the care of Mrs. Landingham (I had to say it) at the Lowell House for disadvantaged youths. Giles expresses outrage at her holier-than-thou attitude, telling her that the tension and terror she inflicted upon those kids has caused this energy. What isn't clear in this episode is what Buffy and Riley have to do with it. Poltergeist energy doesn't lie dormant waiting for a new negative energy, and even if that were the case, there is no negative energy between Riley and Buffy — they're simply acting out what the kids at Lowell House were prohibited from even thinking about. Or are the writers suggesting that their lovemaking is a sham, as Riley will hint at in season five? Giles states that if they stop making love, they'll die, which is never really explained. One possibility is that their lovemaking could be a reference to the "little death"; in French, the word for orgasm is "petit mort," because of the old belief that every time a person had an orgasm, they died a little.

For the most part, this is a stand-alone episode that has little bearing on the ones before and after it. Although, it does contain the Giles highlight of the season when he's caught . . . singing. One only wishes Oz could have been there. He would have truly appreciated the moment.

HIGHLIGHT: The look on Willow's face when she spots Giles at the Espresso Pump.

DID YOU NOTICE? The hallway outside Ms. Holt's apartment is the same one they'll later use for the hallway outside Xander's.

NITPICKS: What kind of ice-cream-truck music is that? Any ice cream jingle I've ever heard coming out of an ice cream truck is happy, tinkly music. This tune was written in a minor key and was so creepy I half-expected the Gentlemen to pop out of some bush.

OOPS: When the gang is standing in front of Lowell House, you can see Spike's reflection in the door.

MUSIC/BANDS: Throughout this episode we hear Crooner's "Parker Posey" (never released on album); "Brit Pop Junkies" (artist unknown); Caviar's "I Thought I Was Found" from their self-titled CD; Lumirova's "Philo" (*Lightning Stroke of Persistent Splendor*); and Fonda's "One of a Kind" (*The Invisible Girl*). As Xander and Anya argue, the song in the background is Face to Face's "The Devil You Know (God Is a Man)," from *Ignorance Is Bliss* (it is also on the *Buffy* soundtrack). And at the café, Giles is covering the Who's "Behind Blue Eyes."

4.19 New Moon Rising

Original air date:	May 2, 2000
Written by:	Marti Noxon
Directed by:	James A. Contner
Guest cast:	Seth Green (Oz), Conor O'Farrell (Colonel McNamara)

Willow has a difficult decision to make about her relationship with Tara when Oz suddenly reappears in Sunnydale.

Marti Noxon can make Willow (and consequently, us) cry like no one else can. "New Moon Rising" was another painful Willow/Oz episode where it seems like everyone's dream had been answered, but the timing was all wrong. In the world of *Buffy the Vampire Slayer* and *Angel*, there are no easy decisions. And no happy endings when it comes to love. Buffy and Angel were soul mates, but were forced to separate for the greater good. When Angel is finally given the opportunity to become human, making everyone's biggest wish for the couple come true, it turns out there were horrible side effects, and he had to sacrifice his happiness for Buffy. And in "New Moon Rising," just as Oz appears to have gotten his wolfiness under control, Willow is realizing her love for someone else.

An interesting analogy is made between Riley's reaction to Oz being a werewolf and Buffy discovering her best friend is gay. Riley can't believe Willow is "that kind of girl" to have dated a demon, but Buffy defends her because of her own past (and future) relationships with dangerous "HSTs." But when Buffy discovers Willow's new relationship, she has a look of surprise on her face that says, "Oh, I didn't realize you were that kind of girl." Just as Buffy quickly accepts Willow because she's her friend, Riley comes to terms with the fact that not all demons are bad, when he goes against the Initiative to try to help Oz.

ALBERT L. ORTEGA

Seth Green

What makes this episode so difficult is that the chemistry between Hannigan and Green — and consequently Willow and Oz — is so real, and because Tara is a new character, we still haven't really seen that onscreen chemistry (but it will happen, just you wait). Just as Angel and Buffy broke up because she was the only thing that could trigger his evil side, Oz needs to walk away because Willow stirs the animal within that's he's trying so desperately to control. When he keeps the werewolf under wraps, it comes out in a far more terrifying way, changing Oz's laid-back, almost catatonic personality into a jumpy, freaked-out ball of jealousy. Watching him and Willow say goodbye in Oz's van is absolutely heartbreaking, and the viewer feels as if he or she is the one breaking up with someone. This final gut-wrenching scene ends the relationship once and for all, and we sigh with disappointment that one of television's most interesting couplings has ended.

HIGHLIGHT: The touching scenes between Tara and Willow.

INTERESTING FACTS: Buffy, holding a crossbow to a scientist's head, threatens to pull a William Burroughs on him if they don't let Oz go. Pretty obscure reference for someone who isn't much of a reader. William S. Burroughs, the surrealist Beat writer famous for *Naked Lunch*, was charged with murder when he tried to shoot an apple off his wife's head with a gun . . . and missed. Also, the Colonel's last name is McNamara; could he be related to the brothers who kidnapped Angel in "The Ring"?

NITPICKS: Oz worries he won't be able to keep in touch now that he's continuing his travels. Can't he get a Hotmail account or something? And when Buffy's hiding out with Riley in the remains of Sunnydale High, where does she get the ceramic coffee mug she's holding?

OOPS: When Riley hits Oz with the dart, you can't see it in his back. But when Riley stands over him, you can.

4.20 The Yoko Factor

Original air date:	May 9, 2000
Written by:	Douglas Petrie
Directed by:	David Grossman
Guest cast:	David Boreanaz (Angel), Conor O'Farrell (Colonel McNamara), Bob Fimiani (Mr. Ward), Jade Carter (Lieutenant Reid)

Spike tries to split the gang up after Adam promises he'll remove his chip if he does so, and Adam puts the final phase of his plan in place. Meanwhile, Angel follows Buffy to Sunnydale to resolve some loose ends.

This episode brings to a climax the tensions that have been building all season. Buffy's been spending so much time with Riley and the Initiative, it's like she's forgotten the Scoobies ever existed. Willow fears that her friends might be "freaking out" about Tara now that the truth about their relationship has come out, and Xander continues to feel invisible, as he did in "Fear, Itself." Giles — who is revisiting his youth through the Who and Peter Frampton — feels unwanted; and Buffy no longer turns to him as a Watcher or a father. Spike, who has been a keen observer throughout the season, has tapped into the weakness of the gang, and ignites it, setting off arguments, tensions, and betrayals all around.

Spike explains the problem as the Yoko Factor, alluding to the theory that the Beatles broke up because of John's obsession with Yoko Ono — in fact, tensions had been building in the band for years. He rightly points out it wasn't Yoko's fault, but she's been blamed for it ever since. Riley is the Yoko, and because of him, the gang assumes, Buffy hasn't had the time of day for them. But the real problem is far more complicated. This isn't the first time Buffy has abandoned her friends when something more interesting came along, but she always ends up coming back, because she values them above all else. And many people lose touch with their close friends after high school, as they move away, enroll in college, take different courses, and follow separate paths. Only those with the strongest friendships can transcend the usual problems and remain close no matter what, and that's something the Scoobies will realize they must do.

Angel's appearance just adds to Buffy's confusion, but it gives a kinder sense of closure to their relationship than in "Sanctuary," the *Angel* episode that preceded it. It was inevitable that the writers would put Riley and Angel together for our amusement, although Buffy is really angry when he arrives. She tells him — again — that she went to L.A. to help him, assuming — as she always does — that he came to Sunnydale just to hurt her and Riley. The thing is, she *didn't* go to L.A. to save Angel, she went to get revenge against Faith. And he didn't come to Sunnydale to hurt Riley, he came to resolve the tensions between him and Buffy.

The tensions among the Scoobies climax in Giles's apartment, when they gang up on Buffy over how she no longer needs them. Her angry reaction is warranted, and you can't help but feel satisfied when she walks out on them. She counterattacks in a way we wish she had been able to do in "Dead Man's Party," and her "friends" deserve her reaction for taking Spike's word over Buffy's.

HIGHLIGHT: Willow getting all dramatic with Miss Kitty Fantastico: "You cannot have more catnip! You have a catnip problem!"

NITPICKS: Why does Riley put on those ridiculous Xander pants anyway? The army pants with a normal T-shirt wouldn't have drawn any attention at all. It's the camouflage vest with heavy artillery that generally makes people do a double take. Also, Angel says he needs Buffy to invite him into her dorm, but how did Sunday and her vampires get into Buffy's room and clear it out in "The Freshman"?

OOPS: When Giles is singing in his apartment he's wearing glasses, but when he jumps up they're gone.

MUSIC/BANDS: When Spike enters Giles's apartment, Giles is singing Lynyrd Skynyrd's "Freebird."

4.21 Primeval

Original air date:	May 16, 2000
Written by:	David Fury
Directed by:	James A. Contner
Guest cast:	Jack Stehlin (Dr. Angleman), Conor O'Farrell (Colonel McNamara), Bob Fimiani (Ward), Jordi Vilasuso (Dixon)

The gang figures out Adam's plan and realizes the only way to bring him down is to work together.

CHRISTINA RADISH

So that's *what he looks like under the makeup! George Hertzberg, who plays Adam*

Just when you thought Maggie Walsh couldn't get more evil, we realize she's implanted a chip in Riley to make him do her will when her plan fell into place. Riley — who's really been an automaton up to this point, anyway — can no longer make his body do what he wants it to, and his will belongs to the whim of Adam.

We discover the final phase of Maggie's — and now Adam's — plan, and are shown a secret lab behind Room 314. The reanimated corpses of Forrest, Maggie, and the doctor are just stupid and disgusting, though, and yet one more reason I was happily bidding adieu to this season. In *Frankenstein*, the creature wanted the doctor to create a woman for him, but Adam creates a legion of workers and soldiers that will help him take over the world. Unlike Frankenstein's monster, Adam doesn't have any more questions — he knows all the answers. Forrest is as cocky and annoying in death as he was in life, and it's satisfying to see him get whupped (but was it really necessary to have his decapitated head spin toward the screen? Yuck!)

The gang realizes they've been duped by Spike, and they come together in one of the coolest and strangest scenes yet. Where the writing of this episode may have been a little dubious, the direction was stunning. The *Matrix*-like moves of Buffy and the wall she creates around her are beautiful, and show how important her friends are to her. When they come together as one being, they are unstoppable, and the most powerful force on earth. The voice-over of the government official explaining how the project failed while we watch the gang escape in slo-mo is another great moment (nothing beats slow-motion scenes on *Buffy*). The Initiative is over (thank God), the gang is back together, and Tara and Riley are now accepted members of the group. A satisfying conclusion to a clumsy and disjointed season.

HIGHLIGHT: The colonel's reaction to Giles's magic gourd: "What kind of freaks *are* you people?!"

INTERESTING FACTS: If this episode reminded you of *The Matrix*, that's probably because it's one of Joss Whedon's favorite films, although he maintains that he never intended the final effect to be so close to the film. He wrote on the Bronze posting board: "We broke the story, magic-girl bests machine-man, and in preproduction realized the structural similarities to *The Matrix*. I became sheepish and insisted we make sure the action looked NOTHING LIKE the film, 'cause I'm not interested in being too derivative. I was VERY SPECIFIC on the subject. Of course, I wasn't around when they were filming it . . . . So IMAGINE THE LAUGHTER when I saw dailies. The incredible lack of laughter. But it was too late to reshoot, and it did look cool, so I lived with it."

NITPICKS: When Willow and Buffy are climbing down the elevator shaft they're talking so loudly, how did they ever think they were going to make a stealthy entrance? Also, Sarah Michelle Gellar lost a lot of weight throughout seasons three and four, and it's more noticeable in this episode than any other. In the final scene with Adam, which required mainly work from her stunt double, someone came up with the bright idea of putting her in a sheer top. The problem is, her double is larger and more muscular, and you could tell it wasn't Sarah throughout the entire scene.

OOPS: At the beginning of the episode, when Anya goes to see Xander, who's still in bed, watch as the top of his cover keeps moving up and down on his chest whenever the camera returns to him.

4.22 Restless

Original air date:	May 23, 2000
Written and directed by:	Joss Whedon
Guest cast:	Sharon Ferguson (First Slayer), David Wells (The Cheese Man), Phina Oruche (Olivia), Michael Harney (Xander's Dad)

Perhaps as a result of some bad cheese, the gang returns home after defeating Adam only to succumb to nightmares.

A glorious cross between *Alice in Wonderland* and *Nightmare on Elm Street*, "Restless" is unprecedented in television. It is a difficult episode that is so jam-packed with information we'll probably be seeing allusions to it for the rest of the series. Joss has set this episode up as the coda to season four, and a sort of mysterious lead-in to the emotionally turbulent season five. On first glance, the episode doesn't make much sense; it seems to be nothing more than a surreal dreamscape. Only later do we realize that Joss has mapped out what is going to come in the next two seasons.

Willow's dream is first. Much like her nightmare in "Nightmares," she discovers she's going to have to once again go onstage, but this time it's different (she refers to it when she says she can't do *Madame Butterfly*, the opera she was forced to sing in that episode). The ensuing psychotic production of *Death of a Salesman* — complete with cowboy, Dutch milk girl, and flapper — is hilarious. Willow has matured and changed so much over the past few years that it seems like the wallflower of high school is long gone. But is she? Has Willow really changed, or is the shy bookworm sitting just below the surface, constantly terrified they'll discover she's no different and start laughing at her again? Tara moves in and out of the dream, reminding Willow that they're going to find out about her, and Buffy keeps asking her why she's wearing a "costume."

Most of Willow's dream makes more sense in light of season six, when the gang discovers that Willow's powers are more devastating than even she could imagine. Being a witch is the first thing she's done in her life that makes her more powerful than everybody else. Willow's dream alludes to both *Alice in Wonderland* — her constant worry that she's going to be late is similar to the White Rabbit in Lewis Carroll's ultimate weird dream sequence — and C.S. Lewis's *The Lion, The Witch, and the Wardrobe*. In that book, four children discover the world of Narnia on the other side of the wardrobe, a world full of magic, but one that's not as wonderful as it seems. Similarly, Willow has come out of her own closet on her relationship with Tara and has entered a world of magic. But she, too, will discover that magic can be very dark and dangerous.

Next comes Xander's dream. His is influenced by *Apocalypse Now*, the infamous war movie based on Joseph Conrad's novel *Heart of Darkness*. In the movie, Captain Willard is sent into the jungles to bring back Colonel Kurtz, a man who has gone mad and become a danger to himself and those around him. But Willard discovers much more about himself on the journey than he'd bargained for. Xander's dream is similar to that journey — he is almost seduced by a woman (Joyce, in a strange Oedipal sequence), he encounters French-speaking people (Anya and Giles are dubbed in French), and he's constantly trying to escape his personal demons. Those demons happen to be his alcoholic parents, who haunt him daily and whom he never talks about. Xander's sequence is played out somewhat in "Hell's Bells" and "Grave," but otherwise it remains a mystery — maybe we'll discover why Buffy called him "big brother" in season seven? Armin Shimerman makes an interesting appearance as the Kurtz-meets-Principal-Snyder character.

Giles's dream is funny and poignant. While Xander and Willow have both been chased by a mysterious creature who seems to be trying to kill them, Giles figures out who the creature is. Buffy features prominently in his dream, as both his daughter and the one who is keeping him in the United States. While he walks through his dream with a rather blasé attitude, there are some jaw-dropping moments that make the viewer wonder what Giles has been keeping from everyone. Olivia appears pregnant and crying — has she asked him to move back to England with him to start a family, and he can't? Buffy can't seem to hit the fake vampire with the Nerf ball, triggering his innate fear that he's no good to her anymore (when she finally hits it, he tells her he has no treats for her, possibly alluding to Buffy telling Wesley that Giles always gives her a cookie when she slays a vampire). Like Willow in her dream, Giles fears he's late and has too many things to do. Does he believe life has passed him by, which is why he's been in a midlife crisis in season four? Willow blames him for what is happening, perhaps because he forgot to mention that their conjoining spell in "Primeval" is what's caused these dreams. His song onstage is hysterically funny (showing everyone why Joss *had* to do a musical episode in season six), and the recurring symbol in his dream is a watch (duh) that neither Slayer seems to pay any attention to. Is his stint as a Watcher over?

Finally, Buffy's dream comes, and it predicts pretty much everything that will happen in season five. Tara keeps reappearing in her dream, trying to give her the Manus card from "Primeval," which Buffy refuses. Tara tells her she's lost her friends, and then delivers, in a chant-like voice, the most important line to sum up season five: "You think you know what's to come, what you are. You haven't even begun." And then she tells her to be back before dawn . . . .

Joyce is stuck in a wall, mice nibbling on her knees, and the last thing Buffy sees of her is her face ("The Body"). Buffy leaves her, even though Joyce tells her that if she tried, she could probably get her out of there. Riley, who calls Buffy "Killer" (which, in "The Gift," she believes is her birthright), is sitting with the human-looking Adam. He tells Buffy he and Adam are very busy naming things (an allusion to Adam's job in the Garden of Eden when he had to name all the animals; there's another biblical allusion when Giles eats an apple in Xander's dream, a reference to both his teaching position and the one who led the others out of Paradise), and Buffy tries to convince them she's not a demon (season six). When she believes they're under attack, she opens her weapons bag to find only mud. This scene foreshadows her helplessness in season five when faced with the impending danger to both Dawn and Joyce. In her own allusion to *Apocalypse Now*, she takes that mud and smears it on her face, as Willard does before he enters Kurtz's camp. Riley tells her she's on her own ("Into the Woods") and she heads into the desert, where she finally confronts the beast that's been attacking her and her friends in their sleep. It's at the moment when she's face-to-face with the First Slayer that she understands she has so much more to learn about herself and her lineage, sparking her need for knowledge in season five.

You could write an entire university paper on "Restless" and its importance to the *Buffy* series, so I'm only skimming the surface here. I urge you to revisit this episode at the end of every season. Oh, and as for the Cheese Man, he doesn't mean anything. He is representative of those ridiculous things that happen in dreams where you wake up and say, "Now why the hell was that purple rhino stamping people's hands as they were jumping off the bridge?"

HIGHLIGHT: Willow holding up the lighter in the Bronze while doing her research.
INTERESTING FACTS: In Xander's dream, he runs into Giles at Sunnydale High, and Giles and Anya begin to speak French. Giles tells Xander that he needs to get back to the house where the others are all asleep, and that the demon that's after him can't find him there. When Xander looks confused, Giles gets frustrated and tells him he doesn't have time for Xander to goof around. Anya shows up and tells him everyone is waiting for him back at the house, and that she'll take him there. Ah, I knew that university French course would come in handy someday. Joss has used French as the weird dream speak before (see Buffy's dream in "Surprise"). Also, Willow writes on Tara's back in Greek; it's the beginning of a poem by Sappho, an ancient Greek lesbian poet. Finally, when Giles is on stage singing, that's Christophe Beck, who writes the scores for *Buffy*, on piano. Four Star Mary is also backing him up.

Season Five

SEPTEMBER 2000 • MAY 2001

Recurring characters in season five: Amber Benson (Tara), Clare Kramer (Glory), Charlie Weber (Ben), Troy T. Blendell (Jinx)

5.1 Buffy vs. Dracula

Original air date:	September 26, 2000
Written by:	Marti Noxon
Directed by:	David Solomon
Guest cast:	Rudolf Martin (Dracula), E.J. Gage (Mover #1), Scott Berman (Mover #2), Marita Schaub (Vampire Sister #1), Leslee Jean Matta (Vampire Sister #2), Jennifer Slimko (Vampire Sister #3)

Buffy faces off against the most famous vampire of all time, Dracula, and discovers something about herself in the process.

As far as season openers go (and they tend to be weak on *BtVS*), "Buffy vs. Dracula" is not only the best of the premieres, but features some of the best one-liners we've heard. It's also the first time a season premiere was written by someone other than Joss Whedon. The show immediately follows up many of the revelations of "Restless," sets up Buffy's quest for season five, and has a lot of fun doing it. If there was one vampire we never thought we'd see on this show, it's Dracula.

At one point in the episode, Giles asks Willow to research Vlad the Impaler. Vlad III Tepes (1431-1476) was one of the princes of Wallachia, a province of Romania, and was later called Dracula, or Dracul. His father was also a prince, but the monarchy did not pass from father to son: the new prince was chosen by a group of noblemen known as boyars. In Romanian, the word "dracul" means "dragon" (Vlad's father, also named Vlad, belonged to a knighthood known as the Order of the Dragon), but the word "drac" means "devil," and "dracula" means "son of the devil." Vlad's father and older brother were murdered, and he eventually assembled an army to overthrow the ruler and become the prince. But he's not remembered so much as a ruler as for the atrocities he committed. Dracula's torture method of choice was impalement, because it was a long, horrible death, and he loved to watch his victims as they died — he often ate his dinner while watching. Of course, he didn't limit himself to impalement — he also boiled victims alive, drove nails into them, skinned them . . . and several other things I shouldn't mention in a family book. He placed his impaled victims at the outskirts of the city, so that invading armies would be scared off and passersby would realize this was not a city where crime was tolerated. Dracula spared no one: he impaled women, men, children, and infants, and both noblemen and peasants. By the time he was deposed in 1462, he had killed between 40,000 and 100,000 people.

One anecdote about Vlad the Impaler stands out. After Vlad was deposed, a thief broke into his house, and an officer rushed in to arrest him. Vlad killed the officer, later saying he did so because a gentleman should never enter another's house without being invited. Perhaps this is why vampires must be invited into homes.

In "Buffy vs. Dracula," all of this myth, plus the usual legends, precede him. We see him shape-shifting into mist and into a wolf; hypnotizing women; turning Xander into a blithering Renfield; making Giles the, uh, unwilling Jonathan Harker to the legendary Three Sisters. But what's so funny about the episode is that everyone becomes enamored of Dracula because of his fame, as if he were a rock star rather than a legendary vampire. Buffy blushes with pride when she realizes he's heard of her; the most famous vampire to walk the earth is the perfect one to make her see how important her role is. Repeating Tara's mantra from "Restless," Dracula establishes season five as the one in which Buffy will understand who she is, what a Slayer is, what her "gift" is, what she has to offer the world, what her limitations are, and what she can do to stop all the madness. Note that Buffy takes offense to the term "killer," but "Slayer" is okay.

Her final scene with Giles — where she asks him to teach her who she is and where she falls in the lineage of Slayers, is touching. He has already told Willow that he's returning to England (he confesses to Willow before anyone else, showing the affinity he has for her); perhaps his revelation in "Restless" — that he's missing out on something and there's no more he can do for Buffy — has jolted him into this decision. Thankfully, Buffy convinces him that he's still a necessary part of her life — in essence, she needs her father around. But she can't keep him around for much longer . . . .

HIGHLIGHT: Xander covering up his allegiance to Dracula: "Like any of that's enough to fight the dark master . . . bator."

INTERESTING FACTS: Rudolf Martin, who plays Dracula, wasn't new to the role. When filming began on the episode, he had just completed the film *Dark Prince: The True Story of Dracula*, where he had played Vlad the Impaler. In that film, he had to present the historical Dracula, whereas in *Buffy* he played the fictional character. And if you saw any chemistry between him and Sarah, it's because they played a married couple on *All My Children* in 1993.

DID YOU NOTICE? Buffy has a new fighting style this season, perhaps because she has a new stunt double. Sophia Crawford, her previous double, and Jeff Pruitt, the stunt coordinator, left the show following a dispute. The new double leans less toward martial arts and more toward wrestling moves.

NITPICKS: Despite Dracula transcending most of the vampire hang-ups — his fangs are permanent, he doesn't get a game face when going into battle — he still needs to be invited into a house, even if he is in the form of mist. How did he get into Buffy's room?

OOPS: When Xander and Willow are walking through the cemetery looking for Buffy, Xander's dialogue is out of synch with his lips.

WILLOW WICCA WATCH: Willow starts the barbecue on the beach with a flick of her wrist, the first time we see her use magic effortlessly to do something trivial. She explains to the gang that magic is all about control, something she sometimes lacks.

RESTLESS MOMENTS: Dracula calls Buffy "killer," as Riley had done. Dracula repeats Tara's line from Buffy's dream.

MUSIC/BANDS: As the gang hangs out on the beach, you can hear Vertical Horizon's "Finding Me," from their *Everything You Want* CD. The scores for season five were written by Thomas Wanker.

5.2 Real Me

Original air date: October 3, 2000
Written by: David Fury

Directed by: David Grossman

Guest cast: Mercedes McNab (Harmony), Bob Morrisey (Crazy Guy), Brian Turk (Mort), Chaney Kley Minnis (Brad), Faith S. Abrahams (Peaches), Tom Lenk (Cyrus)

Buffy's little sister, who is really starting to become annoying, gets captured by Harmony and her minions, and Buffy must try to rescue her.

Buffy's little wha . . .? The final scene of "Buffy vs. Dracula" certainly threw viewers for a loop. "Did that other little stranger girl just call Joyce Mom?" And with "Real Me," Joss Whedon didn't give us any answers. So typical.

Keeping us confused, Joss decides instead to act as if nothing strange were happening. It's a dangerous way to handle a major change, with the potential to alienate viewers, but the great thing about Joss Whedon and the writers on the show are the risks they take, and Dawn is one big risk. Writing in her journal, she opens up to the viewers so we can welcome her (even if we haven't a clue what she's doing there) and she's immediately accepted as part of the gang, making us feel like the outsiders. What is Willow doing calling her Dawnie? Why is Giles letting her ride in the new sporty Gilesmobile? Why are Anya and Xander

Harmony, Glory, and their, um, minion

playing The Game of Life with her? The only thing that makes us go, "Ah, yes, she *is* Buffy's sister," is when Joyce tells Buffy to take care of her for the day and then leaves her in Xander's hands. Seems Joyce is about as competent a mother with Dawn as she is with Buffy.

We see the return of Harmony, yet again, with her minions (a precursor to Glory and her pathetic worshipers), and we feel as frustrated as Buffy when Dawn stupidly invites them in. This act begins the pattern of Dawn being a perpetual victim, with Buffy always saving her, something that will become annoying in season six.

Small hints about Dawn are dropped in this episode. A mentally unstable man approaches Dawn and calls her Miss Curds and Whey, alluding to Buffy's dream in "Graduation Day (Part Two)" when Faith says, "Little Miss Muffet counting down to 7-3-0." And the last line in her journal comes across as major foreshadowing, whether on a supernatural level, or even on an annoying-little-sister level. This episode takes some steps to set up the changes that will occur in season five, including Giles becoming interested in the magic shop, and Buffy's new spiritual training.

HIGHLIGHT: Anya trying to trade in her little pink children for more money.

DID YOU NOTICE? One of Harmony's minions, Cyrus, is played by Tom Lenk, who will later torment Buffy in season six as Andrew, that "other guy" in the Troika.

NITPICKS: Even though Dawn is the quintessential bratty little sister, wouldn't she know better than to disrupt Buffy's training or invite vampires into the house? Also, the gang is acting like this magic shop is the only one in Sunnydale and just keeps changing owners. Yet in "Passion," Jenny had to go down some stairs to the magic shop, so it was clearly a different place, and in "Lover's Walk," the shop was half the size of the one in this episode. Not only does the magic shop keep changing owners, it keeps changing locations.

RESTLESS MOMENT: Now we understand Tara's warning: "Be back before Dawn."

MUSIC/BANDS: The song playing on Giles's car stereo is Edvard Grieg's "Prelude from Holberg Suite," Opus 40.

5.3 The Replacement

Original air date:	October 10, 2000
Written by:	Jane Espenson
Directed by:	James A. Contner
Guest cast:	Michael Bailey Smith (Toth Demon), Kelly Donovan (Other Xander), Cathy Cohen (Building Manager), David Reivers (Foreman), Fritz Greve (Construction Worker)

When Xander is hit with a blast from a Toth demon, he is split in two. One Xander embodies all of his strong points, and the other one his weaknesses.

So what do you do when you're on a limited budget and need to do an episode that requires big-budget split screens? Why, you choose an actor who has an identical twin. That's right, half the scenes in this episode feature Nicholas Brendon's brother, Kelly Donovan, who plays the more suave and together Xander in the scenes where they both appear. Both actors are great in this funny episode where Xander, despite his earlier proclamation to the contrary, pretty much becomes everyone's butt monkey once again. One half of his personality is debonair, the other is a loser.

ALBERT L. ORTEGA

Double take: Nicholas Brendon (right) with his twin brother, Kelly

Xander was by far the best choice of characters to have this happen to. If anyone on the show has a split personality, it's him. At home (as we see at the beginning of the episode), he deals with abusive alcoholic parents, but he never talks about it. He covers up his insecurities and anger with a goofy charm, always ready with one-liners and trying to make people laugh so they won't notice how much pain he's in. Xander is possibly the most complex character on the show, precisely because we never find out what he's gone through. He jokes around one minute and lashes out hurtfully the next. By keeping things bottled up, Xander is turning himself into a time bomb.

However, the split doesn't seem realistic. One Xander is sensible, calm, romantic, smart, and confident. The other is freaky, selfish, scared, and just plain goofy. When he's split, what happens to that fierce loyalty he has to friends? Or that scared child who's worried his friends will find out what his parents are like? All the complexities of his character are gone, and the only thing left is the basic elements of Xander. When they're finally ready to be reunited, the two Xanders are very funny, and start to pick up each other's traits (as Giles says, "He's clearly a bad influence on himself").

But the most poignant and surprising part of the episode is Riley's sudden confession to Xander that he knows Buffy doesn't love him. I mean, the guy's a pretty ineffectual character, but few viewers saw this moment coming. It pegs the turning point in Riley's character, when we actually start to become sympathetic toward him.

HIGHLIGHT: THE SNOOPY DANCE!!!
DID YOU NOTICE? Both Willow and Xander wonder if the other Xander's a robot, and every-

one scoffs at them. Later in the season, that idea doesn't seem so ludicrous. Also, Joyce complains of her "two teenage girl headache." Holy foreshadowing, Batman!

NITPICKS: As soon as Xander signs the apartment papers, he sits down and makes a phone call. How the heck did he get the phone company to hook him up within seconds? And if Willow has moved on with Tara, why does she still get extremely jealous of Anya, turning her nose up at the mere mention of her? Seems like some childhood crushes never go away. And finally, did anyone else *not* shake in their boots when Riley says about the Toth demon, "How hard can I kill him?"

OOPS: There are no *Babylon 5* collector plates, making Xander's collection very rare.

WILLOW WICCA WATCH: Willow casts a very simple spell to make Xander whole again.

5.4 Out of My Mind

Original air date:	October 17, 2000
Written by:	Rebecca Rand Kirshner
Directed by:	David Grossman
Guest cast:	Mercedes McNab (Harmony), Bailey Chase (Graham Miller), Time Winters (Dr. Overheiser)

Riley's heart rate becomes dangerously fast, but he refuses medical help for fear Buffy won't love him if he's a normal guy. Meanwhile, Spike tries to get the chip out of his head.

"Out of My Mind" is an interesting episode for its foreshadowing. Joyce momentarily slips out of consciousness and doesn't recognize Dawn. Tara shows concern for Willow's increasing skill as a witch (as Willow's power increases, Tara slips away from her, the opposite of what is happening with Buffy and Riley). Ben the Intern makes his first appearance. And when Riley confesses to Buffy that, without his strength, he fears she won't love him, she counters, "If that's what I wanted, then I'd be dating Spike." Eek.

Is Riley right? Does Buffy need a bit of evil and brute force in her men? She thought she and Angel were soul mates. She tired of Scott Hope quickly, yet when Parker used her and abused her, she pined for him for weeks. She says she loves Riley, but she often forgets about their plans and prefers to do things without him. The episode features fine performances from both Marc Blucas — who sweats and deteriorates, refusing to do what's best for himself — and Sarah, who looks like she's been slapped in the face when Riley confesses his paranoia to her.

But the real revelation is Spike. He kidnaps the doc, tries to get the chip removed, has good ol' Harm following him every step of the way, and once again has to slouch away, admitting defeat. But the final scene, where he finally discovers something about his relationship with Buffy that he's been refusing to admit for so long, comes as a shock to him and the audience. (And it will be used in the "Previously on *Buffy*" bits forever, it seems. . . .)

HIGHLIGHT: Spike again falling on his face in the middle of a grandiose, epic speech.

DID YOU NOTICE? As Spike watches *Dawson's Creek*, he says Pacey's a "blind idiot" for not realizing Joey doesn't love him, an obvious reference to his own short-sightedness.

NITPICKS: First of all, this government operation is either the most bumbling one around or Riley is partially deaf. There's no way the wiretap would be that noticeable. The writers of the show seem to think it's literally a tap-tap-tapping going on. And what kind of doctor uses a local anaesthetic on *brain surgery?!*

WILLOW WICCA WATCH: Willow creates a ball of bright light to help guide her and Tara through Sunnydale High, and Tara is concerned that Willow has learned so much, so fast.

MUSIC/BANDS: As Riley plays basketball, you can hear Nickelback's "Breathe," from *The State*.

5.5 No Place Like Home

Original air date:	October 24, 2000
Written by:	Douglas Petrie
Directed by:	David Solomon
Guest cast:	Ravil Issyanov (Monk), Paul Hayes (Older Night Watchman), James Wellington (Night Watchman), John Sarkisian (Older Monk), Staci Lawrence (Customer)

When Buffy encounters "the Beast" and assumes it's after her mother, she puts herself into a trance and discovers a horrible secret.

Memories. They make us who we are. Without them, we behave differently, don't know our family and friends, and become a blank slate. Imagine waking up and you've forgotten everything you know. Nothing is familiar, and you don't even know who you are. You'd be like a newborn, forced to begin again and construct your life, which would be very different than the one you had before.

In "No Place Like Home," Buffy discovers that someone has played with her memories, as well as those of her friends and mother. We finally realize who Dawn is after Joss Whedon has been dangling clues before us for three episodes. Although the idea is a little far-fetched (how would the monks know whose memories to play with?) it's still a brilliant one in the Buffyverse, even if the original idea came from "Superstar." At least it gives that episode a reason to exist. . . .

When Buffy realizes her sister isn't real, she's devastated: her memories are a sham and the sister that she loves (despite sometimes wishing her dead) is in fact a ball of energy, and Joyce is getting sicker and Buffy was hoping there might be a supernatural explanation for it. The realization that Joyce might actually be ill is a blow to her, and to make things worse, she's unable to tell her friends about Dawn because she must protect her. Buffy is quite possibly the most put-upon character in the history of television. Is there any other terrible thing the writers can throw her way? Oh wait, this is season five, after all.

When Buffy first realizes that Dawn isn't who she seemed to be, she's in a deep trance. The trance is beautifully filmed, with a Steven Soderbergh-like grittiness and photo-negative effect, and with haunting background music. Her first instinct when she sees Dawn's face flicker out of the family pictures is to assume she's a demon and she's hurting Joyce. It's a great trick to play on viewers, and Joss pokes fun at the similarity between a 14-year-old sister and an evil demon that is threatening to break the family apart, especially since Dawn is *so* bloody annoying in this episode.

"No Place Like Home" also features Buffy's first encounter with "the Beast," later called Glory, who, like Adam, is difficult to fight. Glory is infinitely stronger than Buffy and sends her sailing while Buffy can barely get a punch in. Glory is in search of a "Key," and although we don't know why, we know Buffy has become the Key's protector, and she will spend the rest of the season attempting to fill that role.

HIGHLIGHT: Giles in his wizard outfit, welcoming Buffy to the grand reopening of the Magic Box.

DID YOU NOTICE? Glory continues the Dawn-as-Little-Miss-Muffet motif when she says someone's going to "sit down on her tuffet and make this whole thing stop!"

NITPICKS: Everyone on the show — actors and writers — are big *Harry Potter* fans, but while the obvious references to the series are funny, when Giles calls the Beast "that which cannot be named," it's just a little close to J.K. Rowling's books. I was worried that the Beast would eventually be called Voldemort. Also, Buffy seems quick to accuse Dawn of not being her sister. If a trance told you that your sibling wasn't real, would you immediately dismiss all of your memories to the contrary? And finally, is Dawn the most immature 14-year-old on the planet?

OOPS: Probably to avoid continuity errors, the clock in the Magic Box isn't running. But the motionless second hand makes it too obvious. And watch when Buffy throws Dawn against her bedroom wall. The entire wall caves in and the closet door flies open. Gotta love those Hollywood sets. Finally, when Buffy puts herself into the trance, it seems to take hours for it to take effect. But the incense she'd lit is still burning, and incense sticks only last about 30 minutes.

5.6 Family

Original air date:	November 7, 2000
Written and directed by:	Joss Whedon
Guest cast:	Steve Rankin (Mr. Maclay), Amy Adams (Cousin Beth), Kevin Rankin (Donny Maclay), Ezra Buzzington (Bartender), Megan Gray (Sandy), Teddy Pendergrass (Demon), Brian Tee (Intern)

When Tara's family shows up in Sunnydale, she uses extreme measures to prevent Willow and the gang from discovering her secret.

An interesting stand-alone episode, "Family" focuses on Tara, what the gang thinks of her, and her feelings about how she fits in Willow's life. She might have seemed like an outsider until this episode, but now she's a full-fledged Scooby.

The episode plays on the notion that in patriarchal households, the women are beaten down by the men and made to feel less than human, thus "keeping them in line" and cooking and cleaning. In Tara's case, the men take this tradition to its literal extreme, by convincing the women in the family that they are *not* human. Viewers got their first hint that Tara was a demon in "Goodbye Iowa," when she deliberately messed up Willow's demon locater spell, insinuating that perhaps it was she who didn't want to be found. And in this episode, she casts a spell of her own so the others will be blind to her demony half.

However, would Tara's spell have worked even if she had been part demon? And what impact did it have on Willow and her later addiction? In the "Graduation Day" episodes, we discovered that all of the demons Buffy fights are part human and none are pure demon. Yet when Tara casts the spell, the gang is unable to see Spike and the other demons who attack them, demonstrating that even the part-demons were invisible under the spell. Therefore, if Tara *had* been part demon, she would have been invisible to them also. And it's interesting that Willow forgives Tara so quickly, telling the gang she made a mistake. But unlike Willow, Tara, who has practiced magic since she was a child, learns from her mistake, and we never see her take her magic lightly again. If only Willow had learned from this lesson, too.

Not only does Tara's family ostracize her for being a woman, but the underlying metaphor is that they're shunning her for being gay. There are a lot of hints dropped in this episode that people are talking about the issue without actually talking about it. Up until now, the fact that Willow and Tara are witches has been used as the metaphor, and while this show is rife with metaphors, one wonders if their friends are also using it as a euphemism because they don't know what else to say. Xander and Buffy are at a loss for what to buy Tara for her birthday (they have, after all, been keeping her at arm's length) and Xander's comment — "I just know she likes Willow, and she already has one of those" — while funny, shows that Tara is defined only by the fact she's a lesbian. They didn't have any problem making Oz part of the gang when Willow began dating him, but Tara is different. Buffy and Xander keep telling themselves they don't have a problem with her lifestyle by reiterating how "nice" she is, but it's only near the end of the episode, when they realize just how much she means to Willow, that they finally welcome her into the fold.

Although this episode stands alone, the title indicates that it's about something much larger. Tara's "family" is hurtful and abusive, and in reality, the Scooby gang is her true family. Similarly, Xander and Willow have less-than-perfect home lives, but rely on their friends to get them through, and when Buffy endures some tragic moments this season, she'll need the strength of her friends to keep her going. Sometimes family isn't defined by who has the same DNA as you; it's about who's there to catch you when you fall.

HIGHLIGHT: The beautiful ending, where Tara and Willow float above the dance floor in each other's arms.

NITPICKS: Buffy's father has gone from being an okay father to being the scummiest deadbeat dad around (which is typical of fathers in the Buffyverse). In "Nightmares," he's still a part of her life, and in "Helpless" she says that up until that birthday, he had always gone to the Ice Capades with her. How did he go from being an occasional father to running off to Spain with his secretary, oblivious to his daughters and his ex-wife's condition? While bad fathers who don't have much to do with their kids aren't exactly rare, he seems to have gone downhill really fast.

WILLOW WICCA WATCH: Willow didn't use any spells in this episode, but she made excuses for Tara's, which is something she longs for Tara to do in season six.

MUSIC/BANDS: As Sandy tries to pick up Riley at the bar, Yo La Tengo's "Tears Are in Your Eyes" (*And Then Nothing Turned Itself Inside-Out*) is playing in the background. At Tara's birthday party, we hear Motorace's "American Shoes" (*American Shoes SP*), Vitriol's "Cemented Shoes" (*Cemented Shoes* single), and Melanie Doane's "I Can't Take My Eyes Off You" (*Adam's Rib*) as Willow and Tara dance together.

5.7 Fool for Love

Original air date: November 14, 2000
Written by: Douglas Petrie

Directed by:	Nick Marck
Guest cast:	Juliet Landau (Drusilla), Julie Benz (Darla), David Boreanaz (Angelus), Mercedes McNab (Harmony), Kali Rocha (Cecily Addams), Edward Fletcher (Male Party-goer), Kenneth Feinberg (Chaos Demon), Ming Liu (Chinese Slayer), April Wheedon-Washington (New York Slayer)

When Buffy is seriously hurt on patrol, she wants to learn more about how her predecessors were killed, and turns to the only person who knows: Spike.

A brilliant episode, this was the first of two parts detailing how Spike became a vampire and killed two Slayers. The episode is beautifully filmed, taking us from England in 1880, to China at the turn of the century, to New York City in 1977, and to the present. Spike was a poet, a rebel, and a punk. He developed true fighting skills but is always at the whim of his heart. He's the most soulful soulless character in the Buffyverse.

James Marsters turns in a gorgeous performance — from the stuttering, prudish writer who worries about his mother, to the jumpy, excitable young vampire obsessed with "bagging" a Slayer, to the cold, hard 1970s punk rocker who kills without mercy, and to a combination of all three in the present. Only Marsters could show us such a cruel, cold, calculating person, and have our heart swell for him at the same time when Buffy rejects him. Her harsh words — echoing those of his first love — are a slap in the face to both him and us, and the way he sweeps up the money while weeping is heartbreaking. It's astonishing that he could garner our sympathy in that way, especially after what we know of him. But Spike has always followed his heart. He became a vampire amid the pains of unrequited love, he loved one woman for 120 years, and he's now spurned by a mirror image of his Cecily so many years later.

In his "lesson" to Buffy, he concludes by saying all Slayers have a death wish, and his words to her — "Death is your art" — are the first haunting ones she hears about death. Her quest in season five is to discover who she is and what she's all about, and whether she likes it or not, Spike is telling her the truth. He tells her that someday she will choose death, and when she does, he'll be right there. But he doesn't realize that when that day comes, he won't be doing a little victory dance like he thinks he might. The final scene, with the two of them on Buffy's back porch, is quietly touching. Angel is good because he has a soul that forces him to be. But Spike can be good without a soul. Does this mean he's inherently the better man? (See "Darla" for the conclusion of this episode on *Angel*.)

HIGHLIGHT: When we discover the true meaning behind Spike's nickname, William the Bloody.

NITPICKS: Spike's turned into a vampire in 1880, and later that same year his accent is different, he's using different words, and Angel is lecturing him on how he's getting them all into trouble. How could his behavior have changed so much in less than a year, and then not change much after that?

OOPS: When we flash back to Yorkshire in 1880, Angel is holding Spike up against a wall, choking him. It's not possible to choke a vampire: they don't need to breathe. Also, in China in 1900, Spike has a ponytail, which is also impossible. He is undead, so there's no way his hair could have grown, and his hair was short in 1880. Finally, during the subway sequence near the end, you can see Spike's reflection in the subway windows.

MUSIC/BANDS: Throughout this episode, we hear at the Bronze Crushing Velvet's "xxx" (unavailable on CD), Avenue A's "Run Cold" from *Never the Less*, "Heal Yourself" by Virgil (formerly Elephant Ride), and "Balladovie" by the Killingtons, from their self-titled CD. When we see Spike's past, we hear J.S. Bach's "Partita No. 3 in E Major," and Felix Mendelssohn's "Midsummer Night's Dream."

5.8 Shadow

Original air date:	November 21, 2000
Written by:	David Fury
Directed by:	Daniel Attias
Guest cast:	Kevin Weisman (Dreg), William Forward (Dr. Isaacs), Megan Gray (Sandy)

When the doctors discover a "shadow" on Joyce's CAT scan, Buffy must face the reality that her mother's condition is more serious than she thought. Meanwhile, Glory conjures up a beast to help her find the Key.

"Shadow" is a haunting episode that sets the pace for the remainder of season five. Kristine Sutherland delivers her best performance as she tells Buffy about the shadow that's been found on her CAT scan, and when the biopsy reveals a tumor, Buffy's first instinct is to find out what she can do. Her repeated question — "But what can *I* do about it?" — is never answered to her satisfaction, and she rushes to the gang to get them to conjure up a healing spell.

And therein lies the tragedy of this season: Buffy has fought anything that comes her way, be it vampire, fraternity reptiles, the Gentlemen, or a giant praying mantis. When she meets something that's her match, like Adam, she can band together with her friends to destroy it. But now she's facing something bigger and scarier than anything she's come up against: a brain tumor. There are no fairy tale monsters here. No amount of research and patrolling can stop this. There is absolutely nothing she can do, and yet this "monster" will have a more devastating effect on her than anything before it. Buffy has never met anything she couldn't fight, and now that she's facing something that could kill her mother, all she can do is sit back and watch.

Giles explains to her that the medical and the magical should never be mixed. Tara agrees, adding that the molecules in the human body are so complex you could make things worse. Unfortunately, Willow doesn't seem to be listening. A poignant moment comes at the end, when Buffy chases Glory's (for that is her name) monster and almost enjoys beating on it, because it's something tangible that she can get her hands on. But while she's dealing with an unspeakable emotional hell, she's pushing Riley away from her and into the arms of vampires.

HIGHLIGHT: When Riley finds Spike in Buffy's bedroom, sniffing her sweater.
NITPICKS: Owning a magic shop on the hellmouth, wouldn't Giles have memorized a huge list of items you don't sell together?
OOPS: When Buffy leaps over the rock to wrap the chain around the snake's neck, it's clear that it's not Sarah. Also, during the fight, Glory had hurt Buffy's right shoulder, yet at the hospital, Buffy ices the left.

WILLOW WICCA WATCH: Buffy begs Willow to cast a healing spell on Joyce, and Willow says she'll try to find one but doesn't think it will work, and then Giles and Tara assure her it won't.
RESTLESS MOMENT: In "Restless" Joyce is stuck in a wall and Buffy wants her to come out, but she can't. She says that if Buffy could help her, she might be able to come out, but Buffy turns and walks away. Similarly, here Joyce is caught somewhere where Buffy can't get to her, and when Buffy asks how she can help, everyone tells her she can't.

5.9 Listening to Fear

Original air date:	November 28, 2000
Written by:	Rebecca Rand Kirshner
Directed by:	David Solomon
Guest cast:	Bailey Chase (Graham Miller), Nick Chinlund (Major Ellis), Kevin Weisman (Dreg), Randy Thompson (Doctor Kriegel), Paul Hayes (Night Watchman), April Adams (Nurse Lampkin)

A demon from outer space lands in Sunnydale, preying on mental patients.

The main plot of this episode was just okay, with the queller demon being more of a distraction from the big issue of Joyce's declining health. What was more important about "Listening to Fear" was that Buffy is quickly becoming the mother figure. At the beginning of the episode, she tells Willow that a book of spells is an inappropriate gift for Dawn, while Joyce sits there silent. Later she has to explain to Dawn in laymen's terms what is happening to Joyce, and when Joyce's mental faculties start to decline and she begs Buffy to take her home and look after her, Buffy becomes her nurse and caretaker as well. As she breaks down washing dishes and trying to be a good "mom," our hearts go out to her. She missed out on a normal teenage life, and now she's forced to become a mother and adult very quickly.

Again someone tells Dawn that there's nothing inside of her and that she isn't real; it finally registers with Dawn, triggering her doubts about herself and what is going on, especially when Joyce echoes the man's sentiments. Unfortunately, the rest of the episode is a little too *X-Files*-ish for this viewer's tastes, with both an extraterrestrial crashing to Earth and Riley's troops rushing in to try to clean up the problem.

The episode ends with Buffy playing both mother and daughter to Joyce, as Joyce reveals what she knows about Dawn. Suddenly the scene at the beginning of the episode — where Willow plays a little Jewish Santa — makes perfect sense. Just as children grow up and realize one day that Santa isn't real (despite what Anya says), so too does Joyce suddenly have the knowledge about Dawn. And like the kind parent, Buffy must assure her that yes, she's right, but they'll be okay. Although the look in Sarah Michelle Gellar's eyes in this heartbreaking scene indicates anything but.

HIGHLIGHT: When Giles calls the queller demon a "killer snotmonster from outer space," and then pauses before stating, "I did not say that."
NITPICKS: If the people who've been affected by Glory can see that Dawn is the Key, why doesn't Glory just hang out in the mental ward or follow one of these people around until they point out who the Key is? Hasn't she figured out that her powers have this effect on her victims?

Religion on Buffy

Parents' groups and religious organizations have been deriding *Buffy the Vampire Slayer* for years for its "graphic" horror, sex, and language. One of my personal favorites is the Parents Television Council (check them out at www.parentstv.org), whose advisory board includes Pat Boone, Senator Joseph Lieberman, and Billy Ray Cyrus. Every year they rank the best and worst shows on network television, and the 2001 list of best shows contained such cerebral fare as *Touched by an Angel, Twice in a Lifetime,* and *Who Wants to Be a Millionaire?. Buffy* has held an honorable place on the "worst" list for a few years now, ending up at No. 3 in 2001, up from No. 4 (way to go, *Buffy!*), with *Angel* proudly entering at No. 8.

The council complains that on *Buffy*, "sexual content was at times graphic. In one episode from last season, a boy at a fraternity party became sexually aroused simply by touching a wall, and grabbed his crotch." They then quote in long, explicit detail, a scene where Buffy is explaining to Spike how she would have sex with him (of course, they don't see anything wrong with repeating the words on their Web site for children to read). As for *Angel*, "Last season, sexual content was infrequent but always very offensive. In one episode for example, after having sex with Buffy on a kitchen table, Angel smears chocolate and peanut butter on his chest, inviting Buffy to lick it off."

However, though these groups believe there is nothing wholesome or redeeming on either show, religion plays a major part, and many of the characters are defined by their spirituality. Tara is a peaceful Wiccan who adheres to her religion, using her powers only for good. Willow is Jewish, and has said so on several occasions. Xander is Episcopalian. Angel has a thing for convents, and waxed poetic in his show's second season about how beautiful some of them were. Drusilla was a devout Catholic before Angel sired her. Most important, though, the cross — the symbol of Christianity — literally wards off evil, and Buffy is never seen without one. On other shows, like *7th Heaven*, we're constantly reminded of the power of God. But only on *Buffy* and *Angel* do we actually see the power of God at work. Of course, it's never explained why the Star of David can't ward off evil, too. . . .

OOPS: When Riley and the gang are heading into the woods looking for the meteor, Anya is walking behind Riley. When the camera cuts to show the whole group, she's beside him. Also, when doing research, Willow says the Russian Tunguska meteor hit in 1917, when in fact it landed in June 1908.

5.10 Into the Woods

Original air date:	December 19, 2000
Written and directed by:	Marti Noxon
Guest cast:	Bailey Chase (Graham Miller), Nick Chinlund (Major Ellis), Randy Thompson (Doctor Kriegel), Rainy Jo Stout (Vampire Girl with Riley)

Buffy discovers Riley's dark secret, and he confronts her with an ultimatum.

Just as we get our first taste of hope and joy (as does Buffy), it all falls apart once again. Marti Noxon chose the perfect title for her episode (the first time she's both written and directed, and she does an excellent job), because just as Joyce is "out of the woods" and Buffy is able to breathe again, events inevitably don't go her way and she's forced back into her gloominess, back into the woods.

Riley was never one of my favorite characters — because he's boring, not because of Marc Blucas. Blucas turns in a great performance here, and at the end of the episode I wished he'd stay. Even if you don't like the guy, his fall over the past few episodes would make anyone feel sorry for him. He's so in love with this girl, and it hurts him so much that his feelings are unrequited that, without thinking, he's made a huge mistake. He tells Buffy he's heading to Belize (we'll find out why in "As You Were"), but only after stomping off to Spike's to teach him a lesson. What is so fascinating about the scene with Spike is what Spike tells him, and Spike's immediate retraction. He says he sometimes envies Riley, but then realizes what torture it must be to hold the woman he loves while her thoughts are miles away . . . and then realizes what he's saying and takes it back. What seems like a funny throwaway line is actually a big motivator for Spike in season six (he'd rather have a distant Buffy than no Buffy), and it's surprising how many fans took offense to what happens with Buffy and Spike in the next season, after he's made a speech like this one.

Riley's addiction is a metaphor for either sex or drug addiction. The vampire nest could be interpreted as a crack house or a brothel, and the female vamp who is, um, *sucking* on him, looks like a heroin addict, but Buffy calls her a whore.

Buffy and Riley argue, and while she's more mature with him than she ever was with Angel, once again she makes it everyone's fault but her own, and is so quick to blame Riley for everything instead of looking within herself to see what's wrong with her relationships. That said, what kind of person gives someone an ultimatum and puts her through this kind of hell less than two days after she thought her mother was going to die? This couple was probably never right for one another, and while Buffy and Riley might not see it that way, scenes like this tell us otherwise.

Finally, Xander again comes in from the sidelines to make a big difference in everyone's lives. He chases Buffy and confronts her over what's going on between her and Riley, telling her how stupid she's being. The end of the episode — where Xander walks into Anya's bedroom and tells her how he truly feels about her — shows that it's not just Buffy who's matured. Xander isn't a boy anymore, and this scene is so touching and beautiful that it gives all of us hope for true love.

HIGHLIGHT: Xander's response when Anya says she bathes him: "Only in an erotic, *Penthouse*-y way, not a spongebathy, geriatric sort . . ."

INTERESTING FACTS: This episode was dedicated to the late D.C. Gustafson, otherwise known as Gustav Gustafson, who had worked on the show and was a good friend of Sarah Michelle Gellar.

NITPICKS: I was going to nitpick the fact that Joyce just underwent major surgery and somehow walked away with nothing more than a Band-Aid, but according to Kristine Sutherland, there was a reason the writers did that. Her own mother suffered a brain aneurysm in exactly the same spot as Joyce, and when the writers had initially decided to have the actress's head shaved and have her wear a wig, she explained that the doctor had simply shaved a small area around her mother's temple and bandaged it. Also, I realize Buffy was upset, but why would she set a place on fire and keep the fire department *really* busy for the next few hours like that? Even if it was supposed to be a metaphor for a crack house or a brothel, Buffy still committed arson.

OOPS: After Riley "stakes" Spike, there's no hole in Spike's shirt. Also, during their conversation, Spike opens the bottle of alcohol, the camera cuts away, and when it returns to him, he's opening it again.

MUSIC/BANDS: This episode features "Summer Breeze," by Emiliana Torrini from *Love in the Time of Science*.

5.11 Triangle

Original air date:	January 9, 2001
Written by:	Jane Espenson
Directed by:	Christopher Hibler
Guest cast:	Abraham Benrubi (Olaf), Ranjani Brow (Young Nun)

The fighting between Anya and Willow escalates to a breaking point, placing Xander in the middle and all of Sunnydale in danger.

"Triangle" has its funny moments, but for the most part it's a throwaway episode that pushes the limits of credibility. Would Willow really be that whiny, stealing supplies from Giles the moment he's out of town, and fighting with Anya? We've come to know her as a bit of a goody-goody who knows the difference between right and wrong, and if this is supposed to indicate the beginning of her dangerous addiction, it's rather sudden. Anya is perfectly in character, but Xander seems to take Willow's side one too many times (especially after that speech he delivered to Anya at the end of the last episode).

Would Buffy really cry uncontrollably about the future of Anya and Xander's relationship? No wonder Tara looks so flummoxed; it's completely out of character for Buffy to be crying like that, especially with all the hiccuping and silly comments. It's as if her relationship with Riley were reduced to a joke, where she didn't learn anything and is now projecting her own abandonment issues on everyone else. And would Xander really be pouring his heart out to Spike?

The troll itself is funny (he delivers his lines, clearly scripted to be a caricature, perfectly), but by the end the gag is tiresome, leaving viewers impatient to get back to the real story.

HIGHLIGHT: Willow's reaction to Anya's suggestion that she could try to break her and Xander apart: "Hello? Gay now!"

NITPICKS: Anya yells to Buffy at the end that the troll's strength is in his hammer. And she didn't think to mention that earlier?

OOPS: Anya says she has never driven before (and in "Restless" said she only knew how to "gesture emphatically"), but in "Graduation Day (Part Two)" she told Xander her car was waiting outside and begged him to come with her.

WILLOW WICCA WATCH: Willow seems to go over the edge in this episode: she steals supplies and says it's okay to do so if she's just trying to help Buffy; she tries a spell on the counter and makes the cash register disappear (twice); she stops in the middle of a spell to yell at Anya, completely oblivious to the fact that her spell is going haywire; she's unable to stop the troll at the Bronze or back at the Magic Box.

MUSIC/BANDS: At the Bronze, we hear Blur's "There's No Other Way" from Leisure, and "Bohemian Like You" by the Dandy Warhols, from *Thirteen Tales from Urban Bohemia*.

5.12 Checkpoint

Original air date:	January 23, 2001
Written by:	Douglas Petrie, Jane Espenson
Directed by:	Nick Marck
Guest cast:	Harris Yulin (Quentin Travers), Cynthia LaMontagne (Lydia), Oliver Muirhead (Phillip), Kris Iyer (Nigel), Kevin Weisman (Dreg), Wesley Mask (Professor), Justin Gorence (Orlando)

The Watcher's Council shows up with information about Glory, but must put Buffy and her friends through a series of tests before she is deemed worthy enough to know more.

"Checkpoint" is a very funny episode, but shows once again the inherent incompetence of the Council that is supposed to be giving Buffy her orders. They clearly know nothing about the demon world, choosing instead to rely on their books and information, or writing a thesis on Spike but not daring to come close to him. Buffy's sudden revelation at the end of the episode is dead on, but you wonder how the Council could be so clueless if their society is almost as old as the tradition of slayerdom? One of the best scenes in this episode takes place in Buffy's history class, where her professor seems as clueless to the dangers lurking in Sunnydale as the Council is.

Meanwhile, Glory has realized the clock is ticking, and she needs to find the Key. While it might seem odd that she has chosen to make her earthly presence that of "Her Supreme Vacuousness and Materialism," Glory is the perfect foe for Buffy. If the powers that be were to choose a slayer of demons and vampires, would they choose a big, strong person with superhuman strength and perhaps bionic parts, probably about eight feet tall . . . or would they choose a small, blond, teenage cheerleader? Logic might dictate the former, but it's the latter that is the cunning fighting machine needed in the modern world. Similarly, Glory's looks are deceiving: she might seem to be a flighty girly-girl, but she's hiding a lot of power behind that punch, and someone like Dawn might open up to her and tell her where her Key is. This episode also marks the first time we see the Knights of Byzantium.

The best part of this episode is when we're reminded that the gang fights as a unit, and while merging the essence of Xander, Giles, Willow, and Buffy seemed like a one-time thing, Buffy really does need everyone to be with her. Watching Willow, Tara, and Anya become stuttering messes under the scrutiny of the Council is hilarious, and it's nice to see Willow and Tara declare their sexuality openly, without inhibition, even if it was because they misunderstood the question. Despite the fact that with every appearance the Council seems even more and more useless, "Checkpoint" was a great episode.

HIGHLIGHT: Anya's sudden "Willow's a demon??"

INTERESTING FACTS: Spike and Joyce both watch *Passions*, which actually does feature a character named Timmy. *Passions* is one of the most ridiculous soap operas imaginable, but unlike a lot of stupid shows, it embraces its silliness. Timmy is a doll that can talk and walk around like a regular person, which is why Spike is unconcerned that his life is in danger.

NITPICKS: The woman who interviews Spike has a horrible accent — someone should have given the actress a few more hours with the voice coach. Also, when the Council asks Xander what special skills he has, why doesn't he mention his commando skills? How many other Scoobies can assemble weapons? And finally, when testing Buffy in the training room, why does Quentin Travers continue to speak Japanese when it's clear she can't understand a word of it?

5.13 Blood Ties

Original air date:	February 6, 2001
Written by:	Steven S. DeKnight
Directed by:	Michael Gershman
Guest cast:	Justin Gorence (Orlando), Michael Emanuel (Guard), Joe Ochman (Janitor), Paul Bates (Mental Patient #1), Carl J. Johnson (Mental Patient #2)

Dawn discovers the truth about what she is and, unable to accept that her memories are not real, she runs away from home.

"Blood Ties" turns the current storyline into a metaphor for adoption. Just as many adopted children find out in their teen years that their family is not their biological one, Dawn discovers that Buffy is not her sister and Joyce is not her mother. She goes through the same kind of withdrawal and depression that might be experienced by an adopted child, discovering that her memories, beliefs, and sense of security are all false, and that her family is not her biological one. At the end of the episode, when Buffy convinces Dawn that they are sisters and have Summers blood, it's similar to adoptees realizing that it's the family who raised them that is their real kin.

Just before Dawn discovers the secret, Buffy tells the gang, who are incredibly hurt by what they see as Buffy's betrayal. They forgive her quickly, probably because they realize it isn't their lives she was as worried about as Dawn's. In the early scenes, Anya reveals that there are several demon dimensions, and she's seen a few of them. It begs the question: why does the gang often shun Anya rather than pumping her for information? She was the only person in season three who had been to an Ascension. She's the only one who has visited alternative universes and demon dimensions. How better to understand other demons than to speak to one who had been a demon for over a thousand years?

"Blood Ties" isn't just about the complicated sibling relationship between Dawn and Buffy, but also the one between Ben and Glory. Suddenly many things make sense (while others seem more confusing) and the casting people couldn't have chosen two actors who looked more alike than these two. When Glory corners Dawn in the hospital, we see the two sibling halves that are not human facing off. And while Glory seems to be unbeatable, in this episode the audience discovers two of her vulnerabilities, and now we sit back and wait for the characters to catch up.

HIGHLIGHT: Glory's reaction when she realizes she's been teleported.
INTERESTING FACTS: When Dawn walks into the psychiatric ward, the patients tell her to go away and that they don't want to see her. One of them says, "What's the frequency?" — a reference to a bizarre incident that happened with news anchor Dan Rather. In 1986, he was attacked by a mentally ill man who kicked and beat him, shouting, "Kenneth, what's the frequency?" This inspired R.E.M.'s song, "What's the Frequency, Kenneth?" in 1994. Later it was discovered that the mental patient believed the television media were sending

messages into his head, and he wanted to know the frequency of the signal so he could block it out. In the show, clearly the patient is asking the same thing so he can block out any images or signals of the Key.

NITPICKS: Now that we know Ben and Glory are the same, our minds go back to previous episodes: in the last one, how was Jinx able to leave Glory to meet Ben at the hospital, and then leave Ben to return to Glory? How was Ben/Glory able to move faster?

WILLOW WICCA WATCH: Willow and Tara cast a protection spell on the Magic Box and Buffy's house, which seems to work. Later, Willow casts a teleportation spell on Glory that gives Willow a nosebleed, prompting Giles to show his concern that the spell is more powerful than someone of her ability should be trying.

MUSIC/BANDS: The song playing at Buffy's birthday party is "Holiday" by Star Ghost Dog, from *The Great Indoors*.

5.14 Crush

Original air date:	February 13, 2001
Written by:	David Fury
Directed by:	Daniel Attias
Guest cast:	Juliet Landau (Drusilla), Mercedes McNab (Harmony), Frederick Dawson (Porter), Greg Wayne (Student), Joseph DiGiandomenico (Matt), Walter Borchert (Jeff), Asher Glaser (Boy at the Bronze), Jennifer Bergman (Girl at the Bronze)

Buffy finds out that Spike is in love with her, and she makes it very clear that he has no chance. But when a love from Spike's past returns to Sunnydale, Spike decides to make some choices.

There are fans who love Spike and wish the gang could just open their arms to him, and there are fans who hate him, seeing him as nothing but a cold-blooded killer. This episode deepens the complexities, and can be interpreted both ways. "Crush" is from the point of view of Spike, disrespected by the Scoobies at the Bronze even though he helped them fight Glory, spurned by Buffy despite vowing his devoted love to her, and fighting the demon within him when Drusilla returns to tempt him back to his evil ways. It's as if Spike were a better person than Angel, because he is soulless, yet is still able to love.

But is he as good as the show portrays? When you watch this episode, you feel sorry for him when Xander tells him to go away, when Buffy looks like she'll vomit when he tells her he loves her, when she freaks out on him after he took care of Dawn, and when he discovers that he's no longer welcome in the Summers' home. Since "Fool for Love," you can't help but see him as William, the sentimental poet who was abused by a rich girl who broke his heart. You see him as a really great guy, trying to help Buffy, trying to look after Dawn, and sympathizing with the troubles of the "Summers women."

But try watching this episode as if Spike were an abusive boyfriend, and you'll see a different character emerge. He practices talking to Buffy by using a mannequin, but when he believes the mannequin tells him to go away, he hurls chocolates at it and takes its head off. To get Buffy's love, he chains her up in his crypt and threatens to kill her if she doesn't tell him she's in love with him. He uses Harmony for sex, but tells her to dress up as Buffy and then tries to kill her anyway. When Buffy refuses to go along with his little game, he screams at her, swearing and threatening her. If he were human, he'd be seen as an abusive alcoholic who needs to be in prison, attending anger management courses. He believes he loves Buffy, but wife abusers believe they love their wives, too. Is he kind, or is he a killer?

The problem is, Spike essentially *is* a good person; it's the demon within him that emerges every once in a while to show its ugly face. Unlike Angel, Spike doesn't have a soul that tells him what's right and what's wrong, but he tries as hard as he can to let his human side show through. This inner struggle is what Buffy fails to see; she can see only the demon within him. And until he can keep that demon in check, can Spike really be good?

HIGHLIGHT: Harmony's lame goodbye speech.

DID YOU NOTICE? Willow is wearing a blue ribbon in one of the scenes, which signifies online free speech. At a time when the WB and other networks were shutting down fan sites that weren't making any money, accusing the fans of infringing on copyright, Willow's is an interesting statement to make on the show.

NITPICKS: When Buffy tells Joyce and Willow that Spike has feelings for her, Joyce's first reaction is to ask Buffy if she led him on in some way. Nice mothering, Joyce. Also, the lead-up that Drusilla is in town lasts the first 15 minutes of the episode, but the suspense is gone because the opening credits plainly state, "Juliet Landau as Drusilla." Couldn't they have forgone the formalities for the sake of the suspense? It would have been worth it. And when Spike takes Buffy to the vampire nest, she gets angry that they're not the vampires she's looking for and leaves. Uh, isn't a vampire slayer supposed to slay vampires? Finally, Buffy tells Dawn not to hang out with Spike because he's a vampire and he's dangerous. How can Dawn possibly believe Buffy when every time the Slayer's in a scrape, she gets Spike to take care of Dawn and Joyce?

WILLOW WICCA WATCH: Willow and Tara discuss the nosebleeds and headaches Willow has been suffering since the teleportation spell, showing she was probably in territory she wasn't ready for.

MUSIC/BANDS: This episode featured "Play It by Ear" (*Pure Juice*) and "Happy" by Summercamp, and "Key" by Devics.

5.15 I Was Made to Love You

Original air date:	February 20, 2001
Written by:	Jane Espenson
Directed by:	James A. Contner
Guest cast:	Shonda Farr (April), Adam Busch (Warren), Amelinda Embry (Katrina), Paul Darrigo (Driver)

When Buffy realizes the new girl in town looking for her boyfriend is actually a robot programmed to love only one person, she knows the girl is dangerous.

Love comes to Sunnydale in many forms in this episode. Spike continues to follow Buffy around, showing up at the same parties just to bother her; "puffy Xander" tells Buffy that the right guy for her is out there somewhere, and how lucky that guy will be; Ben runs into Buffy at the party and gives her his phone number, along with a long, confusing speech about coffee; Joyce finally gets back on the dating scene and meets a great guy who happens to *not* be

JONATHAN MOFFAT/ZUMA PRESS

Adam Busch, Amelinda Embry, Sarah Michelle Gellar, and Shonda Farr film a scene from "I Was Made to Love You"

a robot this time; and a young girl who talks a lot like Anya shows up in town looking for her boyfriend (oh, and she *is* a robot).

While the episode is interesting at times (and sets up some future episodes and a character for season six), it was a little fluffy compared to recent shows. The robot, April, was fun (the quick glimpse of the files that Warren had installed in her was hilarious) and sad all at the same time. Buffy empathizes with April, because Riley had walked out on her, just as Warren ditched his creation. But all this girl ever did was love Warren, while Buffy never loved Riley, so the parallel is shaky.

The gang also comes down hard on Spike when he appears at the Magic Box. Obviously Buffy has told them that he tied her up and threatened to kill her, but the way they treat him is so harsh, and not in keeping with how they treat him afterward (they go right back to the begrudging tolerance they always showed him). The harshest is Giles, who shoves Spike and tells him to leave Buffy alone — Giles has become an even more protective father figure in Buffy's life.

The best — and most devastating — part of this episode is the ending. Buffy enters the house and finds the flowers that Brian (an anagram of brain?) has sent for Joyce, and begins calling for her. Finally, here's a guy who is a real gem (and for the first time on this show, I really liked Joyce when she was joking about losing her bra). But when Buffy leans into the staircase calling for her and you see a glimpse of Joyce in the background, your heart sinks. This was the most painful ending to this point, and leads the way for the sheer brilliance of the next episode.

HIGHLIGHT: When Giles tells Buffy he was babysitting Dawn and was subjected to cheerful music sung by people chosen for their ability to dance.

INTERESTING FACT: April was originally supposed to be played by pop singer Britney Spears, but scheduling conflicts prevented her from appearing. And *Buffy* fans everywhere breathed a huge sigh of relief.

DID YOU NOTICE? Some of the robot files included Sex, Fetish, Positions, Give Him Presents, etc. and in the Protect Warren folder, one of the file names was misspelled — "destroy_obsticle.gfd" — showing that Warren should have checked a dictionary before programming. Also, as the robot winds down and begins spouting clichés, she says, "Things are always darkest before . . ." and leaves off the final word — dawn.

NITPICKS: Why would Xander have been so obvious about his sudden crush on April? She enters the party and Xander says to Anya, "Who is *that*?" And why is it that every time Buffy is hurt ("The Freshman," "Harsh Light of Day") she always hurts the same arm, yet doesn't suffer any after-effects? She should get that looked at. . . . Finally, how did Spike find out where Warren lived?

OOPS: When Katrina is unconscious and Buffy carries her to the bench, you can see Katrina's legs moving.

MUSIC/BANDS: At the party we hear "Hideeho" by Mellanova, from their self-titled EP, "OK Nightmare," by Caviar, from their self-titled CD, and "Kawanga!" by the Los Straitjackets, from *The Velvet Touch of Los Straitjackets*.

5.16 The Body

Original air date:	February 27, 2001
Written and directed by:	Joss Whedon
Guest cast:	Loanne Bishop (Voice of the 911 Operator), J. Evan Bonifant (Kevin Berman), Kelli Garner (Kirstie), John Michael Herndon (Vampire), Rae'ven Kelly (Lisa), Tia Matza (Teacher), Randy Thompson (Dr. Kriegel)

When Joyce suddenly dies, Buffy and her friends deal with their grief in various ways.

An absolute masterpiece. "The Body" is hands down the single most terrifying, heartbreaking, painful, and amazing hour of television I have ever seen. The performances by everyone in the cast are second to none. Sarah Michelle Gellar is jaw-dropping. Alyson Hannigan portrays helplessness and confusion beautifully. And Emma Caulfield's innocent, wonderful speech will have you weeping. Joss Whedon lost his own mother, and wrote "The Body" out of that experience. The episode is so realistic, so true to life, that it couldn't possibly have been written by someone who hadn't been through it.

In 1969, author Elizabeth Kübler-Ross released her groundbreaking work, *On Death and Dying*, where she outlined the five stages of grief: Denial and Isolation (this isn't happening), Anger (I'm not ready for this, make it stop), Bargaining (if I promise to be good, will you stay and not die; what could I have done to make her stay?), Depression (I wasn't a good daughter, I could have done things differently, I can't deal with this), and Acceptance (I understand what happened, and while I wish it didn't, I'm not angry anymore). While her simplistic theories were later questioned (she stated that if anyone can't move from one stage to the next in a timely manner, they need psychiatric help, effectively discounting the personal nature of mourning), we see these stages played out in this episode and later ones. Buffy is in shock, denying that Joyce is dead and trying to cover her up to make her warm. She's completely alone, isolated from her friends, her family, and Giles. She steps outside and sees children playing, something everyone has done when they've just lost someone close to them ("How can the sun be shining and people be going about their daily duties when my whole world is collapsing?"). She begins bargaining with herself, believing if she performs CPR, maybe Joyce will come back: "If I had come home earlier, maybe I could have saved her."

Xander represents the anger. He's furious at the world, at Joyce leaving them, at an aneurysm taking the mother figure of the group and leaving Buffy alone. Willow is the helpless and confused one, angry with herself for not being able to choose the right shirt, angry at her closet for not having the perfect apparel for the occasion, upset with others for not understanding her dilemma. Anya is the child, completely innocent and unable to grasp that one day someone could be there, the next they're gone. How does that happen? How can someone just stop . . . being? Anya gives Willow the outlet she needs to vent her anger and frustration, but also allows Willow to mother her, explaining that no one knows the answers. Anya's movement from innocent questions to quiet, confused breakdown is an amazing scene, showing how much Emma Caulfield has grown as an actress and how Anya has matured as a human being.

Dawn is also in denial. Her mother is her mother, she has always been there, and, like Anya, Dawn can't grasp that Joyce is not there. She can't talk to anyone, she's sad and moody, and she gets as close to depression as anyone until "The Weight of the World," where Buffy's depression overwhelms her and shuts her down. Dawn, unable to accept that Joyce is dead, has to go to the morgue to see it for real.

And finally, Tara is acceptance. We discover she's gone through this before. She understands what Buffy's experiencing, but doesn't pretend to know everything. She remains quiet, trying to help Willow choose her sweater, trying to help Xander soothe his hand, and allowing Buffy to talk to someone who's been through the same heartbreak. When Willow almost succumbs to her panic, Tara suddenly moves forward to kiss her; we sit back and sigh that Joss Whedon could be so amazing as to take an onscreen kiss between two women and make it seem normal and everyday. *This* is a true, loving relationship.

Buffy reaches her own tentative acceptance near the end, when Dawn sneaks in to see the body and is attacked by a vampire. While we may think at first, "What the hell is that doing in this episode?" it makes perfect sense. No matter who you lose, or how much your world is caving in on you, life goes on. Buffy has a mission, and she must continue to fight the vampires and demons of the world to save mankind. She couldn't save her mother, no matter how hard she tried, but she can save others. She can save Dawn. And that's her mission now. As Dawn reaches out to touch the body, the screen suddenly goes black, for the body isn't Joyce, it's an empty shell.

And Kristine Sutherland turns in one of her best performances. The camera holds on the body for excruciatingly long periods of time, and you don't see her move a muscle. The blank stare of her eyes haunted every viewer as she gazed at us throughout that final scene.

"The Body" is unmatched on television for its portrayal of grief. We've all seen the daughter run in and yell, "No, no!" while pounding on the mother's chest. Or heard the music swell to heartrending notes as the camera pans back and shows the grief and wailing of the bereaved. But Joss tossed out all the clichés, all the conventions, and presented us with the cold, hard fact of death. There was no music, no noise except the eerie silence that Joyce had left behind. What he gave us was a play in five grueling acts, and he refused to water anything down. "The Body" is a masterwork of immense beauty.

HIGHLIGHT: Every minute of the episode.
INTERESTING FACTS: Asked why Joss decided to keep Joyce's eyes open throughout the episode, Kristine Sutherland gave a detailed explanation: "I think Joss wanted to make it really clear that this was real death. This wasn't about vampires. I know some people have been critical of it, but I think that our society doesn't really grapple with death at all. We make up dead bodies so that they look like they're still alive, and shove them off to funeral homes and pretend they don't exist. Our chickens and turkeys arrive neatly packaged in the grocery store so you can pretend you're not really eating what you're eating. I've found Europeans don't have the same 'Let's clean death up' attitude. You go to the butcher, and it's a lamb, it's a chicken. It's got its head on and its feet on. I can only imagine that their reaction to human death is not quite as antiseptic as ours is, as well. At an Irish wake they lay the body out on the kitchen table and everybody comes to look at it and have a big party. Not

closing her eyes was part of that." Also, while the holiday scene looked a little out of place at the beginning of the episode, it was necessary in order to create the stark contrast with what came later. According to Whedon, "I knew that I had to have opening credits, and I knew that there was no way in God's green earth that I was going to put them over the 911 sequence, so I thought, 'Well, I've got to have a scene.'"

DID YOU NOTICE? The dress Joyce models for Dawn and Buffy is the same one she was wearing when Buffy caught her kissing Ted in "Ted."

5.17 Forever

Original air date:	April 17, 2001
Written and directed by:	Marti Noxon
Guest cast:	David Boreanaz (Angel), Todd Duffey (Murk), Andrea Gall (Customer), Joel Grey (Doc)

Unable to deal with the loss of her mother, Dawn searches for a spell that will bring Joyce back to life. Meanwhile, Ben lets slip to Jinx that the Key is an innocent, narrowing Glory's search.

There are certain events that can happen in one's life where no matter how horrible you act afterward, your friends and family will forgive you. The loss of a parent is one such event. Children have always been given leeway to act childish, rude, or selfish, but as adults we are forced to keep it together, not lose control, and try not to show our emotions. Sarah Michelle Gellar and Michelle Trachtenberg display those traits beautifully in this sad and painful episode.

With the loss of anyone important in our lives, be it a parent, friend, or beloved pet, we can't help but hope it's all a bad dream, that the loved one will return somehow, and we wish that there was some way you could facilitate that. In "Forever," when Dawn tells Willow and Tara that she wants them to help her bring Joyce back, we chalk it up to her youth and immaturity. She also doesn't realize how dangerous her request is — that is, until "Bargaining." Dawn is selfish, rude, and acts so immaturely that you almost want to slap her (talk about wish fulfillment in this episode) until you realize she's so young, and in the past few months has gone through so much. Everyone wants to help make it better. But Willow — who should know better — helps her in all the wrong ways. As does Spike (who knows better, but ignores it, as is his way). Giles tries to help Buffy through her pain, as does Angel (whose "epiphany" had perfect timing) in a short crossover cameo. Tara, on the other hand, knows what Buffy and Dawn have been through, but also realizes you can sometimes make the situation worse by trying to help, so she spends the episode trying desperately to stop what Willow and Spike have put in place. When the Doc tells Dawn that if you raise the dead they sometimes come back a little "off," and Buffy tells Angel she's not a very good grown-up, we get some foreshadowing of the dark sixth season.

The episode features one small, almost forgettable scene that is touching in its subtlety. Just as Buffy has had to put on a brave face to show she's an adult, Giles has to step in as the father figure for everyone and remain the voice of reason and stability. But there is a quick shot of Giles, sitting alone in his apartment and drinking, listening to Cream's "Tales of Brave Ulysses." This is the same song he'd listened to with Joyce in "Band Candy." While that was a comic episode, maybe the moment really meant something to him. Joyce's death has left him with a hole in his life, too, but he'll never let the others see that.

CHRISTINA RADISH

Sisters in arms: Michelle Trachtenberg and Sarah Michelle Gellar

The final scene with Michelle and Sarah is amazing, showing just what these young actresses are made of. Dawn shouts terrible insults at Buffy, who is shocked but remains calm as she tries to explain to Dawn that she's the adult now, and as such, must act a certain way. But when some version of Joyce comes lumbering across the front lawn, Buffy immediately becomes a child again, whimpering and crying out for her mommy, proving that this "adult" thing is going to be far more difficult than it sounds.

HIGHLIGHT: Anya feeling threatened by Dawn's presence in the Magic Box.
INTERESTING FACTS: "Forever" borrows its storyline from the classic American short story by W.W. Jacobs, "The Monkey's Paw." A family receives a monkey's paw, which they are told will grant them three wishes. The father wishes for two hundred pounds, and the next day his son is killed in an accident, with the factory compensating the family with exactly two hundred pounds. The wife, in a fit of insanity, begs her husband to wish for their son to return, and when he does so against his will, they hear an ominous knock on the door. As she rushes to the door and tries to unbolt the lock, the husband realizes the grave

mistake they made, and uses his last wish to make the thing go away, just in time for his wife to throw the front door open and find nothing there.

NITPICKS: Despite her youth and the problems she's gone through, Dawn should be a little more mature. When she drops the egg, she immediately runs back, completely oblivious to the danger to Spike.

WILLOW WICCA WATCH: Willow makes a bad decision when she uses her magic to push one of her books forward on the bookshelf so that Dawn will see it. Why does she do this? Doesn't she understand the danger of putting such tools into the head of a very intelligent and determined 14-year-old girl? Obviously Willow is starting to believe that magic can fix anything.

MUSIC/BANDS: As Xander and Anya talk in bed, we hear Splendid's "Tomorrow We'll Awake" (not available on CD), and Giles listens to Cream's "Tales of Brave Ulysses."

5.18 Intervention

Original air date:	April 24, 2001
Written by:	Jane Espenson
Directed by:	Michael Gershman
Guest cast:	Adam Busch (Warren), Todd Duffey (Murk), Sharon Ferguson (The First Slayer)

Spike's Buffybot is discovered by the gang, who mistake it for the real Buffy. Meanwhile, the real Buffy is out in the desert with Giles on a Slayer quest.

A very funny episode if you can get past the creepiness of the Buffybot and her main function. Just like April in "I Was Made to Love You," the Buffybot talks like Anya and was made by a chauvinist twit who created her for sexual pleasure only (it's unclear why Spike chose to include a slaying function; its only purpose is for the writers to use her in future episodes). Meanwhile, Buffy and Giles embark on a Slayer quest to the desert; she's worried that all of her training is only making her cold and hard to people, and that she will soon lose all emotion, just like she lost Riley.

The desert scenes are interesting and contain the key (no pun intended) to the season finale. It's too bad they're couched in an otherwise comic episode, since the lessons Buffy learns in the desert — death is her gift, she is full of love, and she will be unable to give love only if she is unable to receive it — are profound, dictating the course of the series and Buffy's journey from this point on.

The most disappointing aspect of this episode is that Buffy's friends don't realize the Buffybot isn't real. Somehow, only three episodes before this, they recognized April as a robot immediately, but here, when their best friend is mooning over Spike and speaking in clipped tones, they don't clue in? When the bot is finally alone with Willow, the viewer can't help but assume Willow will make the discovery. No such luck.

Spike redeems himself by the end of the episode, though. He might be a sexed-up vampire who will resort to a Buffy blow-up to satiate his appetite, but he has a heart and is willing to die for Buffy and her sister. He can keep repeating how bad he is until he's blue in the face, but deep down, he'll always be William.

HIGHLIGHT: Giles doing the hokey-pokey in the desert. With his magic gourd.

INTERESTING FACTS: Nicholas Brendon was sick during the filming of this episode, so in several scenes where there was no dialogue, his brother Kelly stood in for him.

NITPICKS: The Buffybot seems aware that Glory is looking for the Key and who that Key is. Why would Spike put that sort of delicate information into his sex toy? And when Spike runs to the elevator to escape Glory's clutches, the door closes on him. Yet when he rides it to the lobby, the doors stay open throughout the entire fight sequence. How? Finally, the ending is inconsistent: when Buffy's pretending to be the bot, she's a little too convincing; she's never actually heard a conversation between the bot and Spike, so how would she be able to repeat exact phrases that were used earlier?

OOPS: When we see Xander and Anya from the robot's point of view, there are three files on her desktop: Make Spike Happy, Slaying, and Locate Spike. The Make Spike Happy file is open and active, yet she's supposed to be in slaying mode, and therefore the Slaying file should be open instead. Later, when we see Willow, the Buffybot is desperately trying to find Spike, and again the Make Spike Happy file is open instead of the more apt Locate Spike file. It appears the show's designers made one screen to show what the robot's point of view would be, without taking the various circumstances into account.

5.19 Tough Love

Original air date:	May 1, 2001
Written by:	Rebecca Rand Kirshner
Directed by:	David Grossman
Guest cast:	Anne Betancourt (Principal Stevens), Leland Crooke (Professor Lillian), Todd Duffey (Murk)

After discovering that Dawn has been cutting classes, Buffy is instructed that if she can't stop her sister from acting up, Dawn will be taken away from her. Meanwhile, Glory thinks she knows who the Key is, and her mistake has terrible consequences.

A shocking episode on all fronts, "Tough Love" jump-starts the push toward the finale that always happens about four episodes from the end. Buffy is forced into a mother role that she's unprepared to take on, and while she seems to be doing everything wrong and being a little rough, we can't blame her. She's never done this before. She's pressured to drop all of her classes to become a full-time guardian to Dawn, but she's hoping she'll be able to return next year, when she's more herself. D'oh.

The focus of this episode is the relationship between Willow and Tara. Many fans who don't like the relationship have suggested there's no chemistry between these two, that there's none of the tension that existed between Willow and Oz. They're missing the subtleties, though. Willow and Tara have one of the most beautiful and realistic relationships on television. They're not always falling all over each other or holding hands or making eyes, they just quietly love one another and are comfortable and happy in each other's presence. We've seen them float above a dance floor because they're so in love; they've worked together as powerful witches to stop Glory and other pending dangers; they understand each other's jokes, even when others are completely baffled by them. Just as Willow came out of her shell gradually and stopped stuttering, Tara is learning to be one of the gang with Willow's support. At other times, Tara is the stronger one, the one who was a Wiccan long before Willow had begun, and has had lesbian relationships before. They comfort each other and take turns being strong. There is so much love between these two, and Amber Benson and Alyson Hannigan are just incredible because they're able to emote very subtly, without resorting to obvious declarations of love. Anya and Xander seem almost like a joke compared to these two, who always stand by each other no matter what.

So when they have their first fight, we're extremely upset. Willow has always been the more sensitive of the two, which is why the argument spirals so quickly into accusations and suggestions. The argument is both well-written and beautifully acted, and when we see just how much it tears up Willow as a result, we know this love is real. But unfortunately, the one moment that Willow lets her guard down is the same one where Glory steps in. What Willow does next is no different than what Giles did in "Passion"; against Buffy's better judgment, when someone hurts the one you love, you take revenge. The one thing viewers take away from this episode is never piss off a powerful witch. The ending, where Willow feeds Tara applesauce, is touching and heartfelt. No matter what, Willow declares that Tara is her girl, her everything, and she will fight what has happened until things get back to normal again.

HIGHLIGHT: When Willow says she can't sleep without Tara and Anya offers to sleep with her: "Wow, now *that* came out a lot more lesbian than it sounded in my head."
WILLOW WICCA WATCH: Somehow, Willow has become a very powerful and dangerous witch when we weren't looking. She finds the most potent spell book in the Magic Box *and* knows how to open it. This is the first time we see her eyes go black when she's performing the dark magicks, although it's not enough to stop Glory. Unfortunately, when she's scared and upset, she can't perform; when she sees Glory with Tara, she stumbles through a spell, unable to remember the words.

5.20 Spiral

Original air date:	May 8, 2001
Written by:	Steven S. DeKnight
Directed by:	James A. Contner
Guest cast:	Justin Gorence (Orlando), Wade Andrew Williams (General Gregor), Todd Duffey (Murk), Lily Knight (Grodi), Karim Prince (Knight)

Glory discovers that Dawn is the Key, and Buffy must do the one thing she thought she'd never have to in order to save her sister — run away.

"Spiral" is a heart-pounding, suspenseful episode full of action and surprises. And we *finally* get an explanation of exactly who Glory is and what the Key can do. The gang escape Glory in a beat-up motorhome they take into the desert, but the Knights of Byzantium catch on and chase them until they're forced to take refuge in a shack in the middle of nowhere. Both Spike and Giles are seriously hurt, and suddenly everyone is crying out for Buffy — Giles is moaning her name, Anya's telling Buffy to get them out of the mess, Dawn is screeching "Bufffaaaaay!" every two seconds, Willow's telling Buffy she needs to help Giles. . . . No wonder the episode ends the way it does. Everyone is pressuring Buffy — even Giles and Xander question her decision to bring Spike along in the first place — and they're not making her job any easier.

The goddess-like Clare Kramer

As they are caught in the shack with nothing to protect them except one of Willow's spells, Buffy gets the scoop from Gregor, the army general who she's captured. He tells her who Glory is and what the Key can do. His story sounds familiar. The writers have cleverly borrowed some parts of John Milton's poem *Paradise Lost*, a story about another angel who fell from grace and decided to get revenge on the God who cast him out. The poem begins in the midst of the story, just after Satan has been cast out of Heaven for trying to rebel against God with his army of angels, and they awaken in the rivers of Hell. Despondent and resigned, the angels listen half-heartedly to Satan telling them they must rally and fight back. He forms a council of angels, who contribute ideas on how they will fight back against God. Beelzebub, Satan's right hand, suggests they forget trying to fight Heaven, that instead they should go to Earth and destroy mankind. Milton explains: "Spirits when they please/Can either Sex assume, or both . . ." — something that Glory/Ben does.

As Satan continues to speak, his angels grow smaller and smaller until they're dwarf-like (think of Glory's minions), and finally he agrees to do what Beelzebub suggested, telling them he will travel to Earth himself. The angels begin to worship Satan: "Towards him they bend/With awful reverence prone; and as a God/Extol him equal to the highest in Heav'n." Although I'm sure they weren't calling him "Your Satany scrumptiousness," as Glory's minions are wont to do. As Satan travels to Earth, he meets a woman at a gate who refuses to let him exit Hell, and she fights to keep him away. When she can resist no longer, she's forced to give him the Key. He enters the Garden of Eden, where Adam and Eve are living happily, and tears their world apart.

Similarly, Glory needs the Key to open the dimensions, but not just one — all of them will blend together and the world will fall into complete and utter chaos. Buffy and Dawn are like Adam and Eve; where Eve was made from Adam's rib, Dawn was made using Buffy's blood. As the truth of the situation comes out, you can almost see the faces of everyone around Buffy thinking that maybe trying to protect Dawn isn't such a good idea after all. Maybe the Knights of Byzantium, whom the gang are fighting and killing, have the right idea. But Buffy doesn't have the power to do what needs to be done. She might have been able to kill Angel to save the world, but Dawn is the only family she has left, and she cannot sacrifice her. The end of the episode is so powerful, fans were left begging for more. What do you *mean* we have to wait an entire week?!

HIGHLIGHT: The conversation between Ben and the female minion about how Glory is ruining his life. Ben: "You know why I wanted to be a doctor?" Minion: "Flattering drawstring pants?"
NITPICKS: If the monks had to put the Key in human form, couldn't they have made it a little

stronger and not quite so pathetic and useless? As Glory is hot on the heels of Dawn and Buffy at the university, Dawn runs about 20 feet before falling over and crying that she just can't go on any longer, forcing Buffy to actually *pick her up* and carry her while running! Dawn clearly doesn't have any sense of self-preservation, and should likely work some exercise into her schedule if running across a lawn leaves her winded. Also, in "Where the Wild Things Are" Willow told Tara she's always been terrified of horses, ever since a childhood pony incident. Yet when Giles is trying to get away from the knights, she yells at him not to hurt the horses.

WILLOW WICCA WATCH: At the beginning of the episode, Willow creates a wall that prevents Glory from entering Tara's dorm room, and then sends Glory reeling back through the air. When they're in the shack, she creates a protective wall that prevents the army of thousands of knights from entering and killing them all. And, of course, she gets the payphone working, which seems to impress Spike more than anything else. Everything she does in this episode is helpful, and without it, they all would have died and Glory would have taken Dawn. Too bad no one remembers any of these good deeds in season six.

5.21 The Weight of the World

Original air date:	May 15, 2001
Written by:	Douglas Petrie
Directed by:	David Solomon
Guest cast:	Dean Butler (Hank Summers), Todd Duffey (Murk), Joel Grey (Doc), Lily Knight (Grodi), Matthew Lang (High Priest Minion), Alexandra Lee (Young Buffy)

Buffy has slipped into a catatonic state upon losing Dawn, and Willow enters her thoughts to try to snap her out of it. Meanwhile, the barrier between Glory and Ben begins to break down and Glory loses control right before the ritual.

A very strange episode that shows how the smallest and most seemingly insignificant of moments can have a profound effect on our lives. After exhausting all of her energies to save Dawn, Buffy finally shuts right down — everything that has happened this season with her and her family seems to have hit her at once. Her mother is dead, her father is AWOL, her sister's not real, and she's been given this cryptic message that apparently explains her very existence: "Death is your gift." She has tried everything on Glory and nothing works, and she's admitted to herself that maybe she can't fight this enemy. And the guilt of not being able to save her mother, and possibly killing her sister, has weighed upon her too heavily.

Meanwhile, Glory is facing a little guilt of her own. Ben begins seeing visions of the hundreds of men Glory has killed, and she begins seeing all the good he has done. For once, Glory feels guilt and other emotions, and she's almost paralyzed by their force. Dawn must suffer not only the terror of knowing she's about to be used in some ritual, but the confusion of not knowing if she can trust anyone long enough to help her. And Buffy's not in any state to help right now.

For the first time, Willow takes charge of the situation, showing that she can be a leader if forced. She orders the gang to complete various tasks, and they become so afraid of her they don't question her at all. Do they think perhaps she would use her magic against them? As she moves into Buffy's mind, we see the moments of this season that have had the biggest impact on her. And all of them have involved her family — the Summers house, the Magic Box where she meets Dawn every day after school, the Summers house circa 1987, and the desert where she learned the message. All of these images are swirling around in her head and bumping into one another, but she can't make sense of them.

It seems that no matter how strong you are, when guilt intervenes, it can be devastating.

HIGHLIGHT: Spike's frustration when no one remembers that Ben is Glory and vice versa.
NITPICKS: Perhaps one of the reasons Glory seems to be losing control is that she hasn't brain-sucked anyone in a while. Why haven't the minions gotten her any fresh humans? And after being impaled by a javelin and almost killed, Giles has bounced back pretty quickly. Same goes for Spike, who had his hands ripped by a sword a few hours earlier and now they show no marks whatsoever.
OOPS: In "Killed by Death," we see Buffy at 10 years old and she has very dark brown hair. In this episode, when we flash back to her at age six, her hair is as blond as it is now. Also, the symbol on Dawn's forehead keeps disappearing and reappearing.
WILLOW WICCA WATCH: Willow uses a separation spell to stop Spike and Xander from fighting, then uses magic to enter Buffy's psyche. As Giles says, that's "extraordinarily advanced" for a witch at her level, but it's required to keep the gang in order and bring back Buffy.

5.22 The Gift

Original air date:	May 22, 2001
Written and directed by:	Joss Whedon
Guest cast:	Todd Duffey (Murk), Joel Grey (Doc), Josh Jacobson (Teen), Tom Kiesche (Vampire), Craig Zimmerman (Minion #1)

Buffy and the gang come together to try to stop Glory, and when the ritual begins early, Buffy must make a difficult decision.

From the "Previously on *Buffy the Vampire Slayer*" to the gut-wrenching conclusion, "The Gift" is an intense, emotionally charged episode that leaves you breathless. If you watched this episode on the WB, you were met with an interesting surprise at the beginning and ending — throughout the show, the network called it the "series finale," leaving some fans wondering if the series was actually going over to UPN or if this was the final instalment. The show opened with a clip from all the pivotal moments of the series, from the first episode right through the fifth season. Then a kid running down an alleyway, being chased by a vampire (wow, I was beginning to forget those things were part of the show) and being cornered, only to be rescued by Buffy. His rather confused line to her, "But you're just a girl," has a ring of irony, since that's what she's been trying to tell everyone throughout the series. In this episode, we discover she's so much more than that.

Every actor on the show pulled out all the stops for this incredible episode. Alyson Hannigan plays the range of her character from weepy to happy to the old giddy Willow we know and love. Amber Benson played the mentally drained Tara as a cross between a child and a brain-sick psychiatric patient. Nicholas Brendon is still Xander, goofy and thinking about sex at all the wrong moments, but we also realize he's a big boy now when he's about to take a huge step. Emma Caulfield shows us another side of Anya, one that is so terrified she's forced to take charge for a moment and come up with two ideas that could possibly save the world. But notice how she stays and helps everyone fight, something she wouldn't have dreamed of doing in "Graduation Day (Part Two)." James Marsters shows a side of Spike we've never seen before. Anthony Stewart Head goes from being angry at Buffy to being a fighting machine, and gives us a surprising reappearance of Ripper that we always knew was in there somewhere. Michelle Trachtenberg shows us a fear of knowing that the world is going to end, but, more importantly to a 14-year-old girl, that she's about to die. And finally, Sarah Michelle Gellar is superb.

Every character takes a step forward in their lives that propels them into season six. Giles stops being a Watcher and becomes a Doer, doing what he must to ensure Buffy's safety. Willow takes a new step after her new skill learned in "The Weight of the World" and begins speaking in people's heads, forcing Spike to take charge when he's needed. And Xander takes a big step into adulthood.

Glory/Ben continue to bounce back and forth, but ultimately it's Glory who will stand at the immense tower her minions and brainsucked victims have constructed for the ritual. A character from a past episode suddenly shows up when Glory is busy with the Slayer, and he is the catalyst for the suspenseful ending.

The finale of this episode was the culmination of the entire beautiful season. As Buffy rushes to save her sister and realizes the bloodletting has begun, she suddenly understands what the prophecy in the desert was all about. Death is her gift. The voice-over, music, and visuals as everyone realizes the sacrifice Buffy is about to make are absolutely stunning — if, of course, you can still see the television despite your teary eyes. Fans mourned over the ending of this episode for months. For many, it was the sight of Spike sobbing at the base of the tower that did it, since we've never seen him like this before. This ending was five years in the making, and so many earlier prophecies that we'd seen before came true, the most potent being Faith's: in "Graduation Day (Part Two)," when she says that Buffy is counting down to 7-3-0, she was referring to the number of days. Exactly two years, or 730 days after that season finale, Buffy would have to make the ultimate choice, and she does. Her friends will have to go on, fighting the good fight, and using the tools she has given them. Even though the day that *Buffy* ends will be a sad day indeed, this episode would have been an absolutely perfect ending to the series. Thank you, Joss.

HIGHLIGHT: The close up of the tombstone at the end. It's exactly the epitaph Buffy's friends would have given her.

INTERESTING FACTS: As Buffy tells the gang that if the ritual starts, they'll all die, and if they come near Dawn, she'll kill them, Spike mutters to Giles, "Well, not exactly the St. Crispin's Day speech, was it?" He's referring to the legendary speech the king gives to his troops and friends in Shakespeare's *Henry V* — he says it's St. Crispin's Day, and from that day on everyone will remember that they fought to save England, and that they'd done it on St. Crispin's Day. The speech rallies an otherwise despondent group of men into a fighting machine, giving them hope that they'll actually win (which isn't exactly what Buffy does here). Giles's response — "We few, we happy few" — is the most well-known line from the speech: he says that not a day will go by, "From this day to the ending of the world,/But we in it shall be rememberèd — /We few, we happy few, we band of brothers."

NITPICKS: While I hate to nitpick this episode at all, there is one little thing. When the Buffybot shows up at the tower to fight Glory, everyone is tricked into believing it's actually Buffy because it talks and looks like her. Yet before and after this moment the bot speaks in clipped sentences. She hasn't been programmed to speak differently, so it was a little unbelievable that she'd sound exactly like Buffy when they needed her to.

Season Six

OCTOBER 2001 • MAY 2002

Recurring characters in season six: Adam Busch (Warren Meers), Danny Strong (Jonathan Levinson), Tom Lenk (Andrew Wells), James C. Leary (Clem), Kali Rocha (Halfrek)

6.1 Bargaining (Part One)

Original air date:	October 2, 2001
Written by:	Marti Noxon
Directed by:	David Grossman
Guest cast:	Franc Ross (Razor), Mike Grief (Klyed), Paul Greenberg (Shempy Vampire), Geoff Meed (Mag), Joy DeMichelle Moore (Ms. Lefcourt), Bru Muller (Teacher), Robert D. Vito (Cute Boy), Harry Johnson (Parent #1), Kelly Lynn Warren (Parent #2), Hila Levy (Pretty Girl), Richard Wharton (Homeowner)

Willow, Xander, Tara, and Anya, still reeling from Buffy's death, try to bring her back to life, while Spike, Dawn, and Giles struggle to move on with their lives.

After giving us one of the most shocking season finales ever, the writers start the new season with a bang, with all of the characters moving in different directions. Many viewers believe that season six was disjointed, partly because it was a dark year, with Buffy trying to come to terms with her life and several characters undergoing major changes. Some critics blamed the upheaval on the fact that Joss Whedon handed over the day-to-day responsibilities to Marti Noxon. But when you watch the season in its entirety, it's actually a lot tighter than it seemed at first.

"Bargaining" opens with the various characters in limbo, not quite able to move on after losing Buffy. Xander and Anya can't find the right time to tell everyone that they're engaged; Spike blames himself for her death; Giles believes he has no place in Sunnydale now that his Slayer is gone; Willow hasn't accepted Buffy's death or mourned properly because she's been planning to bring her back all summer; and Dawn, who first lost her mother and then her sister, finds solace at night with the Buffybot as she tries to convince herself that the piece of machinery is her sister.

The most telling transformation is that of Willow. At the beginning of the episode, she's instructing the Scoobies on how to fight the vampires by speaking inside their minds, not considering whether her actions are an invasion of privacy. Her magic this season will move far beyond merely helping people. She begins using magic on her friends against their will, starting here. But the most disturbing scene is where she sacrifices the baby deer to obtain the last ingredient for her spell. One of the classic books of magicks is the *Lemegeton*, also known as "The Lesser Key of Solomon," and Willow's incantation is taken from the "Ars Almadel," the fourth book of the *Lemegeton*. It is believed that by creating an Almadel, Solomon used magic to call forth the wisdom of the angels to help him govern the four corners of the earth. To make an Almadel (a four-sided symbol made of pure wax), a person writes the names of the angels he will invoke on the sides. On the east side one writes the names that Willow invokes — Adonaij, Hellomi, and Pine. In the center of the structure lies a pentagram within a hexagram. The symbol itself is a telling one (the symbol of Wicca within the Star of David), and a clever wink on the part of the writers. Adonaij is the Hebrew word for God, or Lord of Lords, and Hellomi and Pine are angels. Willow calls upon Jewish deities — Judaism being her original religion — so she can bring forth an angel she will sacrifice to the god Osiris, the Egyptian god of the underworld. Willow has crossed a line, as Xander, Tara, and Anya realize when they see how serious the spell is and the physical impact it has on Willow. Not only has she sacrificed the blood of a Hebrew angel for darkness, but she has defied the central law of Wicca — to never harm nature.

Why did everyone want Buffy back? Willow believes that Buffy could be in a hell dimension and she wants to end Buffy's suffering, but is that really the reason they helped perform the spell or are they being selfish? A telling aspect is the homing device Willow has put into the Buffybot — whenever the bot is injured, it comes back to Willow, just like Willow wishes Buffy would. No one can move on now that Buffy is gone, and each thinks his or her life was better with her in it. The only person who forces himself to move on without Buffy is Giles, who decides to return to England in a scene every fan feared would happen sooner or later. But in their haste to do what they believe is right, the gang doesn't think the spell through, and at the end, as they abandon the grave site and Buffy awakes within her coffin (in a rather graphic scene), we see that their rash behavior will have devastating consequences.

HIGHLIGHT: Tara giving Giles a little rubber monster as a going-away gift, and making it go "Grr, argh," like the Mutant Enemy man.

INTERESTING FACTS: Anthony Stewart Head has been removed from the opening credits, and Alyson Hannigan takes his valued place at the end. Amber Benson, on the other hand, *still* isn't considered a regular. Marti Noxon's name appears with Joss Whedon's as co-executive producer at the end of each episode.

NITPICKS: As if the university wasn't strange enough for a tiny "one Starbucks town," they also have a rather large airport?

RESTLESS MOMENT: In Giles's dream, Spike tells him he must make up his mind about whether he's staying or going.

WILLOW WICCA WATCH: Willow is able to speak inside her friends' heads, and the spell to bring Buffy back produces physical effects on Willow's body.

MUSIC/BANDS: Static X's "Permanence," from *Machine*, plays in the demon biker bar. Season six score composed by Thomas Wanker.

6.2 Bargaining (Part Two)

Original air date: October 2, 2001

Written by:	David Fury
Directed by:	David Grossman
Guest cast:	same as in part one

Buffy comes back to life and must help her friends rid Sunnydale of a demon biker gang.

Where "Bargaining" contained a lot of action, part two involves the emotional side. When Willow realizes the urn has broken and believes the spell was a failure, she starts to mourn Buffy. For the first time since Buffy's death, Willow feels her friend is finally gone.

Meanwhile, Buffy has to fight her way out of her own grave (the Scoobies forgot one important detail about raising the dead — they come to life where they are) and emerges frightened, confused, and alone. Sarah is incredible throughout this episode. As Buffy stumbles onto the street just in time to see the Buffybot drawn and quartered, the sight is not only confusing to her, but symbolic of her character. Throughout season six, she'll feel like she's being drawn in different directions — wanting death, wanting life, wishing her friends would go away, wishing they'd stay near, wanting Spike, not wanting Spike. When she happens upon her friends, it's Xander who realizes exactly what they've done, and given his personality, he'll be beating himself up for it for the rest of his life.

In her confused state, even Buffy's friends don't seem welcoming to her, and she stumbles back to the last place she remembers before she died — Glory's tower from "The Gift." As she stands perched above the very spot she was killed, Dawn appears and the two reenact the final scene from "The Gift," only with the roles switched. As Buffy insists she has to die, Dawn begs her to live, telling her how much they need her. It's exactly like the moment when Dawn told Buffy she had to die to stop the destruction around them, but Buffy told Dawn to live. Even the same music from "The Gift" swells up once again. The ending is different, though, and viewers know the season will be a dark one, for although Buffy is alive, there's only deadness in her eyes.

HIGHLIGHT: Tara sending the ball of light to guide Willow and Xander out of the woods.
INTERESTING FACTS: Tara calls on Aradia to help guide Willow and Xander. Aradia was the daughter of Diana, the goddess of the hunt, and is seen as a protectress of witches.
DID YOU NOTICE? Unfortunately for the writers and director, the way the tower fell was a little too reminiscent of the World Trade Center falling on September 11, 2001. The two-part "Bargaining" was the first *Buffy* episode to air after the tragedy, and viewers cringed when that moment occurred. In the previous hour, Willow had been wearing a red shirt with the number eleven on it, and some fans speculated that it was an homage to the date before realizing the episode had been filmed in the summer. There is an unintentional parallel between the events of 9/11 and the first few episodes of season six — just as Buffy is trying to adjust to a darker, harsher world, so were the viewers.
NITPICKS: Xander becomes angry with Willow for not explaining the seriousness of the spell to him. They were *bringing back the dead* — he didn't think that would be serious? Also, when the demons corner the gang in the alleyway, Razor's graphic threat to rape the women is completely unnecessary. Finally, the writers have perpetuated the myth that one's hair grows after death, since Buffy's hair looks a lot longer than it was when she died. According to forensic anthropologist William R. Maples, "It is a myth that fingernails and hair continue to grow after death. What really happens is that the skin may retract around them, making the hair and nails prickle up and jut out more prominently."

6.3 After Life

Original air date:	October 9, 2001
Written by:	Jane Espenson
Directed by:	David Solomon
Guest cast:	Lisa Hoyle (Demon)

When members of the gang become possessed, they worry that something else might have come back with Buffy.

In Wiccan circles it's called the Threefold Law, or the Karmic Law of Return. The idea that whatever you do will come back to you threefold also exists in Judeo-Christian beliefs: "As you sow, so shall ye reap." Or, in modern terms, what goes around comes around. Wicca is an individualistic religion, where there are no priests, no belief in Satan, and so on; instead one must be self-correcting and responsible. The Threefold Law is that self-correcting influence, helping keep Wiccans on the right track. Wiccans believe that if you affect the universe in a positive way, you will receive three times the strength in positive energy. Similarly, if you affect the universe in a negative way, it will come back to you negatively with three times the strength. The fact that mostly negative things happen to the gang from this point on in the season would indicate that what Willow did was wrong.

In "After Life," the gang discovers the downside to magic, and Xander's concerns that perhaps Willow didn't fill them in on everything become even more pronounced. He wonders if she knew ahead of time that things could go terribly wrong and just didn't say anything. Trust has been breached all around, as Spike has been helping the Scoobies all summer with their demon fighting, yet they didn't let him in on their plan. Willow's selfishness moves to a new level, where her happiness at Buffy's return is tarnished by the fact that Buffy hasn't thanked her for bringing her back.

The scene between Buffy and Dawn is quiet and sad. Dawn has watched her parents get divorced, and no doubt wished her father would come back; she has watched her mother die, and we know she almost tried to bring her back; she watched her sister die and had to endure the Buffybot hanging around; and now her dream has come true and she treats Buffy like a porcelain figurine, almost scared she'll disappear if Dawn says or does the wrong thing. She becomes the mother for a moment, cleaning up Buffy and reassuring her that everything will be okay. Unfortunately, it's one of the last moments of maturity Dawn exhibits for the entire season.

HIGHLIGHT: Spike's heartfelt confession to Buffy that, in his dreams, he's saved her every night since her death.

NITPICKS: Spike tells Buffy that he knows how she feels because he's had to claw himself out of a coffin, too. When? In "Fool for Love," we see Drusilla kill him. She would not have left the body for his family to bury — in "Reunion" on *Angel*, Drusilla keeps Darla's body so she can wait for it to arise, and it's likely she would have done the same with Spike. After being lonely for so long, she wanted a companion. She wouldn't have just left him behind.

WILLOW WICCA WATCH: As Tara and Willow cast a spell to locate the demon, Willow breaks away from Tara and finishes it herself.

RESTLESS MOMENT: In "Restless," Willow was worried everyone would find out about who she really is. In this episode, it seems she knew there was a chance Buffy would come back wrong, and she hopes no one finds out.

6.4 Flooded

Original air date:	October 16, 2001
Written by:	Douglas Petrie, Jane Espenson
Directed by:	Douglas Petrie
Guest cast:	John Jabaley (Tito), Michael Merton (Carl Savitsky, Loan Officer), Brian Kolb (Band Guard), Todd Stashwick (M'Fashnik Demon)

Buffy discovers that she can't pay the bills, and must find a way to make some money. Meanwhile, there's a new evil . . . well, a new big bad . . . um, okay, a new pesky force in town.

When asked what season six was going to be about, Joss Whedon described the overarching theme as "Oh, grow up." "Flooded" forces Buffy into the big bad adult world of full copper repipes and bills she can't pay. This season Willow will discover that you can have a power that sets you apart from others, but you must act responsibly or you can get hurt; Dawn gets older — but doesn't exactly mature; and Anya kick-starts the new theme by telling Xander in a fit of anger that he should grow up and accept the fact that they're going to get married. While season four was about what happens after high school, season six is about becoming an adult and embarking on the rest of your life. For everyone, it's going to be filled with disappointments and obstacles they hadn't anticipated, and because the only adult in their lives has moved to England, they'll have to learn to go it alone.

For a few weeks, however, Giles will be back, if for no other reason than to be reunited with his beloved Buffy. Unlike the rest of the gang, who are simply happy that Buffy is back but don't ask her any questions, Giles is concerned about how Buffy is dealing with everyone. He's seen enough in his life to know what real pain is, and can only imagine what she must be going through. He's also the only one to notice that Buffy seems distracted and behaves differently than before, and when he confronts Willow in the kitchen, the resulting scene is painful and disturbing. Here are the two characters that many fans say are their favorites fighting, insulting one another, and tossing out dangerous threats. We viewers feel torn and uncomfortable, which is exactly how most of the characters feel throughout the season.

And finally, what can I say about the Troika? Warren and Jonathan are instantly recognizable to viewers as two thorns in Buffy's side from previous seasons (although Warren was pretty annoying in season five, and it's surprising they'd bring the character back), and Andrew, a.k.a. "that other guy," is unknown to Buffy because it was his brother Tucker who caused the ruckus (see "The Prom"). Their first few appearances are absolutely hysterical, and later, just as they become tired characters, they will begin to change to darker constructs. Perhaps that Wiccan Threefold Law is personified in these three, considering where their characters will go this season. Their bumbling comic-book-villain quest for world domination (okay, Sunnydale domination) is great, considering how similar these geeks are to most of the writers on the staff . . . and the fans, for that matter.

HIGHLIGHT: Anya and Dawn fight over whether or not Spider-Man was paid to fight crime and they turn to Xander, who drops his head and sighs, "Action is his reward."

INTERESTING FACTS: Giles mentions that he lives in a flat in Bath, which is where Anthony Stewart Head lives.

DID YOU NOTICE? When Buffy gets the phone call from Angel, she says they have to meet, "Not [in] L.A. And not here. Somewhere in the middle." It's a wink to the fact that now the shows are on two different networks, there can no longer be any crossovers, so what Buffy was really saying was "Not on UPN, not on the WB, but somewhere off the networks altogether."

NITPICKS: One of my biggest pet peeves is that Buffy spends most of the season desperately trying to find work to pay the rent, while Tara and Willow are freeloading upstairs. Several fans have argued that they're probably on full scholarships and should be spending all of their time on their studies, but if that's the case, they should be living in a dormitory or Willow should move back home. Neither has paid one dime to Buffy, yet they use the hot water in the house, are living in a room that Buffy could be renting out, and eat the food without contributing to a grocery fund. The "Oh, grow up" principle should start with them. And hey, if Willow can wave her hand and make things appear and disappear, can't she do a full copper repipe job for Buffy or, even better, create money?

OOPS: At the end of the episode, Angel calls Buffy and she immediately leaves. But in "Carpe Noctem" on *Angel*, which had aired the night before this episode, Cordy comes rushing out to Angel and says Willow has called him with the news and is on the phone.

6.5 Life Serial

Original air date:	October 23, 2001
Written by:	David Fury, Jane Espenson
Directed by:	Nick Marck
Guest cast:	Paul Gutrecht (Tony), Noel Albert Guglielmi (Vince), Enrique Almeida (Marco), Jonathan Goldstein (Mike), Winsome Brown (Woman Customer), Christopher May (Male Customer), David J. Miller (Rat-faced Demon), Andrew Cooper Wasser (Slime-covered Demon), Richard Beatty (Small Demon), Clint Culp (Bartender), Mark Ginther (Horned Demon), Derrick McMillon (Ron), Jennifer Shon (Rachel), Jabari Hean (Steve), Alice Dinnean Vernon (Mummy Hand)

The Troika test Buffy with a series of challenges while she tries to find a job.

After a bleak and depressing start to season six, "Life Serial" is hilarious, especially if you know (or are) someone like the geek squad. The Troika are stereotypical comic-book nerds who still live in their parents' basements and learn everything through comics and sci-fi television. There are few things they treasure more than their beloved action figures, and each one is smart academically, but not socially. They falter in just

The Troika, a triumvirate of annoyance

The Many Names of Jonathan

Throughout Jonathan's stint as the most enduring recurring character on Buffy (he's appeared in every season but season five and was even in the unaired pilot), he's been called many names by other students and even the Scoobies. But his two cohorts in season six — Andrew and Warren — are responsible for most of them. These are the names they've called him throughout season six:

Warren:
Whine-athan ("Flooded")
Stretch ("Life Serial")
Frodo ("Gone")
Sparky ("Dead Things," "Seeing Red")
Big Man, Midgetor, Spanky ("Normal Again")
Padawan, Short Round ("Entropy")
Little Man ("Seeing Red")

Andrew:
Deanna Troi, Betazoid ("Seeing Red")
Fuzzball, Jerk-athan, Little Feller ("Villains")
Buttwipe ("Grave")

---

about every task, yet can quote flawlessly from endless sci-fi shows and books. Of course, they were taunted and mocked in high school, and that humiliation provides them with their motivation. These are the extreme versions of kids who got bullied in school.

In a season where the other characters are learning to accept adult responsibility, the supernerds represent kids who are stuck in arrested development. They can't grow up, and are trying to live out comic-book fantasies of little boys. While we feel sorry for Buffy in this episode, we can't help but laugh because the Troika don't yet pose a serious threat like Glory; they're more like an annoying itch she can't reach. "Life Serial" was filled with comic highlights, including their arguments about the proper Death Star, allusions to *Monty Python*, *The X-Files*, and *Star Trek*, fights over who was the best James Bond . . . and, of course, Jonathan's magic bone. The three of them are already developing their own personalities — Warren pretends to be the grown-up but doesn't play well with others and becomes defensive and whiny if his superiority is challenged; Jonathan can be timid but sticks up for himself, even if he's immediately shot down by Warren; and Andrew is the meekest of the bunch . . . as long as you don't say nasty things about Timothy Dalton.

Sarah Michelle Gellar turns in a comic performance of her own, including a sidesplitting fight with a mystical mummy hand. In her growing frustration about everything that has happened to her in recent weeks, she turns to Spike, since he's the one person who wasn't involved in bringing her back. She is able to open up to him as if he were a therapist because she believes he's not one of her real friends and won't be affected by anything she says. In a way, he's a perversion of Giles — he's older than she is and therefore carries more wisdom, yet unlike Giles he won't lecture her or be disappointed in her. As she gets drunk at the demon bar — hilariously gagging with every shot — she discovers the painful side of dealing with the troubles of adulthood: the hangover.

HIGHLIGHT: The *Star Wars* horn in the Troika's van that accidentally goes off at an inopportune moment.

NITPICKS: How did Buffy get into the demon bar with a bottle of alcohol? The bartender never would have allowed it, especially considering she's only 20.

MUSIC/BANDS: In the bar scene, we hear "Kidnapper Song" by the Masticators, from *Masticate!*, and "Boom Swagger Boom," by the Murder City Devils, from their self-titled CD.

6.6 All the Way

Original air date:	October 30, 2001
Written by:	Steven S. DeKnight
Directed by:	David Solomon
Guest cast:	John O'Leary (Kaltenbach), Kavan Reece (Justin), Amber Tamblyn (Janice), Dave Power (Zack), Charles Duckworth (Glenn), Dawn Worrall (Christy), Emily Kay (Maria), Adam Gordon (Carl), Steven Anthony Lawrence (Chunky Kid), Sabrina Speer (Girl), Chad Erikson (Guy), Dominic Rambaran (Paramedic #1), Anthony Sago (Paramedic #2), Lorin Becker (Witch Woman), Lily Jackson (Witchy Poo)

Dawn sneaks out with Janice to hang out with boys on Halloween, and gets a big surprise.

The title of this episode is ironic, for while each character makes a step forward to becoming an adult "all the way," they each make a step backward by the end and remain in limbo. The episode centers on Dawn's new rebellion. She's been stealing from various stores — including the Magic Box — and on Halloween tells Buffy she's going over to Janice's house, only to sneak out to get her first kiss. The moment would have been a step toward adulthood, since every teenager takes that step of lying to their parents about what they're doing, but when she's caught she immediately feels like a little girl again, being lectured by Buffy and Giles. Just as Buffy is about to mature and become the parent figure, she freezes up and asks Giles to assume the role, proving that she can't move forward, either.

Meanwhile, Xander seizes the moment and announces his engagement to Anya, but when Giles sits him down and asks him about downpayments on houses and Anya talks about children, Xander suddenly feels like he's suffocating. Is he moving too quickly? Marriage seemed like the logical next step to him, but perhaps Xander — who has always seemed like the most emotionally immature of the bunch — isn't exactly the marrying type. That said, he's the most sensitive of the group, too, and we know he really does love Anya. Nicholas Brendon and Anthony Stewart Head are great in their scene together, and we can't help but wonder if Giles is saying the things he is to deliberately freak Xander out.

But the relationship that makes the biggest movement forward and backward is Tara and Willow's. Tara finally confronts Willow about her flippant use of magic, but as we saw when Giles tried to do the same, Willow is becoming a very defiant and defensive character. For so many years she was corrected when she did things wrong, taunted by others for the way she was, and always looking to others for guidance; in this season, her inferiority has caught up to her and she's not going to take it anymore. She becomes rude and impertinent with Tara, and even when Xander announces his marriage to Anya she stands there brooding, as if she always secretly hoped they would break up and Xander would remain unhappy. And at the end of the episode, she finally uses her power against Tara in a shocking way. Willow is the hands-down fan favorite on the show, and her character development throughout the season will be the most devastating.

HIGHLIGHT: Giles walking through the cemetery looking for Dawn: "Mist, cemetery, Halloween. Should end well. [Trips and falls; leaps back up.] Bloody brilliant."

INTERESTING FACTS: While the "Lethe's Bramble" is a flower made up for the show, it borrows its name from Lethe, the daughter of Discord in Greek mythology. She gave her name to the spring of forgetfulness in the underworld, also known as the river of Oblivion, and it was believed that when one died, one drank from the river to forget what had happened in one's earthly life. Similarly, when reincarnated, one drinks from the river to forget one's life in the underworld and enter the world anew.

NITPICKS: Buffy somehow kills a vampire by slamming a car door on it. At first it seems like she took the vampire's head off, but when you look at the scene, the door closes around the vampire's waist. There's no way it would have been dusted using that method.

OOPS: Several times during the otherwise terrific fight scene, you can clearly see the face of Sarah's stuntwoman.

WILLOW WICCA WATCH: Willow decorates the living room for the engagement party, threatens to shift the people in the Bronze to an alternate dimension, waves her hand to create silence, and uses a forgetting spell.

RESTLESS MOMENT: In Giles's dream, Buffy acts like she's a little girl and he's her father, and in this episode she forces him to act like the parent to Dawn so she doesn't have to.

MUSIC/BANDS: As if to make up for the dearth of music to this point in the season, "All the Way" is loaded with it. We hear Lift's "Even If (It Is Love)," from their *September EP*. Coin Master's "Body of Binky," from *Schematic*, plays in the park. Anya and Xander discuss wedding plans to the sounds of Strange Radio's "Make Me a Star," from *Pre-Released Pop Radio*. Willow and Anya dance to "Everybody Got Their Something," by Nikka Costa, from *Everybody Got Their Something*. As Dawn and Justin kiss in the car, we hear "Around My Smile" by Hope Sandoval and the Warm Inventions (*Bavarian Fruit Bread*). Man of the Year is onstage at the Bronze, playing "Just as Nice" from *The Future Is Not Now*. When Dawn realizes what Justin is, you can hear Fonda's "The Sun Keeps Shining on Me," from *The Strange and the Familiar*.

6.7 Once More, With Feeling

Original air date:	November 6, 2001
Written and Directed by:	Joss Whedon
Original song music and lyrics by:	Joss Whedon
Songs produced and arranged by:	Jesse Tobias, Christophe Beck
Score by:	Christophe Beck
Choreographed by:	Adam Shankman
Guest cast:	Hinton Battle (Sweet), David Fury (Mustard Man), Marti Noxon (Parking Ticket Woman), Daniel Weaver (Handsome Young Man), Scot Zeller (Henchman), Zachary Woodlee (Henchman), Timothy Anderson (Henchman), Alex Estronel (Henchman), Matt Sims (College Guy #1), Hunter Cochran (College Guy #2)

Sunnydale is taken over by a singing and dancing demon, and everyone begins expressing their innermost thoughts through song.

Adam Shankman choreographs the final scene from "Once More, With Feeling"

Joss Whedon directs Michelle Trachtenberg and Hinton Battle
in "Once More, With Feeling"

This absolutely brilliant episode continues a tradition of working out problems through music. Most musicals, while bright and cheery on the outside, are about very dark topics. A girl who never knew her parents and is now starving to death in an orphanage where she's beaten daily by its caretaker is the premise of *Annie*. A story of another orphan who escapes his orphanage only to be taken in by a greedy man who forces him to steal for him became *Oliver!* And, as we all know, the plotlines of operas are rarely a walk in the park. A few years ago on *Xena: Warrior Princess*, the writers attempted a similar idea. The relationship between Xena and Gabrielle had gotten to a point where Xena tried to kill her best friend and there was nowhere left to go, and they were transported to a land where they had to sing their deepest secrets to one another. The resulting episode was incredible, and it was the most famous musical episode of a television show. And then along came Joss Whedon, with "Once More, With Feeling."

This episode was hyped for weeks on UPN during *Buffy*, so it had a lot to live up to. First, the entire cast opted to sing their own parts, rather than have stand-ins do the vocals for them. Second, Joss — who has no musical background — decided to write all of the lyrics and music, and it was going to be the only episode he would write and direct all season. He is a big fan of Stephen Sondheim, and used him as his muse while he wrote the songs. "I know the words to every one of his songs," he says. "Well, except *Passion*, which I've excised from my brain. It was just wrong." It took six months for Whedon to write all of the music, and the actors had to undergo voice training for three months. The final product was one of the best *Buffy* episodes of all time, and just when you thought the ensemble cast couldn't possibly be more talented, you discover they can also sing. After all, in the year of *Moulin Rouge* and a renewed interest in musicals, it was perfect timing.

Joss explores various genres of music throughout the episode: the show begins and ends with 1950s-television-style theme music and credits; Anya and Xander sing a 1930s-style duet that's both charming and funny as they reveal their insecurities about spending the rest of their lives together; Spike gets the big rock song where he wishes that Buffy would either treat him like a human being or leave him alone; Anya sings a rock opera interlude about her bunny terror within a bigger Broadway number performed by everyone; Tara performs a pop hit that would be welcome on the Lilith Fair tour as she conveys her love to Willow; Giles sings a sad ballad that exposes his fear that Buffy doesn't need him anymore; and Buffy, fittingly, sings the most complex pieces, full of syncopated beats and dissonant chords. Her songs are the most heartfelt and reveal the very things she swore she wouldn't tell anyone, creating a horrified reaction among her friends. Originally there was talk of bringing in a voice double to sing her parts, but when she read the script she insisted on singing them herself. She says, "I basically started to cry and said, 'You mean someone else is going to do my big emotional turning point for the season?'" In the end Gellar does a superb job and displays a great singing voice — why did they even consider having someone else cover for her?

In fact, each of the actors does a fantastic job. Amber Benson has the most stunning voice, showing a surprising range. Brendon and Caulfield are wonderful as they sing and dance about their love for one another, and they're the only pair who harmonize, showing that even though they have worries about their future, they really are a couple that was meant to be together. Even Michelle Trachtenberg shows some singing talent, although we don't hear much of Dawn's voice because the actress refused to do a full song for Whedon. Alyson Hannigan sings about three lines because she was uncomfortable with her singing voice. Marsters and Head, both singing veterans, show a skill we already knew they had, although Marsters's voice is a little shaky at times, since he's more accustomed to rockabilly numbers.

The final song the gang sings, "Where Do We Go From Here?" is appropriately titled, since they've all uncovered their darkest secrets and fears. Now that everything's out in the open, there's going to be a lot of explaining to do.

HIGHLIGHT: "They got the mustard OUT!!"

INTERESTING FACTS: Hinton Battle, who plays Sweet, is the only living three-time Tony Award winner. Also, the episode ran in letterbox format and for eight minutes longer than a normal episode for its first airing only. In future airings, the following was deleted: the overture; the "If We're Together" section of the gang's number at the beginning; a verse from Spike's "Rest in Peace"; Dawn's dance; a verse from "Walk Through the Fire"; and some dialogue. When Xander is in the Magic Box at the beginning of the episode doing his "respect the cruller, tame the doughnut" scene, he's alluding to Tom Cruise's speech in the film *Magnolia* about the importance of masculine superiority. The Parking Ticket Woman is Marti Noxon, writer and executive producer, and the Mustard Guy is David Fury, writer and co-executive producer.

DID YOU NOTICE? If you continue to listen to the song by the Parking Ticket Woman after Xander, Giles, and Anya pass by her, you can catch her scandalous (but hilarious) bribe. Also, at the very end of the episode, the Mutant Enemy man sings his "Grr, argh" in a falsetto.

NITPICKS: I won't reveal which of the gang was responsible for calling Sweet's magic forth, but earlier we see a man under the influence who tap-dances himself into oblivion. Isn't the person who made the music happen responsible for his death? Also, why doesn't Buffy hear anything Giles says in his heartfelt song? She's working out in the same room, and he's singing a few feet away from her.

RESTLESS MOMENT: In Willow's dream, Giles encourages the students to show energy, "especially in the musical numbers," and then says the audience will strip them naked and they have to learn to hide. In this episode, they were unable to hide their feelings, and Sweet stripped them bare emotionally. In Giles's dream, he comes to the revelation of what's following them by getting up on stage at the Bronze and singing.

MUSIC/BANDS: The titles of the songs are generally listed as follows, in sequence: "Going Through the Motions"; "I've Got a Theory"/"If We're Together"; "They Got the Mustard Out"; "Under Your Spell"; "I'll Never Tell"; "No Parking"; "Rest in Peace"; "Dawn's Lament"; "Sweet's Song (Why Don't We Dance a While?)"; "Standing"; "Wish I Could Stay"; "Walk Through the Fire"; "Life's a Show"; "Why Don't We Dance a While? (reprise)"; "Where Do We Go From Here?"; "Walk Through the Fire"/"Rest in Peace (reprise)"

6.8 Tabula Rasa

Original air date:	November 13, 2001
Written by:	Rebecca Rand Kirshner
Directed by:	David Grossman
Guest cast:	Raymond O'Connor (Loan Shark), Geordie White (Vamp #1), Stephen Triplett (Vamp #2), David Franco (Vamp #3)

Willow attempts to do a spell on Tara and Buffy to help them forget the events of "Once More, With Feeling," but it goes awry.

The concept of *tabula rasa*, Latin for "blank slate," was first put forth in 1607 by philosopher Francis Bacon, but was popularized by John Locke in his 1690 treatise *Essay Concerning Human Understanding*. The idea is that each of us is born into the world a blank slate, knowing nothing, and knowledge is written upon us by our experience. You are born with a propensity toward being good, and your personality is imprinted upon you. Charles Darwin later opposed Locke's argument, stating that our emotions are based on instincts, which are partly hereditary. In "Tabula Rasa," the *Buffy* writers tend to side with Darwin.

This episode is a pivotal one — things happen in "Tabula Rasa" that will affect the characters for the rest of their lives, despite the fact that none of them knows who they are anymore. In the musical episode, characters revealed their innermost secrets and acted upon them, and now Buffy and Spike need to work out whether or not they'll have a romantic relationship, or whether Buffy just kissed him because she needed something at that moment and he filled it. Tara has discovered that Willow worked her mojo on her in "All the Way," and insinuates that she'll leave if Willow can't stop. Willow is confused: in high school she didn't date until Oz came along because she was seen as a computer geek. With Oz, she was still shy and quiet, but she was starting along a new path of self-discovery and learning magic. Now, with Tara, she's found her soul mate, one who also used to be a wallflower but whose strength has been brought to the fore through her love for Willow. So Willow is bewildered that her witchcraft — which she believes should be attractive to people because it's so far removed from that other, unattractive (in her opinion) Willow of old — is the very thing that is driving Tara away.

The ensuing mess caused by her spell is hilarious, with Giles and Spike believing they're father and son (before Spike starts to think he's a version of Angel), Anya and Giles thinking they're engaged to one another, Xander and Willow believing they're dating, and Buffy thinking she's a superhero named Joan. Their memories wiped clean, they need to write their own stories. But just as Darwin argued, eventually we rely on our instincts. Buffy figures out that Dawn's her sister, Dawn reverts to whining and complaining, Xander tries to attack a monster but can't, Anya screws up spells and is afraid of rabbits, Giles is constantly annoyed by her, and there's an instant attraction between Tara and Willow.

But when the memories come back, all of the good times go away, and they're left with the dark, desolate world they'd left behind. Giles and Tara move on, and Willow is devastated. Buffy is almost paralyzed by the memories of what she's been through, and as she lies on the ground, completely despondent, we almost understand why Willow attempted the forgetting spell.

HIGHLIGHT: Buffy and Spike preparing to fight the vampires: "Ready, Randy?" "Ready, Joan."

DID YOU NOTICE? Willow makes the same befuddled comment she does in "Doppelgängland" about being "kinda gay."

WILLOW WICCA WATCH: Willow uses a spell to dress herself and then attempts a forgetting spell.

RESTLESS MOMENT: In Xander's dream, Spike and Giles are on the swings. Spike is dressed in a brown suit and tie, and Giles says, "He's like a son to me." Xander then tells Buffy he has to move forward, "like a shark, with feet and much less fins." Spike adds, "And on land."

MUSIC/BANDS: At the end of the episode Michelle Branch performs "Goodbye to You" on-stage at the Bronze. A different version of the song appears on her album, *The Spirit Room*. Joss Whedon saw her perform in Boston and knew that song would be perfect for the ending for "Tabula Rasa." But when he got her album, he found the song overproduced, so Branch and her band recorded it live for use in the episode.

6.9 Smashed

Original air date:	November 20, 2001
Written by:	Drew Z. Greenberg
Directed by:	Turi Meyer
Guest cast:	Elizabeth Anne Allen (Amy), Patrice Walters (Woman), John Patrick Clerkin (Man), Jack Jozefson (Rusty), Rick Garcia (Reporter), Kelly Smith (Innocent Girl), Jordan Belfi (Ryan), Adam Weiner (Simon), Melanie Sirmons (Brie), Lauren Nissi (Girlfriend)

When Willow makes Amy human again, they go on a magic spree. Meanwhile, Spike makes a discovery about Buffy that she doesn't like.

"Smashed" is about rebellion and succumbing to peer pressure, showing once again that members of the gang are in a stasis and can't grow up. In this case, it's Willow and Buffy. Willow has been using magic in a negative way, but has been hiding it from everyone because she knows it's wrong. With Tara using her magic only to protect others, as a good Wiccan should, Willow constantly felt inferior, although she was a far more powerful witch. Now, with only a little bit of goading from Amy (who reminds her that she sat around doing nothing throughout high school), Willow easily yields to the peer pressure and goes wild.

Buffy, on the other hand, was suffering from the opposite problem. Despite Spike's avowed love for her and her attraction to him, she felt superior to him, and to sleep with him would only lower her self-esteem. But when she and Spike begin to fight and he suddenly discovers he can hit her without the chip reacting, she believes she's no better than he is. Later in the season, several viewers complained that the relationship between Buffy and Spike would become abusive and confusing, but if you look at their first encounter in this episode, it begins with fighting, hitting, verbal abuse, and general destruction, and ends with Spike unzipping his fly.

Ultimately, both Buffy and Willow are women who have always done what they were told, rarely rebelled, and fought for good. It's inevitable that when faced with the temptation to be bad for a moment, they'd take it. It's not like Buffy hasn't done it before. . . .

HIGHLIGHT: Spike threatening to hurt Boba Fett (someone should probably explain to the Troika that a limited-edition action figure is worth only about 10 to 20 percent of its full value if it's out of the box — and yes, I know I sound like one of them).

INTERESTING FACTS: Many viewers were shocked by the graphic nature of the final scene of "Smashed," but according to Marti Noxon, it could have been a lot racier. "You should have seen the shot at the end before UPN cautioned us," she says. "It was much, much longer and that last image of them in the smoke — that's CGI smoke we had to add for a couple reasons.

One of the reasons is that we had to shorten that shot dramatically, but we also needed to obscure the action for the network."

NITPICKS: It's hard to believe it took this long for Willow to figure out how to de-rat Amy. She has created protective barriers, can call upon dark magic, and has raised the dead, but she couldn't figure out how to change Amy back into a human being? If I were Amy, I'd be pretty ticked off. Also, there's no way the British Museum would lend a priceless diamond to the Sunnydale Museum if the only security they had was a guy named Rusty.

OOPS: Buffy first hears about the security guard being hurt when the television news report says he's in critical but stable condition, which would suggest he was already in the hospital. Yet when she goes down to the museum to check things out, the guard is just being brought out to the ambulance: considering he's a block of ice, he's hardly in stable condition.

WILLOW WICCA WATCH: Willow de-rats Amy and looks through the police records by holding her hands over her laptop keyboard, and she and Amy perform various mischievous magicks at the Bronze.

MUSIC/BANDS: Virgil is onstage at the Bronze, performing songs from their self-titled album: "Vermillion Borders," "Parachute," and "Here." Willow briefly turns them into Halo Friendlies, who perform "Run Away" from *Halo Friendlies Ghetto Demo*.

6.10 Wrecked

Original air date:	November 27, 2001
Written by:	Marti Noxon
Directed by:	David Solomon
Guest cast:	Elizabeth Anne Allen (Amy), Jeff Kober (Rack), Fleming Brooks (Mandraz), Mageina Tovah (Jonesing Girl), Michael Giordani (Jonesing Guy), Colin Malone (Creepy Guy)

Amy introduces Willow to Rack, a magic "dealer," and Willow becomes addicted to it, putting herself — and Dawn — in danger.

"Wrecked" fleshed out the metaphor of Willow's dark magicks as drugs: she becomes addicted to them, craving the magic more and more until it begins to take a toll on her mind and life. And just as she starts to come down from a particularly horrifying high, she desires more. The metaphor *almost* works, but has a few flaws. Flip back through the **WILLOW WICCA WATCH** segments in the episode guides for previous seasons, and notice how many times Willow's magic has helped the gang — Dawn would have been dead in season five if Willow hadn't kept Glory at bay time and again. Even when it didn't work out right, she performed magic to protect her friends or herself, and until season six, almost never did it to make her life more convenient.

Kids turn to drugs because they mistakenly think it'll make them cooler (these days even smokers are ostracized by other kids), and usually they're under peer pressure. Willow began doing magic because she looked up to Jenny Calendar, and her first big spell in "Becoming (Part Two)" was to help out Buffy. She didn't turn to magic because "all the cool kids were doing it" — she did it to help out her friends. Drugs never have a positive effect on friends and family or make you a more sociable person; if anything, they cause the user to sit in a corner completely stoned while the rest of their friends are hanging out. To suggest that Willow's magic is akin to drug use borders on offensive, suggesting that drugs can make one's life easier and make one more acceptable and helpful to friends. As a metaphor for the perils of excess, however, the concept works beautifully and fits into the season six storyline of adults making bad choices when facing their futures. But "Wrecked" broke down that metaphor by making Rack's place appear to be a crack house, and Rack a creepy drug dealer.

Another problem: the others refer to Willow as a Wiccan because she uses magic. Wicca is a religion; witchcraft is not. Witchcraft can be part of the Wiccan religion if one chooses it to be, but is not necessary to it. Because it promotes individualism, every Wiccan will interpret the religion differently, but they all follow the Wiccan Rede, which states, "An it harm none, do what you will." Although the Rede can't be taken too literally — as many Wiccans point out, by breathing we harm millions of microorganisms; by eating we kill animals and plants — it still promotes a notion of living in har-

Alyson Hannigan at the premiere of "Once More, With Feeling"

mony with others and not hurting anyone on purpose. Willow has hurt people, and will hurt more. Is she still a Wiccan? Did she ever consider herself a Wiccan? In "Listening to Fear" in season five, when she had been studying witchcraft for a few years, she still referred to herself as Jewish. Tara has always been a Wiccan, one who respected the laws of nature and used her magic only for good (with the exception of the spell in "Family," but after seeing the consequences of harmful magic once, she never committed it again). But Willow is something else, and while the writers will still allude to Wicca when referring to Willow, it no longer applies.

In "Wrecked," as Willow goes over the edge and puts her life and Dawn's in danger, Buffy makes some personal decisions — she can't blame Willow for her actions at the end of the episode because she realizes she's made some bad choices herself lately. Dawn won't be quick to forgive, and she shouldn't be, considering everyone keeps leaving her at home alone and forgetting their responsibility to her, and when Willow agrees to take her to a movie, she drags her to Rack's place instead. Willow and Tara are like parents to Dawn (they took care of her for months while Buffy was gone and probably rarely left her alone), and now they act like separated parents, with Tara reassuring Dawn that her leaving had nothing to do with Dawn, and Willow asking Dawn if Tara had said anything about her.

As the episode comes to a close, both Buffy and Willow experience symptoms of withdrawal from their own temptations.

HIGHLIGHT: Anya revealing that Martha Stewart is a witch: "Nobody could do that much découpage without calling on the powers of darkness."

INTERESTING FACTS: This episode is dedicated to the memory of J.D. Peralta, who was Marti Noxon's assistant.

NITPICKS: Neither Dawn nor Willow are wearing seatbelts when the car slams into the pillar — they should both have flown through the windshield.

WILLOW WICCA WATCH: See entire episode. Plus, it would appear Willow told Amy about the forgetting spell; Amy says she has to go home to see her father, and he doesn't realize she'd been gone.

MUSIC/BANDS: As Willow floats on the ceiling at Rack's place, we hear Laika's "Black Cat Bone" from *Good Looking Blues*.

6.11 Gone

Original air date:	January 8, 2002
Written and directed by:	David Fury
Guest cast:	Daniel Hagen (Frank), Susan Ruttan (Doris Kroger), Jessa French (Cleo), Kelly Parver (Girl in Park), Jeffrey Jacquin (Meter Man), Dwight Bacquie (Security Guard), Lyndon Smith (Little Boy), Melina Webberley (Little Girl), Elin Hampton (Co-worker)

Buffy becomes invisible when the Troika hit her with their invisibility ray.

In "Gone" we see that Buffy's going to have a more difficult time moving on than she thought. While Willow has entered her own personal rehab, chugging back water whenever she gets the urge to do magic and facing the day-to-day drudgery of real life, Buffy feels "free" for the first time when she becomes invisible. Free of the judging eyes of her friends, the lustful eyes of Spike, and the scornful eyes of Dawn, Buffy lets loose. Her mini-rebellion is hardly the stuff of Willow's irresponsibility in the previous episode, but her shenanigans show us that when given the opportunity, Buffy will toss responsibility out the window just to taste the freedom of naughtiness. And that includes Spike, despite her vow to stop seeing him.

The best part of this episode was David Fury's clever direction. The camera constantly follows Buffy, even though we can't see her. When she hears Xander's phone message about the serious consequences of remaining invisible, the camera zooms in on her for a reaction, but we still can't see her. The end fight among Buffy and the Troika, where all four are invisible, is hilarious, as the camera jumps around to capture the entire — non-existent — scene.

Despite the recklessness Buffy shows throughout the episode and Dawn's disgust with her careless behavior, Buffy realizes by the end that she doesn't want to remain invisible. She needs to live, and if that involves being a better guardian to Dawn, noticing when her friends are having problems, and getting rid of Spike, then she's going to do her best to do those things. Starting with getting a job. . . .

HIGHLIGHT: Buffy's hasty reaction when the social worker finds a bag of Willow's supplies and mistakes it for marijuana: "It's *magic* weed!"

NITPICKS: At the beginning of the episode, it was obvious that Sarah Michelle Gellar was wearing a wig. Also, Anya mentions putting Buffy at a table with Xander's parents at their wedding. If Buffy's in the wedding party, shouldn't she be sitting at the head table? And finally, could they *make* a bigger deal about Buffy's hair? She cut it off to this length *and* dyed it to within an inch of its life in season two, and no one said a thing. Her hair has gone from long to short to brown to blond to straight to curly, and suddenly everyone's talking about her new hairstyle (which she only grew out again anyway). The media compared it to what happened on *Felicity* when Keri Russell cut her hair off. Sorry, people, we tune in to *Buffy* for the stories and the acting, *not* for Sarah's hair. That said, it *was* pretty cute.

WILLOW WICCA WATCH: Willow almost lifts a book using magic, but stops herself just in time.

MUSIC/BANDS: In this episode, we hear "I Know" by Trespassers William, from *Anchor*.

6.12 Doublemeat Palace

Original air date:	January 29, 2002
Written by:	Jane Espenson
Directed by:	Nick Marck
Guest cast:	Elizabeth Anne Allen (Amy), Pat Crawford Brown (Wig Lady), Brent Hinkley (Manny the Manager), Kirsten Nelson (Lorraine Ross), T. Ferguson (Gary), Marion Calvert (Gina), Douglas Bennett (Phillip), Andrew Reville (Timothy), Kevin C. Carter (Mr. Typical), John F. Kearney (Elderly Man), Sara LaWall (Housewife Type), Victor Z. Isaac (Pimply Teen)

Buffy gets a job at the Doublemeat Palace and gets a creepy feeling about the special ingredient.

"Doublemeat Palace" is probably the weakest episode of the season. As it's the first episode after the hiatus, viewers were expecting something better, but as we've seen in the past — "Killed by Death," "Superstar" — the writers tend to stick the stinkers after the break. That said, as terrible episodes go, this was by no means a "Beer Bad," showing that season six was a lot stronger than critics would have us believe. The central joke was funny: working at a fast-food restaurant, Buffy becomes suspicious of the zombie-like employees and weird, bright environment where everyone speaks in Teamworkese and they don't act like normal people — only to discover this is all normal behavior for fast-food employees. (Anyone who's ever suffered through a late shift on the drive-thru can relate.) However, stretching the punchline out over a full hour doesn't work, and the joke quickly becomes stale.

Just like the zombies in the fast-food restaurant, Buffy is going through the motions of her life — working her shift, scraping off the grill, coming home and desperately trying to get rid of that smell, and having sex with Spike. Not only was the atmosphere of this episode jarring for viewers — that monotonous *Twilight Zone* music added to its disorienting nature — but it fell within a group of episodes where Buffy was unable to make a decision and stick with it. Her "No, no, no . . . okay" attitude with Spike begins in "Smashed" and continues throughout several episodes, despite her vowing each time to stop. She declares in "Gone" that she has a real will to live and enjoy life, but the next time we see her she's zoned out and looks dead to the world. Season six is great if you watch all of the episodes together with no breaks, but when "Wrecked," "Gone," "Doublemeat Palace," "Dead Things," and "As

You Were" aired with several weeks of reruns in between, it seemed like Buffy's indecision and the motionless storyline went on far too long. But even "Doublemeat Palace" is better the second time around.

The other elements of the episode make it worth watching — Willow's adorable confession to Buffy through the drive-thru cow head; Anya's friend Halfrek showing up suddenly and freaking out Xander, only to end up as giddy as Kathy in "Living Conditions"; and Buffy's soylent green freak-out in the restaurant.

HIGHLIGHT: Buffy's reaction to the Doublemeat video at the beginning is hilarious.

NITPICKS: That creepy plant thing at the end was just *way* too over the top for even the most open-minded viewer. And talk about phallic symbols — there's only one thing they could have modeled that after (it was fitting that Willow was the one who "castrated" it). And any sympathy we had for Spike is dashed when they show the alley scene, possibly one of the most disturbing of the season just for that vacant look on Buffy's face.

WILLOW WICCA WATCH: Imbued with a little birthday present from Amy, Willow is able to do magic just by touching things, and spends the episode too scared to do so.

RESTLESS MOMENT: In Xander's dream, he referred to Anya as "my demon" rather than calling her his girlfriend. In this episode, he worries about her demonness and how that could affect their relationship.

6.13 Dead Things

Original air date:	February 5, 2002
Written by:	Steven S. DeKnight
Directed by:	James A. Contner
Guest cast:	Amelinda Embry (Katrina), Marion Calvert (Gina), Rock Reiser (Desk Sergeant), Bernard K. Addison (Cop #1), Eric Prescott (Cop #2)

When one of the Troika's "evil" plans goes awry, they set Buffy up to take a serious fall.

"Dead Things," while keeping some of the characters in limbo, was a great episode that turned the Troika from a trio of funny, nerdy geeks into vile, hateful, misogynist little boys. Warren has always been the darkest of the group, but now we see that his schemes are fueled not only by revenge, but by his need for control (in case having a robot girlfriend didn't tip you off). Katrina (his ex-girlfriend from "I Was Made to Love You") returns and he puts her under a spell, turning her into a love slave for him and his cronies. Warren is incapable of real love, and can only produce spellbound servants like Katrina and April. When everything goes wrong and Katrina is inadvertently killed, the trio need to find a way to kill two birds with one stone. The reluctance of the other two to go along with Warren makes Andrew's later alliance a little surprising, although it makes sense, considering Andrew doesn't mind being someone's whipping boy.

This episode was important for Buffy's new friendship with Tara. Afraid of what her friends might think of her if they thought she was less than human, she recruits Tara to help her discover whether or not she came back wrong. As she said in "Once More, With Feeling," Buffy feels as though she has been expelled from heaven, and for the entire season she beats herself up for it. In "Dead Things," she seems to have realized that she hates herself, and the way she unleashes her fury on Spike was similar to Faith beating up Buffy in "Who Are You?" Buffy has projected her self-hatred onto Spike, which is why she treats him with such contempt. She refuses to reveal her fears to her friends, just as Willow didn't tell anyone about her magic problems, nor Xander his inhibitions about getting married. While everything came out into the open in the musical episode, their true feelings are locked away from their friends immediately afterward, and this will be a season of each character saying, "Why couldn't you tell me this earlier?" while keeping secrets of their own.

Buffy's reaction to Tara's findings comes as a complete surprise, and as Sarah Michelle Gellar turns in her performance of the season, crumpling in front of Tara and practically asking for her scorn, we can't help but feel that even we weren't aware of the fragility of her emotional state.

HIGHLIGHT: Anya dancing at the Bronze: "Come share in the joy of our groove thang!"
NITPICKS: Spike asks Buffy if she trusts him, and she replies, "Never." Yet somehow she leaves Dawn with him to keep her safe? Also, Jonathan and Andrew have never seen Katrina before, yet they've known Warren for a few years — wouldn't they have met her when she was dating Warren? And considering that after he realized April's devotion was artificial, he tired of her quickly, why would he turn around and create another superficial love interest?
MUSIC/BANDS: The Scoobies dance to Red & the Red Hots' "Boo Wah Boo Wah" from *Gettin' Around*. As Buffy stands at Spike's door, we hear "Out of this World" by Bush, from *Golden State*.

6.14 Older and Far Away

Original air date:	February 12, 2002
Written by:	Drew Z. Greenberg
Directed by:	Michael Gershman
Guest cast:	Ryan Browning (Richard), Laura Roth (Sophie), Elizabeth Cazenave (Teacher)

When the gang congregates at the Summers' house to celebrate Dawn's birthday, they realize they're unable to leave.

"Older and Far Away" was a great episode and a lot of fun, but it still had a few annoying moments, the most obvious involving Dawn. Up to this point, we've given Dawn the benefit of the doubt. The poor kid has been through so much, she's granted some leeway by her family and the viewers. We understand her abandonment issues — her father, mother, and sister all left her life, and now that Buffy appears to be back, she's never around the house. But in "Older and Far Away," we know that the "Older" of the title in no way refers to Dawn. She is 15 years old and has tantrums like a six-year-old all the time. Buffy has also seen her father leave and has lost her mother. But when Buffy was Dawn's age, she became the Chosen One, and the fate of her life was written. She quietly endured the pain without letting her parents know what was happening, and allowed her mother to reprimand her for being a "rebellious teen." Dawn would have come stomping into the kitchen moments after being approached by a Watcher and whined that everyone must have stopped loving her for this to have happened.

Michelle Trachtenberg is a superb actress, and was a big *Buffy* fan before joining the show, so it must have been disconcerting for her that the writers were turning her into the least likable character in the series. Throughout the episode, she complains about how no one spends time with her, how Buffy always leaves and never listens to her, and (my personal favorite) how everyone keeps treating her like a little kid. She has every right to be upset about Buffy never being around, but she has to understand that Buffy has been thrown into a mother role and needs to make money so Dawn can eat. It's much harder to steal a loaf of bread than it is a bracelet. And if she'd stop acting like she were three years old, the gang would stop treating her like it. When Hallie shows up and says she could hear Dawn's cries all over town, everyone looks upset and guilty. It's hard for the viewer to feel any sympathy, however, because we know they weren't able to hear the cries over the din of Whiny McWhine's big temper tantrums. The ball of energy has been replaced by a ball of self-centeredness.

The other major nitpick with this otherwise fun episode concerns Willow not doing magic. Xander and Anya are worried about their friend, who's been harpooned by the demon's sword, and they need to get him to a hospital. There's only one person in the house who can get him to safety, but she's in rehab. As Anya and Xander try to guilt her into doing it, Tara steps in and tells them to back off. It would be a proud moment in their relationship if Xander and Anya weren't right. Willow displayed a lot of willpower in "Doublemeat Palace" not to succumb to Amy's "gift," and she could have done it again. We can't help but be confused at the end of the episode when Tara congratulates Willow. You know, for refusing to save someone's life and allowing him to lie on the floor in utter agony. . . .

Despite those beefs, however, "Older and Far Away" was a great episode that allowed Buffy to realize her sister feels unloved, and made us cheer when Tara insulted Spike and stuck up for Willow, and showed that Anya might be having a few second thoughts about the whole marriage thing.

HIGHLIGHT: Tara taunting Spike throughout the episode, especially when he tries to tell her he had a cramp. "In your pants?"

INTERESTING FACTS: Xander says to Dawn that the only thing missing in the scenario is a cornfield, then looks alarmed and adds, "There isn't a cornfield, is there?" He's referring to the classic *Twilight Zone* episode "It's a Good Life," where a young boy has the power to wish his enemies into a cornfield. His family and anyone else who is near him must constantly reassure him that he's a good boy — "Oh, isn't it wonderful that Anthony just banished that bad man to the cornfield!" — because he can read their minds and will send anyone who thinks or says bad things about him away.

DID YOU NOTICE? Dawn's "Get out get out GET OUT!" is exactly the same phrase — and intonation — she used in "Blood Ties." Kudos to Michelle for performing it as a flawless echo of the first. Also, Hallie turns to Spike near the end and says, "William?" It's an inside joke about the actress who plays Hallie, Kali Rocha, who in "Fool for Love," had also played Cecily, the woman who spurned William in 1860. They've never made it clear if Hallie is indeed Cecily (perhaps she married someone rich instead of the "bloody awful poet," got dumped, and set out for some Victorian vengeance?) or if it's just the same actress playing two unrelated roles, as happens often on the show.

NITPICKS: Dawn becomes gloomy when Xander and Willow won't go to the mall with her — did she really want witnesses to her crimes? And what happened to having some friends of her own?

OOPS: When the demon from the teaser reappears inside the Summers house, Buffy refers to it as the demon she had killed earlier, yet in the cemetery when it disappeared into the sword, she assumed it had run away.

6.15 As You Were

Original air date:	February 26, 2002
Written and directed by:	Douglas Petrie
Guest cast:	Marc Blucas (Riley), Ivana Milicevic (Sam), Ryan Raddatz (Todd), Adam Paul (Skanky Vamp), Marilyn Brett (Lady), Alice Dinnean Vernon (Baby Demon Puppeteer)

An old flame of Buffy's shows up in town and reminds her of who she used to be.

"As You Were" was a pretty good episode, considering some fans were dreading the return of Riley. When he first arrives, Buffy is absolutely stunned, and her life flashes before her eyes as she worries he might be thinking bad things about her. Once the initial shock wears off, she assumes he's returned to Sunnydale to take her away from the bleak life she's been living, like a knight in a Kevlar vest. She flirts with him and we see flashes of the old Buffy, joking and looking doe-eyed at him — until his wife shows up.

Sam was an interesting character story-wise, but seemed a little too perfect. She treats Dawn like a grown-up (despite the fact that Dawn stands before Riley with her arms crossed and accuses him of leaving "her"), supports Willow in her rehab, gives Xander wedding tips, and looks up to Buffy as an idol. But her presence makes Buffy step back and reevaluate her life. She and Riley were in similar stages of their lives only a year ago, and while she has stepped backward — sleeping with someone she despises, working at a fast-food joint, and drifting through life as a disinterested observer, rather than a participant — he seems to have moved on, getting married and having a purpose in life. She doesn't notice the pain all over his face and the fact that it seems to hurt him just to look at her. In the end, Riley's return was worth it, because he not only becomes the catalyst that forces her to once and for all move on with her life, but he's rounded out for the fans who viewed him with scorn when he left in "Into the Woods."

The final scene between Buffy and Spike is a sad one. She calls him "William," the name he's always called when a woman rejects him, yet Buffy clearly means him no malice. She's seen that he'll never change, and through Riley's more realistic eyes she's been able to snap out of her self-hatred. Her walk away from him and into the sunlight will be the last time she ever has to deal with him on this subject — or so she thinks.

HIGHLIGHT: Willow happily exchanging e-mail addresses with Sam, and then, for her best friend's sake, muttering to Buffy, "What a bitch."

DID YOU NOTICE? Spike tells Riley that Buffy needs some monster in her man, exactly what he told him in "Into the Woods."

NITPICKS: Buffy closes the Doublemeat Palace and goes home to Dawn, who asks if she can go out to the Bronze with Willow until 11. Assuming it's about 8 or 9 p.m. when they leave, that would mean the Doublemeat Palace closed at 7 or 8 p.m. (since it usually takes about an hour to clean the place after closing). That's ridiculous, since fast-food restaurants typically stay open late for supper. And she lets Dawn stay out until 11 p.m. on a school night? Also, Dawn reminds Buffy to take out the trash — is Dawn's arm broken or something? Finally, that helicopter scene was laughable. Like no one in downtown Sunnydale would have noticed a large black helicopter; why didn't they go out to the helipad in the Sunnydale woods like they did in "Into the Woods"?

6.16 Hell's Bells

Original air date:	March 5, 2002
Written by:	Rebecca Rand Kirshner
Directed by:	David Solomon
Guest cast:	Casey Sander (Tony Harris), Andy Umberger (D'Hoffryn), Lee Garlington (Jessica Harris), Jan Hoag (Cousin Carol), George D. Wallace (Older Xander Harris), Steven Gilborn (Uncle Rory), Daniel McFeeley (Warty Demon), Rebecca Jackson (Tarantula), Mel Fair (Tentacle Demon), Nick Kokich (Demon Teen), Robert Noble (Night Manager), Julian Franco (Young Bartender), Susannah L. Brown (Caterer Girl), Joey Hiott (Josh, Age 10), Abigail Mavity (Sara, Age 8), Chris Emerson (Josh, Age 21), Ashleigh Ann Wood (Sara, Age 18), Megan Vint (Karen)

On the day of Anya and Xander's wedding, Xander gets a visit from a future version of himself who begs him not to go through with it.

If the ongoing pandemonium of Anya and Xander's marriage plans were any indication, this wedding was destined to be bumpy. In "Doublemeat Palace," Halfrek had placed doubt in Anya's mind about her relationship with Xander, and for the first time Anya realized that Xander didn't show respect for her in public, often correcting her in front of others. In "Older and Far Away," she had responded with more panic than anyone in the house when they were suddenly trapped, as if she were comparing their situation to what the rest of her life would be like. Xander had always had his doubts, but his love for Anya kept him confident that the wedding would be fine (although he did consume large quantities of snack foods in the process). But it will be Xander who can't take the big step.

The wedding day is perfectly depicted in all its horrifying potential. Almost everyone has a great wedding story of either the bride falling apart, the groom fainting, some relative getting really drunk and throwing up, or — if you're a lucky guest — all of the above. Xander's parents are truly awful, with his father getting increasingly drunk and humiliating his wife, and his mother spreading the guilt on thick and causing him even more worry than he needs. Anya's friends are all demons of one sort or another, but as the day goes on we discover it's Xander's family who are the monsters. We've heard so many stories about his family and background — usually shrouded in one of Xander's jokes — but now we see the devastating consequences they have on his emotional state. His friends — who are the opposite of his family, offering him love and support — are no match for what his family does to him in this episode.

Emma Caulfield is wonderful as the beautiful, brokenhearted bride who must make the long walk up the aisle . . . alone. "Hell's Bells" was the first of seven fantastic episodes that will drive the rest of the season.

The blushing bride, Emma Caulfield

CHRISTINA RADISH

HIGHLIGHT: The bridesmaids' dresses.
NITPICKS: Who invited Spike?
OOPS: When Buffy rips her dress to fight the demon, she rips only the fringe at the bottom, but in the next shot, it's been ripped halfway up her thigh.
RESTLESS MOMENT: In Xander's dream, his father had pulled his heart out of his chest, and in this episode Xander can't follow his heart because of his fear of becoming like his father.

6.17 Normal Again

Original air date: March 12, 2002
Written by: Diego Gutierrez

|Directed by:|Rick Rosenthal|
|Guest cast:|Dean Butler (Hank Summers), Kristine Sutherland (Joyce Summers), Michael Warren (Doctor), Kirsten Nelson (Lorraine Ross)|

After being stabbed by one of the Troika's demons, Buffy begins to believe she's a mental patient in a hospital and Sunnydale is a delusion.

"Normal Again" is a marvelous slice of postmodernism, where we are forced to step back and question the characters we've come to know and love. What if none of this was real? What if Buffy is completely delusional and has created this wild and wonderful fantasy in her head, and we viewers have just been suspending our disbelief for six years for no reason?

In this episode, we step out of the traditional role as willing viewers and look at *Buffy* as a fictional program. Buffy becomes the writer, the doctors become the critics telling her that season six isn't as tight as earlier seasons, and the characters become flights of fancy, acting out Buffy's will as their creator. The writers of the show cleverly fight back against the criticisms of this season, happily acknowledging that the Troika aren't exactly the stuff *Buffy* villains are made of and the intricate framework of the show isn't as solid as it's been before. We also discover something about Buffy's past that we didn't know previously, which is rare in the later seasons. It was great to see Kristine Sutherland again, although it forces the viewer to wonder, if Sunnydale is the made-up world, why would Buffy have killed her own mother in her fantasy?

In the Sunnydale reality, her friends rally around her to help, catching the demon and creating an antidote. Even Dawn begins to help, although when she realizes she's not in the other world and makes her ridiculously selfish comment, "It's your ideal reality and I'm not even part of it," we wish she'd just shut up and go away. Yes, Dawn, being pumped full of drugs while being a zoned-out psychotic is Buffy's ideal reality. Isn't it everyone's?

The alternate-reality storyline is appropriate for this season simply because Buffy has been looking for ways of escaping her present existence. Once again she'll be faced with the option to drop out of this life and stop living, and what she does to her friends in the process is shocking. This season everyone will hurt the ones they love, and season seven will definitely be one of forgiveness and moving on. And at the end of "Normal Again," we can't help but wonder which reality was the real one.

HIGHLIGHT: Spike and Xander bickering as they search for the demon.
NITPICKS: We know the psychiatric hospital is fake because no real doctor would tell a delusional schizophrenic patient to "will" herself back into reality. Buffy tells Willow she freaked out when she saw her first vampire and told her parents, who promptly committed her to a "clinic." This is inconsistent with "Becoming," where we see her fight her first vampire, return home, and silently cry in the bathroom, away from her arguing parents. Also, she tells Dawn she hasn't been doing her chores lately. When have we ever seen Dawn doing chores?
OOPS: In previous episodes where we've seen Buffy's basement — "Bewitched, Bothered and Bewildered," "What's My Line? (Part Two)," "Flooded" — the space underneath the stairs has been encased in cement. But in this episode it's an open space that Buffy is able to hide under.

6.18 Entropy

Original air date: April 30, 2002
Written by: Drew Z. Greeenberg
Directed by: James A. Contner
Guest cast: Edie Caggiano (Mother)

Anya returns to Sunnydale and tries to exact vengeance on Xander.

Entropy is a complex scientific term that, in its most basic sense, explains the universe's propensity toward chaos. The idea is that, left alone, all things naturally move away from being organized and toward disorder. It's the perfect title for this episode.

When Anya returns and we realize she's again a vengeance demon, we fear this could be a dark and depressing episode. However, Emma Caulfield always plays Anya in a delightful way, even when she's angry, and the ensuing scenes of her approaching Buffy, Willow, Tara, and Dawn to help her get revenge on Xander are hilarious. She reminds Buffy of all the men who have left her, tells Tara and Willow that as lesbians they're supposed to hate men, and, knowing what had happened in "Older and Far Away," thinks Dawn might be an easy target. But Xander's friends are loyal to him, and Anya storms off in frustration.

As the title suggests, when left alone things will go to hell. Dawn's stealing has gotten so out of hand that she can't go into any stores, Buffy tells Spike to move on and walks away, Anya sits alone in the Magic Box, and the little spy cameras that the Troika had hidden in "Life Serial" now become a central part of the story. As Willow hurries to bring the Magic Box camera into focus while certain events are unfolding there, the suspense builds to a chilling climax. The scene at the end involving Xander, Buffy, Spike, and Anya is a painful one, and we again feel sympathy for Spike despite everything he's done. And poor Xander, discovering the truth about Buffy and Spike, is left with the same outrage and disgust Willow had felt in season two when she discovered Xander and Cordelia were together. The only aspect of their lives that seems to be moving toward order is the incredible relationship between Willow and Tara.

But there's one other thing that Buffy and the gang have forgotten about — the Troika.

HIGHLIGHT: Anya trying to convince Willow and Tara that Xander is a bad person because he's a typical man who loves girl-on-girl action.

NITPICKS: Just as she was always so quick to blame Angel, Buffy looks at Spike and says, "Didn't take long, did it?" even after she'd told him repeatedly to move on. After the childish way she treated Angel, and the self-centered way she acted around Riley, which eventually drove him away, when will she wake up and realize the common denominator in her ill-fated relationships is her? Also, that street she and Dawn walk down looks more like a shopping district in L.A., not Sunnydale. The main street in Sunnydale is one narrow lane with a coffee shop, not four lanes of traffic with huge fashion outlets on either side.

RESTLESS MOMENT: Anya tells Xander in the ice cream truck that she's thinking of becoming a vengeance demon again because she thinks "this is going to be a very big year for vengeance." She was off by one year.

MUSIC/BANDS: Xander drinks and thinks of Anya to the tune of Tom McRae's "Sao Paolo Rain," from his self-titled album. When Xander and Buffy walk away from Spike and Anya, we hear Alison Krauss's "That Kind of Love," from *Forget About It*.

6.19 Seeing Red

Original air date:	May 7, 2002
Written by:	Steven S. DeKnight
Directed by:	Michael Gershman
Guest cast:	Amy Hathaway (Dark-Haired Woman in Bar), Nichole Hiltz (Blond in Bar), Garrett Brawith (Frank), Tim Hager (Administrator), Stefan Marks (Guard #1), Christopher James (Guard #2), Kate Orsini (Girl at Bronze)

Spike, Anya, Buffy, and Xander try to put their lives back together, while Buffy attempts to stop the Troika once and for all.

"Seeing Red" was the first of what could be deemed a four-part season finale. Everything that happens between this episode and the end of "Grave" takes place over two days. After love interests including vampires, werewolves, computer demons, praying mantises, vengeance demons, mummy girls, and just plain jerks, we finally find two people who were meant to be together, and who might actually have a happy relationship on the hellmouth. Uh-oh.

While the ending of this episode was a downright shocker, the topic of discussion that popped up on the Internet for weeks afterward was the scene in the bathroom between Buffy and Spike. What really happens there? From Buffy's point of view, if she hadn't stopped him, Spike was going to try to rape her. From Spike's point of view, he didn't see it as rape, but as him proving his love to her. Most rapes occur between two individuals who know one another, often with the aggressor believing they are in love and the victim disagreeing. How could Spike have mistaken her screams and pleas for anything other than what they were? Well, look at their past "lovemaking" sessions: they almost all begin with Buffy insulting him in some way, then he tells her she's less than human and likes the darkness, punches are thrown, and Buffy finds herself having sex with him. Their relationship is filled with abuse — both verbal and physical — and as far as Spike was concerned, this scene was no different. It's Gellar's incredible acting that lets the viewer know he's wrong. She doesn't just look afraid, she looks desperate and weak against him, like a normal woman might in this situation. As soon as they break apart, however, the reality of the situation hits him.

His later discussion with Clem shows the inherent problem with Spike — no matter how gentle he acts, he'll always be part vampire. No matter how bad he pretends to be, he'll always be part human. It's the humanity of William that resides inside of Spike that causes the problem, creating an ambivalence in him that loves Buffy deeply while despising her for making him feel that way. He says to Clem, "What have I done?" immediately followed by "Why didn't I do it?" The two sides will be warring within him forever, unless he can do something to stop it.

Meanwhile, scenes between Xander and Buffy are the most touching of the episode. He is disappointed in Buffy for being with Spike and not telling him, and doesn't understand why her relationships and personal problems — which she used to share with her friends — are now off-limits. Xander has an interesting point — as someone who never hides his true feelings and always says what's on his mind, he wonders why part of growing up has to be shutting up.

And finally, there's Warren. Warren is despicable in this episode, making most viewers

CHRISTINA RADISH

Rest in peace, dear Tara . . .

hope that something terrible would happen to him (ah, the glory of wish fulfillment). In a reenactment of the Charles Atlas "98-pound weakling" advertisement (these guys even act out the ads of their comic books), he fights back against a guy who had bullied him in high school before coming after Buffy. In a truly Freudian moment, Buffy smashes his magic balls and he's left a weak, simpering little boy — but one who's really pissed off. His surprising return after his escape shows he's momentarily given up on the little toys and has a big-boy weapon. The ending of this episode was heartrending, as we had to say good-bye to yet another beloved character. Right up to her final words, "Your shirt," Tara was always thinking of Willow.

HIGHLIGHT: Andrew's sidesplitting "exit" with his jetpack. Possibly the funniest moment of the season.

DID YOU NOTICE? Amber Benson finally appears as a regular in the credits. The producers are sick, sick people. . . .

NITPICKS: Why would the Troika leave their action figures behind in a place that was about to be destroyed? Also, one of the biggest disappointments of this season is the failure of the writers to make Xander the Troika's foil. When the Troika were first being established as this season's "medium-sized bad," it seemed logical that Xander would be the one to figure out who they are, since he's as much of a sci-fi geek as any of them. His eyes glazed over when Willow mentioned the photos of female Vulcans in their lair. In "Smashed," while the rest of the gang are searching through demon encyclopedias, he's reading a D&D manual — and probably was the closest to figuring out who was behind the robbery. And in this episode, while everyone is cross-referencing the strange language they've discovered in the Troika's lair, Xander immediately recognizes it as Klingon (clearly poems written by Andrew to Warren). Why wasn't he more involved with finding them, and why did the writers deny us one great scene with him coming face-to-face with these guys who are so much like him?

OOPS: When the trio show up to the amusement park it's nighttime, but when Warren flips the truck it's still sunset. By the time Buffy shows up, it's night again.

WILLOW WICCA WATCH: In the final seconds of the episode, Willow's eyes turn black, signaling the dark magic is about to happen.

MUSIC/BANDS: Throughout this episode we hear "The Leaves" by Daryl Ann (not available on CD), "Stranded" by Alien Ant Farm, from *ANThology*, and Azure Ray's "Displaced," from their self-titled CD.

6.20 Villains

Original air date:	May 14, 2002
Written by:	Marti Noxon
Directed by:	David Solomon
Guest cast:	Jeff Kober (Rack), Amelinda Embry (Katrina), Steven W. Bailey (Cave Demon), Tim Hodgin (Coroner), Michael Matthys (Paramedic), Julie Hermelin (Clerk), Alan Henry Brown (Demon Bartender), Mueen J. Ahmad (Doctor), Jane Cho (Nurse #1), Meredith Cross (Nurse #2), David Adefeso (Paramedic #2), Jeffrey Nicholas Brown (Vampire), Nelson Frederick (Villager)

Willow turns to dark magicks to help her hunt down Warren.

Could any of us have foreseen that one day our Willow could be capable of the things she does in "Villains"? Alyson Hannigan has given us some phenomenal acting, but over the next three episodes she'll display heights — and depths — we couldn't have thought possible. She is easily one of the best actresses in Hollywood today. In this episode, the metaphor of Willow as an addict actually works. It doesn't matter that she's been "sober" for several weeks now; what matters is how easily she falls off the wagon when thrown into despair. Tara — her light — has been taken from her, and throughout this episode writers will rely on the symbolism of that idea. In Wicca, it is believed that each person is a light in the temple of the Goddess. As Willow enters the Magic Box in the episode's eeriest scene, the lights blow out behind her as she passes by. Tara's light was snuffed out by a gunshot wound; Willow's will dim through her fury. As the words of the dark-arts books move through her hands and into her head through amazing special effects, she becomes the dark arts; the words are imprinted upon her body. Her eyes and hair turn black, and we know that unlike before, Willow won't return from this unscathed.

Meanwhile, Xander finds out Anya has become a vengeance demon again, and while she agrees to help Xander and Buffy find Willow, she declares that she will help Willow on her path of vengeance. Spike has also turned to his evil side, as he enters a cave and declares he wants to "return to his former self." The hatred in his voice suggests that he wants the chip out and wants to be returned to the evil vampire of season two, but he must undergo some trials first. While Willow, Spike, and Anya embrace darkness, Xander, Buffy, and Dawn are left to cope with what's happening.

Finally, Warren discovers that he's just small potatoes in Sunnydale. When he enters the demon bar, he's surrounded by monsters that could crush him in an instant, but he displays such egotism that they're surprised into silence (when they're not doubled over laughing at him). Despite the Troika's tricks all season, no one has heard of them or their antics. When faced with Willow, Warren desperately pulls out all of his toys, big and small, but they're nothing compared to her power. Sunnydale has a dark underground (literally) that is unparalleled in its malevolence, and Warren, Jonathan, and Andrew were far too naive to realize they were mere children in a devil's playground. Warren is vile, but as Willow gets closer and closer to him, we worry about what she might do. We don't want to see Warren die at the hands of Willow — if she kills a human being, she'll never be the same. Unfortunately, the people who might have been able to stop her arrive just in time to see the most graphically violent moment yet. Her final words to Warren, "Bored now," are spoken with no inflection or emotion. She has embraced the dark side that she first glimpsed in season three, and has become the emotionless Vamp Willow of "Doppelgängland." A devastating and brilliant episode.

HIGHLIGHT: Jonathan freaking out in jail that he'll be assaulted by another inmate: "I hear they like the small ones with little hands like their girlfriends'."

DID YOU NOTICE? The cave drawings Spike examines when he first arrives at the cave closely resemble what Willow will later do to Warren. There's even a picture of a man with his mouth sewn shut.

NITPICKS: When Willow comes out of the house, her shirt is covered in blood and she walks right past Xander, and although he's panicking about Buffy being shot, it's strange he didn't ask Willow about the blood on her shirt. Also, after she goes to the Magic Box and sucks up all the magic, she's still wearing the same clothes, which means she must have gone home to change. Why would she take the time to change her clothes when she had to get to the hospital? (We know they're her clothes because it's the same outfit she wore in "Dead Things" when she runs into Tara outside the Magic Box.) And a strange woman dressed in black enters the O.R. and orders the doctors and nurses to leave . . . and they do? I don't think so.

WILLOW WICCA WATCH: Willow does everything from using force fields against her friends to destroying dark demons with her fury, to stepping away unscathed after having an ax lodged in her back. And everything in between.

6.21 Two to Go (Part One)

Original air date:	May 21, 2002
Written by:	Douglas Petrie
Directed by:	Bill Norton
Guest cast:	Jeff Kober (Rack), Jeff McCredie (Police Officer), Michael Younger (Truck Driver)

Now that Warren's out of the way, Willow sets her sights on Jonathan and Andrew, as the rest of the gang try to figure out how to stop her.

This episode was full of great moments — Rack's place turning into the Magic Box; Willow belittling her former, "mousey" self; Clem trying to keep Dawn occupied; and a movement forward for everyone. Xander, who spends the episode beating himself up over the fact that he couldn't save Tara's life, understands how Anya feels for the first time. Buffy tries to hold Willow at bay without hurting her and manages to keep her loved ones safe. Willow gets rid of her old persona and declares, "Six years as a sideman, and now I get to be the Slayer." And Dawn finally wakes up to the fact that she's been acting like a child all year when Willow tells her how sick she is of her whining, "Mom, Buffy, Tara, waah." "Darth Rosenberg" has lost all reason, and as her face turns white with big ugly veins all over it, she has just one goal: kill Jonathan and Andrew, and anyone who gets in her way. What began as vengeance turns into all-out destruction.

If everyone survives, will they be able to forgive Willow? If they could forgive Angel for the deeds of Angelus, they can forgive Willow for the actions of the thing she's become. The creature that is walking and talking like Willow isn't her any longer. As soon as she took in Rack's power, she lost all of her Willowness and she is unreachable by anyone. All that is left is pure rage and madness. We're torn as we watch Buffy and Willow pummeling each other, with Willow spitting out venomous threats and insults at Buffy. Willow needs someone who can break through her magic. What she needs . . . is a Watcher.

HIGHLIGHT: The six greatest words of the season: "I'd like to test that theory."
INTERESTING FACTS: In the "Previously on *Buffy*" segment before this episode, when Willow kills Warren, it's shown from a slightly different angle. The editors used an alternate take for this montage.
NITPICKS: What happened to our dear Clem? One minute he was standing in the waiting room of Rack's place, and then he just disappeared. Perhaps he's back at the crypt finishing his snack-food taste test.

OOPS: As Willow pulls the jailhouse bricks out, the ones we see being pulled from the inside don't correspond with the same ones from the outside.

RESTLESS MOMENT: In "Restless," we discover that Willow's deepest fear is that her innate high school nerdiness is always right below the surface (as she reiterated in "Wrecked"), and in "Two to Go," not only does Jonathan still think of her as high school Willow who "wore floods," but we discover that perhaps her quest for the dark magic stems from that fear. In becoming evil, she effectively kills all remnants of the former Willow, ensuring that people will never think of her that way again.

WILLOW WICCA WATCH: Willow has gone off the deep end and commits too many magicks to name.

6.22 Grave (Part Two)

Original air date:	May 21, 2002
Written by:	David Fury
Directed by:	James A. Contner
Guest cast:	Anthony Stewart Head (Giles), Steven W. Bailey (Cave Demon), Brett Wagner (Trucker)

With Buffy and Giles incapacitated, someone must stop Willow before she raises a force that will destroy the world.

At the beginning of the season finale, it was a surprise not to see the words "Written and directed by Joss Whedon" appear on the screen. But just like in "Primeval," where the gang joins forces to create a super Slayer, the triumvirate of Marti Noxon, Douglas Petrie, and David Fury have combined to create a heart-stopping trilogy detailing Willow's downfall. Joss might not be as involved as he once was, but viewers can rest assured the show is in good hands.

Giles is back — the adult influence that has been missing from the season returns, and everyone is able to make the giant leap they've been trying for all year. As Buffy fills Giles in on the trials and tribulations of the Scoobies he begins laughing. As he's almost falling over with tears running down his face, he allows Buffy to step back from everything that has been happening and realize that maybe it wasn't as bad as she thought it was. Giles is a fantastic character, and it is a welcome relief to have him back.

Giles's love for Willow is partly what saves her in the end. He is able to restore one spark of Willow's humanity, which will ultimately stop her from destroying everything. The unlikeliest hero is also the one most suited to the role — Xander. In "Hell's Bells," Willow says to him, "Do you know how much I love you?" and Xander responds, "Not half as much as I love you." In "Grave," we see that his love for Willow is what will save her, and his continued vows of love as she physically tears him apart provide one of the most wonderful images of the series. He knows Willow better than anyone, and only he can break through to the sweet Willow of old.

So who was the "big bad" of season six? Was it Willow or the Troika? It's a difficult call, since generally the villain of the season dogs the gang throughout instead of becoming dangerous only in the last few episodes. I believe it's neither. The biggest enemy each person faced this season was themselves. Dawn hurt herself by stealing and refusing to grow up. Buffy kept going back to Spike and making all the wrong decisions. Xander's first solid decision of the year only caused pain for everyone around him. Anya got so caught up in her anger, she became a vengeance demon. And Willow didn't have the willpower to stop the one thing that put her life — and those of her friends — in serious jeopardy. *Buffy the Vampire Slayer* has always had a serious psychological angle to it: in "Nightmares," "Fear, Itself," and "Restless," we were privy to some of the gang's deepest fears. In season six, those fears were stretched out over the season, becoming the primary villain and threatening to engulf them all.

As the show draws to a close, we know the series is entering a new phase. Buffy climbs out of a grave for the second time this season, but this time she's in daylight, she's with her sister, and she's filled with love and hope. It's a drastic contrast to the hellish scene in "Bargaining." Dawn has proven to Buffy that she's an adept fighter and takes after her sister. Willow will have a lot to atone for, but she remains a question mark — how can she avoid prison after what she's done? The writers have a major mess to sort out in season seven.

And finally, what can I say about Spike? He went into the cave with the intention of becoming an evil vampire who can hurt people, and instead was tricked by the cave demon, who imbued him with a soul (or did he go to the cave intending to restore his soul?). Many fans were outraged, thinking that they've just turned him into Angel again. However, consider the words "Make me what I was before." He wasn't a vampire with a soul before; he was human. Unless the writers have made a serious logistical mistake, in season seven he should be fully human, which will be very different than Angel's atonement. Angel must redeem himself while still having a craving for blood and a propensity toward violence. Spike, on the other hand, will be human, and the weight of what he's done in his past — considering how gentle William was — could be crushing. (If the writers do make him a vampire with a soul, it will be a major disappointment.)

"Grave" was one of the best finales yet — if not *the* best — and should silence any critics who said season six was weak. Season seven might be the last season of *Buffy*, but this show will go out with a bang.

HIGHLIGHT: Anya's sweet speech to a dying Giles.

DID YOU NOTICE? When Willow tells the fireball, "Fly, my pretty, fly," she's echoing the Wicked Witch of the West in *The Wizard of Oz*.

NITPICKS: Buffy tells Giles that if her time comes, someone else will take her place, but she's wrong. Faith is the active Slayer, and a Chosen One is called only when Faith dies, not Buffy. As long as Faith is locked up in jail, there can be no new Slayer. And could Dawn have chosen a more inconvenient time to argue with Buffy about not telling her things? Or taunt Xander about how Spike would have gone back to help?

OOPS: Willow wipes the blood from her nose at the beginning of the episode, but it's there again in the next shot.

MUSIC/BANDS: At the end of the episode, we hear Sarah McLachlan's "Prayer of St. Francis" from the special two-disc version of *Surfacing*.

"Grr . . . argh"

Angel Episode Guide

The following *Angel* episode guide will feature reviews that are shorter than the *Buffy* ones — while *Angel* is an integral part of the Buffyverse, this book focuses primarily on *Buffy the Vampire Slayer*. Like the *Buffy* episode guide, this one will include some spoilers for the episodes, so you should avoid the entries for the episodes you haven't seen.

STARRING: David Boreanaz as Angel

Charisma Carpenter as Cordelia Chase

Glenn Quinn as Francis Doyle

Alexis Denisof as Wesley Wyndam-Pryce

J. August Richards as Charles Gunn (Season Two)

Amy Acker as Winifred "Fred" Burkle (Season Three)

Season One

OCTOBER 1999 • MAY 2000

Recurring characters in season one: Elizabeth Rohm (Kate Lockley), Christian Kane (Lindsey McDonald), Stephanie Romanov (Lilah Morgan)

1.1 City Of

Original air date:	October 5, 1999
Written by:	Joss Whedon, David Greenwalt
Directed by:	Joss Whedon
Guest cast:	Tracy Middendorf (Tina), Vyto Ruginis (Russell Winters), Jon Ingrassia (Stacy), Renee Ridgeley (Margo), Josh Holloway (Good-looking Boy), Michael Mantell (Oliver), Sam Pancake (Manager), Gina McClain (Janice)

Angel moves to L.A., where he meets up with Doyle and Cordelia.

Within the first five minutes of this episode, the audience already knows this is a much darker and different program than *Buffy*. Gone are the high school teachers and romances. Los Angeles is the real, gritty world, where people go to either find a way to stand out from the rest and become famous, or blend into the walls to be forgotten. The voice-over at the beginning is reminiscent of old detective movies, immediately suggesting that this series will have noir elements. It's strange to see Angel as his own person, not as one of the Scoobies helping out or standing silent and brooding while Buffy gets upset. This is *his* show, and we'll have to get used to it. It will take place mostly at night (for obvious reasons), focusing on the seamy underbelly of L.A.

Glenn Quinn was an excellent choice for Doyle. Previously seen on *Roseanne* as Becky's dopey husband Mark (and hiding his Irish accent), Quinn is someone we recognize, but isn't so linked to that character that he's typecast. He is charming but silly, a personality that audiences immediately latched onto. After the void she left behind in "The Freshman," it was a relief to see Charisma on this show (though Angel wasn't particularly relieved). Cordelia is still her endearing, thoughtless, crass self, and we love her for it. Angel retains his cool attitude, but there's an element of humor in this episode — for example, when he jumps into the wrong mysterious black convertible — and Greenwalt will take Angel's character in some interesting directions in this series.

As a nod to its parent show, there's a subtle but thrilling crossover with *Buffy*: in "The Freshman," Joyce's phone rings and Buffy picks it up, but no one answers. In this episode we see Angel make the call, and hang up once he hears Buffy's voice. In the beginning, *Angel* will have to rely on the mythology and background established on *Buffy* to create a foundation for the show, and it'll take until season two before it's able to stand on its own.

One weakness is the constant repetition of Angel's back story. Doyle confronts Angel and tells the long, sad story of the vampire with a soul, and what happened when he was Angelus. It's something that will be repeated over and over again, as if to fill in the non-*Buffy* viewers on what had come before *Angel*. The problem is, the vast majority of viewers are *Buffy* fans and are all too aware of Angel's history. Not only that, but it didn't make much sense dramatically to have Angel sit and listen to his own story as if he'd never heard it before.

"City Of" was an excellent pilot (with an amazing opening theme song), and the series will pick up where *BtVS*'s "Anne" left off. Russell is a great villain who represents all that Hollywood is about: come to Hollywood, and you'll be destroyed. We're also introduced to Wolfram & Hart, which will be a major force in episodes to come. Angel is the brooding vampire with a past he has to atone for, Doyle is the "sensitive" half-demon, and Cordy is, well, Cordy. Together, they form a very promising team.

1.2 Lonely Hearts

Original air date:	October 12, 1999
Written by:	David Fury
Directed by:	James A. Contner
Guest cast:	Lillian Birdsell (Sharon Richler), Obi Nfedo (Bartender), Derek Hughes (Neil), Johnny Messner (Kevin), Ken Rush (Guy), Tracey Stone (Pretty girl), Jennifer Tung (Neil's Pick-up Girl)

Angel has to find a demon that is preying on lonely people at bars and eviscerating them.

Angel discovers that it's difficult to find a lonely person in L.A. when *everyone* is lonely. It's apparent from the beginning of *Angel* that the show will parallel several of the circumstances, situations, and metaphors on *Buffy* each week. In the first episodes of the season, both Buffy and Angel are trying to acclimatize themselves to their new situations. And in this episode, just as Buffy's soul is sucked from her by a college roommate, a demon in the adult world of the L.A. bar scene is sucking the very life from its victims. We're introduced to Kate, the angry, bitter police officer who trusts no one, and once again Angel reveals his cool Bat-toys (although they don't work as well as Batman's did, and they don't remain a staple of Angel's weaponry). Doyle's visions are more like vague images, unlike the later, specific ones that Cordy will have. David Boreanaz begins to reveal the comic deadpan he is so good at, establishing a slight shift in Angel's character that becomes almost giddiness by the end of season two. "Lonely Hearts" was a strong episode, but it's clear *Angel* will be trying to find its way for a while.

1.3 In the Dark

Original air date:	October 19, 1999
Written by:	Douglas Petrie
Directed by:	Bruce Seth Green
Guest cast:	Seth Green (Oz), James Marsters (Spike), Malia Mathis (Rachel), Kevin West (Marcus), Buck McDancer (Dealer), Ric Sarabia (Sunglass Vendor), Tom Rosales (Manny the Pig), Jenni Blong (Young Woman)

When Oz takes the Ring of Amarra to Angel in L.A., Spike follows to try to get it back.

This was an excellent episode, and the first crossover of characters from *Buffy* to *Angel*. It was also a great example of the painful decisions Angel will have to make now that he's fighting evil full-time. L.A. appears bright and full of promise during the daytime, but at night the evil

CHRIS PIZZELLO/AP/CP PHOTO

David Boreanaz and Glenn Quinn share a laugh after taping a scene during the beginning of season one

comes out. Prostitutes, drug dealers, rapists, and — oh, yes — demons. Spike is the perfect foe for Angel (and at first fans wondered if he might become a regular on the show), and the opening scene of him mocking Angel is brilliant. (For this scene the writers have borrowed the premise of comedian Lenny Bruce's stand-up routine, "Thank You, Masked Man," where he wonders why the Lone Ranger never stuck around for thank-yous.) Unfortunately, Spike explains Angel's curse *again* and Spike's background is also explained (one reason some *Buffy* fans stopped watching was the constant repetition of things we already knew). Oz moves easily from the Scooby gang to the grittier, adult heroes — and his van is one versatile fighting machine. The torture sequence is gritty, but shows how Angel will have to endure intense physical pain as well as emotional pain. But, two questions arise: if vampires don't have to breathe, how does Spike almost strangle him to death? And why does he insist on calling Angel his sire, when Drusilla is the one who made him? Yes, Joss Whedon has said in interviews that a "sire" is the one who teaches you, not necessarily the one who made you, but he was probably covering up this huge inconsistency (in "What's My Line? Part Two," Giles defines a sire as the one who makes another vampire).

1.4 I Fall to Pieces

Original air date:	October 26, 1999
Written by:	Joss Whedon, David Greenwalt
Directed by:	Vern Gillum
Guest cast:	Jan Bartlett (Penny), Andy Umberger (Dr. Ronald Meltzer), Tushka Bergen (Melissa Burns), Carlos Carrasco (Dr. Vinpur Narpudun), Christopher Hart (the hands), Garikayi Mutambirwa (Intern), Brent Sexton (Dead Cop)

Angel must stop a neurosurgeon who is stalking a woman, but things get complicated when he realizes the guy has learned to detach parts of his body.

Big Brother is depicted in a most disgusting way in this realization of every woman's fear. This was an especially creepy episode (the detached hands running around like Thing still give me the willies), but one that began to establish a routine for the show. The doctor's lawyers are none other than Wolfram & Hart (now the viewers know they weren't just limited to the first episode) and Kate becomes involved in the case. Like the high school/hellmouth metaphor in *Buffy*, in *Angel* the demons and nightmares are all based in fact, on very real fears of adults living in the city. One nitpick: Cordelia says she recognizes the yogi from the doctor's book because she'd seen him on public television. When would she have watched public television?

1.5 Rm W/ a Vu

Original air date:	November 2, 1999
Written by:	David Greenwalt, Jane Espenson
Directed by:	Scott McGinnis
Guest cast:	Greg Collins (Keith), Beth Grant (Maude Pearson), Denney Pierce (Vic), BJ Porter (Dennis), Marcus Redmond (Griff), Michael Yavnielli (Lenny)

Cordy's new apartment is haunted by a ghost that seems intent on killing her, but Cordy refuses to seek help because the rent is so cheap.

After "Beer Bad," the *Buffy* episode that aired before "Rm W/ a Vu," any *Angel* episode would have been a relief, but this installment was so much fun, and it introduced a new character — Dennis. The episode was so good because it took us back to Sunnydale High, not only with the reference to "Graduation Day" — "It was a rough ceremony" — but because we discover that Cordy has serious guilt over the way she acted in high school. Despite all the horrible things she said and did to the people around her, we can't help but feel sorry for her as she cowers in her apartment, paralyzed by guilt. It's only when she embraces the bitch within that she's able to escape. This was an excellent look at how what you did in the past can haunt you in the present, and we realize Angel isn't the only one with personal demons.

1.6 Sense and Sensitivity

Original air date: November 9, 1999
Written by: Tim Minear
Directed by: James A. Contner
Guest cast: John Mahon (Trevor Lockley), John Capodice (Little Tony Papazian), Ron Marasco (Allen Lloyd), Alex Skuby (Harlan), Kevin Will (Heath), Thomas Burr (Lee Mercer), Ken Abraham (Spivey), Jimmy Shubert (Johnny Red), Ken Grantham (Lieutenant), Adam Donshik (Uniform Cop #1), Kevin E. West (Uniform Cop #2), Wilson Bell (Uniform Cop #3), Colin Patrick Lynch (Beat Cop), Steve Schirripa (Henchman), Christopher Paul Hart (Traffic Cop)

The police officers in Kate's precinct become simpering, overly sensitive basket cases after a sensitivity training course.

"Sense and Sensitivity" was an unfocused episode because the actors seemed to mistake drunkenness for sensitivity. You can be sensitive without slurring your words and acting totally out of character. We discover that the reason Kate acts like such a hardass all the time is that she's trying to prove to her father that she can be like him, and to her fellow officers that she's not a crying woman. When Angel accidentally touches the cursed "talking stick," the result is hilarious. We see a new side of Angel that leaves him with the lingering feeling that he is capable of being sensitive and should probably try to show it more often. I never thought I'd see the day when Angel would say, "You could be a rainbow, and not a painbow."

1.7 The Bachelor Party

Original air date: November 16, 1999
Written by: Tracy Stern

Directed by: David Straiton
Guest cast: Kristin Dattilo (Harry), Carlos Jacott (Richard Howard Straley), Brad Blaisdell (Uncle John), Robert Hillis (Pierce), Lauri Johnson (Aunt Martha), Ted Kairys (Ben), Kristen Lowman (Mother Rachel), David Polcyn (Russ), Chris Tallman (Rick), William Wayne (Richard's Brother)

Doyle's ex-wife shows up with a new fiancé who wants Doyle to come to his bachelor party, but Doyle doesn't realize what's in store for him.

Doyle becomes more than two-dimensional comic relief in this episode, where we finally find out something about his past, who he is, and how he feels. This episode was funny, although it begged an obvious question: if Harry was a demonologist, wouldn't she have known about her fiancé's ritualistic party game? You'd think she would know more about Anomovic demons than any other kind. Cordelia takes another step toward maturity when she announces she's no longer out to snag someone rich, but wants someone who's brave and interesting. And the big two-hour crossover is set up when Doyle finds a photo of Buffy that puts Angel in a broody funk, and then has a vision that Buffy is in trouble, sending Angel back to Sunnydale.

1.8 I Will Remember You

Original air date: November 23, 1999
Written by: David Greenwalt, Jeannine Renshaw
Directed by: David Grossman
Guest cast: Sarah Michelle Gellar (Buffy), Carry Cannon (Female Oracle), Randall Slavin (Male Oracle)

When Angel touches the blood of a demon and becomes human again, he and Buffy finally have a shot at a normal relationship.

"I Will Remember You" was a heartrending episode, giving fans of the Buffy/Angel relationship (B/A shippers, as they're called online) exactly what they've been waiting for. In one hour, we see a day in the life of "normal" Buffy and human Angel, complete with everything they were previously unable to do. The problem is, we also see what's wrong with that relationship. Angel is rendered as powerless as Buffy was in "Helpless," and Buffy now has to fight to save his life as well as the lives of everyone else. (Not only that, but typically the writers of *Angel* ensure nothing happens on the show that would alter what happens on *BtVS*, so one can watch *Buffy* in syndication without missing anything. The relationship is doomed.)

This episode features the Oracles for the first time, and we're warned of an impending doom that the players on *Angel* will soon have to fight. But the *Angel* plot points are secondary to the Buffy/Angel relationship. In the end, inevitably, the relationship is not to be, and the steps Angel takes to save Buffy from emotional harm just deepen the complexities of his character. As if he didn't have enough pain to carry around, he now bears the knowledge of something Buffy will never know. The final moments of their relationship are the most painful for any fan to watch, and it's interesting that Sarah Michelle Gellar has her finest acting moment of the season . . . on the other show. She is absolutely brilliant, and even more so because of her chemistry with David Boreanaz. Scenes like this prove just how drab the Riley/Buffy relationship is in comparison.

1.9 Hero

Original air date:	November 30, 1999
Written by:	Howard Gordon, Tim Minear
Directed by:	Tucker Gates
Guest cast:	Tony Denman (Rieff), Michelle Horn (Rayna), Lee Arenberg (Tiernan), Sean Gunn (Lucas), Anthony Cistaro (Scourge Commander), David Bickford (Cargo Inspector), James Henrikson (Elder Lister Demon)

L.A. is besieged by an army of the apocalypse, and a prophecy states that only a sacrifice of the Chosen One can stop them.

One of the most moving episodes of *Angel* ever, this one also had viewers asking "Why?" Why did the writers make the decision they did? Why remove a central character? Some viewers held out hope that maybe the ending was only momentary, and Doyle would return in a future episode. When that didn't happen, the show lost some of its viewers, who felt betrayed by the loss of someone they'd come to care about. "Hero" was in the spirit of Joss Whedon's "Don't get too comfortable as a regular on my show" motto (see Jenny Calendar and Principal Flutie, among others), but it showed us what a true hero was, and jump-started Cordelia's path to redemption. While it would appear the sacrifice was made by Doyle, Cordy unwittingly makes a sacrifice of her own, one that will take her to many frightening places in episodes to come. The ending of this episode is a tearjerker, and the story arc was beautifully written and acted. The Scourge, possibly the most terrifying-looking villains in the Buffyverse after the Gentlemen, are dressed up like German S.S. officers (see "I Robot, You Jane"). An excellent episode.

1.10 Parting Gifts

Original air date:	December 14, 1999
Written by:	David Fury, Jeannine Renshaw
Directed by:	James A. Contner
Guest cast:	Maury Sterling (Barney), Carry Cannon (Female Oracle), Randall Slavin (Male Oracle), Alexis Denisof (Wesley Wyndam-Pryce), Henry Kingi (Kungai Demon), Dominique Jennings (Mac), Kotoko Kawamura (Korean Woman), Jason Kim (Soon), Lawrence Turner (Hank)

Cordelia discovers that Doyle left her a "parting gift," and when a new "rogue demon hunter" comes to L.A., the group is reunited with an old acquaintance.

Cordelia has inherited Doyle's visions, and right away she discovers the danger when she's kidnapped and narrowly escapes having her eyes removed in a weird demon auction

Glenn Quinn, our hero

(and there's a mention that Cordelia is a twentysomething — why is she a year older than Buffy?). Doyle may be gone, but now we have Wesley Wyndam-Pryce in his place. The return of Wesley is great — it's always nice to see a familiar face — but once again showed *Angel*'s reliance on old characters from *Buffy*. Only in season two, when the show starts to develop its own myths, does it get out from under its mother show and find its own legs. That said, adding Alexis Denisof to the mix was a stroke of genius — he shines on *Angel* like he was never able to on *Buffy*.

1.11 Somnambulist

Original air date:	January 18, 2000
Written by:	Tim Minear
Directed by:	Winrich Kolbe
Guest cast:	Jeremy Renner (Penn), Kimberleigh Aarn (Precinct Clerk)

Angel fears he may have unknowingly returned to his evil ways when he dreams of murdering people and those very people are found the next day, murdered.

As if we haven't been reminded of Angelus enough, this episode brings Angel's deepest fear into the foreground and makes it a very real possibility. We're introduced to someone who Angel had "sired" (again that complicated word) in the 1700s, and who, like Angel, had some serious issues with his father. Angel opens up to Kate and gains her reluctant trust (although her profile on him is strangely accurate, and we're never told how she got all her information), and while she's the Scully to his Mulder, she quickly accepts that the demon world really does exist, and she becomes a potential ally to the team. Kate's entrance into the world of demonology coincides with Riley's discovery that the world isn't exactly what he thought it was, either, again keeping *Angel*'s storylines a little too close to the ones on *BtVS*. Notice how in this episode Kate appears to be wearing a white version of the commando sweaters that Riley's gang are always wearing.

1.12 Expecting

Original air date:	January 25, 2000
Written by:	Howard Gordon
Directed by:	David Semel
Guest cast:	Daphne Duplaix (Selene), Ken Marino (Wilson Christopher), Josh Randall (Bartender), Louisette Geiss (Emily), Doug Tompos (Dr. Wasserman), Steven Roy (Jason)

Cordelia gets more than she bargained for when she has a date with a guy and ends up nine months pregnant the next morning.

With a gestation period shorter than Gabrielle's on *Xena*, Cordelia wakes up out-to-there the morning after what seemed like the perfect date. Like in "Rm W/ a Vu," Cordelia believes she's gotten this way because of how she's acted in her past (she's quickly becoming a poster child for why you shouldn't bully other kids in school). The incident is a metaphor for dating in the big city, where guys take you on one-night stands and leave you pregnant with their child. The fetus seems to grow so quickly the mother can barely put her life in order. But in this case, her pregnancy also seems to stand for surrogate motherhood — when women agree to carry other people's children — and the pain surrogate mothers endure when they give the child away. This episode was important mostly for how the relationship among the triumvirate strengthens as a result of what happens . . . and the fact that Angel ends up grinning at the end.

1.13 She

Original air date:	February 8, 2000
Written by:	David Greenwalt, Marti Noxon
Directed by:	David Greenwalt
Guest cast:	Bai Ling (Jhiera), Colby French (Tae), Heather Stephens (Demon Girl), Sean Gunn (Mars), Tracy Costello (Laura), P.J. Marino (Peter Wilkers), Andre Roberson (Diego)

Angel tries to help a society of women hoping to avoid painful and life-altering procedures at the hands of men when they come of age.

"She" was an okay episode, but got a little muddled, almost bordering on misogynistic at times. It guest-starred Bai Ling (a.k.a. Ling Bai) a film star in her native China who is known for her outspoken protests against her country's injustices. Bai Ling is best known for playing the attorney who defends Richard Gere in *Red Corner*, a movie where the Chinese judicial system is seriously called into question. The movie was banned in China and Hong Kong, and Bai Ling suffered ostracism as a result. She was scheduled to appear in two films by Chinese directors and they both backed out on her; her passport was revoked, and she has been banned from her native country. By the time the film came out, Bai Ling was already a U.S. citizen, and had been studying acting in New York since 1992 (she left China three years after being involved in the Tiananmen Square riots of 1989). She has since appeared in *Anna and the King* and has had guest roles in other films, including *Nixon* and *The Crow*.

In this episode she appears as Princess Jhiera, a woman who is trying to escape the evil injustices inflicted upon the women of her society when they come of age. These sorts of barbaric practices still occur throughout the world, such as the removal of the clitoris among some tribes in Africa so women can no longer enjoy sex (and will presumably not stray). The episode showed that it's not the women who are dangerous; it's the men who can't seem to control themselves around these women, but the point was made in a too obvious way. And considering vampires have no body temperature, Angel taking a cold shower after being near the princess made no sense. The action sequences were exciting (Bai Ling did all her own stunts) and it would be great to see this actress on *Angel* again. Also, "She" contains the single funniest moment in season one of *Angel*, when David Boreanaz shows off his Elaine Bennis-type dance moves at Cordy's party. Hilarious.

1.14 I've Got You Under My Skin

Original air date:	February 15, 2000
Story by:	David Greenwalt, Jeannine Renshaw

Teleplay by:	Jeannine Renshaw
Directed by:	R.D. Price
Guest cast:	Will Kempe (Seth Anderson), Katy Boyer (Paige Anderson), Anthony Cistaro (Ethros Demon), Jesse James (Ryan Anderson), Ashley Edner (Stephanie Anderson), Jerry Lambert (Rick)

Angel and Wesley try to exorcise a demon that is possessing a little boy, only to be met with a horrible discovery.

"I've Got You Under My Skin" is an excellent first season episode with lots of surprises. Through the story of a child who's possessed by a demon that is making his parents' lives a living hell, we learn more about the other characters on the show. Although, just as the alcoholism in Xander's family is only ever hinted at, in this episode we get a hint that Wesley was abused and tortured as a child (and had bedroom accommodations similar to that of Harry Potter), and suddenly his bumbling and constant attempts to fit in are more sad than pathetic. Because of the demon's accusations, Wesley feels compelled to tell Angel that he really does trust him, and Angel confesses that he feels guilty for not saving Doyle. Also, in the past few episodes Cordy has admitted that her visions have gone beyond pictures in her head, and she's starting to feel the effects of them, a storyline that will become more important in future episodes.

1.15 The Prodigal

Original air date:	February 22, 2000
Written by:	Tim Minear
Directed by:	Bruce Seth Green
Guest cast:	Julie Benz (Darla), John Mahon (Trevor Lockley), Glenda Morgan Brown (Liam's Mother), J. Kenneth Campbell (Liam's Father), Bob Fimiani (Groundskeeper), Mark Ginther (Head Demon), Christina Hendricks (Barmaid), Henri Lubatti (Vampire)

Past and present come together when Kate faces her feelings for her father, and we learn about Angel's relationship with his father.

For those who loved "Becoming" and were clamoring for more back story, this episode had it. Angel was a drunken layabout named Liam who spent his free times in bars and strange women's beds. His father condemned his behavior, and when Liam becomes Angelus we see just how brutal (once again) he was. He kills his family, one by one, relishing the death of his father. It's interesting that David Boreanaz has made Angel such a charismatic character that we can watch scenes like these and still like the guy. Meanwhile, Kate's father is involved in some dirty dealings and is killed by Wolfram & Hart — specifically, Wolfram & Hart vampires — and she blames Angel and "his kind" for what happened. In an interesting juxtaposition, we see Angel's tombstone in 1753, which says "Beloved Son" (an ironic wording since he had been sent away by his father, who hated him), and Kate's father's tombstone in the present day, with the eerily similar wording "Beloved

Father" (in fact, she never saw eye-to-eye with him, and he was a hard and often cruel man).
An excellent episode.

1.16 The Ring

Original air date:	February 29, 2000
Written by:	Howard Gordon
Directed by:	Nick Marck
Guest cast:	Scott William Winters (Jack McNamara), Marcus Red- mond (Tom Cribb), Douglas Roberts (Darin McNamara), Marc Rose (Mellish), Juan A. Riojas (Val Trepkos), Anthony Guidera (Ernie Nellims), Mark Ginther (Lasovic)

Angel is kidnapped and made part of a demon gladiator team that has to fight and kill 21 demons before they'll be set free.

CHRISTINA RADISH

Stephanie Romanov, who plays Lilah Morgan, Wolfram & Hart's resident bitch

When this episode first aired, many people compared it to *Fight Club*, the hit movie at the time, but it's closer to *Gladiator*, which was released in May 2000, after "The Ring" aired. In *Fight Club*, the fighters actually chose to be part of the club. In "The Ring," as in *Gladiator*, the demons have no choice but to fight their way to freedom. The tables are turned in this one as Cordy and Wes have to try to save Angel from certain death, and through Wes's patience and Cordy's ingenuity, they find a way to do it. This episode also brings in Lilah Morgan as a key player at Wolfram & Hart, and while she seems like a black and white character in "The Ring," she'll become far more complex in episodes to come. There's a subtle reference to *Buffy* at the beginning of the episode when Cordy, who's trying to track down demons using an online demon dating service, argues with Wesley, who says books are better than computers any day. The conversation is a cattier version of the same argument Jenny and Giles had in "I Robot, You Jane." Interestingly, the Web site she's checking out, archfiend.org, has actually been registered by someone, but there's no site when you get there. I bet Wolfram & Hart had something to do with this. . . . "The Ring" was okay, but unfortunately was yet another monster-of-the-week episode that plagued the first season of *Angel*.

1.17 Eternity

Original air date:	April 4, 2000
Written by:	Tracy Stern
Directed by:	Regis Kimble
Guest cast:	Tamara Gorski (Rebecca Lowell), Michael Mantell (Oliver Simon)

Angel and the gang meet famous actress Rebecca Lowell, who wants Angel to turn her into a vampire so she can stay young and beautiful (and on a hit sitcom) forever.

"Eternity" was a great episode that paralleled vampires with actors who remain the same age on television forever, and also moved the relationships of Angel, Wes, and Cordy forward, with each one finding out something about themselves. Like Cordelia, who has seen the seedy side of acting in L.A., Rebecca finds out the hard way that even when you make it in Hollywood, your dreams can quickly become a nightmare, thanks to the people you thought were your friends. The scene where she tricks Angel with her happy pill is a terrifying reminder of what lurks beneath the smouldering exterior of our favorite vampire, and although I'm always thrilled to see Angelus rear his ugly head, this scene was particularly frightening because of the danger Rebecca was in. He turns on Wes and Cordy, not to hurt them physically, but to tell them what he really thinks about them. The result is a sobering of the relationship among the trio, but also a strengthening, because now they know where they stand. The opening scene of the episode — where Wes and Angel try to plot an escape from Cordelia's horrific performance — is hilarious, offering a hint of the lighter side of *Angel* that will show itself in season two.

1.18 Five by Five (Part One)

Original air date:	April 25, 2000
Written by:	Jim Kouf

Directed by:	James A. Contner
Guest cast:	Julie Benz (Darla), Eliza Dushku (Faith), Thomas Burr (Lee Mercer), Tyler Christopher (Wolfram & Hart Lawyer), Francis Fallon (Rick)

Faith arrives in L.A. and is immediately hired by Wolfram & Hart to kill Angel.

At the beginning of this episode, Angel, trying to convince someone to testify against a drug dealer, tells him that we all have to face our demons at some point. "Five by Five" is about coming face-to-face with one's demons, and while Angel compared Faith to himself in "Consequences," here we get a more direct parallel. We're taken back to 1898, when Angel first had the curse inflicted upon him (and we think of Faith and her first kill). Darla shuns Angel from her life and tells him he's dirty. He walks the streets haunted by his past deeds, but is forced out of necessity to continue to attack people (just as Faith was shunned by the Scoobies and became a serial killer). Faith now arrives in L.A. and begins attacking people in a bar (to the sounds of Rob Zombie's apt "Living Dead Girl") before getting her mission from Lindsey and Lilah. The scene where she captures and tortures Wesley also throws to Angel, who tortured a Watcher in "Becoming (Part Two)." Like Angelus, Faith has become a monster, only she still has a soul and is haunted by her crimes *while* she is committing them. The fight scene between her and Angel is incredible: ultimately, as she did in "Who Are You," she sees herself as an evil monster who must be destroyed. The final scene, where she begs Angel to kill her while the rain falls, is gorgeous. In a sense, Faith is baptized at this moment, and we hope it signals a new beginning for her. The only nitpick is that Angel calls Giles, who tells him that Faith had left Sunnydale the week before. Actually, she left about two months before, if we look at the fact that "Who Are You" aired at the end of February, and the shows are meant to occur at the same time.

1.19 Sanctuary (Part Two)

Original air date:	May 2, 2000
Written by:	Tim Minear
Directed by:	Michael Lange
Guest cast:	Thomas Burr (Lee Mercer), Alastair Duncan (Collins), Eliza Dushku (Faith), Sarah Michelle Gellar (Buffy), Kevin Owers (Smith), Jeff Ricketts (Weatherby), Adam Vernier (Detective Kendrick)

Angel tries to help Faith admit her mistakes and regain her soul, but Buffy suddenly appears in L.A., wanting nothing but revenge.

A fantastic *Angel* episode, filled with betrayal, complex relationship issues, and more analogies of Faith's predicament being like Angel's. The evil arm of the Watcher's Council shows up in L.A., having followed Faith from Sunnydale, and tries to lure Wesley to help them capture her again. It's interesting that when they corner Giles in "Who Are You," he complies, whereas Wesley is reluctant. Kate (in another sweater that looks like it came off Riley's back) continues her quest to bring down Angel and prove he's evil, while Faith tries to come to terms with the things she's done. Just as all the murders Angel had committed

over a century ago came flooding back to him when he got his soul, now Faith begins to remember everything she did, and can't possibly apologize for.

But the most intriguing part of this episode is the sudden appearance of Buffy. Angel
has discovered that Riley is in the picture, so perhaps that contributes to his lack of sympathy for her, but Buffy, in her own way, is self-centered, refusing to see the other side of the
picture. She accuses him of being in a murderers' club with Faith, flippantly mentions her
new boyfriend, and tells him she could never trust him. All of this, of course, after she's
punched him in the face. She explains that Faith has tortured her family and come after
Buffy, and Buffy just wants to destroy her. Later she tells Faith that no one else has ever made
her a victim. Hmm . . . she seems to have forgotten a certain vampire who tortured her
Watcher, killed Giles's lover, threatened her friends, and tried to kill her mother. Funny how
she forgave him and chastized others for not forgiving him as well. The end of the episode
is one of the most intriguing Angel/Buffy moments we've seen, where he tells her to get out
of "his" city once and for all, and she purposely tries to hurt him once again. This signals
an end to *Angel* being in *BtVS*'s shadow — he tells her to leave him alone, and it's a subtle way of announcing that Buffy will no longer be coming over to *Angel*, which will allow
it to become its own show, with its own mythology, no longer relying on crossovers with
Buffy to bring in new viewers. (See "The Yoko Factor" for the conclusion to this episode
on *Buffy*.)

1.20 War Zone

Original air date:	May 9, 2000
Written by:	Gary Campbell
Directed by:	David Straiton
Guest cast:	David Herman (David Nabbitt), Michele Kelly (Alonna), Joe Basile (Lenny Edwards), Maurice Compte (Chain), Mick Murray (Knox), Sven Holmberg (Ty), Kimberly James (Lena), Rebecca Kingler (Madam Dorion), Sean Parhm (Bobby)

*When Angel Investigations is doing a job for dot-com billionaire David Nabbitt, they en-
counter a vampire-slaying gang, led by Charles Gunn.*

"War Zone" provides our introduction to both David Nabbit (who returns in "To Shanshu in L.A." and "First Impressions") and Gunn, the angry vampire-hunter who goes from
vigilante trying to clean up the streets to pained brother wreaking vengeance for his sister's
death. Gunn's team, truck, and weaponry are very cool, but they lack the strength and quick
reflexes to fight properly, and the gang suffers many casualties. Meeting Gunn brings
back some buried feelings for Angel (not that he ever buries his guilt very deep), and he sees
what the loss of Gunn's sister has done to the young gang leader. We can tell Angel is wondering how many families he destroyed in this way, and later he refers to himself as
Angelus, as if no matter what he does right, the evil will always be percolating right under
the surface. Seeing Gunn's determination, Angel realizes what his own quest should be,
while Nabbitt provides the hefty check that will keep Angel Investigations in business. The
only nitpick to this episode concerns Gunn's gang: when they reappear in "The Thin Dead
Line" they're a mostly African-American gang, but in this episode they're mostly white.

1.21 Blind Date

Original air date:	May 16, 2000
Written by:	Jeannine Renshaw
Directed by:	Tom Wright
Guest cast:	Thomas Burr (Lee Mercer), Sam Anderson (Holland), Jennifer Badger (Vanessa Brewer), Charles Constant (Howard)

Angel tries to find a blind assassin whom Wolfram & Hart is protecting before she kills three children.

This interesting episode, which introduces Holland Manners (played by veteran Sam Anderson, best known from *Perfect Strangers*, as the principal on *Growing Pains*, and from numerous other television and movie character roles), establishes Lindsey as a major character and announces an ancient prophecy that features Angel, one that will become central to the show's premise. We discover Lindsey had an impoverished childhood, so his rise within the ranks of Wolfram & Hart has been propelled mostly by his own desire to rise above his parents. His guilt in this episode is similar to that of Faith's and, like Faith on *Buffy*, he's too impressionable and vulnerable to be saved yet. The fight between Angel and Vanessa is great (imagine fighting a blind foe who can "see" you better than anyone with 20/20 vision), but the pivotal moment is when Wesley begins to decipher the ancient prophecy (making him more important to the team) and discovers that Angel is mentioned.

CHRISTINA RADISH

The cast of Angel *lines up to promote season two. From left, J. August Richards, Elizabeth Rohm, Charisma Carpenter, David Boreanaz, Alexis Denisof, Christian Kane, and Stephanie Romanov*

1.22 To Shanshu in L.A.

Original air date:	May 23, 2000
Written and directed by:	David Greenwalt
Guest cast:	Sam Anderson (Holland), Todd Stashwick (Vocah), Carey Cannon (Female Oracle), Randall Slavin (Male Oracle), David Herman (David Nabbitt), Julie Benz (Darla), Lia Johnson (Vendor)

Angel's fate has been predetermined, but only if he is able to rise to the occasion and fulfill his destiny.

The best episode of season one, "To Shanshu in L.A." is fast-paced, suspenseful, and contains all the elements we'll need to fully appreciate season two. Wesley translates Angel's position in the prophecy to mean that he will die, which leaves Angel unfazed. When Cordy is paralyzed by a barrage of visions filled with pain and heartbreak, and Wesley is rushed to the hospital with severe burns, Angel becomes far more concerned about his friends than his own prophesied future. The pain on Angel's face as he moves between hospital rooms shows just how mature David Boreanaz has become as an actor: his eyes speak volumes. Gunn is recruited to help once again, setting him up as a major part of the show, and when Cordelia is returned to the group, she's a new and improved Cordy — a woman who has seen the pain of the world around her and realizes her mission with the gang is more important than the latest style of Prada shoes. Meanwhile, Wolfram & Hart resurrect an enemy from Angel's past that will jump-start his season two downward spiral. And Wesley realizes his translation might have been a little off (anyone who recognizes the allusion in the show's title can guess the prophecy).

Season Two

SEPTEMBER 2000 • MAY 2001

Recurring characters in season two: Andy Hallett (The Host), Julie Benz (Darla), Sam Anderson (Holland)

2.1 Judgment

Original air date:	September 26, 2000
Teleplay by:	David Greenwalt
Story by:	Joss Whedon and David Greenwalt
Directed by:	Michael Lange
Guest cast:	Justina Machado (Jo), Eliza Dushku (Faith), Matthew James (Merl), Edward James Gage (Mordar), Glenn David Calloway (The Judge)

When Angel accidentally kills a woman's champion, he must come up with a way to save her life before a tribunal kills her.

A touching, strong episode, "Judgment" introduces many of the major elements of season two: the Host and Caritas (both of which are brilliant concepts); Angel's Pinocchio-like quest to become human; the teamwork of Angel Investigations; Merl the parasite demon; Gunn as a strength Angel can rely on; Wolfram & Hart as the continuing nemesis for Angel; and the, um, staggering talent of Angel's singing voice. Ahem. Although the plot of the woman being chased by the Tribunal is a little skewed (we're never told why they're after her or what she's on trial for), it's the subplots that make this episode so good. The karaoke bar is a clever plot device, giving the show some much-needed humor, and Andy Hallett is great as the Host. (And those are some impressive pipes he's got, too.) A native of Osterville, Maine, Hallett was singing in a dinner theater in Los Angeles when Joss Whedon walked in and asked the 25-year-old to audition for the part. Hallett, who was working as a property manager at the time, accepted the invitation, and after three auditions, the part was his. His debut on "Judgment" thrilled fans, and he was kept on for future episodes. The final scene of the episode, where Angel goes to see an old friend, is a pleasant surprise, bringing us full circle to his quest. We see how so many people on both *Buffy* and *Angel* are on personal quests for redemption. A great beginning to what will be a stunning second season.

2.2 Are You Now or Have You Ever Been

Original air date:	October 3, 2000
Written by:	Tim Minear
Directed by:	David Semel
Guest cast:	Melissa Marsala (Judy), Julie Araskog (Over the Hill Whore), J.P. Manoux (Bellhop), John Kapelos (Ronald Meeks), Tommy Hinkley (Private Investigator), Scott Thompson Baker (Actor), Brett Rickaby (Denver), Eve Sigall (Old Judy), Tom Beyer (Writer)

We flash back to 1952, where Angel was staying at a hotel inhabited by a paranoia demon that fed off the souls of the people there.

One of my favorite *Angel* episodes. Finally, a flashback that doesn't take place in the 19th century. In 1952, Angel is more brooding than ever, cooped up in a hotel where he talks to no one and keeps completely to himself. He dresses like James Dean, drinks his blood from a glass bottle, and has brief heroic moments followed by complete apathy toward human beings. He meets Judy, a light-skinned African-American woman who is passing as white. Passing was a common phenomenon in the first half of the 20th century, and there have been several books and poems written about it. One of the best is *Autobiography of an Ex-Colored Man* by James Weldon Johnson, a novel about an African-American man passing as a white man, and how he gives up his heritage in order to be accepted into white society. "Are You Now or Have You Ever Been" flashes between the present, where Angel has asked Cordelia and Wesley to research the Hyperion hotel where he stayed, and the past, where the viewer sees what *really* happened, as opposed to what the newspapers reported.

Even though Angel has a soul in 1952, you wouldn't know it from his actions, and we discover yet one more grisly act of revenge he committed back then. It's going to be an even longer road to redemption for him. The hotel is aptly named — Hyperion, the father of the sun god, was blinded by his enemies at night, but could see during the day. Similarly, the occupants of the hotel become more paranoid in the evenings, committing horrible things, and act with more reason during the day. This episode provides us with a new office for Angel Investigations (at the same time as Giles is acquiring a new "office" for the Buffy gang). A couple of nitpicks, though: when the hotel guests attempt to kill Angel, what they do actually *would* have killed him, since we've seen Angel dust vampires by breaking their necks. Also, in "Becoming (Part Two)" Whistler insinuates that Angel has been living off rat blood for a century, and tells him how to get blood at the butcher's, but here in 1952 we see he's already buying his blood in a bottle. Finally, maybe the writers thought referring to Julie Araskog's character as "Over the Hill Whore" was funny, but I think it's tasteless.

2.3 First Impressions

Original air date:	October 10, 2000
Written by:	Shawn Ryan
Directed by:	James A. Contner
Guest cast:	David Herman (David Nabbit), Chris Barber (Henry), Cedrick Terrell (Jameel), Edwin Hodge (Keenan), Lucas Babin (Joey), Alan Shaw (Deevak), Angel Parker (Veronica), Ray Campbell (Desmond), Christopher Babers (Gunn's Friend)

As Angel begins to have dreams of Darla, Cordelia declares herself Gunn's protector and races off in an effort to save him from what she saw in a vision.

The beginning of the downward spiral. As part of the overall plan Wolfram & Hart have for Angel, Darla is now inhabiting his dreams in passionate ways. He can't seem to get to sleep fast enough, and refuses to tell the others what is happening to him. Meanwhile, without Angel as its center, the team is falling apart, arguing all the time, becoming ineffectual in their fighting and refusing to listen to one another. It's an interesting way to set up what will happen this season, and Cordy breaks away from the group to try to save Gunn on her own. She explains to him that he's a greater danger to himself than anything else is, which, eerily, is what the viewers could later say about Angel.

2.4 Untouched

Original air date:	October 17, 2000
Written by:	Mere Smith
Directed by:	Joss Whedon
Guest cast:	Daisy McCrackin (Bethany Chaulk), Gareth Williams (Mr. Chaulk), Michael Harte (Detective), Drew Wicks (Officer)

As Angel's racy Darla dreams continue, a woman with telekinetic powers who is recruited by Lilah needs him to help her.

Telekinesis, the ability to make objects move by using the mind, has featured in several movies — most notably *Carrie* — and there is still much debate about whether it is possible. Those in the know agree you cannot make an object move by wishing it to, that it has to do with the subconscious. In "Untouched," Bethany is a telekinetic who can't control her powers, and things move and shake whenever she gets upset. There's an insinuation that her father molested her, a scenario common in fictional representations of telekinetic power. In *Carrie*, the title character has an abusive mother who makes her feel dirty for being a pubescent woman. The levitation of the father is an homage to the 1978 Brian De Palma film, *The Fury*, where a telekinetic boy floats in the air above his father. Wesley infuriates Bethany by bringing up her father, and when Wolfram & Hart send her father over in the flesh to coax her home, all hell breaks loose. The tie-in to the ongoing drama is that just as Bethany has no control over her power because of her sexual frustration, Darla has complete control over Angel by satiating his.

2.5 Dear Boy

Original air date:	October 24, 2000
Written and Directed by:	David Greenwalt
Guest cast:	Juliet Landau (Drusilla), Stewart Skelton (Harold Jeakins), Cheryl White (Claire), Matt North (Stephen), Rich Hutchman (Detective Carlson)

Angel finally realizes that Darla is alive, but no one will believe him, especially not Kate.

"Dear Boy" is a heart-pounding episode where Darla rises to new heights of sadism. Not satisfied with haunting Angel only during his dreams, she moves to his waking hours, allowing him glimpses of her. This is enough to convince him she's alive, but his friends find it hard to believe, especially when they see her walk into the sunlight. Darla reports to her bosses that Angel is starting to crack, and good ol' Kate comes back into the picture, desperate to get the goods on Angel and put him behind bars, where she thinks he belongs. She also reveals a racist side to herself; when Kate meets Gunn for the first time, she immediately asks for his ID and gets a fellow officer to run a check on him. We never saw her pull something like that with Wes or Cordelia. In a flashback scene to Angel and Darla in the good old days, we see how they turned Drusilla into a vampire, and the return of Juliet Landau is an absolute thrill, even if it is only for a few episodes. She's as amazing as she ever was on *Buffy*.

Darla finally corners Angel in a convent, where we discover she only *seems* to be working for Wolfram & Hart; instead she sees Angel as her possible salvation, and vice versa. She tells him Angelus is always under the surface, and he should let him out (too bad she missed season two of *Buffy*). Julie Benz and David Boreanaz are powerful in this scene, seeming to dance with one another back and forth, one minute looking like they're in love, the next hating one another. The onscreen chemistry is evident, and the viewer believes they've had a long and shadowed past with one another. The episode ends with a warning that things will only get uglier, and we fans can't wait to see how.

2.6 Guise Will Be Guise

Original air date:	November 7, 2000
Written by:	Jane Espenson

Julie Benz: as Darla, she's the one who started the whole darn thing

Directed by: Krishna Rao
Guest cast: Brigid Brannagh (Virginia Bryce), Todd Susman (Mr. Bryce), Patrick Kilpatrick (Paul Lanier), Art LaFleur (T'ish Magev), Danica Sheridan (Yeska), Saul Stein (Benny)

When Angel goes off to visit a swami at the Host's bequest, Wesley pretends he's Angel to help protect the daughter of a powerful man.

Buffy writer Jane Espenson penned this very funny episode that allowed Alexis Denisof to show his hilarious and brooding sides. Posing as Angel, Denisof pulls off some absolutely brilliant slapstick moments, including entering a house, realizing he's entered uninvited, and hurling himself backwards out of the doorway until he's received permission. Brigid Brannagh guest stars as Virginia, the daughter of another deadbeat dad (yet another of the weekly parallels between *Buffy* and *Angel*, since this episode followed "Family"), who falls in love with "Wesley as Angel." Meanwhile, the Host gets Angel into yet another pickle when he's sent to a swami, someone who looks more like he would belong in Tony Soprano's gang than a spiritual advisor. Yet, despite being a little shady, he seems to hit Angel's problems on the head when he says Angel is his own enemy, that he piles up problems around himself, and that he needs to exorcise himself of Darla, which he could do by finding a pretty blond thing, bedding her, and going all medieval on her before leaving her (you can tell a *Buffy* writer was at the helm of this one).

2.7 Darla

Original air date: November 14, 2000
Written and directed by: Tim Minear
Guest cast: Juliet Landau (Drusilla), James Marsters (Spike), Mark Metcalf (The Master)

Through flashbacks, we see how Darla became a vampire, what life was like when she was with Angel, and how her past is impacting on her present.

A beautiful, beautiful conclusion to the *Buffy* episode "Fool for Love," "Darla" uses some of the same scenes we've already seen, but puts a new spin on them. If you thought it was strange in "Fool for Love" that Angel was standing next to Darla in 1900 — considering he'd gotten his soul back two years earlier — the explanation is here. We find out that Darla was a prostitute dying of syphilis in the Virginia Colony when the Master "saved" her from her condition (it's great to see Mark Metcalf again, and he's just as brilliant as he was in season one). This may be the nitpickiest of nitpicks, but Darla couldn't have been in the Virginia Colony (known as Jamestown) in 1609. The first colonists to Jamestown were 104 men, who arrived from England in 1607. Two other "supplies" of settlers arrived in 1608, but of the newcomers, only two were women — Mrs. Thomas Forrest and her servant, Anne Burras. Burras was married in November 1608, and no further settlers arrived during the following year. So there were no single women in the colony in 1609.

Angelus is impetuous and rude when Darla first introduces him to her sire, and it's no wonder that the Master later has it in for him. Again, the scenery is beautiful, although it's a little confusing that this episode was apparently directed by Tim Minear, and "Fool for

Love" was directed by Nick Marck, when there are overlapping scenes. That said, Minear is quickly becoming the best writer on *Angel* (he's also responsible for "Are You Now or Have You Ever Been" and later "Through the Looking Glass"). The flashbacks between past and present are skilfully written and directed, with each moment having a direct impact on the present action. "Darla," easily one of the best episodes of *Angel*, shows how a crossover is possible without one show being dependent on the other. Together, these two episodes are phenomenal.

2.8 The Shroud of Rahmon

Original air date:	November 21, 2000
Written by:	Jim Kouf
Directed by:	David Grossman
Guest cast:	W. Earl Brown (Menlow), Dwayne L. Barnes (Lester), Michael Hagy (Jay-Don), Tony Todd (Vyasa), Robert Dolan (Bob), R. Emery Bright (Detective Turlock), Tom Kiesche (Detective Broomfield)

Angel poses as a flashy vampire from Las Vegas when he discovers a bunch of demons will try to steal the Shroud of Rahmon, a deadly shroud that can drive people crazy.

This episode opens with a distraught and weary-looking Wesley talking about how everything went wrong. The flashback plot device — where we see the end before the rest of the episode — hasn't been used on *Angel* before, even though it's a staple in detective shows. In this case, it's a little overdone, just because Denisof seems to be almost overplaying his part. We're led to believe that Angel has killed Kate, who is particularly annoying in this episode. When she meets Angel at his apartment, she taunts him by referring to "blindingly sunny courtrooms" and other vampirist remarks. He threatens her, which is just what she wanted him to do, and it gives credence to what happens later. Everyone's involved in this episode — Wesley, Gunn, and Cordelia (in her Monica Lewinsky hair) — and David Boreanaz gets to show us another side of his acting chops as the flashy, smooth-talking vampire from Nevada. However, the episode ends on an unnecessarily foreboding note: Wesley says Angel hasn't tasted human blood in a very, very long time and this will start his downward spiral into gloominess, when, in fact, Angel drank Buffy's blood less than two years before this. The more telling moment occurs earlier, when Angel is almost overcome by the shroud. In his eyes we see the human half of him fighting the demon half, refusing to let it out. But perhaps some of the demon half made it to the surface, because from this point on he's pretty far gone.

2.9 The Trial

Original air date:	November 28, 2000
Teleplay by:	Douglas Petrie, Tim Minear
Story by:	David Greenwalt
Directed by:	Bruce Seth Green
Guest cast:	Juliet Landau (Drusilla), Jim Piddick (Overseer), Evan Arnold (Shempire)

Lindsey reveals to Darla that she's got two months to live, and she becomes desperate for immortality once again.

Another spectacular episode of *Angel* — season two is certainly head and shoulders above season one. Again flashing back and forth between the past and the present, this episode reveals that when Wolfram & Hart made Darla human again, she was reinflicted with the disease that almost killed her human self in the first place. We jump to a time when Darla and Angel were being chased by a vampire hunter named Holtz (which will take on more importance in season three), and when she betrayed Angel to save her own skin. Is she betraying him once again? Can he believe everything she says? And how can he be her salvation? In his mind, he believes that if he can save this one tormented soul, which has been damaged and bruised almost beyond redemption, then maybe he'll be on his own path to salvation. The episode title comes from a series of harrowing trials that Angel must endure to try to save Darla, and only in watching just how much he will risk for her life, she realizes that maybe she's okay the way she is (another parallel with *Buffy* — just as Buffy could do nothing to help her mother, Angel is helpless here). But in an absolutely magnificent ending (my favorite of any *Angel* episode), we discover that Wolfram & Hart has other plans. As anyone would expect with such heavyweights as Minear, Greenwalt, Petrie, and Bruce Seth Green at the helm, this episode is a stunner. My only nitpick would be the scene where Angel enters a hotel room and says it's possible to do so because it's considered public accommodation. That is *way* too much of a stretch.

2.10 Reunion

Original air date:	December 19, 2000
Written by:	Tim Minear, Shawn Ryan
Directed by:	James A. Contner
Guest cast:	Erik Liberman (Erik), Juliet Landau (Drusilla), Stephanie Manglaras (Landlady)

CHRISTINA RADISH

"We are family." Drusilla and her grandmummy-cum-daughter, Darla

When Angel can't stop Darla from being reborn as a vampire, he decides to forget about redemption and spend all of his time hunting her.

A pivotal episode for season two, "Reunion" brings back Drusilla in all her craziness and Darla in her seductive vampiness, and we even see a glimpse of the evil Angelus. A true family reunion. Drusilla is as loopy as ever, but considering the personality change she underwent in season two of *Buffy*, where she ended up loopy but able to carry out her evil duties, here she just seems crazy, like the old Drusilla. It's as if the writers can't separate the old from the new. That said, she's still hilarious in every scene, and it's through her that we can tell how far gone Angel is. After he's failed at every attempt to save Darla, it seems like something in Angel snaps, and he skips over the problem itself and goes to the source, attempting to eradicate Wolfram & Hart. The result is a devastating loss of the humanity he's worked so hard for, and he recognizes the dark path he's on and shuns his friends and coworkers.

2.11 Redefinition

Original air date:	January 16, 2001
Written by:	Mere Smith
Directed by:	Michael Grossman
Guest cast:	Brigid Brannagh (Virginia), Nicolas Survoy (Hunt Acrey), Matthew James (Merl), Brad Kalas (EMT)

Cordelia, Wesley, and Gunn are on their own after being fired by Angel, and Angel's out to wreak vengeance on Darla and Drusilla.

And the dark just keeps getting darker. This gloomy, graphic episode should definitely not be shown to kids. Angel moves deeper within himself, and first gets rid of his dozens of drawings of Darla (in a prophetic way: in the fireplace) before becoming physically and mentally ready to wage war against Darla and Drusilla. Through a monotonous and chant-like voice-over, Angel tells us how he's readying himself, and when he gets close to Darla at one point, he realizes he's still too close to her emotionally to do what he must. Meanwhile, without jobs, Gunn, Wesley, and Cordelia do what any self-respecting Los Angelites do with no money or future: they get drunk and sing karaoke at Caritas. When they receive a vision from the powers that be and answer it, they realize that they might not have Angel's powers, but they have the caring and urge within them to fight the good fight, so they do. But Angel, who finally corners Darla and Drusilla in what turns into a grisly scene, has given up fighting the good fight, and has let part of the demon within him surface so he can destroy what he believes is the true evil.

2.12 Blood Money

Original air date:	January 23, 2001
Written by:	Shawn Ryan, Mere Smith
Directed by:	R.D. Price
Guest cast:	Julia Lee (Anne Steele), Gerry Becker (Nathan Reed), Mark Rolston (Boone), Matthew James (Merl), Jeffrey Patrick Dean (Dwight), Jason Padgett (Holden), Jennifer Rosa (Serena), Deborah Carson (Liza)

Angel begins following a woman who works at a homeless shelter when he discovers she's had dealings with Wolfram & Hart.

While "Blood Money" is an entertaining and satisfying episode, there's a brilliant character choice that might have slipped by a lot of viewers. Anne, a worker at a homeless shelter in L.A., should look familiar to *Buffy* viewers. As Chanterelle in "Lie to Me," she was a vampire worshiper who thought all vamps were like Lestat — romantic and wonderful. She was wrong. In "Anne," she was Lilly (the same character with a name change), who believed Ken, a social worker who convinced homeless kids that there's a better life for them — and she ended up in a hell dimension as a result. At the end of that episode, Buffy told her she could have the name Anne if she wanted, because Buffy was going back to her real name. It looks like she took Buffy up on that. Now, with that past behind her, she's a worker in a homeless shelter (probably to make up for all the kids Ken hurt) and she's faced with yet another dilemma: does she believe the law firm that's offering her a ton of money and is helping raise funds for the shelter, or does she believe a vampire who's been following her, stealing her wallet, and taking pictures of her? Because we know her past, we know what an excruciating decision this is for her, but it seems like Anne's matured, and she makes the right choice for herself. She still doesn't trust Angel, but she believes she's done the right thing. It takes guts to introduce a character to one show that's been partially developed on another without showing any flashbacks or scenes from *Buffy*, but for those who catch on, the payoff is worth it.

2.13 Happy Anniversary

Original air date:	February 6, 2001
Teleplay by:	David Greenwalt
Story by:	Joss Whedon, David Greenwalt
Directed by:	Bill Norton
Guest cast:	Brigid Brannagh (Virginia), Matt Champagne (Gene), Darby Stanchfield (Denise), Mike Hagerty (Bartender), Victoria A. Kellner (Val), Danny LaVaca (Mike), Norma Michaels (Aunt Helen), Eric Lange (Lubber Demon #1)

The Host warns Angel that the world is coming to an end, due to a scientist that is going to attempt to stop time.

A filler episode (Joss only ever seems to write fillers for *Angel* — his real talent is displayed on *Buffy*), "Happy Anniversary" shows that when Angel's not around, Wesley, Gunn, and Cordelia are able to snag clients on their own and solve crimes successfully (the Sherlock Holmes sequence in the parlor is hilarious). It also gives Angel a chance to rant to someone that no matter how much good he does in the world, he'll never be allowed to atone for what he's done in the past. The main plotline involves a scientist who's unable to connect with his girlfriend, so he discovers a way to stop all time just as they're making love. What doesn't realize is that he won't stop time just for them, but for everyone else. It's up to the Host and Angel to prevent him from doing so. The problem here is that in a storyline where we're supposed to watch Angel going deeper and deeper within himself and getting darker and darker, a night out with the Host puts a comic spin on things, hurting the momentum of the season. But it's a momentary lapse, and next week we're back to the brooding.

2.14 The Thin Dead Line

Original air date:	February 13, 2001
Written by:	Shawn Ryan, Jim Kouf

Directed by: Scott McGinnis
Guest cast: Julia Lee (Anne), Jarrod Crawford (Rondell), Mushond Lee (Jackson), Cory C. Hardrict (Ray), Kyle Davis (Kenny), Camille Mana (Les), Darin Cooper (Officer), Brenda Price (Callie), Darris Love (George), Matthew James (Merl), Geoff Koch (Street Cop), Jerry Giles (Desk Seargeant), Steven Barras (Captain)

A gang of zombie cops clamp down on crime in their precinct, but innocent people are dying as a result.

On the surface, this might seem to be another monster-of-the-week episode where we move away from the main plotline and again battle some demon or other. But instead, all the key players are involved, even if they don't realize they're helping each other out. Gunn, Wesley, and Cordelia have a new office and their first client, a woman whose daughter has an eyeball in the back of her head. Meanwhile, Gunn finds out from his former gang members that rogue cops are beating up neighborhood people who are on the streets after dark. Enter Anne again with her homeless shelter, and the police officers attack her place specifically. Meanwhile, Angel is again with Kate, and he visits the shelter to find out for himself if these officers are as bad as everyone says they are. The visual metaphor is interesting: while Wesley and the gang fight from the inside of the shelter, Angel remains on the outside, looking in and trying to do things his way. When Wesley, who believes the officers are good, shows up to try to talk one out of threatening Gunn, he is shot and almost dies. But when Gunn and Cordelia work together to insure that won't happen, the threesome become a full-fledged team. A couple of nitpicks with this episode, however: when Anne sees Cordelia and Wesley for the first time, she doesn't recognize them, even though they were both on the tape that played at the charity event a couple of episodes earlier. And when a tough guy shows up, she just lets him in so that there's no trouble. Does she feel the same way about rapists? What kind of shelter allows the evil inside?

2.15 Reprise (Part One)

Original air date: February 20, 2001
Written by: Tim Minear
Directed by: James Whitmore, Jr.
Guest cast: Brigid Brannagh (Virginia), Gerry Becker (Nathan Reed), Thomas Kopache (Denver), David Fury (First Worshiper), Kevin Fry (Skilosh Demon)

As Wolfram & Hart come under their 75-year review, Angel discovers a ring that can take him to Hell. Meanwhile, Kate loses her job and Cordelia follows up on a non-paying customer.

An amazing episode that brings everything this season to a head, with nearly everyone seeming to give up. Angel stops trying to be nice to the gang (not that he was making great strides with that, anyway) and storms into their office, rude and uncaring, to get what he needs. Virginia, who has been dating Wesley since "Guise Will Be Guise," gives up on the relationship because she can't be with someone in such a dangerous profession (wasn't her dad a wizard?). Meanwhile, the police department, fed up with Kate chasing demons and monsters, forces her to turn in her badge. Furious with herself that she's let down her father, she stops trying to live up to his standards and begins drinking herself to death. Angel gives up on everything, discovering a way to get to Hell and taking it. Jumping on an elevator to Hell with Holland (just because you're dead doesn't mean you're not still contractually obligated to Wolfram & Hart, apparently), he discovers a painful, awful truth, one that will change his entire outlook on his mission and his personal quest. Only Cordelia refuses to give up. Facing an unpaid bill for a job well done (remember that girl with the eye in her skull in the last episode?), Cordy rushes over to the client's place in the middle of the night when promised the payment, not realizing she's heading to her certain doom. "Reprise" is a great climactic episode that builds up to such a height that it can't help but come crashing down. The episode ends with a familiar scene: Angel has sex with Darla, and in the middle of the night sits bolt upright, gasping. Uh-oh.

2.16 Epiphany (Part Two)

Original air date: February 27, 2001
Written by: Tim Minear
Directed by: Thomas J. Wright
Guest cast: Marie Chambers (Mother), Kevin Fry (Skilosh Demon)

Angel has a sudden moment of clarity where he realizes the error of his ways and the long road he'll have to take to get back to where he was.

Well, someone's been reading their James Joyce. Before the 20th century, the word "Epiphany" was used in a Christian context only, to refer to the moment when Christ revealed himself to the Magi. But Irish novelist Joyce changed that when he developed the literary epiphany, a moment of absolute knowledge that suddenly comes in a flash of recognition, usually during an otherwise normal circumstance. One of the most famous literary epiphanies occurs in Joyce's *Portrait of the Artist as a Young Man*, where Stephen Dedalus sees a woman standing in water, holding her skirts up, and is suddenly filled with such a joy he can hardly contain himself. Similarly, in "Epiphany," Angel sleeps with Darla and when it doesn't bring about the "moment of true happiness" that occurred with Buffy, he realizes he's not all evil, he doesn't belong with Darla, and his soul can be saved (when he crawls out on the balcony in pain while the rain whips at him, it's a little much, though, and nothing like what an epiphany should be). He rushes to try to save Kate from committing suicide, the Wheelèd One from being killed, and Cordelia from being, um, implanted. Lindsey appears to have had an epiphany of his own, as he suddenly shows up dressed like the poor redneck he always was, in his Sanford and Son truck, and beats the crap out of Angel. Darla has left town, and Lindsey realizes he's not the lawyer he pretends to be, he's a hick from the wrong side of the tracks and he needs to embrace that. Angel returns to the fold, but in a new capacity.

2.17 Disharmony

Original air date: April 17, 2001
Written by: David Fury

Directed by: Fred Keller
Guest cast: Mercedes McNab (Harmony), Alyson Hannigan (Willow), Pat Healy (Doug Saunders)

Harmony shows up in Los Angeles and immediately hooks up with her old pal Cordelia, who doesn't know that Harmony's a vampire.

"Disharmony" is a really funny, tongue-in-cheek episode that opens with one of David Boreanaz's best lines — "Man, atonement's a bitch" — and makes fun of flighty high school friendships, misunderstandings, and motivational speakers (hey, that last one is too easy!). Harmony comes back into Cordelia's life, and all the leaps and bounds in Cordy's maturity seem to take a backseat when she meets her vacuous former buddy. When Harmony comes into her room and admits she's changed, Cordelia mistakes her for a lesbian and is absolutely hilarious. Willow, who seems to be the Sunnydale contact for Angel Investigations, tells Cordelia what Harmony meant, prompting one of the best Cordelia gaffes on the show: "Harmony's a vampire? I thought she was a great big lesbo! . . . Oh, yeah, really? That's great . . . good for you!" When Angel and Wesley catch on, they try to stake her, but Cordelia won't let them. It's inter-

Mercedes McNab, who plays Harmony, the dopiest vampire in the lair

esting that after Harmony treated her so terribly in "The Wish" — pretty much the last time they had any contact — Cordelia is so quick to forgive her, whereas with Angel she makes it clear that they're not friends and he'll have to try very hard to regain her trust. Clearly, Angel means more to her than Harmony. The motivational speaker is very funny, telling the vampires how they can get ahead in the world by creating an army of like demons, while contributing to the "food bank." At the end of the episode, we discover that Cordelia's emotions may not run as deeply as we thought. No matter how far from Sunnydale she is, she'll always have a little Harmony in her.

2.18 Dead End

Original air date: April 24, 2001
Written by: David Greenwalt
Directed by: James A. Contner
Guest cast: Gerry Becker (Nathan Reed), Michael Dempsey (Irv Kraigle), Mik Scriba (Parole Officer), Pete Gardener (Joseph Kramer), Stephanie Hash (Wife), Steven De-Relian (Bradley Scott)

CHRISTINA RADISH

Christian Kane, who plays the evil, sad, and slightly insane Lindsay McDonald

Lindsey is fitted with a human hand that has a mind of its own, and Cordy has a graphic vision that's tied to Lindsey's surgery.

One thing about those epiphanies — they tend to leave one with a new sense of humor. In the last episode and all those following, Angel is less broody and more giddy. He jokes around with the gang, plays a practical joke on Lindsey, and cracks jokes about who he used to be. Although it's fun at first, after a while one longs for the old Angel from season one. "Dead End" was a very eerie episode with an almost grotesque conclusion, and it marks the last appearance of Christian Kane. Kane, who is a singer in L.A. when he's not acting, gets a chance before he goes to show off his vocal talents (not to mention his guitar-playing) and when the Host and Cordelia — and even Gunn — start fawning endlessly over him, I half expected an ad to pop up letting us know where Christian Kane would be appearing next. It was a nice touch, but gratuitous. He puts in a great final performance, ranting and raging all over the screen, and the very graphic vision is a portent of things to come. It seems the main reason Doyle was able to stomach the visions was because of his demon half. Cordelia is a human being, and the visions are beginning to take their toll on her.

2.19 Belonging

Original air date:	May 1, 2001
Written by:	Shawn Ryan
Directed by:	Turi Meyer
Guest cast:	Jarrod Crawford (Rondell), Darris Love (George), Brody Hutzler (Landok), Kevin Otto (Seth), Lynne Maclean (Claire)

When a beast suddenly appears in Caritas through a portal, the Host begs Angel Investigations to kill it, and tells them about his home, where the beast came from.

"Belonging" is the first of an amazing four-episode arc centering on Pylea, the world where the Host used to live, where things are black and white, all champions or slaves, with no art or music. The Host is a little more nervous than usual when the beast comes through the portal, and it's Cordelia's vision of a girl opening a portal in a library that forces the team to hunt down the beast. Meanwhile, each member of the team is having doubts about who they are and the paths they've chosen. Gunn fights his former gang, which loses a member because their strength is dwindling without him. Wesley calls his father to tell him he's now in charge, only to be reminded of how many times he's screwed up before (ah, yet another unpleasant father on *Buffy* and *Angel*). Cordelia gets a gig on a commercial, but the director treats her like dirt, telling her she doesn't make him want to sleep with her and calling her "princess" (in her skimpy outfit, there isn't a mark on her stomach, despite being impaled by a massive spike in "Lover's Walk"). Angel is having problems asking Wesley for instructions when he's so used to giving them. And the Host — whom we discover is actually Krevlornswath of the Deathwok Clan (Lorne for short) — is dealing with issues of inferiority that had forced him to leave Pylea in the first place. All these problems come together when the gang accidentally opens another portal, bringing forth Landok from Pylea, and in order to send him back they must figure out how to open yet another portal. Unfortunately, things don't go as well as they'd hoped, and they will all be forced to face their personal demons in a different land.

2.20 Over the Rainbow (Part One)

Original air date:	May 8, 2001
Written by:	Mere Smith
Directed by:	Fred Keller
Guest cast:	Persia White (Aggie), Susan Blommaert (Vakma), Michael Phenicie (Silas), Daniel Dae Kim (Gavin Parks), Brian Tahash (Constable), Drew Wicks (Blix), William Newman (Old Demon Man)

Cordelia ends up in Pylea and is turned into a slave, and the others try to figure out how they can rescue her.

The title of this episode is borrowed from the 1939 film *The Wizard of Oz*, and it's appropriate — we're not in Kansas anymore. Cordelia is immediately captured and called a "cow," and she meets Fred, the girl in her vision who had disappeared from the library five years earlier. Unfortunately for her, she has a vision in the middle of her chores and the villagers believe she is cursed. Meanwhile, Angel is desperate to get to her, because he believes he's worked so hard to earn her trust and get her back into his life, and he can't deal with not having her with him now. But it's Lorne who must make it through the biggest emotional conundrum in this episode: does he return home to Pylea and face his dreadful past, or stay in L.A. and continue trying to forget where he came from? Gunn faces the

CHRISTINA RADISH

The adorable Andy Hallett, who looks very different from his character, The Host

opposite problem; unlike Lorne, he longs to get back to his roots and believes his new life is holding him back. The scene where the men all finally make it to Pylea is hilarious, as Angel discovers the sun there is different than the earth's sun — "Can everyone just notice how much fire I'm not on?" — while Lorne finds out that sometimes you just can't go home, and Wesley and Gunn realize that humans aren't exactly welcome in Pylea.

2.21 Through the Looking Glass (Part Two)

Original air date:	May 15, 2001
Written and directed by:	Tim Minear
Guest cast:	Mark Lutz (Groosalugg), Tom McCleister (Lorne's mother), Michael Phenicie (Silas), Brody Hutzler (Landok), Brian Tahash (Constable), Adoni Maropis (Rebel Leader), Andrew Parks (Priest #1), Joss Whedon (Numfar)

Cordelia has been made the princess of Pylea, while Angel finds Fred and rescues her, before becoming a demon that she'll need rescuing from.

Be careful what you wish for, yadda yadda yadda. In "Through the Looking Glass," everyone is subverted — they discover that when they finally get what they thought they wanted, it wasn't what they'd expected. The episode title is taken from Lewis Carroll's classic sequel to *Alice's Adventures in Wonderland*, where Alice steps through a mirror and everything in the Looking Glass world is the opposite of what it should be. People and institutions appear to be the same, but on closer inspection are the mirror versions of what she is used to. Similarly, Cordelia, who two episodes ago was mocked by a director and called "princess" in a sneering tone, now becomes a princess (wearing only a little more clothing than on the commercial). However, she'll soon discover that her situation is only slightly different than it was in her world; here she is still directed by a group of monks who despise her and use her to achieve their own ends. And Angel, who thought he loved this world because he seemed more human than vampire, discovers there's a dark side to the world, and to him. Lorne explained in "Over the Rainbow" that in Pylea everything is black and white; there is no gray. Therefore, Angel can't be both a demon and a human at the same time as he is on earth so he's a human at first, and then pure demon. Fred, who was brilliant in her world, is a raving lunatic in Pylea, constantly scrawling on the wall of a cave, trying to convince herself she's not dead yet. Wesley is finally the undisputed leader, and he realizes that Wolfram & Hart are everywhere, even in Pylea. They're not just a law firm, as Holland suggested in "Reprise," but a metaphor for pure evil. As Cordelia prepares herself to com-shuck with the Groosalugg, she's faced with a horrible surprise, and one of the most shocking endings on *Angel*.

However, this episode also contains the single funniest moment on either *Buffy* or *Angel*: Numfar's dance of joy. Similar to Monty Python's "Ministry of Silly Walks" sketch, it's made even funnier because it's going on in the background. And if you saw it and thought, "Now, that seems like something Joss Whedon had a hand in," you'd be right — Numfar *is* Joss Whedon. The night the episode first aired, writer Tim Minear posted the following at the Bronze: "The Dance of Joy and Honor both came from Joss. He did it in the room when we were breaking the story, and it was too brilliant to entrust into any other hands, so I asked if he'd do it in my episode — and sure enough, he did. It took a moment for the cast to even recognize him, as he was in full demon makeup. But then they noticed that I was letting an extra sit in my chair and saying nothing . . . the only extra on the set who could fire me!" A sidesplitting series highlight.

2.22 There's No Place Like Plrtz Glrb (Part Three)

Original air date:	May 22, 2001
Written and directed by:	David Greenwalt
Guest cast:	Mark Lutz (Groosalugg), Tom McCleister (Lorne's Mother), Michael Phenicie (Silas), Brody Hutzler (Landok), Lee Rehmerman (Second Rebel Leader), Andrew Parks (Priest #1)

When Angel finds out that Cordelia is with the Groosalugg, he's determined to fight it to save her. Meanwhile, Wesley has found a rebel army that he leads in storming the castle.

A great season ender (even if many people, having just seen "The Gift," taped it to watch later when they were able to think clearly again). Cordelia must try to put Lorne back together again, while Angel faces the truth about his demon self while talking with Wesley and Fred. As on *Buffy*, there are moments that foreshadow certain storylines for season three: Fred moons over Angel and tells him the others might judge him but she wouldn't; Angel looks disappointed when Cordelia says she doesn't love him, she loves the Groosalugg; Cordelia uses a sword, which Angel will teach her more about later. Wesley finally makes an effective leader, learning the first rule about battle — some people will get killed, and you try to allow the least number of casualties, not to prevent casualties altogether. The priests become more powerful, but not more powerful than the gang when they're finally together. Once again, we see that apart, everyone flounders with their personal demons and self-doubt, but when they're together, things get done right. The episode had a great ending: everyone realized that while things seemed like fun for a while in Pylea, eventually everyone ends up feeling like Lorne, that L.A. is a place for all of them because no one belongs there. But they realize just as quickly that things aren't all peaches at home, either. Especially when they return and a sorrowful-looking Willow is waiting there for them. . . .

Season Three

SEPTEMBER 2001 • MAY 2002

Recurring characters in season three: Keith Szarabajka (Daniel Holtz), Laurel Holloman (Justine Cooper), Daniel Dae Kim (Gavin Park), Jack Conley (Sahjhan), John Rubinstein (Linwood Murrow), Mark Lutz (Groosalugg)

3.1 Heartthrob

Original air date:	September 24, 2001
Written and directed by:	David Greenwalt

Guest cast: Ron Melendez (James), Kate Norby (Elisabeth), Matthew James (Merl), Koji Kataoka (Pilgrim), Sam Littlefield (Young Man Hostage), Dalila Brown-Geiger (Sandy), Christian Hastings (Vamp #1), Bob Fimiani (Codger Demon), Robert Madrid (Rough Man), Bob Morrisey (Dr. Gregson)

When Angel kills a vampire he knew in the 18th century, her boyfriend hunts him down and opens some emotional wounds.

It's been three months since the events of season two, and the gang is having a tough time moving on. Cordelia pines for Pylea, where she had been worshiped, Fred has created a new cave for herself that she refuses to leave, and Angel is trying to deal with the loss of . . . "the B-word" by going to a monastery. But the theme of the episode was two-fold: what it's like to have pain in your heart, and how to move on from things. As will happen for the rest of this incredible season, we will flash back in time to when Angel and Darla were being hunted by Daniel Holtz, a vampire hunter first mentioned by name in "The Trial," and we will see how Angel's actions in the past have dictated what will happen to him in the present. While Angel has to deal with an angry, vengeful vampire in this episode, his bigger battle is with himself. Will he be able to move on from Buffy's death? And if so, will he betray her by doing so? The theme cleverly touches on the fact that *Buffy* and *Angel* are now on different networks and the fledgling spin-off must find its own way now, without relying on she-who-must-not-be-named. Meanwhile, Fred must overcome her agoraphobia and pull herself out of her new prison, Cordelia is dealing with her mind-numbing headaches . . . and Wesley has a fine new haircut that makes him more of a heartthrob himself. And, of course, there's the shocking ending, where we discover that Darla might have a little future of her own soon. "Heartthrob" was an excellent episode, even if it had one niggling inconsistency: Angel is unable to enter Fred's room, yet as he stated in season two and will say again in "Benediction," a vampire can enter a hotel room because it's public accommodation (a feeble addition to the myth, but one with which they need to stay consistent).

3.2 That Vision Thing

Original air date: October 1, 2001
Written by: Jeffrey Bell
Directed by: Bill Norton
Guest cast: Frank "Sotonoma" Salsedo (Shaman), David Denman (Skip), Mitchell Gibney (Innocuous Man), Alice Lo (Old Chinese Woman), Kal Penn (Young Man in Fez), Justin Shilton (Young Man), Ken Takemoto (Old Chinese Man), Bob Sattler (Masked Man)

Cordelia's visions begin leaving physical marks on her body, and Angel vows to find out what's going on.

A very exciting episode right up to its graphic conclusion, "That Vision Thing" featured a storyline the writers had been leading up to all of last season. Cordelia has been suffering

---

A Buffy/Angel Timeline

879 — Anya becomes a demon.

c. 1000 — The Master becomes a vampire.

1609 — The Master visits a dying Darla and makes her a vampire.

1727 — Liam is born.

1753 — Darla turns Liam into a vampire, Angelus, and he kills his family.

1760 — Darla introduces Angelus to the Master, but the meeting doesn't go well.

1764 — Angelus and Darla kill Daniel Holtz's family in York, England.

1765 — In France, Holtz's army traps Darla and Angelus in a barn, but Darla hits Angelus over the head and escapes on a horse.

1767 — With vampires James and Elizabeth, Angelus and Darla are surrounded by Holtz's men in Marseilles, France, but they escape.

1771 — Holtz captures Angelus in Rome with the help of a monsignor and begins to torture him, but Darla saves Angelus and shoots Holtz with an arrow.

1773 — The time traveler Sahjhan visits Holtz and makes a deal with him to take him to 2001 where he can kill Darla and Angelus.

1800 — Angelus turns Penn into a vampire, and Penn becomes his protégé.

1838 — Angelus kills a young man named Daniel in Dublin, Ireland.

1860 — Angelus stalks Drusilla, making her crazy by killing her family, and ultimately sires her.

1880 — William is rejected by Cecily, and Drusilla finds him and sires him.

1898 — Darla kidnaps a gypsy girl and Angelus kills her, and the gypsies place a curse on him. Spike, Dru, and Darla massacre everyone in the camp.

1899 — The town of Sunnydale is officially established.

1900 — Spike, Darla, and Dru are in China during the Boxer Rebellion, and Spike kills his first Slayer. Angel rejoins them and tries to convince Darla he's changed, but she knows he's lying.

1914 — Anya curses a man named Stewart Burns in Chicago, and it will come back to haunt her.

1920 — Angel is in Juarez, Mexico, with Boone.

1930s — Angel is in Montana during the Depression.

1952 — Angel is staying at the Hyperion hotel when he rediscovers why he hates humans.

1969 — Spike attends Woodstock and kills a flower child.

1977 — Spike kills his second Slayer in New York City.

1981 — Buffy is born.

1989 — Spike and Dru are in Prague and she is attacked by an angry mob.

1996 — Whistler finds Angel in an alleyway in New York City, sucking blood from rats. Buffy is approached by Merrick to become a Slayer, and ends up burning down her school gym.

1997 — Buffy and her mom move to Sunnydale.

---

migraines and worse as the visions begin to take their toll, but she quietly endures them and refuses to let the others know how serious they've become. As far as she's concerned, she's finally part of a team where she's not a hindrance or the screaming girl who always gets kidnapped, as she was in Sunnydale. Without her powers, she's nothing more than the flighty Cordelia she was in the first season of *Angel*, sitting around the office answering phones and buying doughnuts. But in this episode, she fears for her life for the first time, terrified that the powers that be are trying to kill her for reasons she can't understand. Meanwhile, Angel is forced to sacrifice the greater good for someone who has become extremely important to him. The scene where he meets Skip — an absolutely brilliant character — is very funny, as they chitchat about commuting to work while standing around in a hell dimension. But what Angel does in the end isn't so funny, and his actions will have terrible consequences. And over at Wolfram & Hart, the anti-Cordelia, Lilah, is waging a war with Gavin Park, who will try to come after Angel "in his own way."

3.3 That Old Gang of Mine

Original air date:	October 8, 2001
Written by:	Tim Minear
Directed by:	Fred Keller
Guest cast:	Jarrod Crawford (Rondell), Matthew James (Merl), Khalil Kain (Gio), Heidi Marnhout (Fury #1), An Le (Fury #2), Madison Gray (Fury #3), Josh Kayne (Cowering Demon), Sam Ayers (Tough Guy Demon), Giancarlo Carimona (Gang Kid), Steve Niel (Huge & Horrible)

When harmless demons around L.A. are found dead, Gunn worries it could be the work of his former gang members.

COURTESY RISING STARS ENTERPRISES

Jarrod Crawford,
a.k.a. Gunn's friend Rondell

J. August Richards is a terrific actor, and it's great to see episodes that give us further insight into his intriguing character, although this one fell a little flat. Rehashing a plot we already covered in "The Thin Dead Line," Gunn is again taunted by his former gang, including a newcomer named Gio who sees Gunn as a sellout and traitor. But while in "The Thin Dead Line" Gunn was torn between his past and his present, here the lines are more clearly drawn. His gang have lost their ability to fight what's wrong, and instead paint every demon with the same brush. The episode brings up an interesting point that is later discussed in "Villains" on *Buffy*: what is worse, a human being who is a murderer, or a demon who is completely harmless? Why is it okay to slaughter demons just because they're demons, but human beings are off-limits no matter what they do? It's an interesting argument, and one played here for irony, since Gio's remark to Gunn that he's a "demon lover" eerily echoes racist remarks that have probably been used against the street gang. This episode is important for the evolution of Gunn's character, and the destruction — again — of Caritas.

3.4 Carpe Noctem

Original air date:	October 15, 2001
Written by:	Scott Murphy

Directed by: James A. Contner
Guest cast: Rance Howard (Marcus Roscoe), Paul Benjamin (Fellow Resident), Steven W. Bailey (Ryan), Marc Brett (Health Club Man), Paul Logan (Woody), Misty Louwagie (Christina), Lauren Reina (Escort #1), Magdalena Zielinska (Escort #2)

An elderly man switches bodies with Angel, who must find a way to contact his friends before succumbing to the ravages of aging.

"Carpe Noctem" was a lot of fun, if only to see David Boreanaz playing a rude, womanizing sex fiend. After being called a eunuch by Cordelia, Angel is tossed into the body of an elderly man, where he essentially *does* become a eunuch while Marcus goes wild with Angel's body. Meanwhile, Fred has fallen in love with Angel, believing him to be her white knight that has saved her from a life of torture and imprisonment. When Cordelia tells Marcus-in-Angel's-body that he must tell Fred there can be no office romances, the ensuing scene displaying a *Three's Company* confusion is hilarious. Marcus believes Fred is a man and this Angel guy must have been gay (and the leather pants don't help much). Marcus is played by Rance Howard, who is Ron Howard's father (his late wife, Jean Speegle Howard, played the real Nathalie French in "Teacher's Pet" on *Buffy*). The episode had its sad moments as well, when Fred catches "Angel" in a surprising moment and is completely devastated. The episode showed how easy it is to succumb to temptation, and how difficult it must be for Angel day after day to resist letting the demon in him come out — not just the vampire, but the sexually active man. And discovering that Buffy is alive at the end of the episode (which corresponded with Buffy hearing from him in "Flooded") will definitely send his world into a tailspin.

3.5 Fredless

Original air date: October 22, 2001
Written by: Mere Smith
Directed by: Marita Grabiak
Guest cast: Gray Grubbs (Roger Burkle), Jennifer Griffin (Trish Burkle)

Fred's parents show up in L.A. and she tries to evade them, hoping they won't take her home with them.

"Fredless" featured Amy Acker's best performance to date. Up to this point she's been a stuttering mass of nerves, but in this episode she showed a new side of her character. We discover that Fred has convinced herself her stint in Pylea never happened, and that it was all a figment of her imagination that is still playing out as a fairy tale in her head. She tries to stay away from her parents because she doesn't want to know the truth — that if they can see her, all of her suffering was real, and she doesn't want to cope with that reality. The Burkles, who show up on the doorstep of the Hyperion like Rooster and Lily in *Annie*, were probably the first set of positive parents we've seen on either *Buffy* or *Angel*. They are a breath of fresh Texas air in our dark L.A. show (although their muttering about "calling

CHRISTINA RADISH

Our dear Fred

them in sooner than we think" was strange, and never explained). The episode was very funny at parts, including Cordy's even better-than-usual barbs, increased flirtiness between her and Angel, Fred singing "Row, Row, Row Your Boat" to the Host and nearly knocking him over, and Angel freaking out in a sewer because his cellphone went off. (Though that moment certainly begs the question, how come that phone *never* rings or keeps a signal aboveground, yet deep in the sewers he has no problem talking on it?) By the end of "Fredless," Fred has become a firm member of the gang, and she literally erases the remnants of her fairytale from her life in a beautiful final scene, with the help of her new friends.

3.6 Billy

Original air date: October 29, 2001
Written by: Tim Minear, Jeffrey Bell
Directed by: David Grossman

Guest cast: Justin Shilton (Billy Blim), Richard Livingston (Congressman Blim), Jeniffer Brooke (Clerk), Gwen McGee (Detective), Cheri Rae Russell (Female Officer), Kristoffer Polaha (Dylan), Rey Gallegos (Sanchez), Joy Lang (Amber), Timothy McNeil (Cab Driver), Charlie Parker (Guy)

The gang must take action when Billy, the man Angel freed from a hell dimension, begins causing men to hate women.

"Billy" was a very creepy episode, showing us a new — and scary — side of Wesley, while developing Cordelia's character even further. One of the best aspects of *Angel* is the transformation Cordy has undergone. Throughout season three, you can't help but recall the über-bitch she used to be in Sunnydale, and compare that to the incredible woman she has become. "Billy" explores the helplessness of women and the men who prey on it. The show opens with Angel teaching Cordelia how to swordfight so she can defend herself. Not only is she a quick study, but soon she's overpowering him when he least expects it. (Though how many times must Cordy remind Angel that someday she might have to kill *him*? I mean, what's that doing to the guy's self-esteem?) Billy Blim, who Angel had freed in "That Vision Thing," reappears and begins wreaking havoc by causing men to become misogynist psycho-killers. Throughout the episode, we see Cordelia come to terms with the fact that Billy is roaming free so she could be saved, and Lilah discovers what helplessness is herself. Will the women continue to be helpless, or can they rely on their own strength to get them out of their predicaments? Meanwhile, Wesley succumbs to Billy's powers at the Hyperion, and the ensuing terror between him and Fred is suspenseful and frightening: it definitely borrows from the film *The Shining*, with Wesley hunting Fred through the hotel corridors, wielding an ax. All work and no play might make Wes a dull boy, but in the end he's left with his own personal horror — that he actually possesses within himself the power to be brutal and cold, just like the father he tried so desperately to please. His guilt at what he was able to become will fester throughout the season, until he makes the biggest mistake of his life.

3.7 Offspring

Original air date: November 5, 2001
Written by: David Greenwalt
Directed by: Turi Meyer
Guest cast: Steve Tom (Stephen Mills), Heidi Marnhout (Fury #1), An Le (Fury #2), Madison Gray (Fury #3), Robert Peters (Arney), Sergio Premoli (Monsignor), Van Epperson (Bus Driver), Peyton and Christian Miller (Johnny), Kathleen McMartin (Mom), Theresa Arrison (Johnny's Mom)

Darla arrives in L.A. and announces to Angel that he's about to be a father, causing disappointment in Cordelia and worry in Wesley.

A fantastic episode that sets in motion everything else that will happen in season three. "Offspring" gives us another flashback to the 18th century, where Holtz was chasing Angelus, and Darla was intent on causing Holtz more pain and misery. In the present, Darla returns to Angel, looking very pregnant, which shocks and hurts Cordelia. Angel had earlier re-assured Cordelia that nothing had happened between him and Darla, and after he's spent the last several months regaining Cordy's trust, it's gone in an instant when she realizes he's betrayed her. This episode is also when Angel first discovers he might have feelings for Cordy, and while she seems oblivious to the fact that she feels the same way, there is definitely a chemistry between them. The contrast between his relationship with Darla in the past — where they banded together on a destructive killing spree across Europe and didn't love each other so much as enjoy mutual emotional torture — and his healthier, more equal and loving relationship with Cordelia shows how far Angel has come. But a visit from his lover of the past — carrying their child of the future — forces his worlds to collide. While Angel marvels at the fact that he might actually have a child, Wesley stands back from the action, asking the more technical questions. What could the child be? How could two vampires have possibly created a living thing? Could this child be the destructive force predicted in the Nyazian scrolls? When Wesley begins to find answers, everything falls apart. What no one counted on, of course, was the reappearance of Angel's arch-nemesis. The last few minutes of this episode are amazing.

3.8 Quickening

Original air date:	November 12, 2001
Written by:	Jeffrey Bell
Directed by:	Skip Schoolnik
Guest cast:	Jose Yenque (Vampire Leader), Matt Casper (Cyril), Bronwen Bonner-Davies (Caroline), Michael Robert Brandon (Psychic), William Ostrander (Captain), Kasha Kropinski (Sarah), John Durbin (Dr. Fetvanovich), Angelo Surmelis (Tech Guy)

The gang try to figure out what they will do when Darla's baby is born, and Angel's old enemy is in town to deliver some vengeance.

The good just keeps getting better. "Quickening" is like part two of "Offspring," with "Lullaby" being part three. Each episode takes place immediately after the one before it, building up the suspense. In fact, if you look at all the episodes from this point on and mark them on a calendar, the rest of the season takes place over about a month. "Offspring" brings together all the elements of Angel's life and current predicament: Darla, the baby, the gang, Holtz, and Wolfram & Hart. Darla wants to get rid of the baby, the gang ponders how to kill it when it's born, Holtz doesn't realize the baby exists, and Wolfram & Hart want to dissect both it and Darla (and in this episode, Lilah gets her hands on the scrolls that Wesley has been working so hard to interpret). For anyone who follows that other sci-fi show featuring a butt-kicking gal, a very similar storyline occurred in *Xena: Warrior Princess* when Xena wanted to kill Gabrielle's child and the Greek gods tried to destroy Xena's daughter. On *Angel*, both those elements come together. Angel wants to believe that the child will be fine, while his friends are convinced it's an evil thing that could destroy them. Just as he did in "That Vision Thing," Angel lets his heart get in the way, opting to save someone close to him and possibly sacrifice the greater good in the process. Meanwhile, Holtz gets caught up on the last 127 years he's missed, with the help of Sahjhan, the time traveler that brought him there, but he's so intent on killing Angel and Darla that he doesn't care about anything else happening around him. The parallel is perfect: Angelus killed Holtz's wife and children, and Holtz is about to kill the father. They're both about to get a surprise.

Of course, the episode wasn't completely serious. The comic highlight of "Quickening" was the answering-machine message when Cyril calls his Master: "[Female voice] Hi, you've reached the Tittles. We can't come to the phone right now. If you want to leave a message for Christine, press one. [Male voice] For Bentley, press two. [Dark, deep voice] Or to speak to or worship Master Tarfall, Underlord of pain, press three." It's moments like this, within a darker and more serious episode, that set *Buffy* and *Angel* apart from all other shows.

3.9 Lullaby

Original air date:	November 19, 2001
Written and directed by:	Tim Minear
Guest cast:	Jim Ortlieb (Scroll Translator), Robert Peters (Arney), Bronwen Bonner-Davies (Caroline), Kasha Kropinski (Sarah)

As the evil forces close in on Darla and Angel discovers that Holtz is back, Darla prepares to give birth to the baby.

Wow. Each episode in this arc is better than the one before it. "Lullaby" explores the pain of losing a child and what it's like to be a parent. Once again we go back to the 18th century, and just when the viewer is hoping Angel will drive a stake through Holtz, we see what it was like for him to come home and discover that not only did Darla and Angelus massacre his family, but they turned his daughter into a vampire. We see the pain and rage that Holtz felt, and we sympathize with him entirely. He was tortured in the way that Angelus loved to torture people; killing just wasn't satisfying enough. In the present, Darla is shocked to discover that she loves the child inside her, and for the first time she doesn't want to get rid of it. But, she doesn't want to give birth to it either, because she knows once the baby's soul has left her body, she'll be the same ruthless, soulless creature she was before. As Caritas — ironically, the bar's name is Latin for "mercy" — blows to bits (again) and Holtz comes face-to-face with the two vampires he despises more than any other, the viewers are treated with one of the most incredible sequences ever seen on *Angel*. Darla discovers what a mother is and acts accordingly, and Holtz devises a new plan that will cause Angel infinitely more pain than death. A piece of trivia: John Rubinstein, who plays Linwood Murrow at Wolfram & Hart, is the son of famous piano virtuoso Artur Rubinstein, and is a composer in his own right.

3.10 Dad

Original air date:	December 10, 2001
Written by:	David H. Goodman
Directed by:	Fred Keller
Guest cast:	Kira Tirimako (Doctor), Stephanie Courtney (Gwen)

Angel becomes fiercely protective of his newborn son as demons move in to try and kill the infant. Meanwhile, Holtz recruits a woman for his new gang of warriors.

After the last three episodes built to such a stunning conclusion, it's only natural that this episode seems a little slower and not as enjoyable. Not only that, but we have to listen to a 240-year-old vampire making baby talk with his son, and the goo-goo's and babba's, funny for about two minutes, are sickening by the end of the show. I prefer my Angel to be broody, thank you. "Dad" is where the gang finds out that raising a baby who plays an important part in an ancient prophecy isn't as easy as it might seem. Web sites have gone up offering rewards for his capture; biker demons have shown up to kill the baby; Wolfram & Hart has installed cameras throughout the Hyperion to watch the goings-on . . . and boy, can that kid fill a diaper. Angel won't let anyone near the baby, instead developing a "serious mama bear vibe," as Lorne observes. While Wesley tries to decipher the text to discover exactly what the child's part in the prophecy will be, Angel must learn to trust his friends and understand that raising a baby is a group effort. One nitpick, though: how is it that Lorne immediately hears the hum of the Wolfram & Hart cameras, but Angel's highly attuned vampire hearing never picked up on it?

3.11 Birthday

Original air date:	January 14, 2002
Written by:	Mere Smith
Directed by:	Michael Grossman
Guest cast:	David Denman (Skip), Patrick Breen (Nev), Max Baker (Hyperion Clerk), Heather Weeks (Tammy), Aimee Garcia (Cynthia)

When Cordelia receives a powerful vision that puts her in a coma, she has an out-of-body experience where she's told that she has to give up the visions or she'll die.

Another excellent episode from Mere Smith. Like "The Wish" on *Buffy*, we're given a what-if scenario that shows what could have happened if Cordelia hadn't met up with Angel at the party in "City Of." It also allows Cordelia to take yet another step away from the Cordy of Sunnydale and become more mature. For the first time in her life, she fits into a group of real, genuine people, not the phony clique she had in high school. She feels like they care about her, and as she matures, she sees her personal growth reflected back through the admiration of those around her. Because of this, she is reluctant to give up the visions, even when Skip (it was great to see him back again) shows her graphically what could happen if she doesn't. It's only when she overhears Angel telling the conduits Cordy is nothing more than a flighty rich girl, that she steps back aghast and chooses a life of fame over goodwill. (The theme song to her TV show, *Cordy!* is sung by *Buffy* executive producer Marti Noxon.) We soon discover that despite the powers that be saying that Doyle's "parting gift" was a mistake, perhaps it was fated after all. Meanwhile, with the help of dear Dennis, the rest of the gang discovers that Cordelia has been keeping medical records, medications, and her condition a secret from them, and she'll need to build up some trust with them again. Watch for Wesley's reference to "Parting Gift."

The charismatic one

3.12 Provider

Original air date:	January 21, 2002
Written by:	Scott Murphy
Directed by:	Michael Grossman
Guest cast:	Jeffrey Dean Morgan (Sam Ryan), Eric Bruskotter (Brian), Sunny Mabrey (Allison), Tony Pasqualini (Harlan Elster), Alan Henry Brown (Head Nahdrah), David Ramirez (Pizza Chef), Brett Wagner (Nahdrah Prince), Benjamin Benitez (Tattoo Vamp #2)

In an attempt to boost business and raise money for the new Connor Fund, Angel instructs the gang to take on any case, and nearly gets them all hurt.

Like "Dad," this episode had its funny moments but was pretty much filler. Angel begins to move away from his path of atonement and toward his new path, a college fund for his son Connor. As Wesley and Gunn try to chase off one girl's zombie stalker boyfriend while Fred and Lorne try to help out the Nahdrahs by deciphering their puzzle and Cordelia plays babysitter, Angel clears out a vampire nest for a guy who can't exactly pay up. Angel's flip attitude toward the guy — "You're a true champion!" "Yeah, whatever" — is hilarious, but the rest of the episode is taken up with more of Connor crying while Wes and Gunn fawn over Fred. It's interesting how one episode ago there were hundreds of demons after Connor, and now everyone just leaves him in the hotel with Cordelia. Meanwhile, over in vengeance land, Holtz is teaching his new protégé, Justine, a thing or two about obeying orders and fighting demons. At first it appeared as though he was playing Merrick to her Buffy, but after this episode there are no further scenes in cemeteries.

3.13 Waiting in the Wings

Original air date:	February 4, 2002
Written and directed by:	Joss Whedon
Guest cast:	Mark Harelik (Count Kurskov), Summer Glau (Prima Ballerina), Thomas Crawford (Manager), Don Tiffany (Security Guard)

The spirits of two lovers take over Angel and Cordelia at the opera, causing them to act out a love scene that happened over 100 years before.

A beautifully directed episode by the one and only Joss Whedon, "Waiting in the Wings" incorporated lush music, gorgeous costumes, and some of the finest acting we've seen yet. Normally that wouldn't be a surprise coming from the master, but on *Angel*, Whedon's work sometimes falls flat. Borrowing from the second season *Buffy* episode "I Only Have Eyes for You," Joss uses the concept of two present-day people succumbing to the will of former lovers in trouble. He aptly uses *Giselle* as the ballet backdrop for the story. In *Giselle*, a nobleman who falls in love with a peasant girl is exposed as a liar by the gamekeeper, who is also in love with the girl, and she dies of a broken heart. In the second act, the two men visit her grave, and as night falls, the wilis appear. The wilis were vengeful spirits of virgin brides who died

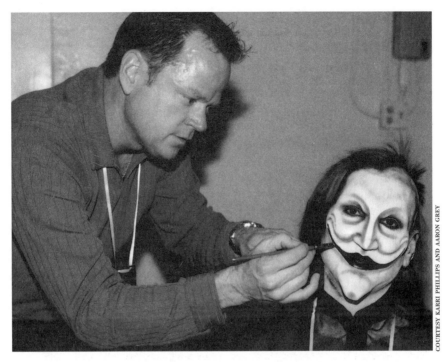

*Makeup artist Dayne Johnson puts the finishing touches on one of the demons
from "Waiting in the Wings"*

the night before their wedding and they find young men and force them to dance themselves to death. Giselle's spirit rises from her grave to join them, and the gamekeeper is killed and the nobleman saved by her love, although she now realizes she'll be a wili forever.

In "Waiting in the Wings," the roles have been switched. When Kurskov discovered his favorite ballerina was in love with another, he trapped her into dancing forever in a ghostly ballet performance that is the same night after night. But because she's a spirit, her essence traps Cordelia and Angel, forcing them to do a dance of their own. The ensuing love scenes between Cordelia and Angel are hot and steamy, but their love scene, like the ballet, is not real — it's "an echo." The scene between Angel and the ballerina is touching, and Joss must have seen something in Summer Glau, since he signed her on to be a main character in his new show, *Firefly*. Meanwhile, both Wesley and Gunn make a play for Fred: Gunn says they laugh at all the same jokes, while Wesley is thrilled that he's finally found someone who reads the same science journals and understands difficult mathematical problems like he does. But when it comes to love, we act with the heart, not the head, and when Wes discovers that Fred has chosen Gunn, his depression and sadness are almost overwhelming. Season three definitely belongs to Alexis Denisof, who turns in one great performance after another. This season his character develops from the sort of bumbler whose lack of grace covers up his true pain to a tormented man whose troubled past catches up to him and encroaches on his present. We're only given clues about his upbringing, but the clues are enough to round out the character and insinuate that terrible things have happened to him. As the episode comes to an end, Wesley is not alone in his unrequited love — an unexpected blast from the past arrives just in time to whisk Cordelia away from Angel.

3.14 Couplet

Original air date:	February 18, 2002
Written by:	Tim Minear, Jeffrey Bell
Directed by:	Tim Minear
Guest cast:	Bernard K. Addison (Monster), Fanshen Cox (Anita), Steven Hack (Lionel), Marisa Matarazzo (Susan), Scott Donovan (Jerry), Bob Rumnock (Business Man), Vanie Poyey (Pillow Fight Woman), Michael Otis (Pillow Fight Man)

Angel feels jealous when the Groosalugg can do things he can't, and Wesley ponders the consequences of office relationships.

Mark Lutz, the sad, sweet, and bulky Groosalugg

COURTESY RISING STARS ENTERPRISES

"Couplet" begins immediately after "Waiting in the Wings," as everyone tries to pick up the pieces of their lives. Gunn and Fred couldn't be happier, but Wesley quietly stews in his office wondering why he wasn't chosen. The scenes between Angel and Groo at the beginning are amusing, as Angel stands on his tiptoes to look taller, complains that Groo is too bulky to fight alongside, and makes fun of his tactics. But when the two fight together, Angel realizes Groo can do certain things that he can't — including com-shuck with the girl that Angel loves. Cordelia is thrilled that Groo has come back, but the viewer sees that maybe Cordy has feelings for Angel, too; she just doesn't acknowledge them or realize they're even there. She cuts Groo's hair and makes it short and spiky, and dresses him up in Angel's clothes (although he ends up looking more like a Backstreet Boy than Angel). She is physically attracted to Groo, but worries she'll lose her "visionity" and won't be valuable to Angel anymore. Meanwhile, Gunn and Fred make a near-fatal error, incurring a lecture from Wesley. The relationship between Gunn and Fred had a lot of potential, but it's never convincing. The two actors have little chemistry onscreen, and seem to be going through the motions whenever they're together. But when Wesley makes a grisly discovery with the scrolls at the end of the episode, suddenly everything else seems unimportant. One interesting note: When this episode first aired on the WB, Verizon Wireless did one of those annoying "Can you hear me now? Good" commercials that took place in the Hyperion. Interesting, considering Angel's cellphone never works *anywhere*.

3.15 Loyalty (Part One)

Original air date:	February 25, 2002
Written by:	Mere Smith

Directed by:	James A. Contner
Guest cast:	Wendy David (Aubrey), Enrique Castillo (Doctor), Susan Martino (Mother #1), Annie Talbot (Mother #2), Marci Hill (Nurse), Chris Devlin (Holtzian Man), Thom Scott II (Holtzian Man #2)

When Wesley discovers the prophecy that Angel will kill Connor, he exhausts every source he has trying to prove it wrong.

The first of a trio of stunning episodes, "Loyalty" moves away from the lovebird theme and gets back on track with the Angel/Holtz/Connor/Sahjhan saga. Holtz's army is becoming more powerful, and because it's made up of ordinary people who have lost loved ones, therefore giving them a desire for vengeance, they can blend in more easily without raising the suspicions of Angel and the gang. Angel seems to be drinking a lot more blood than usual, Fred and Gunn have decided they won't break up just because Wes is uncomfortable, and Cordelia's not around (Angel sent her on vacation with Groo, and she won't reappear until "Double or Nothing"). But the focus of this episode is Wesley. He alone bears the weight of his new knowledge, and he's so convinced it's wrong he can't bear to share it with anyone. His quest throughout the episode is heroic, although the seriousness of the prophecy is undermined by that stupid drive-thru statue he talks to. The statue is so distracting you almost miss its very important words. It's sad that the creative low point of the season is found in an otherwise amazing episode. When Wes finally confronts Holtz, he puts in motion the factors that will change all of their lives forever, and his path is determined when Angel utters his astounding comment at the end.

3.16 Sleep Tight (Part Two)

Original air date:	March 4, 2002
Written by:	David Greenwalt
Directed by:	Terrence O'Hara
Guest cast:	Marina Benedict (Kim), Jeff Denton (Lead Guitar), Jhaemi Willems (Drummer), J. Scott Shonka (Commando #1), Robert Forrest (Warrior #2)

Wesley kidnaps Connor to prevent the fulfilment of the prophecy, and sets in motion several tragic events.

"Sleep Tight" was the stuff season finales are made of. This episode had everything: suspense, intrigue, betrayal, loss . . . and vengeance. As Angel continues to chug down the blood like it's, well, blood, the others start to notice changes in him: he is talking and acting differently, getting a little too excited about killing demons, and becoming annoyed with Connor. When they discover the reason why, it's absolutely chilling. Lilah turns out to be even more of a coldhearted bitch than we thought possible, Justine goes from merely unsympathetic to downright despicable, Holtz takes his vengeance to a level even he didn't think he could, and Sahjhan reveals a long-standing feud with Angel (who has no idea who Sahjhan is). Of course, the most interesting change in character happens to Wesley. Holtz gives him 24 hours to deliver Connor to him to prevent his death at the hands of Angel, as the prophecy states will happen. But Wes has plans of his own, and it's obvious by the way he packs up his vehicle that he had no intention of delivering the child to anyone. Throughout the season he has been battered, rejected, betrayed, and filled with pain, and he's come a long way from the prim Watcher he was in season three of *Buffy*. He's surrounded by the friends who give him the only solace he's had in his life, but by the end of the episode, fans feared he would be no more. As Wes lies bleeding to death, Angel watches his son disappear from his life at the hands of Holtz, and the look on his face is heartbreaking. On another show, the lead character would have been screaming, beating the ground, and crying, but David Boreanaz conveys a father so filled with suffering he's completely paralyzed and speechless. Not only is his son gone, but he's filled with the pain of knowing that he had inflicted this very pain on Holtz 130 years before. No matter how much good Angel does, he will always pay for the sins of Angelus.

3.17 Forgiving

Original air date:	April 15, 2002
Written by:	Jeffrey Bell
Directed by:	Turi Meyer
Guest cast:	Kay Panabaker (Girl), Kenneth Dolin (Bum), Tripp Puckell (Holtzian), Sean Mahon (Truck Driver)

As Gunn and Fred search frantically for Wesley, Angel tries opening a portal to get his son back.

"Forgiving" is a whirlwind of an episode. Angel becomes dark once again and tortures Linwood for information (although, he is someone from Wolfram & Hart, so technically he's only barely human). When Lorne tells them that Wes took Connor (and beat Lorne up in the process), Fred and Gunn go to Wesley's house and find his diaries, discovering exactly why he did what he did. Fred is overwhelmed by relief; knowing that Wesley was only trying to act in Connor's best interest, she believes it'll be easier for everyone to forgive him now. Justine continues her yawn-invoking rampage to destroy Angel, while Angel manages to use dark magic (and Lilah) to open up a portal. Sahjhan reveals a devastating truth that makes Wesley's decision even more tragic. The ending of this episode is the most powerful and unexpected thus far, however, and I defy any viewer to watch it without trembling. David Boreanaz is brilliant. Just as with *Buffy* in season six, our loyalties are now officially divided, as we watch the cracks in the friendships become a deep, insurmountable chasm.

3.18 Double or Nothing

Original air date:	April 22, 2002
Written by:	David H. Goodman
Directed by:	David Grossman
Guest cast:	Jason Carter (Repo-Man), Patrick St. Esprit (Jenoff), John David Conti (Male Elderly Demon), P.B. Hutton (Female Elderly Demon), Nigel D. Gibbs (Doctor)

A soul-sucker demands payment of Gunn's soul, after Gunn had sold it to him seven years ago.

In this episode, we flash back to where Gunn sold his soul to Mr. Jenoff seven years earlier in order to obtain something he wanted. The theme of "Double or Nothing" is pertinent to what is happening in the show's main storyline — just as Gunn believed he had no future "living in a gangsta's paradise" and therefore was able to sacrifice it for his present happiness, Angel also believed he had no future until Connor came along. Gunn now sees that he was wrong and that his future lies with Fred, while Angel has had his future ripped from him. The episode had its highlights: Repo-Man is played by Jason Carter, the Terence Stamp sound-alike who is best known as Ranger Marcus Cole on *Babylon 5*, and Groo's welcome to him — "Hail to you, potential client!" — is priceless. The writers are careful not to drop the other storyline, and keep us updated on Wesley, Angel's grief and movement forward, and Cordelia discovering what had happened in her absence. But "Double or Nothing" was ultimately disappointing because of Angel. The guy goes to a monastery in Sri Lanka for three months to work through his grief over losing Buffy, yet when his son is snatched from him and sucked into a hell dimension, he gets over his sorrow within a week and is playing cards in a casino? While we still see some broodiness in Angel, his sudden change in temperament is uncharacteristic. The return of Cordelia *should* have been a positive moment, if she hadn't come back with that god-awful haircut and dye job.

3.19 The Price

Original air date:	April 29, 2002
Written by:	David Fury
Directed by:	Marita Grabiak
Guest cast:	John Short (Phillip J. Spivey), Wayne Ford (Kid), Waleed Moursi (Manager)

Angel discovers the consequences of practicing dark magic when the Hyperion is overrun with translucent, slug-like creatures.

We haven't had a *Buffy* writer on *Angel* for a long time now, and seeing David Fury's name in the credits was exciting. He uses a theme and a term — thaumogenesis — from "After Life," when Willow and the gang discover that when they brought Buffy back, something else came along for the ride. In this episode, a bunch of creatures are lurking about the Hyperion on a desperate search for water, trying to escape something called the Destroyer. We see a new wing of the hotel that was never previously explored; Cordelia's powers make her all glowy, astonishing even Angel; Groo worries that Cordy loves Angel and not him; and Lorne hangs around in a Quentin Crisp hat not doing much of anything, as has been typical of the character for the entire season. While season three is by far the best of the seasons of *Angel*, the lack of development in Lorne's character has been a big disappointment. But the finest moment belongs to Wesley, who has been shunned by the only people he loves, yet who are quick to use him when the situation calls for it. Gunn asks for his help, but never returns to say thank-you or even to just talk to him. Wesley's impassioned speech about staying alive for his friends is a touching moment, one that seems wasted on Gunn. While Angel still retained some depression in the previous episode, he actually borders on giddy in this one, excited that they finally have a case to work on. But as in "Forgiving," the ending of this episode will make you forget everything that came before it.

3.20 A New World

Original air date:	May 6, 2002
Written by:	Jeffrey Bell
Directed by:	Tim Minear
Guest cast:	Vincent Kartheiser (Connor), Erika Thormahlen (Sunny), Anthony Starke (Tyke), Deborah Zoe (Mistress Meena)

Connor is back in town, but he's suddenly a teenager — and he's pretty pissed off.

"A New World" was a great episode, although it lags a bit as Connor shows up and then immediately leaves again. We see him wandering the streets of grimy L.A. and hooking up with a drug-addicted girl, and while the plot is a little slow when Connor (now called Steven, but for the purposes of the episode guide I'll call him Connor) is with her, it picks up in the scenes at the Hyperion. Vincent Kartheiser is excellent, and here's hoping he sticks around for a while (if for no other reason than to pull in a younger female audience). When Angel does catch up to him he gains some of Connor's trust by saving his life, and tells him he is not alone. But as someone who has had to work out difficult situations himself, Angel understands Connor's need to be alone. Fred, on the other hand, was increasingly annoying throughout this episode, telling everyone that only Wesley would know what to do in their situation. This coming from the person who, in "Double or Nothing," visited Wes in the hospital and told him never to come to the hotel again. They won't listen to Wes's side of the story, yet Fred believes he would help them in their time of need? Speaking of Wesley, Lilah has swooped in on her broomstick to recruit him for Wolfram & Hart, but will Wesley give in? A couple of nitpicks: "The Price" takes place in the middle of the night, yet at the beginning of this episode, which takes place about 10 minutes later, it's midday. Also, that *Matrix* rip-off opening scene was laughable, and I hope they didn't blow their entire budget on it. It would have been slightly fascinating if we hadn't already suffered through countless takeoffs of the same special effects.

3.21 Benediction

Original air date:	May 13, 2002
Written and directed by:	Tim Minear
Guest cast:	Vincent Kartheiser (Connor)

Angel continues to vie for Connor's trust and discovers things they have in common, but Holtz has other plans.

David Greenwalt will be gone by the time *Angel* begins its fourth season, which will be unfortunate, but on the positive side, Tim Minear will get more responsibility. The episodes with Daniel Holtz are the best ones this season, simply because he is such a complex character. His need for vengeance often borders on loathsome, yet we cannot blame him because we know what he's been through. He lost everything that meant something to him at the hands of Darla and Angelus, and has spent the last 16 or so years in a hell dimension. In "Benediction," he wears the ravages of time and torture on his face, and appears to have aged about 40 years as a result. He encourages Connor to be with Angel, and tells him he belongs with his real father, but he's lying. Connor will become the final pawn in Holtz's complex plan to avenge the deaths of his family. Despite the fact that he truly believes he loves Connor, he will now set forth to destroy Connor's life as well as Angel's. Meanwhile, Connor attacks Angel's "demon" friends and we catch another glimpse of Cordelia's rather confusing new power. Skip had told her she would have to be part-demon, but she appears to be part-angel instead, and her soothing "Let it go, honey" is so far removed from the original Cordelia that we can't help but look upon this woman's growth with awe (although it's interesting that while Connor later seems to have super-hearing, in this scene he can't hear the gang talking about him as they stand 10 feet away from him). The fight scene involving Angel and Connor is superb, and shows just how much they really do have in common. The final few moments of the episode — with Holtz's voice-over reading the letter he has just given to Angel, while Justine aids Holtz in putting his vengeance to rest, and Connor begins a quest for retribution of his own — are stunning.

3.22 Tomorrow

Original air date:	May 20, 2002
Written and directed by:	David Greenwalt
Guest cast:	Vincent Kartheiser (Connor), David Denman (Skip)

As Angel begins to make plans for Connor's future, he doesn't realize Connor is planning Angel's. Meanwhile, Cordelia realizes she loves Angel, and races to tell him so.

Up until this year, there was a sort of unwritten rule about the season finales of *Buffy* and *Angel*: never end it on a cliffhanger. Finish all of the storylines, bring the arc to a close, and next season use the first few episodes as a transition from the previous season before launching into a new story arc. But "Tomorrow" drops many surprises into our laps and leaves the people we love in limbo, forcing us to suffer through a long, excruciating summer for resolution. The Groosalugg finally confronts Cordelia about her love for Angel, and when she is unable to reciprocate his undying love for her, he leaves. Groo was rather annoying when he first showed up, but by the end of the season he had become a delightful Anya-like character who was trying to fit into the L.A. scene. As if his departure isn't bad enough, Lorne — many fans' favorite character — announced his impending departure for Las Vegas. There's a good chance his gig won't work out and he'll be back (we can only hope), but at this point in the storyline, when the writers took this fantastic character and turned him into a pseudo-babysitter and hanger-on in flashy threads, there was really nowhere else for him to move. In "The Price," the gang discovered a huge dance hall in the other wing of the hotel; maybe he'll come back and become the proprietor of a 1940s-style swing club.

But the biggest changes happen with Cordelia and Angel. These two characters have been moving toward their destinies all season, and while Cordy's allowed her to move up, so to speak, Angel's torture sent him down into the depths. The punishment that Connor and the loathsome Justine subject Angel to is a clever plot device, while Cordy's fate had some fans scratching their heads. The ending left us hanging with a ton of unanswered

COURTESY RISING STARS ENTERPRISES

Despite his apparent departure from Angel *at the end of season three, Andy Hallett's beloved character, Lorne, will be back in season four*

questions, but also left us begging for more. And considering "The Adventures of Gunn & Fred" would be canceled after about 30 minutes, it's inevitable that most of the main characters will still be central in season four. If season four even comes close to matching the brilliance of season three, we're in for a major treat.

"Thank you, thank you very much."

Trivia Quiz Answers

SCORING:

81–100   "You've never had any tiny bit of sex, have you?" (i.e. I am very impressed!)

71–80   "Lady of Buffdom, Duchess of Buffonia, I am in awe."

51–70   "You're a cross-referencing fool."

31–50   "You're Deanna Troi. Get used to the feeling, Betazoid."

11–30   "I'm pathetic! Illiterate! I'm Cletus, the slack-jawed yokel!"

0–10   Have you heard about this show called *Buffy the Vampire Slayer*? You should watch an episode.

DIFFICULT, SCHMIFFICULT
Questions for Newbies

1. Xander
2. Sunnydale Razorbacks
3. *Sunnydale Press*
4. Mr. Gordo
5. A Chaos demon
6. Scorned Women ("The Wish")
7. Stevenson Hall
8. Gachnar
9. "Wind Beneath My Wings" ("Something Blue")
10. Belize
11. Warren likes Sean Connery, Jonathan prefers Roger Moore, and Andrew thinks Timothy Dalton was the best Bond
12. A CD holder
13. Strawberries
14. Seabreeze
15. Liam
16. *Songs for the Love Lorne*

"TIME FOR A LITTLE RESEARCH"
The Next Level

1. Hemery High
2. Capricorn on the cusp of Aquarius
3. 1937 ("The Harvest")
4. The Order of Aurelius
5. Collin
6. The Restfield Cemetery
7. Dematorin
8. 1775
9. Sam Zabuto
10. Nighthawk
11. Mr. Platt
12. 1430 ("Lover's Walk")
13. Cleveland
14. 1,120 years old ("Doppelgängland")
15. Ethnomusicology ("The Freshman")
16. Lilac One
17. 62.3°F
18. Room 118
19. 17
20. A Radiohead album
21. The flowering onion
22. 5124
23. Donny
24. Shrimp ("Triangle")
25. 1630 Ravello
26. 220
27. 12
28. Devon
29. 1727
30. When he was 21
31. An Ethros demon
32. *On Your Own*
33. Tuna and ice cream, sometimes mixed together ("Tomorrow")

IS IT GETTING WARM IN HERE?
The Slayer-Sized Questions

1. Cosmetology school ("The Witch")
2. The Advent of Septus
3. Tuscany ("When She Was Bad")
4. 185
5. Near Route 17
6. E flat diminished ninth ("What's My Line? Part Two")
7. D-
8. 43
9. $18 a day
10. Cocorific
11. Breaker's Woods
12. Mr. Sanderson from the bank
13. Marmaduke ("Bad Girls")
14. Her name is Edwina and they married in 1903
15. Monkey ("Consequences")
16. Taparrich
17. Wolf House
18. Dr. Engleman
19. February 25, 2000
20. Mr. Fogerty
21. Anya Christina Emanuella Jenkins
22. At a publishing house
23. 147
24. 40 Siamese cats
25. Methane ("Smashed")
26. $1.92
27. $20 million
28. 212
29. Mercy
30. *Life Lessons*
31. Tan, date, or sing in public
32. Zen
33. Count de Leon

34. 57
35. Montserrat Retirement Home
36. In his left butt cheek ("Fredless")
37. Wife Caroline, and children Sarah and Daniel
38. 378
39. 35 ("Dad")
40. 171 Oak

TROIKIAN TRIVIA
or, I Bow Before Anyone Who Can Answer These Questions

1. Aunt Maureen, Uncle Ken, cousin Jordy ("Phases")
2. 2:27 a.m.
3. Capital murder for bombing Flight 1402
4. Reverend Chalmers
5. The Velvet Underground's *Loaded*
6. 05/01
7. A straight, 4-5-6-7-8 of clubs
8. 1-7-8-3
9. 1481 Hyperion Ave.
10. 213-555-0162
11. NKO 714 ("To Shanshu in L.A.")

Bibliography

"So a Werewolf, Two Lesbian Witches, and a Vengeance Demon Go into a Magic Shop . . ."

"Bidding War Set to Erupt Over *Buffy the Vampire Slayer*." Associated Press. January 9, 2001.

Bonin, Liane. "Blood, Simply." *Entertainment Weekly Online*. May 15, 2001.

——. "Pulling Up Stakes." *Entertainment Weekly Online*. May 8, 2001.

The Bronze Posting Board. Online.

"Buffy the Vampire Slayer Season Finale to Be Delayed Until Later in the Summer." Associated Press. May 24, 1999.

"Buffy Tunes Into Teens." *New York Daily News*. March 30, 1997.

Carson, Tom. "Buffy Battles Teendom's Demons." *The Village Voice*. June 7, 1997.

"The Creator Speaks." *E! Online*. Accessed April 16, 2002.

"Emma Thompson Lends a Hand; Vampire Slayer Undead." *National Post*. June 1, 2001.

Ervin-Gore, Shawna. "Interview with Joss Whedon." *Dark Horse Comics*. Online. Accessed April 17, 2002.

Ferrante, Anthony C. "New Kicks for Buffy the Vampire Slayer." *Fangoria*. January 1998.

Fienberg, Daniel. "*Buffy Goes Prime Time*." *The Daily Pennsylvanian*. April 10, 1997.

Gellar, Sarah Michelle. Interviewed with Howard Stern. *The Howard Stern Show*. March 10, 1998.

——. "Stop Blaming Hollywood for Violent Behavior." Associated Press. March 2000.

Hine, Thomas. "TV's Teen-agers: They're Insecure, World-weary and (of Course) Misunderstood." *Houston Chronicle*. November 10, 1997.

Jacobs, A.J. "Interview with a Vampire Chronicler." *Entertainment Weekly*. May 2, 1997.

Johnson, Neala. "Buffy's End Is Nigh — Really." *The Courier-Mail*. May 2, 2002.

"Joss Whedon Embarks on First-ever Comic-book Endeavor." *Dark Horse Comics*. Online. Accessed April 17, 2002.

Kingwell, Mark. "Buffy Slays Ally." *Saturday Night*. May 1, 1998.

Lee, Patrick. "Joss Whedon Gets Big, Bad, and Grown Up with Angel." *Science Fiction Weekly*. Online. 1999.

Martinez, Jose. "Buffy's Screaming Good Summer Vacation." *Venice*. October 1997.

McEntire, Torrie. "He Just Slays 'Em." *Zap2It*. Online. April 1997.

Millman, Joyce. "Why Must I Be a Teenage Vampire Slayer in Love?" *Salon*. Online. June 8, 1998.

Moore, Richard. "Growing Up with Buffy." *Cult Times*. March 2000.

Nazzaro, Joe. "Beauties, Beasts, and Bad Eggs." *TV Zone*. October 2000.

Nickson, Kevin. "Maybe She's Born With It." *Starburst*. September 2001.

"Noxon Confirms Buffy Season 8." *Sci Fi Wire*. Online. June 20, 2002.

Persons, Mitch. "Angel, Vampire Private Eye." *Cinefantastique*. 1999.

——. "*Buffy the Vampire Slayer*: Bringing Classic Horror to a Whole New Audience." *Cinefantastique*. March 1998.

Pierce, Scott D. "Buffy Is Way Cool." *Deseret News*. June 2, 1997.

"Q&A with Alyson Hannigan." *YM*. August 2001.

Queenan, Joe. "High Stakes." *TV Guide*. May 17-23, 1997.

"Raising the Stakes." *The New Zealand Herald*. December 16, 1999.

Rice, Lynette. "'Slayer' It Ain't So." *Entertainment Weekly Online*. March 16, 2001.

Robinson, Tasha. "Joss Whedon." *The Onion*. Online. September 5, 2001.

"The Slayer Speaks." *E! Online*. Accessed April 20, 2002.

Springer, Matt. "Back to the Basics." *Buffy the Vampire Slayer Official Magazine*. May 2002.

Tucker, Ken. "Ouija Broads." *Entertainment Weekly*. October 30, 1998.

"Two Guys and a Girl's Fillion Flies to *Firefly*." *Zap2It*. Online. February 11, 2002.

The Cast of Buffy

Sarah Michelle Gellar

Altschull, Beth. "Sing When You're Winning." *Big Hit*. March 2002.

"Beauty Tips of the Gods." *National Post*. October 6, 2001.

Brady, James. "Sarah Michelle Gellar." *Parade Magazine*. July 6, 1997.

Bryce, Alan. "Interview: Sarah Michelle Gellar." *Adhoc*. Online. Accessed April 5, 2002.

Carrillo, Jenny Cooney. "My Wizard Time in Oz." *TV Guide*. November 2001.

Carter, Alan. "Young Love in the Afternoon." *Entertainment Weekly*. 1992.

Collymore, Terrie. "Teen Queen." *Soap Opera Digest*. 1994.

Dunn, Jancee. "Love at First Bite: Sarah Michelle Gellar." *Rolling Stone*. April 2, 1998.

"Five Alive." *Dreamwatch*. January 2001.

Gellar, Sarah Michelle. Interviewed by Jay Leno. *The Tonight Show with Jay Leno*. December 17, 1997.

———. Interviewed by Rosie O'Donnell. *The Rosie O'Donnell Show*. February 17, 1998.

Graham, Jennifer and Jeanne Wolf. "Slay Anything." *YM*. January 1998.

Hiscock, John. "Sarah Stakes a Claim to Fame." *NZ TV Guide*. December 11-17, 1999.

Hobson, Louis B. "To Die For." *Calgary Sun*. December 1, 1997.

Krantz, Michael. "The Bard of Gen-Y." *Time*. December 15, 1997.

Kutzera, Dale. "Sarah Michelle Gellar Is the Heroine Who Battles Monsters and Teen Angst." *Femme Fatales*. July 1997.

"Like Mother, Like Daughter." *Daytime TV*. 1994.

Martinez, Jose. "Buffy's Screaming Good Summer Vacation." *Venice*. October 1997.

O'Toole, Lesley. "Kiss or Kill." *Pavement*. April/May 1999.

Pearlman, Cindy. "Interview with Sarah Michelle Gellar." *Chicago Sun-Times*. September 1997.

Rochlin, Margy, and Lawless. "Slay Belle." *TV Guide*. August 2-8, 1997.

Roesch, Scott. "Sarah's Summer." *Mr. Showbiz*. Online. March 18, 1998.

Rush, Michael S. "Learning Life's Lessons." *Daytime TV*. 1993.

"Sarah Tells All!" *Big Hit*. September 1999.

Stewart, Carolyn. "Aussie Guys are Yummy." *Big Hit*. June 2001.

——. "I'm Coming to Australia." *Big Hit*. May 2001.

Strauss, Bob. "Q&A With Sarah Michelle Gellar." *E! Online*. Accessed April 16, 2002.

"Strong * Smart * Sexy." *bliss*. January 2002.

Thompson, Malissa. "Interview with Sarah Michelle Gellar." *React*. October 27-November 2, 1997.

Wofford, Tom. "Amber Benson." *Black and White*. January 18, 2001.

Wolf, Jeanne. "Listen Up with Sarah Michelle Gellar." *TV Guide*. Online. March 31, 1998.

——. "Q&A with Sarah Michelle Gellar." *TV Guide*. Online. March 31, 1998.

Anthony Stewart Head

Agarwal, Manish. "Giles Ahead." *Time Out London*. January 9-16, 2002.

Anderson, Kate. "Heading Back Home." *Xposé*. Fall 2001.

Billen, Andrew. "Buffy's Favourite Brit." *Evening Standard*. December 19, 2001.

Bonin, Liane. "True Brit." *Entertainment Weekly Online*. January 9, 2001.

Boris, Cynthia. "Anthony Stewart Head Is Watching Buffy." *Mania*. Online. May 3, 1998.

Ferrante, Anthony C. "Spike Heel." *Fangoria*. April 2000.

McLean, Gareth. "Oh, You Slay Me." *The Guardian*. February 19, 2002.

Persons, Mitch. "*Buffy the Vampire Slayer*: Bringing classic horror."

"Spooky Head." BBC. Online. February 25, 2002.

Vaardal, Sean. "*Buffy the Vampire Slayer* Star Anthony Head at Home in Somerset with His Partner and Two Children." *Hello!* July 10, 2001.

Alyson Hannigan

"Alyson Hannigan: Truth or Dare." *Smash Hits*. February 2001.

"*Buffy Cast Teases New Eps*." *Sci Fi Wire*. Online. June 21, 2002.

Gibson, Thomasina, and John Binns. "Will Power!" *Cult Times*. July 2000.

Mosby, John. "Willow Blossoms." *Dreamwatch*. October 2000.

Persons, Mitch. "*Buffy the Vampire Slayer*: Bringing classic horror."
Sloane, Judy. "Alyson Hannigan." *Xposé*. December 1997.
Whitby, Kate. "Where There's a Willow. . ." *Big Hit*. September 1999.

Nicholas Brendon

Bonin, Liane. "Blood, Simply." *Entertainment Weekly Online*. May 15, 2001.

Brendon, Nicholas. Interviewed by Sinbad. *Vibe*. CBS. May 4, 1998.

"Monster Mash." *InStyle*. October 2001.

"Nicholas Brendon: Interview with TheWB.com." *TheWB.com*. January 2001.

"Nicholas Brendon on Getting His Xander Up." *E! Online*. Accessed April 1, 2002.

O'Hare, Kate. "'Buffy's' Xander Grows Up and 'Star Trek's' Stewart Honored." *Zap2It*. February 1, 2001.

Owen, Rob. "High School Horror on *Buffy the Vampire Slayer*: Teen Angst Trumps the Supernatural." *Albany Time Union*. September 15, 1997.

Perenson, Melissa J. "Xander the Great." *Cult Times*. May 2000.

Pierce, Scott D. "Role on Buffy Has Opened Delightful New World for Actor." *Deseret News*. June 5, 1998.

Rudolph, Amanda. "He's a Keeper." *InStyle*. May 1998.

Simpson, Paul, and Ruth Thomas. "Nick — Caged!" *EON Magazine*. February 18, 2000.

Wolf, Jeanne. "Q&A with Nicholas Brendon." *TV Guide*. Online. June 15, 1998.

Seth Green

Baldwin, Kristen. "Green's Day." *Entertainment Weekly*. May 14, 1999.

Crane, Robert. "Seth Green." *Playboy*. September 2000.

Elias, Justine. "Where Wolf?" *Entertainment Weekly Online*. July 30, 2001.

Green, Michelle Erica. "Werewolf of Sunnydale: The Wizard of Oz." *Mania*. Online. May 3, 1998

"Green Not Bailing on Buffy." *SciFi.com*. Online. October 4, 1999.

"Live Star Chat with Seth Green." *UltimateTV*. Online. June 15, 1998.

Moro, Eric. "A Return to *Buffy*'s Oz Seems Most Unlikely." *Cinescape*. Online. January 25, 2002.

Morris, Wesley. "Seth Green: A Busy Actor's Hairy Adventures." *San Francisco Chronicle*. August 15, 2001.

"Q&A with Seth Green." *Teen People*. September 2001.

James Marsters

Ash, Roger. "James Marsters Interview." *Worlds of Westfield*. Online. February 1999.

"Chat with James Marsters." *TV Guide*. Online. November 14, 2000.

Darnell, Steve. "Small-town Kid Makes Bad." *Chicago Tribune*. February 11, 2000.

Ferrante, Anthony C. "Spike Heel." *Fangoria*. April 2000.

Gardner, Michael. "In Bed with Buffy." *Cult Times*. March 2001.

Roberts, Dave. "Raising the Stakes." *Starburst*. February 1999.

Schilling, Mary Kaye. "Interview with a Vampire." *Entertainment Weekly*. November 2000.

Stewart, Carolyn. "I'm Coming to Australia." *Big Hit*. May 2001.

"Who's Hot." *Ultimate TV*. Online. Accessed April 2, 2002.

Emma Caulfield

Amatangelo, Amy. "Taming her inner demons." *Boston Herald*. March 4, 2002.

"Buffy Baddie Finally Gets Regular." *TV Guide*. September 25, 2000.

"Demon on Heels." *Buffy the Vampire Slayer Official Magazine*. Summer 2001.

"Emma Caulfield." *Razor*. November 2001.

"Emma Caulfield: Demon Turned Human Confectionary." *Loaded*. February 2001.

"Emma Caulfield TeenHollywood Online Chat." *Teenhollywood.com*. May 17, 2001.

Mosby, John. "Anya Horribilis." *Dreamwatch*. June 2000.

Springer, Matt. "Hollywood Zen." *Buffy the Vampire Slayer Official Yearbook*. Cinescape Special Edition, 1999.

Michelle Trachtenberg

Bonin, Liane. "Sibling Revelry." *Entertainment Weekly Online*. December 18, 2000.

"From Out of the Ether Comes a New Dawn." *E! Online*. September 18, 2000.

"Interview with Michelle Trachtenberg." *CosmoGirl*. September 20, 2000.

Koltnow, Barry. "Young Actress is a Natural-born 'Spy.'" *Orange County Register*. July 9, 1996.

"The New Girl in Sunnydale." *TheWB.com*. September 23, 2000.

Rudolph, Ileane. "Sisters in Arms?" *TV Guide*. August 12, 2000.

Amber Benson

Avery, Don. "Amber's Burning Bright." *Jump*. Spring 2001.

The Bronze Posting Board. Online.

"DiCaprio's Defence." *MrShowbiz*. Online. April 16, 1998.

"DiCaprio Sued Over Plum Role." *MrShowbiz*. Online. April 15, 1998.

Harvey, Alec. "Is There Life After Death on 'Buffy'?" *The Birmingham News*. July 25, 2002.

Lockman, Scot. "Birmingham Actress Casting a Spell on TV's Buffy." *Birmingham Weekly*. June 2000.

McGrath, Stephanie. "Buffy's Amber Benson Talks about Leo Movie." *AllPop*. Online. February 15, 2001.

Nazzaro, Joe. "Any Witch Way You Can." *Starburst*. September 2001.

Radish, Christina. "All I Know Is That She Likes Willow, and She's Already Got One of Those..." *Cult Times*. March 2001. Special Issue.

Spelling, Ian. "Ready to Go." *Xposé*. Summer 2001.

Springer, Matt. "Every Little Thing She Does." *Buffy the Vampire Slayer Official Magazine*. Summer 2000.

The Cast of Angel

David Boreanaz

"*Angel*'s Boreanaz a Dad in Real Life." *Zap2it*. Online. May 2, 2002.

Bernard, April P. "Interview with a Vampire." *Teen People*. November 1999.

Boreanaz, David. Interview with Keenan Ivory Wayans. *The Keenan Ivory Wayans Show*. Fox. January 26, 1998.

——. Interview with Regis Philbin and Kathie Lee Gifford. *Live With Regis and Kathie Lee*. ABC. May 15, 2001.

"Buffy the Vampire Slayer's David Boreanaz." BBS Bulletin Board Chat. *TV Guide*. Online. September 17, 1997.

Carrillo, Jenny Cooney. "I Believe in Angels." *Dreamwatch*. February 2001.

Kappes, Serena. "David Boreanaz." *People*. Online. February 2001.

Malkin, Marc S. "Lucky Dog!" *Twist*. April/May 1998.

Morrow, Terry. "*Angel* Looks for His Piece of TV Heaven." *Teenhollywood.com*. Online. September 24, 2001.

Prichard, Marnie. "Interview with a Vampire." *Philadelphia Style*. February 2002.

Snead, Elizabeth. "Soul Man: David Boreanaz." *The Movies*. February-March 2001.

Charisma Carpenter

Carpenter, Charisma. Interview with Keenan Ivory Wayans. *The Keenan Ivory Wayans Show*. Fox. January 8, 1998.

"Charisma Carpenter." *ONE Magazine*. January 2002.

"Charisma Carpenter Star Chat." *UltimateTV*. Online. April 15, 1997.

Feldman, Len P. "Angel's Charismatic Star." *Gist*. Online. October 12, 1999.

Pierce, Scott D. "'Day Player' Role on Buffy Evolves into Angel Stardom." *Deseret News*. October 4, 1999.

Villanueva, Annabelle. "L.A. Woman." *Cinescape*. March 2000.

Wolf, Jeanne. "Q&A with Charisma Carpenter." *TV Guide*. Online. May 7, 1998.

Alexis Denisof

"AOL Chat with Alexis Denisof." AOL. Online. January 16, 2001.

Hewett, Rick. "The Young Actor Who Is Making Mrs. Merton Laugh Again." *Daily Mail*. August 20, 1997.

Higgons, Jenny. "Demon Scene." *Gist*. Online. Accessed April 9, 2002.

Kempster, Grant. "Head Music." *Xposé*. December 2000.

O'Hare, Kate. "Crossover Love." *Zap2It*. Online. September 25, 2001.

——. "Newest *Angel* Actor Finds His Wings." *Arizona Republic*. February 13, 2000.

Springer, Matt. "Vogue Demon Hunter." *Buffy the Vampire Slayer Official Magazine*. Spring 2000.

J. August Richards

"3 Questions with J. August Richards." *Cinescape*. January 2001.

"J. August Richards Chat." *AmuZnet and Yahoo*. Online. October 5, 2000.

Lowry, Brian. "One Actor's Odyssey." *Los Angeles Times*. August 13, 2000.

Amy Acker

"Angel's Acker a Genre Vet." *SciFi Wire*. Online. October 16, 2001.

Godwin, Jennifer. "Amy Acker Interview." *BuffyNewsWire*. Online. July 22, 2001.

Gross, Ed. "Fred Time Stories." *SFX*. March 2002.

Kuhn, Sarah. "A Girl Named Fred." *IGN*. July 17, 2001.

Stokes, Mike. "The Chosen One." *Buffy the Vampire Slayer Official Magazine UK*. March 2002.

Episode Guides

"Ars Almadel." *Classics of Magick*. Online. June 8, 2002.

Ausiello, Michael. "Death Becomes Buffy." *TV Guide*. Online. March 8, 2001.

Boris, Cynthia. "*Buffy the Vampire Slayer*'s Robia LaMorte and Robin Sachs: A Re-occurrence in Sunnydale." *Mania*. Online. May 3, 1998.

The Bronze Posting Board. Online.

The Bronze VIP Posting Board Archives. Online.

The Buffy and Angel Music Pages. Online.

Chase, Bailey. Interview with author. E-mail. May 9, 2002.

"The Claddagh Ring." *Claddagh Jewellers*. Online. July 3, 1998.

Cobo, Father Bernake. *Inca Religion and Customs*. Trans. and ed. Roland Hamilton. Austin: University of Texas Press, 1990.

Crosby, Johanna. "Angel's Devilish Sidekick." *Cape Cod Times*. October 2, 2000.

Day, John. *Molech: A God of Human Sacrifice in the Old Testament*. Cambridge: Cambridge University Press, 1989.

Fisher, Amber Laine. *Philosophy of Wicca*. Toronto: ECW Press, 2002.

Gellar, Sarah Michelle. "Stop Blaming Hollywood for Violent Behavior." Associated Press. March 2000.

Good News Bible. Toronto: Canadian Bible Society, 1976.

Gordon, Stuart. *The Encyclopedia of Myths and Legends*. London: Headline Book Publishing, 1994.

Grimal, Pierre. *The Dictionary of Classical Mythology*. Trans. A.R. Maxwell. Hyslop Oxford: Blackwell Publishers Ltd., 1996.

Holman, C. Hugh, and William Harmon. *A Handbook to Literature*. New York: MacMillan Publishing Co., 1986.

Kempster, Grant. "Head Music."

Kuhn, Sarah. "The Tara Files." *IGN*. Online. November 7, 2000.

Lee, Patrick. "*Buffy* Boy Marc Blucas Fills Angel's Shoes." *Science Fiction Weekly*. Online. February 28, 2000.

Maples, William R., Ph.D. *Dead Men Do Tell Tales: The Strange and Fascinating Cases of a Forensic Anthropologist*. New York: Bantam Doubleday, 1994.

Marc-Blucas.com. Online.

Milton, John. *Paradise Lost*. Ed. Merritt Y. Hughes. New York: MacMillan Publishing Co., 1962.

Moseley, Michael E. *The Incas and Their Ancestors: The Archaeology of Peru*. London: Thames and Hudson, 1992.

Nazzaro, Joe. "Beauties, Beasts, and Bad Eggs." *TV Zone*. October 2000.

Schilling, Mary Kaye. "Interview with a Vampire." *Entertainment Weekly*. November 2000.

——. "Vamping It Up." *Entertainment Weekly*. November 9, 2001.

Shakespeare, William. *Henry V*. New York: Bantam, 1988.

Sibbald, Vanessa. "*Buffy* Sex Scene Had to Be Trimmed." *Zap2It*. Online. November 27, 2001.

Simpson, Paul, and Ruth Thomas. "Death Becomes Her." *SFX*. October 2001.

Spelling, Ian. "Bad Blood." *Sci-Fi TV*. February 2001.

Stoppard, Tom. *Rosencrantz and Guildenstern Are Dead*. London: Faber and Faber, 1991.

Tong, Diane. *Gypsy Folktales*. San Diego: Harcourt Brace Jovanovich, 1989.

Tsu, Lao. *Tao Te Ching*. Trans. Gia-Fu Feng and Jane English. New York: Vintage Books, 1989.

Virtual Jamestown. Online. Accessed July 11, 2002.

"What Does the Saying 'The Whole Nine Yards' Mean?" *Ask Yahoo!* Online. October 12, 1998.

Additional Sources

"Amber Benson." *TheWB.com*. Online. March 27, 2001.

Anderson, Dennis. "Vampire-Slayer Buffy Battles Master." Associated Press. May 29, 1997.

"Anthony Head." *The Transylvanian Conventions — 1992 Guests*. Online. July 3, 1998.

"Banned Leo-Tobey Pic to Debut in Berlin." *MrShowbiz*. Online. December 14, 2000.

Barber, Paul. *Vampires, Burial, and Death: Folklore and Reality*. New Haven: Yale UP, 1988.

Barker, Lynn. "Michelle and Jim: Together at Last." *TeenHollywood.com*. Online. August 9, 2001.

Bouw, Brenda. "Buffy Goes to College: Gellar Stars in Mobster Film *Harvard Man*." *National Post*. July 31, 2000.

Brady, James. "Sarah Michelle Gellar." *Parade Magazine*. July 6, 1997.

"Breakthroughs '97 — Sarah Michelle Gellar." *People*. December 29, 1997.

"*Buffy* creator zooms to space with *Firefly*." *USA Today*. December 24, 2001.

"*Buffy the Vampire Slayer*'s David Boreanaz." BBS Bulletin Board Chat. September 17, 1997. *TV Guide*. Online. June 15, 1998.

"'Buffy' Tunes into Teens." *New York Daily News*. March 30, 1997.

"Buffy's Estranged Dad Found Dead." Associated Press. October 11, 2001.

"Buffy's Tara Branches Out." *SFX*. November 2001.

"Can an Actor from Modesto Break into Hollywood's Circle of Fame?" *Modesto Bee*. May 14, 2000.

Carrillo, Jenny. "Buffy Roundtable." *Dreamwatch*. March 2001.

Collymore, Terrie. "Teen Queen." *Soap Opera Digest*. 1994.

Dearsley, Jayne and Ed Gross. "SFX Probe: James Marsters." *SFX*. November 2000.

Decker, Sean. "An Interview with Kevin Williamson." October 5, 1997. *Horror Movie*. Online. June 13, 1998.

——. "Interview with the Vampire Slayer." October 1997. *Dungeon of Darkness*. Online. March 31, 1998.

"Do as the Roma Do." *Soap Opera Weekly*. 1993.

Douglas, Adam. *The Beast Within*. London: Chapmans, 1992.

Douglas, Drake. *Horrors!* Woodstock, N.Y.: The Overlook Press, 1989.

Dunn, Samantha. "Heavenly Day." *InStyle*. January 2002.

Ervin-Gore, Shawna. "James Marsters." *Dark Horse Comics*. Online. February 26, 1999.

Feldman, Len P. "Death Becomes Him." *Gist*. Online. Accessed April 2, 2002.

Francis, Rob. "Which Witch Is Which?" *Dreamwatch*. October 2000.

"Friends." *Soap Opera Weekly*. 1993.

Gellar, Sarah Michelle. Interviewed by David Letterman. *Late Show with David Letterman*. CBS. New York. November 20, 1997.

——. Interviewed by Jay Leno. *The Tonight Show with Jay Leno*. NBC. New York. September 8, 1997.

Goods, Lorraine. "Sarah Michelle Gellar: Cult of the Vampire." *People*. Online. March 18, 1998.

Graham, Jefferson. "*Buffy* Star Likes Demands of Action-Comedy Role." *USA Today*. March 28, 1997.

——. "The Ratings Slayer: Box Office Bomb Has Turned into a Hit on Television." *USA Today*. March 28, 1997.

Green, Michelle. "Stake-ing a Claim in *The Vampire Slayer*." *Mania*. Online. May 3, 1998.

Grossberg, Josh. "Gellar: I'm Gone If *Buffy* Leaves the WB." *E! Online*. January 22, 2001.

Hensley, Dennis. "Miracle Worker." *Movieline*. November 1997.

——. "Stars and Strips." *SKY*. February 2001.

The Internet Movie Database. Online.

"Interview with Alyson Hannigan." *MrShowbiz*. Online. July 1999.

"Interview with Emma Caulfield." BBC. Online. August 23, 2001.

"Interview with Modesto's Vampire." *Modesto Bee*. December 17, 1999.

"Interview with the Cast of *Swans Crossing*." *Teen Party*. 1992.

"James Marsters on How He Likes Spike." *E! Online*. Accessed April 2, 2002.

"J. August Richards Online Chat." *TV Guide*. Online. November 17, 2000.

Kappes, Serena. "Michelle the Slayer's Sister." *People.com*. Online. November 17, 2000.

Kemp, Anthony. *Witchcraft and Paganism Today*. London: Michael O'Mara Books, 1993.

Kuhn, Sarah. "Demon Girl, Interrupted." *IGN*. April 13, 2000.

——. "Spike Speaks." *IGN*. Online. June 5, 2000.

——. "Tara's Turn." *IGN*. Online. March 2000.

Littleton, Cynthia. "FX Network Bags *Buffy* Reruns at $650,000 Per Episode." *Variety*. February 25, 1998.

Lonard, Brad. "Red Hot and Cool." *Juice*. December 2000.

Lyons, Shelly. "Alyson Hannigan's 'Willow' — Wallflower by Day, Assistant Slayer by Night." *Ultimate TV*. Online. May 11, 1998.

Maslin, Janet. "Steamy TV: Coffee Opera." *The New York Times*. November 22, 1992.

Mason, Charlie, with Michael Ausiello. "Hoof and Mouth Disease Strikes *Buffy*." *TV Guide*. Online. September 19, 2001.

Meers, Erik, and Paula Yoo. "Killer Charm." *People.com*. Online. March 1999.

Miller, Bruce R. "Staking a Claim." *Sioux City Journal*. March 7, 1997.

Moore, Frazier. "High School Horrific." *TV Week — The Washington Post*. March 30, 1997.

Moran, W. Reed, with Stephen A. Shoop, M.D. "Nicholas Brendon faces down stuttering demon." *USA Today*. May 15, 2001.

Noll, Richard. *Vampires, Werewolves, and Demons: Twentieth Century Reports in the Psychiatric Literature*. New York: Brunner/Mazel, 1992.

Norton, Peter B. et al, eds. *The New Encyclopedia Britannica*. 15th ed. Chicago: Encyclopedia Britannica, Inc., 1995.

O'Hare, Kate. "*Angel* Stars Eager to Spread Wings." *TV Week*. July 17, 1999.

"Once Bitten." *TheWB.com*. Online. 2001.

"Passion — Alyson Hannigan: Beanie Babies." *Teen People*. April 1998.

"Petcabus Awards." *The Petcabus Awards Homepage*. Online. July 6, 1998.

Pond, Steve. "Sarah Michelle Gellar's New Order." *Juice*. March 2002.

Richardson, David. "Demons and Angel." *Cult Times*. September 1999.

——. "Hell Hath No Fury." *Cult Times*. October 1999.

Romando, Tony. "Emma Caulfield." *FHM*. May 2001.

Rudwin, Maximilian. *The Devil in Legend and Literature*. 1931. La Salle, Ill.: The Open Court Publishing Co., 1989.

Schollmeyer, Josh. "Revenge of the Nerds." *Wicked Magazine*. Spring 2001.

Schorow, Stephanie. "Stakeout." *The Boston Herald*. May 19, 1997.

Sebald, Hans. *Witch-Children: From Salem Witch-Hunts to Modern Courtrooms*. Amherst: Prometheus, 1995.

Senn, Harry. *The Were-Wolf and Vampire in Romania*. Boulder: East European Monographs, 1982.

"She Hath No Fury." *TV Guide*. December 25-31, 1999.

Simpson, Lisa. "Man of Style." *InStyle*. February 2001.

Solin, Sabrina. "Girl Meets Boy." *Seventeen Magazine*. August 1994.

Spelling, Ian. "She Savors a Slice of 'Pie.'" *New York Times*. August 8, 2001.

——. "Voice of an Angel." *Starlog*. July 2001.

"Spike Live: *Buffy*'s Biting Vampire Drops By for a Chat." *E! Online*. December 13, 1999.

Spragg, Paul. "Half Price." *Xposé*.

"Star Boards — Sarah Michelle Gellar." *E! Online*. March 31, 1998.

Steinbach, Sheila. "Daytime's Hottest Young Stars." *Soap Opera Update*. 1993.

Stentz, Zack. "Beyond *Buffy*: Sidekick Alyson Hannigan Has Her Own Following." *TVQuest*. November 1998.

Stewart, Carolyn. "WILLOWLOVESOZ." *Big Hit*. October/November 1999.

423. "Up Close with Emma Caulfield." *Big Hit*. September 2001.

Strauss, Bob. "*Buffy* Star Sarah Gellar Nurtures Her Film Career."

Detroit Free Press. November 10, 1997.

Thomas, Mike. "A Virtual Gentleman: Anthony Head Says Goodbye to His 'Nice Guy' Image in *VR5*." *Cult Times.*

Thompson, Bob. "She Buffs up the Teenage Image." *Toronto Sun.* December 3, 1997.

Turner, Alice K. *The History of Hell.* New York: Harcourt Brace & Co., 1993.

Weeks, Janet. "The Devil in Angel." *TV Guide.* November 20-26, 1999.

Yovanovich, Linda. "Young Blood." *OnSat.* July 14, 1997.